176238

WITHDRAWN

Guide to

PLAY SELECTION

COMMITTEE ON PLAYLIST

*National Council
of Teachers of English*

JOSEPH MERSAND
Chairman

FRANCIS GRIFFITH

MARCUS KONICK

PAUL KOZELKA

M. JEROME WEISS

Guide to
PLAY
SELECTION

SECOND EDITION

A PUBLICATION OF THE

*National Council
of Teachers of English*

APPLETON-CENTURY-CROFTS, Inc.

New York

PREFACE

THE PUBLICATION of Milton Smith's *Guide to Play Selection* in 1934 met a need that had long been felt for a volume that could assist directors of theatre groups in schools, colleges, and communities in the selection of plays suitable for production and study by their organizations. In 1952, after the book had long been out of print and practically unobtainable, the National Council of Teachers of English organized the Committee on Playlist to prepare a new volume. The original members consisted of Paul Kozelka, Professor of Speech at Teachers College, Columbia University; Francis Griffith, Principal of Richmond Hill High School, New York City; the late A. M. Drummond, Professor of Drama, Cornell University; and Joseph Mersand, Chairman of the English Department, Jamaica High School, New York City. Later the Committee was enlarged to include Marcus Konick, Chairman of the English and Foreign Language Department, Edison High School, Philadelphia; and M. Jerome Weiss, Assistant Professor of Education, Pennsylvania State University.

Guide to Play Selection, Second Edition, represents the co-operative thinking and action of all members of the Committee on Playlist. The list of plays was approved by all of its members. Whenever it has seemed advisable to retain the plays included in the first edition, we have done so, with the complete permission of Professor Smith. Where there seemed no reason to revise the original summaries, we have retained them, bringing up to date such matters as royalties and sources of publication. For such willing co-operation, the Committee on Playlist wishes to express its sincere thanks to Professor Smith.

The introductions to the various sections in the book were all written by Dr. Konick, who also furnished most of the bibliographies and the new section on television plays. The other completely new section on guidance plays was contributed by Dr. Weiss, one of the authorities in this interesting field of educational dramatics. Clark Weaver, Editor of *Players Magazine*, supplied from his magazine photographs of actual productions of plays for reprinting in this volume. Mrs. Ruth Mayleas of the Greater New York Chapter of ANTA and Leon C. Miller, Editor of *Dramatics*, also co-operated in submitting illustrations. To them and to the directors of the college dramatic groups involved, the Committee on Playlist expresses its gratitude. The appearance of the book has been enhanced by these photographs, while at the same time readers may obtain a good idea of how some of these plays looked in actual stage production.

The criteria used by members of the Committee for retaining plays from the original edition as well as for including new plays produced or published since 1934 need some explanation. All plays in the present volume are considered meritorious by the Committee on Playlist from the standpoint of being eminently suitable for production by school, college and community theatres, based on our own experiences as well as on a study of school and college dramatic production in recent years. Directors of such groups should study the summaries as well as our additional comments as to the degree of difficulty or sophistication of each play. Others may, of course, differ with our judgments, but such differences of opinion are wholesome. We have examined literally thousands of long and short plays before making the final selection of these 430 long plays and 294 short plays. Many of them were seen, produced, or read by one or more members of the Committee.

The 1934 edition had eighty-nine anthologies in which the recommended plays appeared. This revision has enlarged the number to 536 collections, containing a great many of those originally listed and the most important ones that have been published in the past two decades. Information as to the publisher of individual plays and royalties has been supplied for each play that was still in print, and whenever such information was available. Where such information is lacking in the summaries, reference to the Index of Plays will indicate which anthologies can be utilized. At least one source has been supplied for every play.

After each play in the Index of Plays the number in bold-face type represents the page on which the summary appears. The numbers in lighter type immediately following indicate the numbers of the anthologies in which these plays can be found. The second index, of authors, will show at a glance the wide representation of their works; and the bold-face numbers following each name indicate the pages on which summaries of their plays appear.

In a book of this type, errors are bound to slip in although we have checked and rechecked every item. The members of the Committee would welcome any corrections. The manuscript was read by Professor Lauren L. Brink of the University of Nevada and Miss Elsie W. Todd of Gardena High School, Gardena, California, for whose valuable criticisms we are thankful. Miss Ruth D. Keener of the editorial staff of Appleton-Century-Crofts and Dr. J. N. Hook, Executive Secretary of the National Council of Teachers of English, have been of inestimable help in seeing the book through the press. We wish to express our gratitude to Mrs. Estelle J. Mersand for her valuable assistance in preparing the indexes and reading proof.

It is the hope of the Committee on Playlist to prepare periodic supplements to this edition of *Guide to Play Selection* to keep it up to date; so that it may continue to be of service to our many colleagues interested in the study and production of the best in educational theatre.

COMMITTEE ON PLAYLIST, N.C.T.E.

JOSEPH MERSAND, *Chairman*
FRANCIS GRIFFITH
MARCUS KONICK
PAUL KOZELKA
M. JEROME WEISS

CONTENTS

ILLUSTRATIONS

LIST OF PUBLISHERS AND AGENTS

ABELARD-SCHUMAN, Ltd., 404 Fourth Ave., New York 16, N.Y.

ACTORS EQUITY ASSN., 226 W. 47 St., New York 36, N.Y.

GEORGE ALLEN AND UNWIN, Ltd., 40 Museum St., London, W.C.1.

ALLYN AND BACON, Inc., 150 Tremont St., Boston, Mass.

AMERICAN BOOK CO., 55 Fifth Ave., New York 3, N.Y.

AMERICAN THEATRE WING, Inc., 161 W. 93 St., New York 25, N.Y.

APPLETON-CENTURY-CROFTS, Inc., 35 W. 32 St., New York 1, N.Y.

EDWARD ARNOLD, Ltd., 41 Maddox St., London, W.1.

ATLANTIC MONTHLY PRESS (See LITTLE, BROWN & Co.).

RICHARD BADGER, Inc. (Out of business).

WALTER H. BAKER Co., 569 Boylston St., Boston 16, Mass.

BALLANTINE BOOKS, Inc., 101 Fifth Ave., New York 3, N.Y.

BANNER PLAY BUREAU, Inc., 619 Post St., San Francisco 9, Calif.

BARNES & NOBLE, Inc., 105 Fifth Ave., New York 3, N.Y.

BEACON PRESS, Inc., Beacon St., Boston 8, Mass.

G. BELL AND SONS, Ltd., York House, 6 Portugal St., London, W.C.2.

BLAKISTON (See McGRAW-HILL BOOK Co.).

BOBBS-MERRILL Co., Inc., 730 N. Meridian St., Indianapolis 7, Ind.

BRENTANO PUBLISHING Co. (Out of business).

CURTIS BROWN Ltd., 575 Madison Ave., New York 22, N.Y.

F. BRUCKMANN, Munich.

CAMBRIDGE UNIVERSITY PRESS, 32 E. 57 St., New York 22, N.Y.; Bentley House, 200 Euston Rd., London, N.W.1.

CASSELL & Co., Ltd., 37–38 St. Andrew's Hill, Queen Victoria St., London, E.C.4.

CAXTON HOUSE, Inc., 9 Rockefeller Plaza, New York, N.Y.

CENTURY (See APPLETON-CENTURY-CROFTS).

P. F. COLLIER & SON Corp., 640 Fifth Ave., New York 19, N.Y.

COLUMBIA UNIVERSITY PRESS, 2960 Broadway, New York 27, N.Y.

CORNELL UNIVERSITY EXTENSION DIVISION, Ithaca, N.Y.

COWARD-McCANN, Inc., 210 Madison Ave., New York 16, N.Y.

CROFTS (See APPLETON-CENTURY-CROFTS).

THOMAS Y. CROWELL Co. 432 Fourth Ave., New York 16, N.Y.

CROWN PUBLISHERS, Inc., 419 Fourth Ave., New York 16, N.Y.

T. S. DENISON & Co., 321 Fifth Ave., S., Minneapolis 15, Minn.

J. M. DENT & SONS, Ltd. Aldine House, 10–13, Bedford St., Strand, London, W.C.2.

DIAL PRESS, Inc., 461 Fourth Ave., New York 16, N.Y.

DICKSON (*Out of business*).

DODD, MEAD & Co., Inc., 432 Fourth Ave., New York 16, N.Y.

DOUBLEDAY & Co., Inc., Garden City, N.Y.

DRAMATIC PUBLISHING Co., 179 N. Michigan Ave., Chicago 1, Ill.

DRAMATISTS PLAY SERVICE, Inc., 14 E. 38 St., New York 16, N.Y.

DUELL, SLOAN, & PEARCE, Inc., 124 E. 30 St., New York 16, N.Y.

THE DRYDEN PRESS, Inc. (*Refer to* HENRY HOLT & Co.).

DUFFIELD PUBLISHERS (*Out of business*).

E. P. DUTTON & Co., Inc., 300 Fourth Ave., New York 10, N.Y.

ELDRIDGE PUBLISHING Co., Franklin, Ohio

EVERYMAN'S LIBRARY, E. P. Dutton & Co., 300 Fourth Ave., New York 10, N.Y.

EXPRESSION Co., Magnolia, Mass.

FABER & FABER, Ltd., 24 Russell Sq., London, W.C.1.

FARRAR & RINEHART (*See* RINEHART & Co.).

SAMUEL FRENCH, Inc., 25 W. 45 St., New York 36, N.Y.

GARDEN CITY PUBLISHING Co. (*See* DOUBLEDAY & Co.).

GINN & Co., Statler Building, Boston 17, Mass.

GLOBE BOOK Co., 175 Fifth Ave., New York 10, N.Y.

VICTOR GOLLANCZ, Ltd., 14 Henrietta St., Covent Garden, London, W.C.2.

H. W. GRAY Co., Inc., 159 E. 48 St., New York 17, N.Y.

GREENBERG: PUBLISHER, 201 E. 57 St., New York 22, N.Y.

HAMISH HAMILTON, Ltd., 90 Great Russell St., London, W.C.1.

HARCOURT, BRACE & Co., 750 Third Ave., New York 17, N.Y.

HARPER & BROTHERS, 49 E. 33 St., New York 16, N.Y.

GEORGE G. HARRAP AND Co., 30–41 Parker St., Kingsway, London, W.C.2.

HASTINGS HOUSE, PUBLISHERS, Inc., 151 E. 50 St., New York 22, N.Y.

HARVARD UNIVERSITY PRESS, 79 Garden St., Cambridge 38, Mass.

D. C. HEATH & Co., 285 Columbus Ave., Boston 16, Mass.

HEATH, CRANTON Ltd., 6 Fleet Lane, Farrington St., London, E.C.4.

HEINEMANN, Ltd., 99 Great Russell St., London, W.C.1.

HENRY HOLT & Co., Inc., 383 Madison Ave., New York 17, N.Y.

HOUGHTON MIFFLIN Co., 2 Park St., Boston 7, Mass.

INDIANA UNIVERSITY PRESS, Bloomington, Ind.

HERBERT JENKINS, Ltd., 3 Duke of York St., St. James's, London, S.W.1.

JOHN LANE, THE BODLEY HEAD, Ltd., 28 Little Russell St., London, W.C.1.

JOHN LEHMANN, Ltd., 25 Gilbert St., London, W.1.

J. B. LIPPINCOTT Co., E. Washington Sq., Philadelphia 5, Pa.

LITTLE, BROWN & Co., 34 Beacon St., Boston 6, Mass.

LOEB LIBRARY (*See* HARVARD UNIVERSITY PRESS).

LONGMANS, GREEN & Co., 55 Fifth Ave., New York 3, N.Y.; 20 Cranfield Road, Toronto 16, Canada

LOW C. SAMPSON & Co., Ltd., 25 Gilbert St., Oxford St., London, W.1.

J. JOHN W. LUCE & Co., 212 Summer St., Boston, Mass.

The MACMILLAN Co., 60 Fifth Ave., New York 11, N.Y.; 70 Bond St., Toronto 2; 10 St. Martin's St., London, W.C.2.

McGRAW-HILL BOOK Co., 330 W. 42 St., New York 36, N.Y.

DAVID McKAY Co., Inc., 55 Fifth Ave., New York 3, N.Y.

MENTAL HEALTH MATERIALS CENTER, 1790 Broadway, New York 19, N.Y.

MERLIN PRESS, Inc., 309 Lafayette St., New York 12, N.Y.

MODERN AGE BOOKS (*Out of business*).

MODERN LIBRARY, Inc., 457 Madison Ave., New York 22, N.Y.

FREDERICK MULLER, Ltd., 110 Fleet St., London, E.C.4.

NATIONAL ASSOCIATION FOR MENTAL HEALTH, 10 Columbus Circle, New York 19, N.Y.

NATIONAL THEATRE CONFERENCE, Cleveland, Ohio.

THOMAS NELSON & SONS, 19 E. 47 St., New York 17, N.Y.; 35 Paternoster Row, London, E.C.4.

NEW DIRECTIONS, 333 Sixth Ave., New York 14, N.Y.

NICHOLSON & WATSON, Ltd., 32–33 Gosfield St., London, W.1.

NOBLE & NOBLE, PUBLISHERS, Inc., 67 Irving Place, New York 3, N.Y.

NONESUCH PRESS, 19 Clivedon Pl., London, S.W.1.

NORTHWESTERN PRESS (*See* T. S. DENISON & Co.).

W. W. NORTON & Co., Inc., 55 Fifth Ave., New York 3, N.Y.

OCCU-PRESS, 489 Fifth Ave., New York 17, N.Y.

THE ODYSSEY PRESS, Inc., 55 Fifth Ave., New York 3, N.Y.

OXFORD UNIVERSITY PRESS, Inc., 114 Fifth Ave., New York 11, N.Y.; Amen House, 480–486 University Ave., Toronto 2; Amen House, Warwick Sq., London, E.C.4.

PENGUIN BOOKS, Inc., 3300 Clipper Mill Rd., Baltimore 11, Md.

PITMAN Publishing Corp., 2 W. 45 St., New York 36, N.Y.; Sir Isaac Pitman & Sons, Ltd., 381–383 Church St., Toronto; 39–41 Parker St., Kingsway, London, W.C.2.

PLAYS, Inc., 8 Arlington Street, Boston 16, Mass.

PRENTICE-HALL, INC., Englewood Cliffs, N.J.

PRINCETON UNIVERSITY PRESS, Princeton, N.J.

G. P. PUTNAM's SONS, 210 Madison Ave., New York 16, N.Y.

RANDOM HOUSE, 457 Madison Ave., New York 22, N.Y.

Row, PETERSON & Co., 2500 Crawford Ave., Evanston, Ill.

RINEHART & Co., Inc., 232 Madison Ave., New York 16, N.Y.; 103 St. Clair Avenue, W., Toronto 7, Canada.

THE RONALD PRESS Co., 15 E. 26 St., New York 10, N.Y.

SCOTT, FORESMAN & Co., 433 E. Erie St., Chicago 11, Ill.

CHARLES SCRIBNER's SONS, 597 Fifth Ave., New York 17, N.Y.

MARTIN SECKER & WARBURG, Ltd., 7 John St., London, W.C.1.

SHEED & WARD, 840 Broadway, New York 3, N.Y.; 33 Maiden Lane, London, W.C.2.

SIDGWICK & JACKSON, Ltd., 1 Tavistock Chambers, Bloomsbury Way, London, W.C.1.

SILVER BURDETT Co., Park Ave. & Columbia Rd., Morristown, N.J.

SIMON & SCHUSTER, Inc., 630 Fifth Ave., New York 20, N.Y.

THE L. W. SINGER Co., Inc., 249 W. Erie Blvd., Syracuse 2, N.Y.

WILLIAM SLOANE ASSOCIATES, 425 Fourth Ave., New York 16, N.Y.

ST. MARTIN'S PRESS, Inc., 103 Park Ave., New York 17, N.Y.

SMALL, MAYNARD & Co. (*Out of business*).

R. R. SMITH, PUBLISHER, Inc., Topside, W. Rindge, New Hampshire.

STAGE GUILD (*Out of business*).

SWEET & MAXWELL, Ltd., 2–3 Chancery Lane, London, W.C.2.

WILLIAM TARG, 25 Fifth Ave., New York 11, N.Y.

THEATRE ARTS BOOKS, 333 Sixth Ave., New York 14, N.Y.

TUDOR PUBLISHING Co., 221 Fourth Ave., New York 3, N.Y.

UNIVERSITY OF CALIFORNIA PRESS, Berkeley 4, Calif.

UNIVERSITY OF CHICAGO PRESS, 5750 Ellis Ave., Chicago 37, Ill.

UNIVERSITY OF DENVER PRESS (*Out of business*).

UNIVERSITY OF NORTH CAROLINA PRESS, Chapel Hill, N.C.

UNIVERSITY OF TEXAS PRESS, Austin 12, Texas.

UNIVERSITY OF WISCONSIN PRESS, 430 Sterling Ct., Madison 6, Wisc.

VANGUARD PRESS, Inc., 424 Madison Ave., New York 17, N.Y.

THE VIKING PRESS, Inc., 625 Madison Ave., New York 22, N.Y.

GEORGE WAHR, 105 N. Main St., Ann Arbor, Mich.

IVES WASHBURN, INC., 55 Fifth Ave., New York 3, N.Y.

WHITESIDE, Inc., 425 Fourth Ave., New York 16, N.Y.

WHITLOCK'S, New Haven, Conn.

WHITTLESEY HOUSE (*See* McGRAW-HILL BOOK Co.).

JOHN WILEY & SONS, Inc., 440 Fourth Ave., New York 16, N.Y.

THE WORLD PUBLISHING Co., 2231 W. 110 St., Cleveland 2, Ohio.

THE WRITER, Inc., 8 Arlington St., Boston 16, Mass.

YALE UNIVERSITY PRESS, 143 Elm Street, New Haven 7, Conn.

PART I

Full-Length Plays

GREEK AND ROMAN DRAMA

Origins of the Greek Theater

THE DRAMATIC IMPULSE is as old as man. There is evidence of an Abydos Passion Play in Egypt perhaps five thousand years ago. The Book of Job in the Bible is dramatic in form. Yet it is to ancient Greece and Rome we must look for the most important influences on our drama.

In Greece, as in many other places, the drama seems to have originated in religious dances and ceremonies—in this case in honor of the god Dionysus. These performances were a strange combination of the mystic and beautiful with animal high spirits and almost incredible coarseness. From the religious elements tragedy developed, and from the vulgar, comedy, the satyric and popular dramatic forms. Beginning in 534 B.C., in Athens, there was a week set apart each year for the competitive presentation of plays. Prizes were awarded to the winning playwrights, who at that time also produced, directed, and acted in their own plays. The "angels", who were proud to pay expenses of the presentations as a gesture of religious faith, had already been enlisted.

THE THEATER

The original theater consisted of a circular playing space, called the orchestra, surrounded on two-thirds of its circumference by the spectators. On the open side of this circular space was a building (*skene*) which formed the background for the play, and behind which the actors changed their costumes. It usually had three doors: from that left of the spectators the actors entered who came from outside Athens, from the right those who came from the city or harbor. The central, more imposing entrance represented the door of a palace. In comedies the scene commonly was taken to represent a street, and the doors those of houses.

Theaters were later built of stone and the *skene* became more elaborate. It was decorated with columns and statues, grew to two stories in height, (the lower projecting to form an additional stage), and at each end a building was erected which might serve as a temple or house. There were no curtains and little or no painted scenery. By the end of the fifth century, B.C., there were such contrivances as a crane to deliver gods from "heaven"; the *eccyclema*, a revolving or movable platform in the central arch, on which small interior scenes might be presented or dead bodies revealed; and sound effects like thunder were quite common.

PRODUCTION

At first all acting was done in the orchestra, and the chorus was most important. It danced and chanted or sang a commentary on the performance of the actors, giving advice, protesting, teaching love of the gods, preaching patriotism, and the like. However, Thespis first created an actor in opposition to the chorus and its leader. Aeschylus created a second, and Sophocles a third. In addition, Aeschylus divided the original chorus of fifty into four groups of twelve (later increased to fifteen).

Gradually the role of the chorus was reduced, but it never vanished, though its songs became more and more mere interruptions of the action. There were never more than three speaking actors on the stage at one time, although some silent parts were introduced. Instead, each actor might don several masks and do several parts. Only men were permitted on the stage. The actors were regarded with respect. They formed an organization which was strong enough to win them freedom from military service and from taxes.

Costumes were elaborate. In tragedy, high boots with thick soles were worn, the gowns had long sleeves, and the masks (which might contain small megaphones) were attached to high-piled headdresses. In comedy, birds, animals and insects were frequently represented in both costumes and masks, low-heeled shoes were worn, and the costumes were grotesquely padded before and behind. Much of this was made necessary because of the large audiences, which might number 15,000.

At its height, during the fifth century, B.C., there were certain other conventions in the plays. Each competing tragic playwright was required to write three tragedies and a satyr play, all to be produced in one day, beginning at dawn. No violence might be shown on the stage. Although time might elapse and locales change *between* plays, within the individual play certain "unities" were to be observed. The unity of time required the action to be comprised within twenty-four hours, the unity of place forbade moving from city to city, and that of action demanded one dominant theme. Only the last was unviolated and is considered of importance today. These unities were first suggested by Aristotle, were then elaborated upon by Seneca, and finally given a rigidity the ancients never intended by the French classicists.

The work of three great Greek tragic playwrights has come down to us. We are still profoundly moved by the majesty of Aeschylus, the humanity and dramatic power of Sophocles, and the strange mixture of realism, sentimentality, and sensationalism to be found in Euripides. In comedy, the political

OEDIPUS TYRANNUS
Sophocles

●

THE CRUCIFIXION
York Cycle of Mystery Plays

LOVE'S LABOR'S LOST
Shakespeare

•

MACBETH
Shakespeare

VOLPONE
Ben Jonson

●

THE IMAGINARY INVALID
Molière

ARMS AND THE MAN
G. Bernard Shaw

●

THE IMPORTANCE OF BEING EARNEST
Oscar Wilde

and personal satire, vivacity and humor of Aristophanes have never been surpassed.

Unfortunately this golden age could not last. The fantastic and uproarious Old Comedy of Aristophanes was replaced by the increasing realism and contemplation of the Middle and New Comedy, best expressed in Menander's dramatizations of home and street life.

The Roman Theater

The Romans adopted the Greek drama as early as 364 B.C., but had little taste for its finer elements. In their hands, the theatrical building itself became very elaborate. The two-thirds circle of spectators was contracted to a semicircle; all acting was moved from the orchestra to an elaborate stage decorated with columns and carving. A roof was sometimes erected over the stage, and an awning could be spread to protect the spectators. Curtains were frequently employed, and they could be rolled down into troughs in the floor of the stage. All the stage machinery of the Greeks was elaborated by the Roman engineering genius. Vitruvius describes scenery mounted on three-sided prisms, permitting three types of sets: a majestic architectural setting for tragedies, a street scene showing two adjacent houses with a garden shrine between for comedy, and a conventionalized landscape of caves, fountains, and rocks for satyr plays.

In tragedy, the Romans copied the sensationalism of Euripides and produced no first-rate tragedian of their own. The plays of Seneca are mere closet dramas. Even the great Greek tragedies were used chiefly as opportunities for tasteless pageants and parades of captured booty. In comedy, the vulgarity and bold humor of Plautus were preferred to the cultivated humor of Terence. Most of the Roman populace flocked rather to the gladiatorial combats in the arena, the naval battles between the triremes in the flooded Coliseum, or if they tolerated comedy, it increasingly became comedy of an unspeakably indecent sort. It was small wonder that the Church opposed drama as it was practiced in Rome. The invading Goths had little appreciation of it, and it eventually disappeared with the collapse of the Empire.

Modern Production

Today we find the great plays of the Greeks tremendously appealing. Modern arena theaters offer a sympathetic background, and the plays are well suited to the outdoor theater. Behind a proscenium arch, single, simple settings will suffice. The choruses may be recited to musical accompaniment, abridged, or sometimes even omitted. The plays may be produced by all men, all women, or mixed casts. The style of acting in ancient times was rather elocutionary, but the modern, more subtle style has been found very effective. The *Medea* as adapted by Robinson Jeffers, and *Antigone* as interpreted by Anouilh (twice performed on television in the year 1956), to say nothing of such treatments of classic themes as *Tiger at the Gates,* demonstrate conclusively the appeal of classical drama today.

BIBLIOGRAPHY

ALLEN, J. T., *Stage Antiquities of the Greeks and Romans* (Longmans, Green, 1927).

BIEBER, MARGARETE, *The History of the Greek and Roman Theater* (Princeton University Press, 1939).

CHENEY, SHELDON, *The Theatre* (Tudor, 1949), Chs. II, III, and IV.

Encyclopædia Britannica; see Drama, Classics, Theater, Costume Design, etc.

FLICKINGER, R. C., *The Greek Theater and Its Drama* (University of Chicago Press, 1922).

HAIGH, A. E., *The Theater* (Oxford, 1907).

KNIFFIN, HERBERT, *Masks* (Manual Arts, 1931), Chs. I and II.

MATTHEWS, BRANDER, *The Development of the Drama* (Scribner, 1903), Chs. II and III.

NICOLL, ALLARDYCE, *World Drama* (Harcourt, Brace, 1949).

SUMMARIES OF PLAYS

AGAMEMNON. Aeschylus (translated by Gilbert Murray).* *The slaying of Agamemnon by his wife, Clytemnestra, and her lover, after his return from the Trojan War.* Tragedy. 1 exterior. 4 m., 2 f., chorus of old men. Ancient Greek costumes. This play is the first of one of the few extant trilogies, and together with *The Libation Bearers* and *The Furies* makes a powerful three-act play. Needs experienced players and direction. OXFORD, 85¢.

ALCESTIS. Euripides (translated by Gilbert Murray). *Admetus' life is saved by the offer of Alcestis to give up hers, but Hercules saves both because of Admetus' kindness to him.* Drama. 1 exterior. 7 m., 3 f., and chorus of women and attendants. Greek costumes. A happy ending makes this one of the most delightful Greek plays for high schools. OXFORD, $1.25.

ANTIGONE. Sophocles (translated by Gilbert Murray). *Antigone rebels against Creon's edict that her brother shall not be given proper burial, and is punished by death, bringing destruction on the family of Creon.* Tragedy. 1 exterior. 6 m., 3 f., chorus of Theban elders. Greek costumes. One of the most famous and beautiful of the Greek tragedies. Needs experienced players. OXFORD, 85¢.

ELECTRA. Euripides. *Electra and Orestes murder their mother, who has killed their father, Agamemnon; Orestes is banished.* Tragedy. 1 exterior. 7 m., 2 f., chorus of women, and followers of Orestes. Greek costumes. (First of trilogy: *Electra, Orestes, Andromache.*) Dramatic, suitable for college. Translated by Gilbert Murray, OXFORD, $1.25; translated by A. S. Way, Loeb Library, HARVARD, $3.00. *Royalty, $25.00.*

* Royalty on all Gilbert Murray translations on application to ALLEN & UNWIN, London.

IPHIGENIA IN TAURIS. Euripides. *Iphigenia has sworn to slay the first Greek who arrives at the Temple, but when her brother Orestes arrives she breaks her vow, and by her influence and her cunning saves him and escapes with him.* Drama. 1 exterior. 5 m., 2 f., chorus of women. Greek costumes. Dramatic and beautiful, good for experienced players. Translated by Gilbert Murray, OXFORD, 85¢; translated by A. S. Way, Loeb Library, HARVARD, $3.00. *Royalty, $25.00.*

LITTLE CLAY CART, THE. King Shudraka (translated by Ryder and Morgan). *A charming story of love and corrupt politics which manages to have meaning 1400 years after its composition.* Comedy in various scenes. Interiors and exteriors. 26 m., 6 f. Ancient Indian costumes. FRENCH, MSS. *Royalty, $25.00.*

LYSISTRATA. Aristophanes. *Lysistrata leads a revolt of Athenian women, who deny themselves to the men of Athens until peace with Sparta is consummated.* Farce. 1 exterior. 7 m., 7 f., choruses of men, women, and ambassadors. Greek costumes. Interesting plot and idea; one of the most playable of the Greek comedies. Translated by B. B. Rogers, Loeb Library, HARVARD, $3.00. *Royalty, $25.00.* Modern Stage Version by Gilbert Seldes, FARRAR & RINEHART.

MEDEA. Euripides (translated by Gilbert Murray). *Jason in order to marry a princess, deserts Medea and dooms her to banishment; she sends poisonous gifts to the bride and kills her sons.* Tragedy. 1 exterior. 5 m., 2 f., 2 children, chorus of Corinthian maidens. Classical costumes. A difficult but dramatic tragedy, requiring emotional actress. OXFORD, 85¢.

OEDIPUS REX. Sophocles (translated by Gilbert Murray). *Oedipus, the King of Thebes, in order to overcome the plague that is afflicting his people, vows to find the murderer of his predecessor, King Laius, and finds to his horror that it is himself, so that he has fulfilled the prophecy, and killed his father and married his mother.* Tragedy. 1 exterior. 5 m., 1 f., 3 children, chorus of Theban elders. Greek royal costumes. The masterpiece of Greek drama, a noble and dignified play, demanding advanced acting and direction. OXFORD, 85¢.

PHORMIO. Terence. *Phormio, the usual parasite, helps himself, and incidentally his friends, by his schemes.* Farce. 1 exterior. 11 m., 2 f. Roman costumes. Easy to produce. *No royalty.*

PROMETHEUS BOUND. Aeschylus (translated by Gilbert Murray). *Prometheus, the Titan, has incurred the anger of Zeus through giving the use of fire to man, and is nailed to a mountain peak for his presumption.* Tragedy. 1 exterior. 6 m., 1 f., chorus of nymphs. Imaginative costumes suitable to theme. Poetic, easy to produce. OXFORD, 85¢.

TROJAN WOMEN. Euripides (translated by Gilbert Murray). *The women of Troy bemoan their fate after the fall of the city.* Tragedy. 1 exterior. 3 m., 5 f., chorus of women. Trojan costumes. Powerful and difficult tragedy. OXFORD, 85¢; translated by A. S. Way, as "Daughters of Troy," Loeb Library, HARVARD, $3.00. *Royalty, $25.00.*

TWINS, THE (MENAECHMI) Plautus. *Entanglements result from the resemblance of twin brothers.* Farce. 1 exterior. 6 m., 4 f. Roman costumes. (This play is the source of Shakespeare's *Comedy of Errors.*) Broadly humorous farce, easy to produce. *No royalty.*

MEDIEVAL AND RENAISSANCE PLAYS

Development of Medieval Drama

THE MIME and the pantomime, jugglers, acrobats, and storytellers were the only dramatic survivals of Rome's fall. In the monastery or convent Terence might be read surreptitiously, a German nun (Hrotswitha) might apologetically compose imitative plays, or a pedantic debate grow dramatic, but the new drama had different roots.

In the tenth century the ritual of the church service was elaborated by tropes. These grew to elementary dialogue and staging, which dramatized the liturgy and thus earned the name of liturgical drama. It was but a step to dramatizing the Bible (mystery plays), the lives of saints (miracle plays), and ethical and religious principles (morality plays). The earliest of these were first presented in the church, but their popularity, the demand that they be given in the vernacular, the increasing realism and comedy, and the exigencies of more colorful production caused them to be moved out onto the church porch. This did not satisfy the growing secular spirit, and they were adopted by guilds or bands of amateurs and taken into the market place where they developed into great cycles of thirty or even fifty plays.

Meantime interludes came to be used between the courses of a feast or to while away an evening. These sometimes resembled the monastic debates, sometimes the moralities, sometimes the farces of Plautus. On the other hand, jugglers, acrobats, and minstrels remained popular, and dramatic elements were evident in the popular dances and celebrations like the Feast of the Boy Bishop.

PRODUCTION

The mystery, miracle and morality plays were performed on the continent on a long stage with simultaneous spot settings representing Heaven, a temple, the jaws of Hell, etc. In England they were performed on two-story wagons called pageants, and in many places on improvised, raised stages. The costumes and properties were sometimes very ornate, but hardly authentic. Trapdoors were frequently employed, and fireworks and comic antics delighted the audience.

Today these plays can sometimes be used at Christmas time. The morality, *Everyman*, has been performed in many languages, on stage and television. Many of these plays, like the Oberammergau Passion, are profoundly moving, while not a few have a fresh, homely realism and humor which are charming. They are suitable for outdoor or arena production, for at best they were performed originally with no background, sometimes only with curtains, and later only with crudely painted scenery.

Drama of the Renaissance

The Renaissance turned attention to the classical drama, notably the comedies of Terence and Plautus and the tragedies of Euripides and Seneca. The courts and schools led in production, but the professional companies, which had developed out of the morality plays and interludes, quickly followed. At first these plays were presented in the original, then translated into the vernacular, and finally imitated, influencing Shakespeare, Jonson, Racine, and other playwrights down to our own day.

PRODUCTION

In Italy the first theaters resembled the Roman, but were roofed; in France, the long, narrow indoor tennis courts were converted into playhouses; while in Spain the city squares and in England the innyards, with their galleries surrounding a central court, provided the model. The first English theater was built in 1576. The Globe and similar theaters were round in shape with three tiers of galleries for spectators. From one wall a large forestage jutted out almost into the middle of the pit where, for a smaller fee, the audience might sit on backless benches or stand. At the rear of this stage, on which most of the acting was done, was a smaller curtained innerstage for caves, banquets, and the like. Above it, was a curtained upper stage which might be used for a balcony, the summit of a hill, or the crow's nest atop a ship's mast. Over these two stages was a musicians' gallery. Over this a roof, supported by two pillars, protected part of the forestage. On either side were doors for exits and entrances onto the forestage, and above these were windows. In its attic was a crane to lower spirits, while below it the stages were equipped with trapdoors. The theater as a whole had no roof. Thus, with the help of the description in the actors' lines, any locale might be suggested, and swift movement was possible, unencumbered by scenery change. This is still the *sine qua non* of the production of any Elizabethan play. Thus, with a Shakespearean play, a permanent or semi-permanent set can be used, with a few simple platforms and an extra set of travellers (or transverse curtains). An outdoor or arena theater is eminently satisfactory. Indeed, Leslie Hotson has recently suggested[1] that Shakespeare himself presented certain of his plays "in the round."

All the roles in these plays were taken by men and boys. Since all performances, except in closed theaters like the Blackfriars, were in daylight, no artificial lighting was required. Costumes were elaborate, but contemporary for the most part.

The plays were announced by a flag flying from the roof of the playhouse, by criers, sometimes by a parade of actors, and, as early as 1564 in England, by playbills. Over London Bridge to the Bankside thronged a motley crowd of nobles, ladies wearing masks to preserve their anonymity, tradesmen, apprentices, pickpockets, and women of uncertain reputation. The disorder inside the theater, aggravated by the dandies sitting on the stage and the

[1] Hotson, J. L., "Shakespeare's Arena," *Atlantic*, February, 1954, pp. 62–66:

orangewomen selling refreshments, constituted a challenge to any actor. The action was accordingly dramatic, the diction rich and sonorous, the comedy broad or witty by turns—all in all, such variety and power as to command attention.

Other Dramatic Forms

The court was especially fond of the masque, which had been imported from Italy. It was frequently written in charming verse ornamented with fantasy, compliment, and allegory, elaborately costumed and masked, accompanied by music of the foremost composers, enacted by the nobles themselves, and set with all the ingenuity and artistry the time could muster. It influenced Shakespeare in his *Midsummer Night's Dream* and many another play, and eventually helped to seal the doom of the open-air theater and to proclaim the rise of the scenic designer.

A quite different form was developed in Italy. This was the *commedia dell'arte*. It employed stock characters like the bragging soldier, the hoodwinked husband, and the young lovers. Dialogue and stage action were improvised to a prepared scenario. It achieved both popular and court success, spread throughout Europe, but slowly degenerated into mere medicine shows. However, it had a profound effect on Molière and Shakespeare, and left us with an inheritance of memorable characters like Pierrot, Pierrette, Pantaloon, and the Doctor. An experiment in *commedia dell'arte* is a must for budding actors.

This golden age of the drama was to degenerate into morbid heroics instead of tragedy, and licentious realism in place of comedy. It was brought to an inglorious end in England when the Puritans closed the theaters in 1642. Still the rich tragedies, gay comedies, and elaborate fancies of the Elizabethan Age provide us with some of our greatest theater today.

BIBLIOGRAPHY

CHAMBERS, E. K., *Elizabethan Stage* (Oxford, Clarendon Press, 1923), Vols. II and III.

CHAMBERS, E. K., *The Medieval Stage* (Oxford, Clarendon Press, 1903), Two vols.

CHENEY, SHELDON, *The Theatre* (Tudor, 1949), Chs. VI, VII, VIII, IX, X, XIII.

CHUTE, MARCHETTE GAYLORD, *Shakespeare of London* (Dutton, 1949).

DEBANKE, CECILE, *Shakespearean Stage Production: Then and Now* (McGraw-Hill, 1953).

HARTLEY, DOROTHY, *Medieval Costume and Life* (Scribner, 1931).

MATTHEWS, BRANDER, *The Development of the Drama* (Scribner, 1903), Ch. IV.

NICOLL, ALLARDYCE, *Stuart Masques and the Renaissance Stage* (London, Harrap, 1937).

NICOLL, ALLARDYCE, *World Drama* (Harcourt, Brace, 1949), Parts II, III, and IV.

REESE, MAX MEREDITH, *Shakespeare, His World and His Work* (St. Martin's Press, 1953).

WEBSTER, MARGARET, *Shakespeare without Tears* (McGraw-Hill, 1942).

SUMMARIES OF PLAYS

AS YOU LIKE IT. William Shakespeare. *Rosalind, banished by her uncle, the usurping Duke, is followed to the Forest of Arden by her cousin, Celia, and there meets Orlando, her father, the banished Duke, his court, and some poetical shepherds.* Romantic comedy. The Forest of Arden. 17 m., 4 f., attendants. Royal and pastoral costumes. A charming and romantic play of atmosphere rather than plot. Ben Greet Edition, DOUBLEDAY. Globe Theatre Streamlined Version, BAKER, *50¢. No royalty.*

COMEDY OF ERRORS, THE. William Shakespeare. *The confusion caused by two twin brothers, and their twin servants, who meet in Ephesus after a separation of seven years.* Farce comedy. 11 m., 5 f., attendants. A delightful and amusing play which may be acted in a street set in the manner of a Roman comedy. Based on Plautus' *The Twins.* Classical costumes. Good for schools. Ben Greet Edition, DOUBLEDAY. Globe Theatre Streamlined Version, BAKER, *50¢. No royalty.*

COMUS. John Milton. *Comus, an enchanter, captures a lady who is traveling through a wood, but she is rescued by her two brothers and by a spirit sent by Jove.* Masque. 1 interior, 2 exteriors. 6 m., 3 f., many extras. Imaginative costumes. The most beautiful and famous English masque, which can be made delightful with music and dances. *Original music, by Henry Lawes, arranged by Sir Frederick Bridge, published by Novello, may be obtained from* H. W. GRAY, 159 E. 48 St., N.Y.C., *No royalty.*

EVERYMAN. Anonymous. *Everyman, in the midst of life, is summoned by God's messenger, Death, and finds himself deserted by all his worldly friends, but goes bravely to his grave accompanied by Faith and Good Deeds.* Drama. 5 m., 12 f. Imaginative costumes. The most famous English morality play. May be made moving and interesting by artistic playing and costuming. Successfully produced by many schools. FRENCH, *50¢. No royalty.*

FAUSTUS, THE TRAGICAL HISTORY OF DOCTOR. Christopher Marlowe. *Dr. Faustus, the famous medieval scholar, sells his soul to the devil for twenty years of youth and power, and regrets it in the end.* Tragedy. 16 m., 2f. Medieval costumes. Dramatic, and has a few fine scenes. Needs cutting, clever acting, and competent directing. Can be made very impressive. Crofts Classics, APPLETON-CENTURY-CROFTS, *45¢. No royalty.*

FRIAR BACON AND FRIAR BUNGAY. Robert Greene. *Edward, Prince of Wales, infatuated with Margaret, sends his friend Lacy, Earl of Lincoln, who loves her himself, to woo her for him; through the magic of Friar Bungay, and the more powerful magic of Friar Bacon, the tangle is solved, and Edward marries Eleanor of Castille, and Lacy marries Margaret.* Romantic comedy. 25 m., 4 f., attendants. Medieval and clerical costumes. One of the Elizabethan plays most adaptable to the modern stage. *No royalty.*

GAMMER GURTON'S NEEDLE. Anonymous. *Gammer Gurton's needle is lost, and through the machinations of Diccon, the village ne'er-do-well, the entire parish is set by the ears; but when Hodge, Gam-*

mer Gurton's man, changes his breeches, the needle is discovered. Farce. 6 m., 4 f. 16th-century popular costumes. The earliest English farce-comedy. Broad, but actable, and amusing. Arranged by Stuart Walker. *Royalty, $10.00 to* FRENCH.

HENRY IV, Part I. William Shakespeare. *Prince Hal spends his time carousing with Falstaff and his low friends, much to the distress of his father, Henvy IV, but finally shows his true worth and valor by overcoming Hotspur and helping put down the rebellion.* Historical drama. 19 m., 3 f., extras. Historical costumes of period. Often combined with *Henry IV,* Part II, and cut to make one performance. Crofts Classics, APPLETON-CENTURY-CROFTS, *45¢.* Acting Edition, FRENCH, *50¢. No royalty.*

HENRY IV, Part II. William Shakespeare. *Prince Hal continues his reformation, is made King on the death of his father, and reproves and discards Falstaff.* Historical drama. 37 m., 4 f., extras. Historical costumes of period. A continuation of Part I. See above. New Complete Acting Edition, FRENCH, *$1.50. No royalty.*

HENRY V. William Shakespeare. *Prince Hal, now Henry V, proves his virtues, and wins glorious victories in France.* Historical drama. 28 m., 4 f. Historical costumes of period. A continuation of *Henry IV.* One of the best historical plays. Acting Edition, FRENCH, *50¢. No royalty.*

JULIUS CAESAR. William Shakespeare. *Brutus, a noble Roman patriot, is drawn into the conspiracy against his friend, Julius Caesar, kills him, but is in turn outwitted and defeated by Caesar's friends, led by Antony and Octavius.* Historical tragedy. 31 m., 2 f., attendants. Roman costumes. A noble and difficult play, but possible for skilled amateurs. Can be made stirring and moving. Crofts Classics, APPLETON-CEN-

TURY-CROFTS, *45¢.* Ben Greet Edition, DOUBLEDAY (out of print, but available in libraries). Globe Theater Streamlined Version, BAKER, *50¢. No royalty.*

KNIGHT OF THE BURNING PESTLE, THE. Beaumont and Fletcher. *A grocer and his wife in the audience insist on a play about a London merchant, instead of the romantic play the actors have prepared, and nominate their apprentice, Ralph, to play the lead, thus bringing about a complicated double play full of misunderstandings.* Burlesque comedy. 19 m., 5 f., attendants. Elizabethan bourgeois costumes. A burlesque on the romantic extravagance of knight-errantry and on certain Elizabethan playhouse customs. Demands skilled playing and a sophisticated audience, but can be made very delightful. Needs cutting. *No royalty.*

LOVE'S LABOR'S LOST. William Shakespeare. *Ferdinand, King of Navarre, with three knightly followers, has made a fantastic vow to spend three years in seclusion, but affairs of state cause him to interview the Princess of France and three attending ladies, and the inevitable happens.* Comedy. 13 m., 6 f. Royal costumes. Witty and amusing with clever acting. *No royalty.*

MASTER PIERRE PATELIN. Anonymous. *Patelin, a thieving shepherd, escapes justice by the aid of a rascally lawyer, and by turning his own trick against the lawyer succeeds in cheating him too.* Farce. 5 m., 1 f. Medieval costumes. The most famous of the French medieval farces. Can be played in 2 interiors, or out-of-doors before two or three houses in in the manner of a Roman comedy. Amusing and easily actable, but short for full evening. *No royalty.*

MERCHANT OF VENICE, THE. William Shakespeare. *Bassanio, a young Venetian nobleman, borrows money* *from his friend Antonio in order to woo an heiress, Portia of Belmont; Antonio borrows the money from Shylock and pledges a pound of flesh, which he is about to lose, when Shylock is outwitted by Portia, disguised as a lawyer, so all ends happily.* Romantic comedy. 14 m., 3 f. Italian (Renaissance) costumes. In spite of its unbelievable plot, one of the most dramatic and actable of the romantic plays. *No royalty.*

MERRY WIVES OF WINDSOR, THE. William Shakespeare. *Falstaff, in love with two ladies of Windsor, fails to keep them separated, and they trick him into a series of amusing and trying experiences.* Farce comedy. 16 m., 4 f. Elizabethan bourgeois costumes. One of the most playable of Shakespeare's farce-comedies. FRENCH, 50¢. *No royalty.*

MIDSUMMER NIGHT'S DREAM, A. William Shakespeare. *A quarrel between Oberon and Titania, King and Queen of the Fairies, brings about confusion between two pairs of lovers, who have fled to the forest near Athens, and to a group of mechanics, led by Bottom the weaver, who are rehearsing a play to be played before Duke Theseus; but a general reconciliation brings about a happy ending.* Romantic comedy. 11 m., 10 f., fairies and attendants. Royal and workmen's costumes. Needs music, dances, and attractive staging. Suitable for out-of-doors. Henry Thomas Edition for Junior High, BAKER, 50¢; Globe Theater Streamlined Version, BAKER, 50¢. *No royalty.*

MUCH ADO ABOUT NOTHING. William Shakespeare. *Hero, an Italian princess, betrothed to Claudio, is slandered by Don John, and denounced by Claudio, but the villainy is discovered and all ends happily, and in the confusion of the plot Beatrice and Benedick who have both forsworn love and matrimony, are tricked into becoming lovers.* Romantic comedy. 16 m., 3 f. Renaissance costumes. A witty and delightful comedy. May be played out-of-doors. Crofts Classics, APPLETON-CENTURY-CROFTS, 45¢. Winthrop Ames Edition, BAKER, 75¢. *No royalty.*

RALPH ROISTER DOISTER. Nicholas Udall. *Ralph, a foolish dandy, is tricked by his friend, Mathew Merygreeke, who pretends to help him win the love of Dame Custance; she, however, remains true to Gawyn Goodluck, who carries her away from the defeated Ralph.* Comedy. 9 m., 4 f. 16th-century costumes. One of the earliest English comedies, can be made amusing and picturesque. *No royalty.*

ROMEO AND JULIET. William Shakespeare. *Romeo and Juliet, offspring of two noble families of Verona, secretly marry; Juliet, to avoid another marriage, takes a magic opiate, and Romeo, believing she is dead, kills himself, thus bringing about her death.* Tragedy. 13 m., 3 f., extras. Italian Renaissance costumes. One of the most colorful and actable of the Shakespearean tragedies. Needs advanced playing and directing. Crofts Classics, APPLETON-CENTURY-CROFTS, 45¢. New Complete Acting Edition, FRENCH, $1.50; Globe Theater Streamlined Version, BAKER, 50¢. *No royalty.*

SHOEMAKERS' HOLIDAY, THE. Thomas Dekker. *A young nobleman, Lacy, in love with Rose Eyre, the daughter of a master shoemaker who has become Lord Mayor of London, disguises himself as a Dutch shoemaker, works in the shop, and wins Rose and the forgiveness of the King.* Comedy. 17 m., 4 f. (Elizabethan) workmen's costumes. Pleasant old comedy for advanced players. *No royalty.*

TAMING OF THE SHREW, THE. William Shakespeare. *A rich gentleman of Padua, Baptista, refuses to allow his gentle younger daughter, Bianca, to marry until his shrewish* *older one, Katherine, is married. Bianca's wooers find a willing victim in Petruchio, who tames Katherine into a more submissive wife than Bianca.* Farce comedy. 13 m., 5 f., attendants. Italian Renaissance costumes. A rollicking farce-comedy, often played. New Complete Acting Edition, FRENCH, *$1.50*; Globe Theater Streamlined Version, BAKER, *50¢. No royalty.*

TEMPEST, THE. William Shakespeare. *Prospero, rightful Duke of Milan, has been banished from his dukedom and cast upon a desert island with his daughter, Miranda. By aid of his magic, after a period of years, he brings his enemies to the island, revenges himself, and causes Miranda to marry the son of one of his pardoned enemies, the King of Naples.* Comedy. 15 m., 4 f., extras. Italian royalty and seamens' costumes. One of the most charming and delightful comedies. Needs music, dances, and skillful direction. Crofts Classics, APPLETON-CENTURY-CROFTS, *45¢.* Globe Theater Streamlined Version, BAKER, *50¢. No royalty.*

TWELFTH NIGHT. William Shakespeare. *Orsino, Duke of Illyria, loves Olivia, a noble lady, who has fallen in love with Viola, one of the Duke's servants disguised as a page. The appearance of Sebastian, Viola's twin brother whom she thought dead, brings about the denouement, for Olivia marries Sebastian, and the Duke marries Viola.* Romantic comedy. 12 m., 3 f. Royal costumes suitable to period. One of the best Shakespeare plays for schools, charming and effective, with humorous and poetic scenes. Crofts Classics, APPLETON-CENTURY-CROFTS, *45¢.* William Warren Edition, BAKER, *75¢;* Globe Theater Streamlined Version, BAKER, *50¢;* New Complete Acting Edition, FRENCH, *$1.50. No royalty.*

WINTER'S TALE, THE. William Shakespeare. *Leontes, King of Sicilia, suspicious of his wife, banishes her and their daughter, Perdita; sixteen years later he finds his daughter as the betrothed of Florizel, Prince of Bohemia, is convinced of his wife's innocence, and his wife whom he believes to be dead returns from her place of seclusion and forgives him.* Comedy. 22 m., 8 f. Royal costumes suitable to period. Difficult, but interesting, with fine lines and beautiful characters. HEATH, *$1.64. No royalty.*

PLAYS FROM 1650 TO 1870

DURING THIS PERIOD classicism and romanticism in turn held sway, but the dominating influences were remarkably the same. Shakespeare's tragedy and Molière's comedy of manners provided the models for playwrights. The theater buildings were ornate and derived from those of the Italian courts. Moreover, wherever the drama flourished in Europe, the picture was quite similar.

When, in 1660, Charles II and his court returned to England from their exile in France, they found the theaters empty except for an opera now and then. As in France, only a few theaters were licensed. The dissolute court took these over, sat on the stage, brawled in the pit, and made assignations against the background of an ailing stage. The brilliant, unmoral comedies and the falsely heroic tragedies strove in vain for attention. To bolster their appeal, producers turned to elaborate stage settings and tricks of production.

Theaters

Like the baroque Italian court theaters, the new buildings were decked out in columns, festooned with carved garlands, cupids and goddesses. They usually contained horseshoe-shaped galleries rising tier upon tier to the painted ceiling. The floor of the auditorium was slanted. Normally the orchestra seats still had no backs and the best seats were in the boxes. The stage was framed by an ornate proscenium arch, although a huge apron, upon which most of the acting took place, still projected deep into the pit. The stage floor during much of this period was also slanted, giving us our modern terms *upstage* and *downstage*. The actors made their entrances and exits through two to six proscenium doors or between the wing pieces (for there were no practical doors in the sets). Inigo Jones had introduced the architectural perspective settings of the Italians, and the masques had had their influence. There were no box sets, but rather wing pieces and shutters which were placed in channels called grooves and might be closed from each side to form a new set. In the back, painted drops were used. A front curtain rolled up, but it rose only after the triple overture and prologue and then did not lower again till after the epilogue. Because the theaters were now roofed, it was necessary to use candles and lamps. Chandeliers could be raised and lowered. Foot-candles and lamps were employed, sometimes being floated in a trough to prevent fire. In some places footlights are still called *floats*. Sometimes these footlights were equipped with devices for dimming and coloring. Every trick effect was tried: clouds, elevators, trapdoors, wind and rain, horses, and decapitations. Costumes were elaborate but not historically accurate, and Gar-

13

rick played both *Hamlet* and *Macbeth* dressed like an eighteenth-century gentleman. Women now appeared on the stage, but they were not always of a type to ennoble it. The solid citizen stayed home and frowned at the wickedness of the theater.

Conditions Improved

Finally, in 1698, Jeremy Collier attacked the immorality of the stage, and slowly some improvement was shown. This was accomplished by the writing of brilliant and more circumspect dramatists like Sheridan and Goldsmith, and by the influence of great actors like David Garrick (who finally ejected the gallants from the stage), Mrs. Siddons and Edmund Kean. Because of the influence of the *classicists* and the example of Racine, Shakespeare had fallen into disrepute, but now, though rewritten without comic relief and undue violence, he was performed once more. The rising middle classes who supplanted the aristocracy about the middle of the eighteenth century came to the theater once again. Unfortunately they had as little taste for great poetry and majestic tragedy as for the sparkling and licentious comedy of manners. They preferred something more realistic, but the early efforts degenerated into sentiment and melodrama. In the nineteenth century poets like Shelley, Byron, and Tennyson were not able to write really successful plays, but on the continent the romantic movement inspired the dramas of Dumas and Hugo, Schiller and Lessing. A sense of form was taught by those tailors of the well-made play, Scribe and Sardou. The American drama, which was born during this period, likewise gave promise. A better day was coming for the theater.

From the mixed harvest of over two centuries we can select many plays which are still popular on the stage and television screen today. There are charming, witty English comedies of manners like *She Stoops to Conquer* and *The Rivals,* eminently suitable for school production. The neoclassic tragedies of Racine, the rich farce-satires of Molière, and the comedies of Goldoni are theatrical treasure. Actors and audiences deserve the opportunity to sample many styles of dramatic writings which are well illustrated in the list below.

BIBLIOGRAPHY

BENTLEY, GERALD EADES, *The Jacobean and Caroline Stage, Dramatic Companies and Players* (Oxford, Clarendon Press, 1941).

BOAS, F. S., *An Introduction to Eighteenth-Century Drama, 1700–1780* (Oxford, Clarendon Press, 1953).

BOSWELL, ELEANORE, *The Restoration Court Stage, 1660–1702* (Harvard, 1932).

CHENEY, SHELDON, *The Theatre* (Tudor, 1949), Chs. XIV, XV, XVI, XVII, XVIII, XIX.

HUGHES, GLENN, *A History of the American Theatre, 1700–1950* (French, 1951).

MATTHEWS, BRANDER, *Development of the Drama* (Scribner, 1903), Ch. VII.

NICOLL, ALLARDYCE, *A History of English Drama, 1660–1900* (Cambridge (Eng.) University Press, 1952–1955), Vols. I–IV.

NICOLL, ALLARDYCE, *World Drama* (Harcourt, Brace, 1949), Parts V, VI, VII, VIII.

QUINN, ARTHUR HOBSON, *A History of the American Drama, from the Beginning to the Civil War* (Appleton-Century-Crofts, 1946).

SUMMERS, MONTAGUE, *The Restoration Theatre* (Macmillan, 1934).

UHLER, J. H., *Best Eighteenth Century Comedies* (Crofts, 1929), Ch. XIV.

SUMMARIES OF PLAYS

BEAUX' STRATAGEM, THE. George Farquhar. *Aimwell and Archer, two London beaux who have dissipated their fortunes, go to the country as master and man to win a country heiress, but fall in love, and amend their ways.* Comedy. 4 interiors. 11 m., 5 f. 18th-century costumes. A brilliant and playable old comedy. *No royalty.*

BENEFICENT BEAR, THE. Carlo Goldoni (translated by Barrett H. Clark). *Monsieur Geronte has a gruff exterior but a kind heart, and finally saves his nephew, Delancour, from financial ruin, and his niece, Angélique, from an undesirable marriage.* Comedy. 1 interior. 5 m., 3 f. French costumes, early 18th century. Interesting and easy to produce. FRENCH, 50¢. *No royalty.*

CONTRAST, THE. Royall Tyler. *Maria, unwilling fiancée of Mr. Dimple, a scheming, unfaithful fop, meets her ideal in Colonel Manly, morally impeccable but lacking in social grace. When her father accidentally discovers the true qualities of both suitors, he sees the wisdom of her choice.* Comedy. 3 interiors, 1 exterior. 5 m., 4 f., servants. American costumes, late 18th century. One of the earliest social comedies with an American background. *No royalty.*

CRICKET ON THE HEARTH, THE (arranged by Gilmour Brown from the novel of Charles Dickens). *Beautiful little play based on Dickens' well-known story.* Drama in 3 acts. 2 interiors. 7 m., 8 f., extras (including 12 children). Excellent parts, requiring rather advanced acting. Early Victorian costumes. FRENCH, 75¢. *Royalty, $10.00.*

CRITIC, THE. Richard B. Sheridan. *The highly esteemed critic, Mr. Dangle, goes in company with Messrs. Puff and Sneer to the rehearsal of the former's tragedy; the tragedy is rehearsed to the comments of the critics.* Burlesque comedy. 2 interiors. 14 m., 5 f., extras. Costumes of 1777 and Elizabethan. An amusing and satirical burlesque for experienced amateurs. *No royalty.*

DAVID GARRICK. T. W. Robertson. *David Garrick promises Ada's father to cure her of her infatuation for him, and although he finds he loves her, he keeps his word by acting like a drunken boor; but the scheme is disclosed, and they are finally married with her father's blessing.* Romantic comedy. 2 interiors. 8 m., 3 f. 18th-century costumes. Romantic comedy for unsophisticated audience, not difficult with good actor for title role. *No royalty.*

FAN, THE. Carlo Goldoni (translated by Henry B. Fuller). *Signora Can-*

dida breaks her fan, and her lover, Evaristo, buys her another, but, too bashful to present it to her directly, he gives it to Giannina to present, causing misunderstanding and difficulties, which are at length overcome. Comedy. 1 exterior. 10 m., 4 f. Italian costumes, 18th century. Rather difficult to stage, but gay, romantic, and colorful. FRENCH, 75¢. *No royalty.*

FANCHON THE CRICKET. George Sand (translated by August Waldauer). *Fanchon is called "The Cricket" because she is thought by the villagers to be very ugly and lazy. Her conduct in the climax situation proves the nobleness of her character, and she finally marries the son of a rich farmer.* French costumes, middle 19th century. Drama in 5 acts. 3 interiors, 2 exteriors. 9 m., 8 f. Good characters, striking situations, interesting for advanced amateurs. *No royalty.*

FASHION. Anna Cora Mowatt. *Mrs. Tiffany, coached by her French maid and financed by her husband's forgeries, tries to be a lady of fashion. Her daughter, about to marry a continental cook posing as a count, is saved by the revelations of her governess, Gertrude—the one upright person in this shallow world of fashion. Gertrude is finally acknowledged as heiress by Mr. Tiffany's honest farmer friend, Adam Trueman, who averts general disaster.* Comedy. 6 interiors. 8 m., 5 f. Often performed as a revival, in costumes of 1850, with staging of the period. FRENCH, 50¢. *No royalty.*

GOOD-NATURED MAN, THE. Oliver Goldsmith. *Young Honeywood is in love with Miss Richland, but is too humble to press his suit, until after he is arrested for debt, at the instigation of his uncle, who wishes to teach him a lesson. Through the agency of Miss Richland, Honeywood is released, and all ends happily.* Comedy. 3 interiors. 10 m., 5 f. English costumes, late 18th century. A play of

comic situation and good character drawing, not too difficult. *No royalty.*

LADIES' BATTLE. E. Scribe & E. Legouvé (translated by T. W. Robinson). *Two ladies fall in love with a spy they have saved from capture, and then turn against each other in a struggle for him.* Comedy in 3 acts. 1 interior. 7 m., 2 f. Costumes, early 19th century. Very effective, famous old play. *No royalty.*

LONDON ASSURANCE. Dion Boucicault. *Grace Harkaway is forced by her father's strange will to marry Sir Harcourt Courtley or lose her inheritance. His son, however, under an assumed name, outfaces his father, wins Grace, and all is forgiven.* Comedy. 1 exterior, 2 interiors. 9 m., 3 f. 19th-century English costumes. Famous old play with humorous and involved situations, not too difficult for production in high schools. *No royalty.*

MERCHANT GENTLEMAN, THE. Molière (translated by Curtis H. Page). *M. Jourdain, a rich merchant, resolves to be a gentleman, but is tricked by all.* Farce. 1 interior. 12 m., 5 f., extras. French costumes, 17th century. A famous satiric comedy, that can be made colorful with music, dances, and costuming. *No royalty.*

MISER, THE. Molière. *Harpagon, a miser, is in love with the dowry of the girl his son wishes to marry, and also treats his daughter badly, but is left in the end with only his cash box.* Drama. 1 interior. 11 m., 4 f. French costumes, 17th century. The only serious play by Molière suitable for amateurs; excellent parts, needs good actor in the title role. Dramatic and effective. *No royalty.*

MISTRESS OF THE INN, THE. Carlo Goldoni (published as MIRANDOLINA, adapted by Lady Gregory). *Mirandolina, the mistress of the inn, challenged by a misanthropic cava-*

lier, forces him to succumb to her charms, but in spite of this, and two other noble lovers, finally marries Fabrizio, a faithful servant. Comedy. 3 interiors. 5 m., 1 f. Italian costumes, 18th century. Not much plot, but excellent characterizations and comic situations. Possible for all-girl cast. FRENCH, $1.25. Royalty $25.00.

PHAEDRA. Racine (translated by Robert Henderson). Phaedra, the wife of Theseus, hearing that he is dead, reveals her love for her stepson, Hippolytus; Theseus returns, and to revenge herself on Hippolytus, who has scorned her advances, Phaedra accuses him. As he is about to flee with his sweetheart, Aricia, Hippolytus is slain; Phaedra confesses and dies. Poetic tragedy. 1 interior, 3 m., 5 f. Classic Greek costumes. One of the most famous of the French classical tragedies, moving and difficult. No royalty.

RASMUS MONTANUS. Ludwig Holberg. (translated by Oscar James Campbell & Frederic Schenck) Rasmus Montanus, the son of a poor peasant, returns from the university, and with his newly acquired manners and information he sets the village by the ears, argues with the bailiff, quarrels with his family and his prospective father-in-law, and is subdued finally by a lieutenant who threatens to draft him for the army. Farce. 1 interior, 1 exterior. 8 m., 3 f. Danish costumes, 18th century. A famous Danish farce, broad and rollicking, excellent for amateurs. No royalty.

RIVALS, THE. Richard B. Sheridan. Bob Acres, a country squire, finds himself an unwilling rival to Captain Jack Absolute for the hand of Lydia Languish, a romantic lady, who does not wish to marry Jack unless his father, Sir Anthony, and her aunt, Mrs. Malaprop, object to the affair. Comedy. 5 interiors, 4 exteriors (can be reduced). 8 m., 4 f. English costumes, 18th century. The most famous and often played of the 18th-century comedies. Crofts Classics, APPLETON-CENTURY-CROFTS, 45¢. FRENCH, 50¢; BAKER, $1.00. No royalty.

SCHOOL FOR SCANDAL, THE. Richard B. Sheridan. Sir Peter Teazle has married a young wife, with whom he is continually quarrelling, but is finally reconciled to her, after discovering that his respectable nephew, Joseph Surface, is a villain, and the ne'er-do-well Charles Surface is an honorable man. Comedy. 7 interiors, 12 m., 4 f., servants. English costumes, 18th century. Sheridan's best comedy, and probably the best high comedy in the English language; brilliant, satiric, and witty. FRENCH, 50¢; BAKER, $1.00. No royalty.

SHE STOOPS TO CONQUER. Oliver Goldsmith. Charles Marlowe, a bashful gentleman, is sent to the country by his father to woo an heiress, Kate Hardcastle. He mistakes her father's house for an inn, and her for a barmaid, and wins her by mistake. Farce comedy. 3 interiors, 1 exterior. 7 m., 4 f., servants, etc. English costumes, 18th century. The classical comedy of mistaken identity; humorous; much played. Crofts Classics, APPLETON-CENTURY-CROFTS, 45¢. BAKER, 75¢. No royalty.

WAY OF THE WORLD, THE. William Congreve. In order to win Millamant, Mirabell, a philosophic gentleman, plots to have Lady Wishfort, Millamant's guardian, fall in love with Sir Rowland, who is really Mirabell's servant in disguise. The plot is discovered. However, Mirabell saves Lady Wishfort's fortune from the scheming Fainall, and everything is forgiven. Comedy. 2 interiors, 1 exterior. 6 m., 8 f., servants. English costumes of Restoration. A complicated but brilliant comedy of manners for mature players and sophisticated audiences. Crofts Classics, APPLETON-CENTURY-CROFTS, 45¢. No royalty.

MODERN PLAYS

MODERN DRAMA has been shaped by many forces, not so much local as world-wide. First, its inspiration is in the past: in the drama and poetry of Shakespeare, in the technique of Scribe, in the tragedy of Sophocles, in the realism of Ibsen, in the pure poetry of the Oriental theater. But it also reflects the consequences of the Industrial Revolution in its preoccupation with social problems. It mirrors the scientific development of the age in its stage machinery, in its obsession with the here and now, its psychological insight, and its fear of new Frankenstein monsters the laboratory bids fair daily to create. With the questioning of long-held religious beliefs, the modern theater seeks new security, a new vision, a new poetry, or flees madly down the paths of pure entertainment and fantasy. In a world freed of barriers to communication, it experiments with many styles of writing, acting, and setting.

Theaters

In all this, the theater is aided by a stage technique unparalleled in history. The newest buildings are increasingly simple and functional, and reflect the democratic spirit of our era. In the nineteenth century for the first time all seats were turned to face the stage in a wedge-shaped arrangement, reserved seats became common, and seats in the orchestra were first given backs and made comfortable. Now, ornate galleries and boxes are disappearing, except in the older opera houses, and the emphasis is no longer upon spectator display but on visibility and audibility.

On the stage, gas and then electricity made lighting an art capable of the most subtle control, creating a stage setting out of light itself. Revolving stages, elevator stages, stage wagons, and a thousand devices are powered now by electricity. To bring everything under its control, the so-called picture frame stage has developed: the stage apron has contracted and all acting takes place within the proscenium arch. The slanted stage and cumbersome methods of scene shifting have vanished. The box set has replaced drop and wings for interiors. Every phase of modern art, from the painstaking realism of Belasco to the cubism of Picasso has been reflected in scenery design. We have had permanent sets and space sets, and out of it all a remarkable flexibility has been achieved.

Production

From the second quarter of the nineteenth century, increasing care was taken to secure historical accuracy in costuming. Makeup also developed into a fine art, which has been further stimulated by the need for greater veri-

18

similitude in the movies and television. The tendency toward realism, the revolt against melodrama, and the requirements of the camera have turned acting away from rhetoric and toward subtlety, restraint, and inner truth.

Realism

Realism is still one of the most important influences in our theater. The inspiration stems considerably from Continental playrights like Ibsen, Strindberg, Hauptmann, and the Russians. It has had many diverse effects, including the naturalism of Galsworthy, the local color of Synge, the "purposeful laughter" of Shaw, and the abstract questioning of Pirandello.

To support the realistic drama, several concepts developed. One of these was that of the "fourth wall," by which it is suggested that the stage represents life, with the audience as eavesdroppers. Another is the doctrine of artistic distance—that the actors must seem unaware of the audience and that the audience must not intrude on the stage illusion lest its artificiality be exposed.

These and other concepts have not been unquestioned. Realism itself has developed a thousand facets: the problem play, the folk drama, the psychological play, and many others. But essentially realism is not a separate entity and can mingle with many other attitudes, as in the historic drama, expressionism, and the like. Theories and practices of all types have given tremendous variety and power to the modern theater. For instance, in the field of stage setting, the realism of Belasco inspired the revolt of Gordon Craig and Adolphe Appia. The concept of the fourth wall has been eliminated by arena staging.

Theater Organization

There has also been a change in theater organization. The old repertory theaters and versatile companies of actors have been replaced by special casting for each play which, instead of running for a night or two, may be played for hundreds of performances. Although a star-system continues, the ensemble effect of an entire production, including the smallest role and the most minute details of stage setting, has become more important. Accordingly, the producer and director have assumed greater significance, as we can see in the example of Max Reinhardt. On the other hand, the social status of the actor has also improved, as was demonstrated dramatically when Henry Irving became the first actor to be knighted at the English Court.

Theaters were organized into circuits, which froze out many companies. As a result of improved transportation, New York became the theater capital of the United States, as Hollywood did of films, and both of television. With expensive staging, the cost of play producing rose, and commercialism became rampant, making it virtually impossible for new playrights and actors to secure a hearing. This has stimulated the growth of the "independent" or "little" theater. As early as 1887 André Antoine established the Théâtre Libre in Paris, and the illustrious list includes the Freie Bühne in Berlin, the

Provincetown Players, and a host of member groups. Many of these survived only a short time, but some proved stronger, like the Washington Square Players who developed into the Theater Guild. George Pierce Baker's "47 Workshop" at Harvard is significant of the influence the universities have had on both the independent and commercial theaters. The government too has taken a hand and subsidized national theaters in many countries, and some of these have achieved distinction. For a brief time the U.S. government supported the Federal Theatre in the depression of the 1930's.

We are today in the midst of tremendous theatrical ferment, unequalled in the history of the world. America has achieved a significant place in this, and there is hardly a town where living drama is not presented with considerable frequency. Add to this the popularity of radio, film, and television plays and we see a theatrical activity which is without precedent. Naturally, all the plays written to satisfy this need are not good, and haste of composition is hardly a guarantee of quality. Herewith we present a list of worthwhile plays of the last few generations—plays of all types and countries, plays among which surely anyone can find the means of creating that unforgetable moment of spiritual exaltation worthy of the name and in the distinguished tradition of great theater.

BIBLIOGRAPHY

GENERAL

Cheney, Sheldon, *The Theatre* (Tudor, 1949).

Craig, Gordon, *On the Art of the Theatre* (Small, Maynard, 1924).

Nicoll, Allardyce, *A History of Late Nineteenth Century Drama, 1850–1900* (Cambridge, [Eng.], University Press, 1946).

Simonson, Lee, *The Stage Is Set* (Harcourt, Brace, 1932).

AMERICAN

Blum, Daniel, *A Pictorial History of the American Theatre* (Greenberg, 1950).

Cagey, Edmond M., *Revolution in the American Drama* (Columbia University Press, 1947).

Clurman, Harold, *The Fervent Years* (Knopf, 1945).

Flexner, Eleanor, *American Playwrights, 1918–1938* (Simon & Schuster, 1938).

Freedley, George and Reeves, John A., *A History of the Theatre* (Crown, 1941).

Gassner, John, *The Theatre in Our Times* (Crown, 1954).

Houghton, Norris, *Advance from Broadway* (Harcourt, Brace, 1941).

Hughes, Glenn, *A History of the American Theatre, 1700–1950* (French, 1951).

Jones, Margo, *Theatre-in-the-Round* (Rinehart, 1951).

Krutch, Joseph Wood, *The American Drama Since 1918* (Random House, 1939).

Langner, Lawrence, *The Magic Curtain* (Dutton, 1951).

Macgowan, Kenneth and Melnitz, William, *The Living Stage* (Prentice-Hall, 1955).

Morehouse, Ward, *Matinee Tomorrow: Fifty Years of Our Theatre* (Whittlesey House, 1949).

Morris, Lloyd R., *Curtain Time* (Random House, 1953).

O'Hara, Frank Hurlburt, *Today in American Drama* (University of Chicago Press, 1939).

Quinn, Arthur Hobson, A *History of the American Drama from the Civil War to the Present Day* (Appleton-Century-Crofts, 1943).

BRITISH

Cunliffe, J. W., *Modern English Playwrights* (Harper, 1927).

Dickinson, Thomas H., *The Contemporary Drama in England* (Little, Brown, 1931).

Hudson, Lynton Alfred, *The English Stage, 1850–1950* (London, Harrap, 1957).

Reynolds, Ernest, *Modern English Drama: A Survey of the Theatre from 1900.* (London, Harrap, 1949).

Robinson, Lennox, *The Irish Theatre* (London, Macmillan, 1939).

Speaight, Robert, *Drama Since 1939* (London, Longmans, Green, 1947).

EUROPEAN

Clark, Barrett H., *European Theories of the Drama* (Crown, 1947).

Clark, Barrett H., and Freedley, George, A *History of Modern Drama* (Appleton-Century-Crofts, 1947).

Clark, Barrett H., A *Study of the Modern Drama,* 2nd rev. ed. (D. Appleton-Century, 1938).

Gassner, John, *Masters of the Drama,* 3rd ed. (Dover, 1954).

MacLeod, Joseph, *The New Soviet Theatre* (London, Allen & Unwin, 1943).

Macgowan, Kenneth and Jones, R. E., *Continental Stagecraft* (Harcourt, Brace, 1922).

Moderwell, Hiram L., *The Theatre of Today,* new ed. (Dodd, Mead, 1927).

Nicoll, Allardyce, *World Drama: from Aeschylus to Anouilh* (Harcourt, Brace, 1950).

Wilson, N. Scarlyn, *European Drama* (London, Nicholson & Watson, 1937).

SUMMARIES OF PLAYS

ABE LINCOLN IN ILLINOIS. Robert E. Sherwood. *The critical years of Lincoln's early manhood up to the moment of his election as President.* Biographical play. 7 interiors, 3 exteriors. Costumes 1830–60. 25 m., 7 f. Many of the single scenes may be used as one-act plays. DRAMATISTS PLAY SERVICE, *90¢; Royalty, $25.00 ($10.00 for one-act play).*

ABRAHAM LINCOLN. John Drinkwater. *An episodic depiction of dramatic events in the great President's career.* Drama in 6 scenes. 6 interiors. Flexible cast (30 m., 4 f., extras).

Costumes, Civil War. Difficult; demands advanced direction. FRENCH, MSS. Royalty, $25.00.

ACCENT ON YOUTH. Samson Raphaelson. *A sophisticated comedy showing that age is no barrier to love. A middle-aged playwright falls in love with a young woman, but gracefully stands aside for a time, even helps a young man attempting to win the affections of the girl.* Comedy in 3 acts. Interior. Modern costumes. 6 m., 3 f. For advanced casts. FRENCH, $1.00. Royalty, $35.00.

ADDING MACHINE, THE. Elmer Rice. *The play shows, in stark outline, the life history, and, in its later scenes, the death history of Mr. Zero, a cog in the vast machine of modern business.* Drama in 7 scenes. 5 interiors, 2 exteriors. 14 m., 9 f. Modern costumes. Powerful and expressionistic play, suitable only for very advanced amateurs and sophisticated audience. FRENCH, $1.00. Royalty, $50.00.

ADMIRABLE CRICHTON, THE. James M. Barrie. *The family of Lord Loam are shipwrecked on an island where Crichton, the butler, takes command, winning the affection of Lord Loam's daughter, Lady Mary. They are rescued and return to civilization, Lady Mary to her former suitor and Crichton to his old position.* Fantasy in four acts. 2 interiors, 1 difficult exterior. Modern costumes. 13 m, 12 f. Satiric play, offering excellent roles. FRENCH, $1.00. Royalty, $35.00 first performance, $25.00 each subsequent performance.

AH, WILDERNESS! Eugene O'Neill. *Richard, a high school senior and a confirmed rebel, disturbs his family and the average Connecticut small-town they live in with his anarchic, reactionary views, and his violent behavior. He falls passionately in love with a neighbor's girl, and, despite several discouraging events, the play ends on a tenderly understanding,* warm note. Comedy in 3 acts. 3 interiors, 1 exterior. Costumes, about 1900. 9 m., 6 f. For advanced casts. FRENCH, $1.00. Royalty, $50.00.

ALADDIN AND THE WONDERFUL LAMP. Elizabeth Brown Dooley. *Dramatization of the original story, except for the addition of a speaking camel in an otherwise entirely romantic plot.* Romantic comedy in 6 scenes. 2 interiors, 1 exterior (simplified for small stage space and easy changes. Oriental costumes. May be played in an hour and a half, including intermissions). 8 speaking parts (m. or f.) and 8 extras. FRENCH, 50¢. Royalty, $5.00.

ALICE IN WONDERLAND. Lewis Carroll. As dramatized by Mrs. Burton Harrison: 3 acts. 1 exterior, 1 interior. 30 or fewer characters. Modern and imaginative costumes. An excellent adaptation of the story, easy for school children or adults. DRAMATIC PUBLISHING CO., 25¢. No royalty. As dramatized by Alice Gerstenberg: 4 interiors, 3 exteriors. About 20 characters. Fantastic costumes and some 19th-century. This version has been used in schools and professionally, and is preferred except for royalty considerations. LONGMANS, GREEN, 90¢. Royalty, $15.00 if no admission is charged; otherwise $25.00.

ALICE IN WONDERLAND. Eva Le Gallienne & Florida Friebus. (Completely revised version of Lewis Carroll's *Alice in Wonderland and Through the Looking Glass.*) *A journey into a world of complete illusion.* Fantasy in two parts. Exteriors and interiors. More than 50 characters, mostly speaking parts. Modern and imaginative costumes. Extras. FRENCH, $1.00. Royalty, $25.00.

ALICE-SIT-BY-THE-FIRE. J. M. Barrie. *Alice returns with her husband from India to England, must readapt herself to her home and children. There is a misunderstanding between Alice and daughter Amy about a* *"lover".* Comedy in 3 acts. 2 interiors. 3 m., 6 f. Modern or 1905 costumes. FRENCH, $1.00. *Royalty, $35.00 first performance, $25.00 each subsequent performance.*

ALIEN CORN. Sidney Howard. *The tragic love affair of the talented young daughter of a German musician, whose musical career is hampered by the commonplace surroundings of the college town in which she and her father are forced to live.* Drama in 3 acts. Interior. 11 m., 3 f. Sophisticated. Modern costumes. FRENCH, $1.00. *Royalty, $25.00.*

ALISON'S HOUSE. Susan Glaspell. Pulitzer Prize, 1931. *The story concerns the family of Alison Stanhope, a famous poet who had died eighteen years before (action takes place December 31, 1899), and whose home is about to be sold.* Drama in 3 acts. 2 interiors. 5 m., 6 f. Modern costumes. FRENCH, $1.00. *Royalty, $25.00.*

ALL MY SONS. Arthur Miller. *The story is concerned with the fortunes of the Keller and Deever families, set in a structure of almost unbearable power. The climax shows the reaction of a son to his guilty father.* Intense drama. Exterior. 6 m., 4 f. Modern costumes. DRAMATISTS PLAY SERVICE, 90¢. *Royalty, $35.00–$25.00.*

AMPHITRYON 38. Jean Giraudoux (adapted by S. N. Behrman). *Follows the outlines of the legend of Amphitryon, Alkmena, and Jupiter, in which Jupiter descends to Earth, impersonates the General Amphitryon—Alkmena's husband—and makes love to her.* Brilliant comedy. Interior. 3 exteriors (stylized). 6 m., 5 f. Greek costumes. DRAMATISTS PLAY SERVICE, 90¢. *Royalty, $25.00.*

ANASTASIA. Guy Bolton (adapted from play by Marcelle Maurette). *Prince Bounine trains a peasant woman to masquerade as the Czar's daughter Anastasia, with heartbreak-* *ing consequences.* Drama in 3 acts. Interior. 8 m., 5 f. Russian, royal and peasant costumes. Tense. FRENCH, $1.00. *Production limited.*

ANDROCLES AND THE LION. G. Bernard Shaw. *A Christian tailor, Androcles, pulls a thorn from the foot of a lion, and later, in the arena in Rome, is thrown to the same lion, who recognizes and saves him.* Comedy in a prologue and 2 acts. 2 exteriors, 1 interior. 16 m., 2 f; extras. Early Christian & Roman costumes. A satire on persecutions, mad and hilarious, and not too difficult. PENGUIN, 50¢. *Royalty on application to* FRENCH.

ANGEL STREET (GASLIGHT). Patrick Hamilton. *Demoniac story of the Manninghams of Angel Street in the Nineteenth Century. Handsome, sinister Manningham, under the guise of kindliness, is slowly torturing his wife into insanity. He is under suspicion, and finally caught for a murder committed fifteen years ago in that same house.* Victorian thriller in 3 acts. Interior. 3 m., 2 f. (2 policemen). 1880 costumes. Popular, suspenseful theater. FRENCH, $1.00. *Royalty, $50.00.*

ANIMAL KINGDOM, THE. Philip Barry. *Story of a man and two marriages, one with benefit of the clergy. Tom Collier, a nonconformist at heart, and confused by our common animal heritage, found it difficult to discover which was wife and which was mistress.* Comedy in 3 acts. 2 interiors. 5 m., 4 f. Modern costumes. High comedy, sparkling dialogue. FRENCH, $1.00. *Royalty, $50.00.*

ANNA CHRISTIE. Eugene O'Neill. *A character study of a young woman who falls in love, and her struggle to deserve the love she inspires.* Drama. 2 interiors, 1 exterior. 8 m., (a few extras), 2 f. Modern, waterfront costumes. For advanced groups. *Royalty, $35.00–$25.00 to* DRAMATISTS PLAY SERVICE.

ANOTHER LANGUAGE. Rose Franken. *The members of the Hallam family are ruled with an iron hand by Mother Hallam. One of the daughters-in-law tries to escape the deadly family uniformity.* Comedy in 3 acts. 2 interiors. 6 m., 5 f. Modern costumes. Comedy of modern American family life. FRENCH, *$1.00. Royalty, $35.00.*

ANOTHER PART OF THE FOREST. Lillian Hellman. *Family drama of the parents of the Hubbards of* The Little Foxes. *The story and eventual downfall of rich, despotic, and despised Marcus Hubbard.* Interior. 8 m., 5 f. Modern costumes. Intense, hard-hitting drama. DRAMATISTS PLAY SERVICE, *90¢. Royalty, $50.00–$25.00.*

ANTIGONE. Jean Anouilh (translated by Lewis Galantière). *Modern version of the Greek legend of Antigone, reflecting war-tyrannized France. Struggle between Antigone and her uncle Creon over the burial of her brother, bringing about her cruel death, and dooming the entire family.* Tragedy, no act division. Interior. 8 m., 4 f. Modern costumes (formal attire). Gripping, tender drama for advanced groups only. FRENCH, *$1.00. Royalty, $25.00.*

ARMS AND THE MAN. G. Bernard Shaw. *Captain Bluntschi, Serbian soldier, fleeing from the Bulgarians, is sheltered by Raina Petchoff, a Bulgarian lady engaged to Sergius. After the war Bluntschi returns on military business with Major Petchoff and wins Raina from Sergius, who marries Raina's maid.* Comedy in 3 acts. 2 interiors, 1 exterior. 6 m., 3 f. Balkan costumes, early 20th century. Brilliant and worthwhile comedy, requiring good acting. FRENCH, *35¢. Royalty, $25.00.*

ARSENIC AND OLD LACE. Joseph Kesselring. *Two charming and innocent ladies who populate their cellar with the remains of socially and religiously "acceptable" roomers, and the antics of their brother, who thinks he is Teddy Roosevelt, are the subject of this ready-made hit.* Comedy. Interior. 11 m., some minor bits; 3 f. Modern costume. Suitable for all groups. DRAMATISTS PLAY SERVICE, *90¢. Royalty, $35.00–$25.00.*

BARRETTS OF WIMPOLE STREET, THE. Rudolf Besier. *The love of Robert Browning rescues Elizabeth Barrett from her semi-invalid existence in the house of her domineering father.* Romantic comedy. Interior. 12 men (9 of them young), 5 women (all but one of them young). 19th-century costumes. Suitable for all groups. DRAMATISTS PLAY SERVICE, *90¢. Royalty, $50.00–$25.00.*

BAT, THE. Mary Roberts Rinehart & Avery Hopwood. *The thrilling solution of a bank robbery in a country house, where four people are trying to secure the treasure and the real culprit is unsuspected until the very end.* Mystery comedy in 3 acts. 2 interiors. 7 m., 3 f. Modern costumes. One of the best of the thrillers. Good characters. FRENCH, *$1.00. Royalty, $25.00.*

THE BEAUTIFUL PEOPLE. William Saroyan. *An assortment of charming, weird characters and their idiosyncracies represents Mr. Saroyan's belief that love is the only thing which matters in the world.* Comedy in 3 acts. 7 m., 2 f. Interior. Modern costumes. FRENCH, *$1.00. Royalty, $25.00.*

BEGGAR ON HORSEBACK. Marc Connelly & George S. Kaufman. *A young composer dreams he is marrying an unattractive girl for her money, thus becoming a slave of gold and of an impossible family.* Fantasy in 3 acts. Several exteriors and interiors. 15 m., 5 f. (an optional pantomime calls for an additional 6 m., 2 f.). Modern and fantastic costumes. A rich combination of romance and satire. FRENCH, *$2.50. Royalty on application.*

BELINDA. A. A. Milne. *Belinda, supposedly a widow, presents her daughter as her niece and keeps two suitors dangling; her husband returns.* Comedy in 3 acts. 1 interior, 1 exterior. 3 m., 3 f. Modern costumes. Light, charming, witty comedy. FRENCH, $1.00. Royalty, $50.00.

A BELL FOR ADANO. Paul Osborn (from the novel by John Hersey). *Major Joppolo endears himself to the hearts of the people in the small Sicilian town just after its liberation, by acquiring a bell for the town—a symbol of its moral well-being—though this act brings about his doom in the army.* Drama. Interior. 22 m., 5 f. Modern costumes. Play on an aspect of Democracy. DRAMATISTS PLAY SERVICE, 90¢. Royalty, $35.00–$25.00.

BELVEDERE. Gwen Davenport. *An American family is surprised to find Lynn Belvedere who answers their ad for a baby sitter, a very precise and impeccable male. The play deals with Belvedere's hilarious adventures with his two charges.* Comedy in 3 acts. Interior. 5 m., 4 f., 2 children. Modern costumes. This play is the source for the film *Sitting Pretty.* FRENCH, $1.00. Royalty, $25.00.

BERKELEY SQUARE. John L. Balderston. *Peter Standish relives the romance of a forefather while retaining his twentieth-century viewpoint. His eighteenth-century sweetheart becomes more vital to his happiness than his modern fiancée, and he breaks his engagement.* Fantasy in 3 acts. 2 interiors. 7 m., 8 f. Costumes 1784 and modern. Requires skillful acting and direction. FRENCH, $1.00. Royalty, $25.00.

BERNARDINE. Mary Coyle Chase. *Several prankish youths, "nice" Dead End kids, imagine themselves in the ideal town, where the relations between them and grown-ups are completely reversed, a teen-age Utopia featuring the ideal female, Bernar-* dine. Simple, stylized scenery. 13 m., 6 f. Modern costumes. DRAMATISTS PLAY SERVICE, 90¢. Royalty, $50.00–$25.00.

BEYOND THE HORIZON. Eugene O'Neill. *Robert Mayo discovers too late that his marriage with Ruth is a mistake. He struggles against maladjustment until misery and poverty ruin his home, crush Ruth's spirit, and break his own health. Then he welcomes death as an escape into the wide world of his dreams.* Tragedy in 3 acts. 1 interior, 2 exteriors. 6 m., 3 f., 1 child. Modern, rural costumes. Poetic and interesting for very advanced groups only. DRAMATISTS PLAY SERVICE, 90¢. Royalty, $35.00–$25.00.

BILLY BUDD. Louis O. Coxe & Robert Chapman (from the novel by Herman Melville). *Billy Budd, a pleasant guileless sailor, is caught between duty and maritime law. He stoically accepts the death penalty for a rightful, guiltless act.* Drama. 2 interiors, exterior. Costumes, British Navy, 1798. 22 m. DRAMATISTS PLAY SERVICE, $1.50. Royalty, $50.00–$25.00.

BLIND ALLEY. James Warwick. *A professor of psychology saves his wife and himself from a notorious killer through his skillful use of psychoanalysis.* Melodrama in 3 acts. Interior. 7 m., 4 f. Modern costumes. Skillful and dramatic use of psychology. For advanced groups. FRENCH, $1.00. Royalty, $25.00.

BLITHE SPIRIT. Noel Coward. *The ghost of Charles' first wife plots his death that he may join her. Instead, his second wife is killed, and now he is plagued by both women's blithe spirits.* A farce in 3 acts. Interior. 2 m., 5 f. Modern costumes. FRENCH, $1.00. Royalty, $50.00.

BORN YESTERDAY. Garson Kanin. *Highly informal education of ex-chorus girl Billie, makes a responsible* *citizen of her and awakens her to the realization that Harry Brock, the vulgar and egotistical millionaire junkman who had kept her, had used her as a tool for his crooked schemes with Washington higher-ups.* Comedy. Interior. 12 m., 4 f. Modern costumes. DRAMATISTS PLAY SERVICE, 90¢. *Royalty, $50.00–$25.00.*

BOTH YOUR HOUSES. Maxwell Anderson. *A young and idealistic Congressman is pitted against a group of old-time politicians, all at work on a big appropriations bill. When honesty fails, he makes the bill ridiculously dishonest. Ironically, the bill now passes through both Houses.* Satire in 3 acts. Interiors. 13 m., 3 f. Modern costumes. For advanced groups. FRENCH, *$1.00. Royalty, $25.00.*

BOY MEETS GIRL. Bella & Samuel Spewack. *Studio waitress and her fatherless baby get involved with two Hollywood writers.* Comedy. 2 interiors. 14 m., 5 f. Modern costumes. *Royalty, $25.00 to* DRAMATISTS PLAY SERVICE.

BRAIN STORM, THE. Bettye Knapp. *Willoughby Adams and Inner Willy, his materialized inner self, provide some fantastic and refreshing comedy as the latter urges shy Willoughby into college football stardom and eventual manhood.* Comedy in 3 acts. Interior. 8 m., 10 f. Modern costumes. Row, PETERSON, 85¢. *Royalty, 20% of receipts: max. $25.00.*

CAINE MUTINY COURT-MARTIAL, THE. Herman Wouk. *The court-martial proceedings against a young lieutenant who relieved his captain of command in the midst of a harrowing typhoon on the grounds that the captain was psychopathic in the crisis, and was directing the ship and its crew to destruction.* Tragedy in 2 acts. Interior. 19 m. (6 nonspeaking). Costumes of the U.S. Navy, World War II. Powerful psychological drama requiring skilled acting. FRENCH, *$1.00. Royalty, $50.00.*

CANDIDA. G. Bernard Shaw. *Candida, the charming wife of a clergyman, has to choose between her husband and a young poet, Marchbanks, and finally chooses her apparently self-sufficient husband as "the weaker."* Comedy in 3 acts. Interior. 4 m., 2 f. Costumes, 1905 or modern. Fast and witty. Needs experienced actors. PENGUIN, *35¢. No royalty.*

CANDLE-LIGHT. P. G. Wodehouse (from the German of S. Geyer). *Prince Rudolph's valet falls in love with a pretty voice over the telephone, invites his charmer to his master's first-floor apartment, and then, naturally, sheds his livery and becomes a Prince; Prince Rudolph returns unexpectedly and sardonically accepts the situation by donning his valet's livery.* Comedy in 3 acts. Interior. 5 m., 3 f. Modern costumes. FRENCH, *$1.00. Royalty, $25.00.*

CAPTAIN APPLEJACK. Walter Hackett. *Ambrose Applejohn, a bored young Englishman, rents a house on the coast in hopes of finding adventure, and finds it, both in reality and in a dream in which he is Captain Applejack, a pirate.* Comedy in 3 acts. 2 interiors. 6 m., 5 f. Modern and fantastic costumes. Exciting and amusing play, very popular and not difficult. FRENCH, *$1.00. Royalty, $25.00.*

CHARLEY'S AUNT. Brandon Thomas. *An Oxford undergraduate impersonates a wealthy aunt for his two friends and all three become involved in a mad, comic tangle with their sweethearts, especially when the real aunt turns up under an assumed name.* Farcical comedy in 3 acts. Exterior, 2 interiors. 7 m., 5 f. Costumes, 1892. Suitable for all groups. FRENCH, *$1.00. Royalty, $25.00.*

CHEAPER BY THE DOZEN. Perry Clark (from the book by Frank B. Gilbreth, Jr., & Ernestine Gilbreth

Carey). *Dad, a terrific efficiency expert, believes that what will work in his factory will also work in the home. He introduces "organization," equivalent to martial law, into his large family with at once hilarious and disastrous results.* Comedy in 3 acts. Interior. 9 m., 7 f. Modern costumes. Extremely easy to cast and produce. DRAMATIC PUBLISHING CO., 85¢. Royalty, $25.00.

CHERRY ORCHARD, THE. Anton Chekhov (translated by Stark Young) *An estate, its beautiful trees and grounds symbolic vestiges of the dying Russian aristocracy, is auctioned off to the son of a boorish peasant who has succeeded in industry. The family of Mrs. Ranevsky, once proud landowners, depart to take up their lives anew elsewhere under the solemn chorus of the woodsmen's axes, as the cherished trees make way for a factory.* Drama in 4 acts. Exterior, 2 interiors. 10 m., 5 f. Costumes, Russian, 1903. FRENCH, $1.00. Royalty, $25.00.

CHILDREN'S HOUR, THE. Lillian Hellman. *A malicious youngster starts an entirely unfounded scandal about two women who run a school for girls, which precipitates tragedy for the two women. Later it is discovered that the gossip was pure invention, but by that time irreparable damage has been done.* Drama. 2 interiors. 2 m., 12 f. Modern costumes. DRAMATISTS PLAY SERVICE, 90¢. Royalty, $35.00–$25.00.

CHRISTMAS CAROL, A. Charles Dickens (adapted by Cora Wilson Greenwood). *The well known story of the conversion of Scrooge.* Comedy in 9 scenes. 8 m., 6 f., 1 extra. 19th-century costumes. Good dramatization for schools. FRENCH, 50¢. *No royalty.* Dramatized by George M. Baker, arranged for 1 interior. 6 m., 3 f., extras. BAKER, 50¢. *No royalty.*

CIRCLE, THE. Somerset Maugham. *Lady Kitty returns to the family with Lord Porteous, for whom she deserted her husband and son, Arnold, thirty years ago. The spectacle of their degeneration delays, but finally fails to deter, Elizabeth, Arnold's unhappy wife from deserting him and eloping with Teddie.* Social comedy. 1 interior. 5 m., 3 f., servants. Costumes of 1920's. Good characters; excellent adult entertainment. BAKER, $1.25. Royalty, $25.00.

CLEMENTINE. Anne Coulter Martens & William Davidson. *The pranks of Clementine, a very peppy tomboy, set the whole neighborhood in a tizzy, and rouse the ire of the Women Voters.* Comedy in 3 acts. Interior. 5 m., 7 f. Modern costumes. Easy to cast and produce. DRAMATIC PUBLISHING CO., 85¢. Royalty, $25.00.

COME BACK, LITTLE SHEBA. William Inge. *The story of a deep-seated frustration brought about by the unmatched marriage between Doc and Lola, and of its inevitable and furious eruption.* Drama in 2 acts. Interior. 8 m., 3 f. Modern costumes. For advanced groups only. FRENCH, $1.00. Royalty, $50.00.

CONNECTICUT YANKEE IN KING ARTHUR'S COURT, A. John G. Fuller (from the book by Mark Twain). *The Yankee, a young electrical engineer, is knocked out by his experiment and wakes up to find himself in the Court of King Arthur. From then on, the striking contrast between the old and the new develops into a series of highly imaginative and ludicrous events, with philosophical overtones.* Comedy. Interior. 6 m., 6 f. Medieval royal and one modern costume. Suitable for all groups. BAKER, 85¢. Royalty, $25.00.

COPPERHEAD, THE. Augustus Thomas. *Milt Shanks, a Union patriot, allows himself to be hated and distrusted by his neighbors, his wife, and his son, rather than reveal the fact that he is a secret agent for the government and not a "copperhead";*

he confesses the truth only after forty years, when the past seems about to ruin the happiness of his granddaughter. Drama in 4 acts. 2 exteriors, 1 interior (can be played in 1 changed interior). 9 m., 6 f. Costumes of 1860's. First 3 acts, 1861–1863; last act, 1903. Strong play of varied appeal, difficult, but worth producing. FRENCH, $1.00. Royalty, $25.00.

CORN IS GREEN, THE. Emlyn Williams. *Miss Moffat, an English spinster, settles in a Welsh mining village where she starts a school for the boys of the neighborhood, against the prejudice of local folk and the wealthy squire.* Comedy. Interior. 10 m. (extras), 5 f. (extras). Modern costumes. DRAMATISTS PLAY SERVICE, 90¢. Royalty, $35.00–$25.00.

COUNTRY GIRL, THE. Clifford Odets. *Georgie Elgin, the country girl, is a lovable, faithful, forgiving woman whose long years of devotion to her actor husband, Frank, have almost obliterated her own personality, as she strives to save him from downfall and despair between acting parts. Only in the tragic end of the play is her work recognized.* Drama. 5 simple interiors. 6 m., 2 f. Modern costumes. DRAMATISTS PLAY SERVICE, 90¢. Royalty, $50.00–$25.00.

CRADLE SONG, THE. G. Martinez-Sierra (English version by John Garrett Underhill). *Teresa, a foundling, is brought up in a convent where the nuns lavish upon her all the tenderness generally absent from their lives. She finally falls in love and leaves them on her wedding day.* Romantic drama in 2 acts. 2 interiors. 4 m., 10 f., extras. Modern costumes, mostly nuns' costumes. A charming, amusing and pathetic story told with Spanish grace and a delicate touch. Ideal for all groups. FRENCH, $1.00. Royalty, $50.00.

CRADLE TROUBADOUR. Dorothy Rood Stewart. *Peg Markley and her neighbor, Lou Haller, hire young Touchy Williams, an aspiring psychiatrist, as baby-sitter. There is comic pandemonium when Peg's cousin arrives unexpectedly, and the baby disappears.* Comedy in 3 acts. Interior. 8 m., 7 f., extras. Modern costumes. Row, PETERSON, 85¢. Royalty, 20% of receipts to $25.00.

CRAIG'S WIFE. George Kelly. *Mrs. Craig, unassailably selfish, succeeds during one evening in alienating the affections not only of her husband, who is driven from his home, but also of her friends and relatives.* Drama in 3 acts. Interior. 5 m., 6 f. Modern costumes. Character study of biting satire, requiring advanced acting ability. FRENCH, $1.00. Royalty, $50.00.

CRUCIBLE, THE. Arthur Miller. *The Puritan purge of witchcraft in old Salem. Small lies—children's lies—build and build until a whole town is aroused and 19 men and women go to the gallows for being possessed of the devil.* Drama. Single-unit set. 10 m., 10 f. 17th-century Puritan costumes. DRAMATISTS PLAY SERVICE, 90¢. Royalty, $50.00–$25.00.

CURIOUS SAVAGE, THE. John Patrick. *Mrs. Savage, a widow, wants to dispose of $10 million in the best possible way, in spite of the efforts of her grown-up step-children to get their hands on it. She leads these children a merry chase, which takes her even into a sanatorium. There she is relieved to find people interested in her, not her money. With the help of the friends in the sanatorium, she arrives at a solution.* Comedy. Interior. 5 m., 6 f. Modern costumes. DRAMATISTS PLAY SERVICE, 90¢. Royalty, $35.00–$25.00.

CYRANO de BERGERAC. Edmund Rostand (a new adaptation and arrangement by Edna Kruckemeyer). *Cyrano, a clever but homely cavalier,* *loves Roxane, who in turn loves a handsome but stupid soldier, Christian. Cyrano woos Roxane for Christian and does many noble, unselfish deeds; years later, as he is dying, Cyrano learns that she loves him.* Heroic comedy in 5 acts. 2 interiors. 3 exteriors. 30 m., 16 f. Costumes, seventeenth-century French. In this version, the more difficult scenes have been simplified, making the play suitable for all groups. Offers excellent parts to a large number of actors. FRENCH, *$1.00. Budget play.*

DADDY LONG-LEGS. Jean Webster. *Judy, a pretty little drudge in a New England orphanage, is given a chance for education by a visiting trustee, and achieves fame, happiness, and a wealthy husband.* Comedy in 4 acts. 4 interiors. 6 m., 7 f., 6 children. Modern costumes. Sentimental but effective play, not difficult to produce. FRENCH, *$1.00. Royalty, $25.00.*

DAMASK CHEEK, THE. John van Druten & Lloyd Morris. *A literate and charming comedy of manners concerning a middle-aged and repressed English spinster who is sent to America to live with her aunt in the hope of finding a husband.* Comedy in 3 acts. Interior. 3 m., 6 f. Costumes, 1909. FRENCH, *$1.00. Royalty, $35.00.*

DANGEROUS CORNER. J. B. Priestley. *The gradual revelation of the truth about a murdered man disrupts his family and friends and shows them up for the rotters they are.* A combination mystery play and psychological study. Drama in 3 acts. Interior. 3 m., 4 f. Modern costumes. For mature casts only. FRENCH, *$1.00. Royalty, $25.00.*

DARK VICTORY. George Brewer, Jr. & Bertram Bloch. *Judith, a spoiled, casual socialite, discovers that alcohol and random affairs cannot replace love and devotion, but only after submitting to an operation which gives her but a few months to live with her new-found love.* Drama. 2 interiors. 7 m., 7 f., extras. Modern costumes. DRAMATISTS PLAY SERVICE, *90¢. Royalty, $25.00.*

DARKNESS AT NOON. Sidney Kingsley (based on the novel by Arthur Koestler). *A Soviet Commissar with considerable power in the party, is jailed for treason. The play deals with his torment and frustration in his cell, with flashbacks explaining his sentence and the unjust hearings leading up to his execution.* Tragedy in 3 acts. Interior. 18 m., 3 f. Modern and Russian military costumes. Powerful, suspenseful play. For advanced casts only. FRENCH, *$1.00. Royalty, $50.00.*

DATE WITH JUDY, A. Aleen Leslie. *Judy gets into innumerable comic situations, as she tries to win the nomination for Queen of the school dance.* Comedy in 3 acts. Interior. 5 m., 9 f. Modern costumes. DRAMATIC PUBLISHING CO., *85¢. Royalty, $25.00.*

DEAR BRUTUS. James M. Barrie. *Lob brings together at an English country house nine people who all have the common desire to have a second chance at their lives; in a magic woods they are given this second chance, but only one profits by it.* Fantastic comedy in 3 acts. 1 interior, 1 exterior. 4 m., 6 f. Modern costumes. Difficult but worth the effort. FRENCH, *$1.00. Royalty, $35.00 first performance, $25.00 each subsequent performance.*

DEAR RUTH. Norman Krasna. *A young girl carries on a romantic cor-*

respondence with an overseas soldier, in her elder sister's name. There is much confusion when the soldier returns and woos the older sister, who is already engaged. Comedy. Interior. 5 m., 5 f. Modern costumes. DRAMATISTS PLAY SERVICE, 90¢. *Royalty,* $25.00.

DEATH OF A SALESMAN. Arthur Miller. *The tragic story of Willie Loman who, in his last days as a failing salesman, seeks to find out just where and how he has failed to win success and happiness with his wife, his sons, and his business associates.* Tragedy. Interior- and exterior-unit setting. 8 m., 5 f. Modern costumes. DRAMATISTS PLAY SERVICE, 90¢. *Royalty,* $50.00–$25.00. *Fee for use of music of original production,* $5.00 *per performance.*

DEATH TAKES A HOLIDAY. Alberto Cassella (rewritten by Walter Ferris). *Death suspends all activities for three days during which period he falls in love with a beautiful girl, and through her realizes why mortals fear him.* Drama in 3 acts. Interior. 7 m., 6 f. Modern costumes. Suitable for all serious groups. FRENCH, $1.00. *Royalty,* $50.00.

DEEP ARE THE ROOTS. Arnaud D'Usseau & James Gow. *The play explores race prejudice and the Negro problem. A Negro war hero returns to his home in the South, and is welcomed by the white family that employed him. However, one of the women of the family falls in love with him, and the hero is overwhelmed by the prejudice which prevents his being treated not only as a hero, but as a man.* Drama. Interior. 7 m., 4 f. Modern costumes. DRAMATISTS PLAY SERVICE, 90¢. *Royalty,* $50.00–$25.00.

DESIRE UNDER THE ELMS. Eugene O'Neill. *Eben, though fighting his young stepmother, Abbie, for the inheritance of the farm, is seduced by her. His unsuspecting old father wills*

the farm to the illegitimate baby. To prove to Eben that she really loves him and did not intend to trick him in this way, Abbie kills the infant. Tragedy in 3 acts. Interior. 4 m., 1 f., many extras. Modern rural costumes. DRAMATISTS PLAY SERVICE, *Royalty,* $35.00–$25.00.

DESPERATE HOURS, THE. Joseph Hayes. *A home is invaded and its inhabitants held captive by three escaped criminals.* Drama of suspense in 3 acts. Unit set. 11 m., 3 f. Modern costumes. Suitable for all groups. FRENCH, $2.75. *Royalty on application.*

DETECTIVE STORY. Sidney Kingsley. *McLeod, a detective, has a mania for punishing lawbreakers, to the point where he often loses sight of human values and compassion. When his wife becomes involved in an abortion case, McLeod's world collapses about him.* Drama. Interior of a police station. 24 m. (several can be doubled), 8 f. (several nonspeaking extras). Modern costumes. DRAMATISTS PLAY SERVICE, 90¢. *Royalty,* $50.00–$25.00.

DEVIL'S DISCIPLE, THE. George Bernard Shaw. *Dick Dudgeon, the "devil's disciple," is unable to live up to his misanthropic ideals. He finds himself saving the life of a clergyman, but gets sentenced to death by the British. Reprieve comes just as he is about to die heroically.* Drama in 3 acts. 4 interiors, 1 exterior. 10 m., 3 f., extras. Costumes of American Revolution. Suitable for advanced groups only. PENGUIN, 50¢. *Royalty,* $25.00 to BAKER.

DIAL M FOR MURDER. Frederick Knott. *A man plans to murder his wife for her money. When the murderer he hired is unwittingly killed, the husband takes the opportunity to have his wife convicted of the murder, almost succeeding in his plan.* Melodrama. Interior. 5 m., 1 f. Modern costumes. DRAMATISTS PLAY

SERVICE, 90¢. *Royalty,* $50.00–$25.00.

DINNER AT EIGHT. George S. Kaufman & Edna Ferber. *A small dinner party, honoring an English title, discloses dramas of love, jealousy and greed beneath the white ties and the pearls.* Drama in 3 acts. 6 interiors. 14 m., 11 f. Modern costumes. FRENCH, $1.00. *Royalty,* $50.00.

DIVINE FLORA, THE. Florence Ryerson & Colin Clements. *Etta Dean, a shy, awkward, motherless girl of fifteen, had been brought up so strictly by her grandmother that she is known to the high school wolf pack as Little Miss Prune Puss. She gets involved with two boys who believe they are on the way to becoming the greatest advertising men in the world.* Comedy in a prologue and 3 acts. Exterior and interior. 12 m., 14 f. (extras). Modern costumes. FRENCH, $1.00. *Royalty,* $25.00.

DOCTOR KNOCK. Jules Romains (translated by H. Granville-Barker). *Dr. Parpalaid sells his worthless practice to Dr. Knock, a quack, who proceeds to build a lucrative practice through the diffusion of "medical science."* French comedy in 3 acts. 2 interiors, 1 exterior. 9 m., 5 f. French costumes, post World War I. Fresh, interesting story; leading character roles need advanced acting. Scenery for first scene difficult; may be changed. FRENCH, MSS. *Royalty,* $50.00.

DOUBLE DOOR. Elizabeth McFadden. *The theme is the battle for power that goes on in an old New York family and culminates on the verge of murder.* Drama in 3 acts. Interior. 7 m., 5 f. Costumes, 1910. FRENCH, $1.00. *Royalty,* $25.00.

DOVER ROAD, THE. A. A. Milne. *Two eloping couples stop at the house of a strange philosopher, thinking it is an inn, and decide that after all they do not want to elope.* Comedy in 3 acts. 1 interior. 6 m., 4 f. Modern costumes. Not much action, but suitable for advanced amateurs, probably not high schools. FRENCH, $1.00. *Royalty,* $50.00.

DRAGON, THE. Lady Gregory. *Nualla, the princess, has consistently refused all suitors, among them King Manus of Scorcha, who comes disguised as a cook to woo her; when the dragon arrives to devour Nualla, Manus defeats it and marries her.* Fantasy in 3 acts. 1 interior. 7 m., 6 f., the dragon, extras. Fantastic costumes. Irish fairy-tale, not exciting but pleasing. Difficult. *Royalty,* $25.00 to FRENCH.

DREAM GIRL. Elmer Rice. *A charming but dreamy and overimaginative young woman who runs a bookstore finds escape into a romantic world of unreality by daydreaming. The play is a dramatization of some of these dreams.* Comedy-fantasy. Sets are simple to suggest background of dream scenes. 25 m. (several bits), 7 f. (some bits). Modern costumes. DRAMATISTS PLAY SERVICE, 90¢. *Royalty,* $50.00–$25.00.

DRUID CIRCLE, THE. John van Druten. *An embittered professor nearly wrecks the lives of a young man and a young woman whose love for each other has been accidentally revealed to him through a letter written by the boy to the girl. The professor uses this to humiliate the young people, unconsciously venting upon them his own perverse cruelty for the disappointments suffered in his own life.* Drama. 2 interiors. 5 m., 6 f. Modern costumes. DRAMATISTS PLAY SERVICE, 90¢. *Royalty,* $50.00–$25.00.

DULCY. George S. Kaufman & Marc Connelly. *Dulcy Smith, a young bride, eager to be of help to her husband who is considering a merger with a rich capitalist, invites the capitalist and his family for a weekend. Their brief association becomes an unbroken series of hilarious trage-*

dies, Dulcy's final blunder crowning her efforts with success. Comedy in 3 acts. Interior. 8 m., 3 f. Modern costumes. FRENCH, *$1.00. Royalty, $25.00.*

EAST LYNNE. Ned Albert. *Isabel deserts her husband and child, suspecting the former of unfaithfulness, and runs away with a former suitor. It isn't long before she realizes her tragic mistake, and rejoins her family.* Melodrama in 3 acts. Interior. 5 m., 8 f. Modern costumes. FRENCH, 75¢. Budget play.

EDWARD, MY SON. Robert Morley & Noel Langley. *An ambitious and unscrupulous man is shown at various periods during his spectacular career. His life is motivated largely by devotion to his only son, who turns out to be a failure.* Drama. 6 interiors. 10 m., 4 f. Modern costumes. DRAMATISTS PLAY SERVICE, 90¢. *Royalty, $25.00.*

ELIZABETH THE QUEEN. Maxwell Anderson. *Elizabeth the Queen delights in Essex, royal favorite and popular general, as a courtier and lover, but is jealous of him as a military leader and hero.* Romantic drama in 3 acts. 4 interiors, 1 exterior. 16 m., 7 f. (extras). Elizabethan costumes. FRENCH, *$1.00. Royalty, $25.00.*

EMPEROR JONES, THE. Eugene O'Neill. *Emperor Jones, once a pullman porter and convict, now finds himself fleeing from his tribal subjects. The memories of his misdeeds, in the form of hallucinations and sounds, pursue him through the forest, and drive him to suicide.* Drama in 8 scenes. 1 interior, 6 exteriors. 3 m., 1 f., many extras. West Indian costumes. A tense, poetic study of primitive fear. APPLETON-CENTURY-CROFTS, $1.00. *Royalty, $35.00–$25.00. to* DRAMATISTS PLAY SERVICE.

ENCHANTED, THE. Jean Giraudoux (adapted by Maurice Valency). *A*

young lady in a French provincial town is obsessed with belief in spirits and other aspects of make-believe. A government inspector regards her traffic with the supernatural as a threat to the order, security and safety of the state. Comedy in 3 acts. Interior and exterior. 9 m., 11 f. Modern costumes. Suitable for all groups. FRENCH, *$1.00. Royalty, $50.00.*

ENCHANTED COTTAGE, THE. Arthur W. Pinero. *An invalid veteran marries an unattractive girl in order to escape his mother's petty tyranny. After the marriage, each partner thinks the other has changed for the better, Oliver becoming strong and Laura pretty. In truth, it is their love which allows them to live in an enchanted cottage.* Fantastic comedy in 3 acts. 1 interior, 1 exterior. 5 m., 4 f., extras. Modern costumes. Suitable for advanced groups. BAKER, 85¢. *Royalty, $25.00.*

ENCHANTED APRIL, THE. Kane Campbell. *Four women, strange to one another, lease an Italian castle through an advertisement in a London newspaper, to live there for the month of April, away from the society of men. The husbands of two of them and the lover of Lady Caroline invade the retreat.* Comedy in Prologue and 3 acts. 2 interiors. 4 m., 6 f. Modern costumes. Light and amusing comedy. For advanced amateurs. .FRENCH, *$1.00. Royalty, $25.00.*

END AS MAN. Calder Willingham. *Life in a military academy, and the process by which boys are turned into men. Jocko, a rich, spoiled, brutal and vicious upperclassman abuses the lowerclassmen, until he is finally court-martialed and expelled.* Melodrama in 3 acts. 2 interiors. 14 m. Modern military costumes. FRENCH, MSS. *Royalty on application.*

ENEMY, THE. Channing Pollock. *Carl Behrend, aspiring Austrian author of*

a successful pacifist play, The
Enemy, *is drafted into the army,
leaving his bride of a month, Pauli,
and his father, a pacifist university
professor. On the eve of his home-
coming, Carl is killed.* Drama in 4
acts. 1 interior. 7 m., 3 f. Modern costumes, World War I. Moving and
effective pacifist propaganda, for advanced amateurs. Successful in high
schools and older groups. LONGMANS,
GREEN, 90¢. *Royalty,* $25.00.

**ETHAN FROME. Owen Davis &
Donald Davis** (from the novelette by
Edith Wharton). *Ethan Frome attempts to escape from his complaining wife, Zenobia, with Mattie, their
house-drudge. Their attempts are
devastatingly unsuccessful and the
two runaways are reduced to maimed
and resentful invalids under the
wife's care.* Drama. Interiors and exteriors. 7 m., 4 f., extras. Modern
New England rural costumes. DRAM-
ATISTS PLAY SERVICE, $1.00. *Royalty,*
$25.00.

**EVE OF ST. MARK, THE. Maxwell
Anderson.** *Quizz, a GI in the Philip-
pines, talks with Janet in her home
on the eve of St. Mark, the time
when, according to legend, those who
are about to die are able to talk with
those they love.* Drama in 2 acts and
several scenes. 1 set. 13 m., 8 f. Modern costumes, World War II. Suitable
for all groups. DRAMATIC PUBLISHING
Co., 85¢. *Royalty,* $25.00.

EXCURSION. Victor Wolfson. *A Har-
lem-Coney Island tub is about to be
taken out of service, but its captain
rebels and heads the tub for a magic
island south of Trinidad, where his
passengers may begin life anew.*
Comedy. Permanent set (ship's cabin
and deck). 18 m., 10 f. Modern costumes. DRAMATISTS PLAY SERVICE,
$1.00. *Royalty,* $25.00.

**FAMILY PORTRAIT. Lenore Coffee &
William Joyce Cowen.** *The last three
years of Christ's life.* Drama in 3 acts.
Interior, 3 exteriors. 12 m., 10 f.

Biblical costumes. FRENCH, *$1.00.
Royalty,* $25.00.

FAMILY REUNION, THE. T. S. Eliot.
*A son of a contemporary English
family is haunted by the impression
that he killed his wife.* Verse play in
2 parts. Interior. Modern costumes.
7 m., 4 f. FRENCH, $2.75. *Royalty,*
$25.00.

**FANNY'S FIRST PLAY. G. Bernard
Shaw.** *Fanny O'Dowda has written a
play to which well known critics are
invited. The play: Mr. and Mrs.
Lilley are disgraced because their
son, who was to marry Margaret
Knox, is thrown in jail after a brawl.
However, Margaret is also in jail for
hitting a policeman, so the young
people are drawn together. The
critics declare the play a success.*
Comedy in prologue, 3 acts, and epilogue. 3 interiors. 12 m., 5 f. Modern
costumes. Witty and interesting play,
sometimes played by colleges. *Royalty,* $25.00 to FRENCH.

**FATHER KNOWS BEST. Robert
Young.** *Father, after reading a newspaper story about teen-tage elopement, has decided young people must
be watched carefully. The best way
to do that is to keep them home, even
if it means having the whole town's
social life centered in the Anderson
household.* Comedy in 3 acts. One
set. 7 m., 10 f. Modern costumes,
DRAMATIC PUBLISHING Co., 85¢.
Royalty, $25.00.

**FATHER OF THE BRIDE. Caroline
Francke** (from the novel by Edward
Streeter). *A wedding, planned as a
simple affair with a few friends, turns
out to be an extravaganza, with mass
confusion reigning within the family.*
Comedy. Interior. 11 m., 7 f., 3-4
extras. Modern costumes. Recommended for high school groups.
DRAMATISTS PLAY SERVICE, $1.00.
Royalty, $35.00–$25.00.

FIREBRAND, THE. Edwin J. Mayer.
Adventure and comedy as the Duke

falls in love with Angela and takes her away to his summer palace, while the Duchess invites Cellini to the palace also, as her lover. Romantic comedy in 3 acts. 1 interior, 2 exteriors. 8 m., 4 f., extras. Costumes, early 16th century. FRENCH, $1.00. *Royalty, $25.00.*

FIRST LADY. Katharine Dayton & George S. Kaufman. *The conflict centers on the feud between two Washington hostesses who show no quarter in their struggle for the position of First Lady.* Comedy. 2 interiors. 14 m., 11 f., extras. Modern costumes. DRAMATISTS PLAY SERVICE, $1.00. *Royalty, $25.00.*

FIRST LEGION, THE. Emmet Lavery. *Drama concerning a group of Jesuit priests living in their chapter house.* Drama in 3 acts. 3 interiors. 11 m. Costumes, priests' cassocks and civilian clothes. FRENCH, $1.00. *Royalty, $25.00.*

FIRST MRS. FRASER, THE. St. John G. Ervine. *Mrs. Fraser gracefully refuses to accept the second time the man who has divorced her for a chorus girl, and subtly matches wits with her grown sons.* Comedy in 3 acts. 1 interior. 4 m., 4 f. Modern costumes. Witty social comedy for adults, requiring suave acting; simple production. BAKER, $1.25. *Royalty, $25.00.*

FLIES, THE. Jean-Paul Sartre (adapted by Paul Bowles). *The ancient Greek legend of Orestes, retold in the modern idiom, with political and philosophical overtones.* Tragedy in 3 acts. 2 interiors, 2 exteriors. 8 m., 6 f., extras. Greek costumes. *Royalty, $25.00 to* FRENCH.

FOREVER ALBERT. Bettye Knapp. *Uncle Albert is the imp behind all the comic problems that arise in Ben's family.* Comedy in 3 acts. Interior. 7 m., 7 f. Modern costumes. Row, PETERSON, 85¢. *Royalty, 20% of receipts to $25.00.*

FOURPOSTER, THE. Jan de Hartog. *A chronicle of a husband and wife from their wedding night in 1890 until they pack and move 35 years later.* Comedy in 3 acts. Interior. 1 m., 1 f. Costumes, 1890–1925. FRENCH, $1.00. *Royalty, $50.00.*

FRESH FIELDS. Ivor Novello. *Two sisters inherit a mansion without the income necessary for its upkeep. The Pidgeon family moves in as paying guests.* Comedy in 3 acts. Interior. 3 m., 6 f. Modern costumes. Suitable for all groups. FRENCH, $1.00. *Royalty, $25.00.*

FRONT PAGE, THE. Ben Hecht & Charles MacArthur. *A reporter is sick of his profession and marries in an attempt to escape it, only to be pulled back by its irresistible lure. A man about to be hanged escapes and is finally discovered in the reporter's office.* Drama. Interior. 17 m., 5 f. Modern costumes. FRENCH, $1.00. *Royalty, $50.00.*

GENTLE PEOPLE, THE. Irwin Shaw. *Two middle-aged cronies who love to fish seek in each other's company a refuge from domestic difficulties. Their peace is threatened by a gangster, who is quickly taken for a boat ride, from which he fails to return.* Comedy. 3 interiors, 2 exteriors. 10 m., 3 f. Modern costumes. DRAMATISTS PLAY SERVICE, $1.00. *Royalty, $25.00.*

GEORGE WASHINGTON SLEPT HERE. Moss Hart and George S. Kaufman. *Newton Fuller is one of those little Americans who dreams of a little place in the country to call his own. He is talked into buying such a place, along with all its tribulations.* Comedy. Interior. 9 m., 8 f. Modern Costumes. DRAMATISTS PLAY SERVICE, $1.00. *Royalty, $25.00.*

GIOCONDA SMILE, THE. Aldous Huxley. *The friendship of a devoted husband, a pathetically invalid wife, and a woman friend of the family is* *the groundwork for intrigue and murder, resulting in tragic consequences from mistaken motives.* Drama in 3 acts. 2 interiors, 1 inset. 5 m., 5 f. Modern costumes. A powerful, fast-moving play that offers many acting possibilities. FRENCH, *$1.25.* Royalty, $35.00.

GIRLS IN UNIFORM. Christa Winsloe (adapted by Barbara Burnham). *Manuela proclaims her adoration for her German girls' school teacher, and is severely punished for it by the tyrannical head mistress who regards this outburst as depravity.* Drama in 3 acts. 6 interiors. 28 f., extras. Modern costumes. Especially suited for women's colleges and advanced casts. FRENCH, MSS. *Royalty, $35.00.*

GLASS MENAGERIE, THE. Tennessee Williams. *Amanda Wingfield is a faded tragic remnant of Southern gentility who lives in poverty in a dingy St. Louis apartment with her son Tom and daughter Laura. Tom is an alcoholic and Laura lives in a world of illusion, bordered by a zoo of delicate glass animals and her wheel chair.* Drama. Interior. 2 m., 2 f. Modern costumes. DRAMATISTS PLAY SERVICE, *$1.00. Royalty, $50.00–$25.00.*

GOLDEN BOY. Clifford Odets. *Joe, once a musician, becomes a prizefighter. He turns increasingly brutish, and in his last fight, kills his opponent. With both his hands broken and his spirit crushed, he seeks relief in a wild ride which ends in death for both Lorna and him.* Drama. 4 interiors, 2 exteriors. 17 m., 2 f. Modern costumes. Offers good opportunity in sharp dialogue and vivid characterization. DRAMATISTS PLAY SERVICE, *$1.00. Royalty, $25.00.*

GOOD HOPE, THE. Herman Heijermans (translated by Lilian Saunders & Caroline Heijermans-Houwink). *The departure of a crew in a rotten schooner and her loss at sea reveals the agony of those who are left hus-*

bandless, loverless, and sonless ashore. Drama in 4 acts. 2 interiors 11 m., 7 f. Dutch costumes. FRENCH, *$1.25. Royalty, $25.00.*

GOOD HOUSEKEEPING. William McCleery. *The mother of a normal American family raises pandemonium when she sets out, armed with a big psychology book, to make everybody happy.* Comedy in 3 acts. Interior. 4 m, 5 f. Modern costumes. Ideal for amateur and little theatre groups, high schools, and the like. FRENCH, *$1.00. Royalty, $35.00.*

GRASS HARP, THE. Truman Capote. *The pure in heart, like the meek, inherit the earth. A trio finds temporary refuge, in a tree house, from the selfishness and cant of the small town they live in.* Comedy-fantasy. 1 interior, 1 exterior. 10 m., 8 f. Modern costumes. Provides parts that demand skillful acting. DRAMATISTS PLAY SERVICE, *$1.00. Royalty, $50.00–$25.00.*

GREAT BIG DOORSTEP, THE. Frances Goodrich & Albert Hackett. *The Crochets find a magnificent doorstep floating down the Mississippi River. They set it up in front of their poor shanty and try to live up to its meaning.* Comedy in 3 acts. Exterior. 5 m., 7 f. Modern costumes. DRAMATIC PUBLISHING CO., *90¢. Royalty, $35.00.*

GREAT GOD BROWN, THE. Eugene O'Neill. *A drama of symbolism in which Dion Anthony, the artistic, and Billy Brown, the practical, are rivals for Margaret's hand. Dion wins her, but his genius fails to materialize, and he is forced to take a job under Billy's management. Dion drinks himself to death and Billy assumes his personality and attempts to live a double life. Eventually Billy is shot by the police when, as Dion, he supposedly murders Billy.* Fantastic drama in 4 acts. 1 exterior, 5 interiors. 9 m., 5 f. A complicated production, necessitating the clever use of masks to show variations in personality, and requiring very expert acting and direction. *Royalty on application to* DRAMATISTS PLAY SERVICE.

GREEN GROW THE LILACS. Lynn Riggs. *The basis for* OKLAHOMA, *the musical play. Romance and jealousy, as Laurey's love for Curly, the cowhand, inflames a dark-minded ranchhand.* Romantic drama in 6 scenes. 10 m., 4 f., cowboys, girls, extras. Modern costumes. FRENCH, $1.00. *Royalty on application.*

GREEN PASTURES, THE. Marc Connelly. *The religious and racial aspirations of the Negro people.* Dramatic fable. Choruses and spectacular scenes required, but many of these can be greatly simplified. Cast calls for 59 actors, but many are bit parts. Modern and fantastic costumes. Very effective as a theatrical spectacle. DRAMATISTS PLAY SERVICE, $2.75. *Royalty, $25.00.*

GREEN VALLEY. Frank Wattron. *The fighting Berry clan—stirred from their eternal rest by Everheel's rampaging tractor—drive that unscrupulous land operator away from their valuable land.* Comedy-fantasy in 3 acts. Exterior. 5 m., 4 f., extras. Costumes, Modern and Forty-Niner. Row, PETERSON, 85¢. *Royalty, $25.00.*

GUARDSMAN, THE. Ferenc Molnár (translated by Grace L. Colbron & Hans Bartsch). *An actor tests his actress wife's fidelity by masquerading as a guardsman and making love to her.* Comedy in 3 acts. Interior. 4 m., 3 f. Modern costumes. For advanced casts and little theatre groups. FRENCH, $2.50. *Royalty, $25.00.*

HAIRY APE, THE. Eugene O'Neill. *When a stoker is described as a "filthy beast," he begins to realize that he does not belong to the human family. He wanders around New York and finally ends up at the zoo, where he hails the gorilla as brother, only to be crushed to death by it.*

Drama. 5 interiors, 2 exteriors. 6 m., 2 f., extras. Modern costumes. One of O'Neill's most striking dramas; for advanced groups only. *Royalty, $35.00–$25.00 to* DRAMATISTS PLAY SERVICE.

HAPPY TIME, THE. Samuel Taylor (based on the story by Robert Fontaine). *Bibi Bonnard, youngest member of a gay, uninhibited French family in Ottawa, grows up and learns what it is to truly be a man.* Comedy. 2 interiors. 8 m., 4 f. Modern costumes. A happy and carefree theatrical treat. DRAMATISTS PLAY SERVICE, $1.00. *Royalty, $50.00–$25.00.*

HARRIET. Florence Ryerson & Colin Clements. *The dramatic life and struggles of Harriet Beecher Stowe, the author of* UNCLE TOM'S CABIN. Comedy-drama in 3 acts. 3 interiors. 7 m., 10 f. Costumes, mid-Victorian. Ideal for advanced groups. FRENCH, $1.00. *Royalty, $50.00.*

HARVEY. Mary Coyle Chase. *The play is named after the white rabbit who accompanies the lovable hero Elwood. When he is finally despatched to a mental hospital for observation, his sister is given the treatment instead.* Comedy in 3 acts. 2 interiors. 7 m., 6 f. Modern costumes. DRAMATISTS PLAY SERVICE, $1.00. *Royalty, $50.00–$25.00.*

HASTY HEART, THE. John Patrick. *A wounded Scotch soldier learns, during his last few weeks of life in a hospital in the Orient, the true meaning of love for his neighbor.* Comedy-drama. Interior. 8 m., 1 f. Costumes, World War II. DRAMATISTS PLAY SERVICE, $1.00. *Royalty, $50.00–$25.00.*

HAVING WONDERFUL TIME. Arthur Kober. *A comedy about those city men and women who seek relaxation in two short summer weeks at a camp.* Comedy. 2 sets. 17 m., 14 f. Modern costumes. DRAMATISTS PLAY SERVICE, $1.00. *Royalty, $25.00.*

HAY FEVER. Noel Coward. *Weekend guests at the house-party of the eccentric family headed by Judith Bliss, retired actress, readjust their personal interests and escape in pairs.* Farcical comedy in 3 acts. Interior. 4 m., 5 f. Modern costumes. Good example of artificial drawing-room comedy. FRENCH, *$1.00. Royalty, $50.00.*

HE WHO GETS SLAPPED. Leonid Andreyev. (translated by Gregory Zilboorg). *To forget the theft of his wife and his literary work, a mysterious gentleman submerges his personality and becomes "He," a circus clown. When the beautiful little Consuelo, bare-back rider, is about to be given by her avaricious guardian to a wealthy and degenerate baron, "He" mercifully poisons her.* Tragedy in 4 acts. 1 interior. 9 m., 2 f., extra actors and actresses. Fantastic & modern costumes. Interesting variety of character roles, costumes, and make-ups; demanding a mature and experienced actor for the lead. FRENCH, *$1.00. Royalty, $25.00.*

HEAVEN CAN WAIT. Harry Segall. *Joe Pendleton, a prizefighter and heaven-bound, delays the trip, returns to earth in various peoples' recently deceased bodies, and creates much more comic confusion.* Comedy-fantasy. Interior. 5 m., 2 f., extras. Modern costumes. DRAMATISTS PLAY SERVICE, *$1.00. Royalty, $25.00.*

HEIRESS, THE. Ruth & Augustus Goetz (from the novel by Henry James). *Catherine falls prey to a fortune hunter who proposes to her. Her father forbids the marriage, and the young man draws away from her proposed elopement. When he returns and again proposes, she leads him on only to rebuff him in the end.* Drama. Interior. 3 m., 6 f. 19th-century costumes. DRAMATISTS PLAY SERVICE, *$1.00. Royalty, $50.00–$25.00.*

HELL-BENT FER HEAVEN. Hatcher Hughes. *A young mountaineer returns from the war to find his mother and sweetheart imposed upon by a young religious fanatic, and aids his father and grandfather to expose the imposition.* Drama in 3 acts. Interior. 5 m., 2 f. Modern costumes. A powerful, imaginative play of mountain life. Difficult, but not beyond advanced amateurs. FRENCH, MSS. *Royalty, $25.00.*

HIGH TOR. Maxwell Anderson. *A romantic fantasy and a satire on modern materialism. High Tor, towering above the Hudson, serves as the scene for the conflict between idealistic young Van Dorn and hardfisted, double-dealing realtors.* Romantic comedy. Exterior. 14 m., extras. 2 f. Costumes, modern and 17th-century Dutch. DRAMATISTS PLAY SERVICE, *$1.00. Royalty, $35.00–$25.00.*

HOLIDAY. Philip Barry. *Because John Chase sees something more worthwhile in life than making money, he is denounced by his wealthy fiancée and prospective father-in-law; but he is compensated by gaining the love of Linda, her sister, whose ideas harmonize with his.* Comedy in 3 acts. 2 interiors. 7 m., 5 f. Modern costumes. Brilliant play for advanced amateurs. FRENCH, *$1.00. Royalty, $50.00.*

HOLY NIGHT. Gregorio Martinez-Sierra. (English version by Philip Hereford). *On Christmas eve, the Virgin and Child come forth from their cathedral pedestal and venture into the world. When she is required to return, she compassionately leaves her baby to redeem the rabble who have gathered about them.* A miracle play in 3 scenes, 1 interior, 2 exteriors. 12 m., 6 f., many extras. Modern Spanish costumes. Dignified and elaborate; requires expert direction, but not difficult to play. BAKER, *$1.00. Royalty, $10.00.*

HOME OF THE BRAVE. Arthur Laurents. *Under heavy psychological pressure of thinking he has failed in his duty to a dying buddy, a Pacific-stationed GI becomes partially paralyzed so that he cannot walk. It takes much help and understanding to make him realize that he is no different from any one else, with no differences determined by blood or religion.* Drama. Several short scenes. 6 m. Costumes, World War II. DRAMATISTS PLAY SERVICE, *$1.00. Royalty, $35.00–$25.00.*

HOTEL UNIVERSE. Philip Barry. *The suicide of a young man starts a series of psychological revelations in which each character tries to solve his own problem and relives some crisis which altered the course of his life.* Full-length drama without intermission. Exterior. 5 m., 4 f. Modern costumes. Requires experienced interpretation and direction. FRENCH, $1.00. Royalty, $50.00.

HOUSE OF BERNARDA ALBA. Federico García Lorca (translated by James Gordon Lujan & Richard O'Connell). *Widowed as the play opens, the stern matriarch Bernarda declares to her five daughters that they will enter a traditional 8-year period of cloistered mourning. One girl revolts, and the family is thrown headlong into a tragic climax of honor and revenge.* Tragedy in 3 acts. 3 interiors. 10 f., (10–20 extra women). Costumes, 1890's. The greatest of modern Spanish tragedies. *Production restricted. Royalty on application to* FRENCH.

HOUSE OF CONNELLY, THE. Paul Green. *The contrast of a decaying society with the new and living forces of the present in a play of the old and the new South.* Drama in 4 acts. Interior, 2 exteriors. 4 m., 6 f., about 20 extras. Modern costumes. *Royalty, $25.00 to* FRENCH.

HOUSEPARTY. Kenneth Phillips Britton & Roy Hargrave. *A college student who was being blackmailed by a young woman is put on trial for the murder of a woman, who had accidentally fallen and killed herself, —in his fraternity house!* Melodrama in 3 acts. Interior. 9 m., 9 f., extras. Modern costumes. FRENCH, $1.00. Royalty, $25.00.

I REMEMBER MAMA. John van Druten. *Mama, with the help of her husband and Uncle Chris, brings up their children in their modest San Francisco home during the early years of the century.* Source of the television series. Comedy. 1 interior. 1 exterior. 9 m., 13 f. Early 20th-century costumes. DRAMATISTS PLAY SERVICE, *$1.00. Royalty, $35.00–$25.00.*

IDIOT'S DELIGHT. Robert E. Sherwood. *A group of international vacationists are marooned in an inn high in the Alps, just before the outbreak of what threatens to be a world war. An American vaudeville couple are the only ones left, as the others make good their escape, and these two succumb to the first onslaught of war with bravery and a useless sort of idealism.* Satire on warmongering. 17 m., 10 f. (many bits). Modern costumes. For advanced groups. DRAMATISTS PLAY SERVICE, *$1.00. Royalty, $25.00.*

IF I WERE KING. Justin Huntley McCarthy. *François Villon, leader of the vagabonds at the time of Louis XI, becomes king for a day but forfeits his life. He is saved by Katherin de Vaucelle's promise to marry him.* Romantic drama in 4 acts. Exterior, 3 interiors. 20 m., 9 f. Costumes, Louis XI. FRENCH, $1.00. *Royalty on application.*

I'LL LEAVE IT TO YOU. Noel Coward. *Mrs. Dermott is a destitute widow with five children. Her brother Daniel returns from South America reputedly wealthy, and rivalry to be his heir spurs the young people to work and success.* Comedy in 3 acts. 1 interior. 4 m., 6 f. Modern costumes. Good lines; very suitable for advanced high schools. FRENCH, $1.00. Royalty, $25.00.

IMAGINARY INVALID, THE. Molière *Argon, an imaginary invalid, wishes to make his daughter, Angélique, marry a physician, for his convenience; she loves Cleante and refuses, and is saved from being sent to a convent only through the machinations of the maid, Toinette, who disguises herself as a physician and brings about a permanent cure.* Comedy in 3 acts. Interior. 8 m., 4 f. Costumes, Louis XIV. Croft Classics (translated by Morris Bishop), APPLETON-CENTURY-CROFTS, 45¢; (translated and adapted by Merritt Stone), FRENCH, 75¢. No royalty.

IMPORTANCE OF BEING EARNEST, THE. Oscar Wilde. *Jack, in order to escape from his usual surroundings, has invented a wild, younger brother, Earnest, who takes the fancy of Cecily Cardew, his ward; complications ensue when his friend, Algernon, introduces himself to Cecily as Earnest.* Farcical English social comedy in 3 acts. Exterior, 2 interiors. 5 m., 4 f. Modern costumes. One of the most brilliant, well-known plays in English. FRENCH, $1.00. No royalty.

IN ABRAHAM'S BOSOM. Paul Green. *Pictures the struggles of a mulatto son of a white man in a Southern community to achieve status. Although he wants to achieve higher goals for himself and others, he fails because of his own inadequacies and an unfortunate marriage.* Drama in 7 scenes. 2 exteriors, 3 interiors. 9 m., 3 f. Modern costumes. FRENCH, MSS. Royalty, $25.00.

IN A GARDEN. Philip Barry. *Terry, a playwright, decides to withdraw from playwriting, but is urged on by Compton, a scheming friend, who gives him for a plot: "Every wife in her heart is another man's mistress." The almost tragic incidents that fol-low are the result of Terry's trying to prove this with his wife.* Drama in 3 acts. 1 interior. 4 m., 2 f. Modern costumes. A romantic and unusual play for mature and experienced amateurs. FRENCH, $1.00. Royalty, $50.00.

INNOCENTS, THE. William Archibald (adapted from Henry James's THE TURN OF THE SCREW). *A young governess arrives at an English estate to assume charge of two precocious, orphaned youngsters who are influenced by the spirits of a former caretaker and maid, both of them evil and perverse.* Melodrama in 2 acts. Interior. 1 m., 3 f., and boy and girl aged 10–13. 19th century. FRENCH, $1.00. Royalty, $50.00.

INSPECTOR CALLS, AN. J. B. Priestley. *A young girl's suicide touches off a series of strains and contrasts in an apparently close-knit and friendly, respectable British family.* Drama. Interior. 4 m., 3 f. Modern British costumes. DRAMATISTS PLAY SERVICE, $1.00. Royalty, $50.00–$25.00.

INSPECTOR GENERAL, THE. Nikolai Gogol. (acting version by John Anderson). *Satire on official crookedness and human stupidity.* Satiric farce in 3 acts. 2 interiors. 15 m., 4 f. Costumes, Russian, 1830. FRENCH, $1.00. Royalty, $25.00.

IT'S A GREAT LIFE. Robert Finch. *The farcical goings-on in the Peabody household, what with managing the budget, a romantically-inclined teenage daughter, and a time-wasting 17-year-old son.* Farce-comedy in 3 acts. 1 exterior. 6 m., 8 f. Modern costumes. Easy production. Row, PETERSON, 85¢. Royalty, 20% of receipts; max. $25.00 per performance.

IVORY DOOR, THE. A. A. Milne. *Perivale and Lilia lose a kingdom by going through the Ivory Door, but discover happiness and truth.* Fantastic comedy in prologue and 3 acts. 1 interior, 2 exteriors. 12 m., 4 f., child. Costumes fanciful. Can be made colorful and interesting. Rather sentimental, not difficult. FRENCH. *$1.00. Royalty, $50.00.*

JANE EYRE. Helen Jerome (based on Charlotte Brontë's novel). *Jane is finally able to marry Rochester after his lunatic wife succeeds in setting their house afire and destroying herself in the process.* Play in 3 acts. 2 interiors. 10 m., 12 f. Costumes, 1850. FRENCH, *$1.00. Royalty, $25.00.*

JOAN OF LORRAINE. Maxwell Anderson. *Play within a play, the outer play showing a group of actors rehearsing on a bare stage, preparing to produce a Joan of Arc play. The title-role actress learns through the rehearsal that each person has his own kind of faith and idealism.* Romantic drama. Interior. Joan of Arc in traditional costume, rest modern. 18 m., 5 f. DRAMATISTS PLAY SERVICE, *$1.00. Royalty, $50.00–$25.00.*

JOHNNY JOHNSON. Paul Green. *Assured by Wilson that the last war would end wars, pacifist Johnny enlists, and ends by selling toys on the street.* A legend in 3 acts. 49 m., 6 f. 13 scenes (simple). Modern costumes. FRENCH, *$2.00. Royalty, $50.00; Music, $2.50.*

JOURNEY'S END. R. C. Sherriff. *Shows the effect of war on a small group of young English officers.* Drama in 3 acts. Interior. Modern British military uniforms. A tragic and moving piece, for advanced casts only. FRENCH, *$1.25. Royalty on application.*

JUNE GRADUATE. Jean Provence. *The story of a boy who loses himself, and almost his whole future, at one of the most important crossroads of his life, when he is about to enter college and finds he must work his way through, and that his fiancée is scheming and worthless.* Comedy-drama in 3 acts. 1 interior. 5 m., 7

f. (extras, if desired). Modern costumes. ROW, PETERSON, *85¢. Royalty, 20% of receipts to $25.00 per performance.*

JUNE WEDDING. Marrijane & Joseph Hayes. *The amusing experiences of the Perry family during the week of Linda Perry's marriage to Gordon Gavin, thanks to kid-sister Dandy who cooks up an intrigue.* Comedy in 3 acts. Interior. 6 m., 8 f. Modern costumes. FRENCH, *$1.00. Royalty, $25.00.*

JUNIOR MISS. Jerome Chodorov & Joseph Fields. *13-year-old Judy Graves, who loves Fuffy, her confidante, and who wants to be 16, must rescue her father from his love (imagined by her) for his boss's daughter.* Comedy. Interior. 11 m., 6 f. Modern costumes. DRAMATISTS PLAY SERVICE, *$1.00. Royalty, $25.00.*

JUNO AND THE PAYCOCK. Sean O'Casey. *A compelling story dealing with modern Irish city life. Exceptional example of keen character analysis.* Tragedy in 3 acts. Interior. 14 m., 5 f. Modern costumes. Quite difficult. FRENCH, *$1.25. Royalty, $25.00.*

KIND LADY. Edward Chodorov (adapted from a story by Hugh Walpole). *A dignified and aristocratic middle-aged woman, in London, is surrounded by a family of crooks who attempt to convince the outside world that she is insane, in order to confiscate her property. She finally wins the battle, however.* Melodrama in 3 acts. Interior. 6 m., 8 f. Modern costumes. Intensely exciting drama. FRENCH, *$1.00. Royalty, $25.00.*

KING OF HEARTS, THE. Jean Kerr & Eleanore Brooke. *The story tells about Larry Larkin, who draws a comic strip, and who is also the world's No. 1 egotist. Larry's fiancée is rescued from a fate worse than death by Dignan, who originally was to take Larry's place during the lat-*

ter's honeymoon; at the drawing board, that is. Comedy. Interior. 6 m., 2 f., 2 small boys, 1 dog. Modern costumes. Witty, pointed, biting, and original. DRAMATISTS PLAY SERVICE, *$1.00. Royalty, $50.00–$25.00.*

KISS AND TELL. F. Hugh Herbert. *Happy intrigue is caused by Corliss Archer, going on sixteen, who would so like to be grown up that she devastatingly tries to conceal the secret that her friend Mildred married Lennie, Corliss's brother.* Comedy. Interior. 9 m. (incl. boys), 6 f. (incl. girls). Modern costumes. DRAMATISTS PLAY SERVICE, *$1.00. Royalty, $35.00–$25.00.*

KISS FOR CINDERELLA, A. James M. Barrie. *An undernourished servant girl dreams of a prince, and in her delirium attends a ball as Cinderella, meets her prince, and finds him again on her return to reality, in the person of a friendly policeman.* English comedy in 3 acts. 4 interiors. 19 m., 7 f., extras. Modern costumes, military & court. The dream is a fine, fantastic scene. Not too difficult. FRENCH, *$1.00. Royalty, $35.00 first performance, $25.00 each subsequent performance.*

LADIES IN RETIREMENT. Edward Percy & Reginald Denham. *The story of Lucy Fiske, ex-actress, who is murdered by her companion, Ellen, so that Lucy's two sisters may share the cottage with her.* Mystery drama. Interior. 1 m., 6 f. Modern costumes. DRAMATISTS PLAY SERVICE, *$1.00. Royalty, $35.00–$25.00.*

LADY IN THE DARK. Moss Hart. *Liza, successful magazine editor, goes through a series of wishful dreams. A psychoanalyst gives her back her belief in herself and her sanity.* Interiors. 9 m., 11 f. Modern costumes. Dramatic fantasy with music. DRAMATISTS PLAY SERVICE, *$1.00 Royalty, $50.00–$25.00.*

LADY PRECIOUS STREAM. S. I. Hsiung. *Romantic drama of love, tell-ing of the devotion of a wife to her adventurous husband, of his prowess as a warrior and his ultimate return.* Chinese play in 4 acts. Chinese costumes and scenery. Poetic, colorful fantasy, appealing to all classes of theatre-goers. FRENCH, *$1.00. Royalty, $25.00.*

LADY'S NOT FOR BURNING, THE. Christopher Fry. *Philosophical humorist Thomas Mendip wants to die, and so confesses to an alleged murder. Jennet Jourdemayne is accused of witchcraft, but does not want to die. Jennet and Thomas fall in love, and live happily on.* Poetic fantasy. Interior. 8 m., 3 f. 15th-century English costumes. Delightful. DRAMATISTS PLAY SERVICE, *$1.00. Royalty, $50.00–$25.00.*

LADY WINDERMERE'S FAN. Oscar Wilde. *Lady Windermere is about to leave her husband, but is saved from this and other fatal steps, by Mrs. Erlynne, a notorious lady to whom she objects, but who is really her own mother who has made the mistakes in the past from which she saves her daughter.* English comedy in 3 acts. 3 interiors. 7 m., 9 f. 19th-century British costumes. Brilliant, but difficult and sophisticated. Considered Wilde's best play. FRENCH, *$1.00. No royalty.*

LAMP AND THE BELL, THE. Edna St. Vincent Millay. *Beatrice and Bianca, loving and inseparable stepsisters, are estranged by Bianca's marriage to Mario, whom both women love, and by the death of their father, upon which Beatrice becomes the queen; they are reunited only after many years as Bianca is dying.* Poetic drama in 5 acts. 6 interiors, 5 exteriors. 17 m., 29 f., extras. Elaborate costumes of Italian Renaissance. Excellent for all-girl cast. Difficult. BAKER, *$2.00. Royalty, $25.00.*

LATE CHRISTOPHER BEAN, THE. Sidney Howard. *The Haggett family realizes too late the value of the paintings left by Bean, the great artist who had lived with them when alive. The servant, Abby, owns the most precious of the paintings and will not part with it, for Bean had secretly been her husband.* Comedy in 3 acts. Interior. 5 m., 4 f. Modern costumes. Good for high school and college production. FRENCH, $1.00. Royalty, $25.00.

LATE GEORGE APLEY, THE. John P. Marquand & George S. Kaufman. *George Apley is the personification of old Boston tradition. The story centers about his two children who heroically strive to break away from the shackles of family and tradition.* Comedy. 2 interiors. 8 m., 8 f. Modern costumes. DRAMATISTS PLAY SERVICE, $1.00. Royalty, $50.00–$25.00.

LETTERS TO LUCERNE. Fritz Rotter & Allen Vincent. *The animosity a Polish girl feels towards her German friend, Erna, whose brother she loved at the outbreak of war, is dispelled when she learns that Erna's brother preferred suicide to bombing Warsaw.* Drama in 3 acts. 2 interiors. 4 m., 9 f. (Can be done in one set, and all-female cast). Modern costumes. FRENCH, $1.00. Royalty, $35.00.

LIFE WITH FATHER. Howard Lindsay & Russel Crouse (based on Clarence Day's book). *Father and his wife Vinnie, their young sons, relatives and friends, are all involved in the tremendous struggle between father and mother to have father properly baptized.* Comedy. Interior. 8 m., 8 f. Costumes, late 1880's. DRAMATISTS PLAY SERVICE, $1.00. Royalty, $50.00–$25.00. (*Check whether play is released for non-professional production in your area*).

LIFE WITH MOTHER. Howard Lindsay & Russel Crouse (based on Clarence Day's book). *Mother attempts to provide an engagement ring for one of her sons, who wants it for his fiancée.* Comedy. 2 interiors. 8 m., 8 f. Costumes, late 1880's. DRAMATISTS PLAY SERVICE, $1.00. Royalty, $50.00–$25.00.

LILIOM. Ferenc Molnár (translated by Benjamin F. Glazer). *Liliom was a ne'er-do-well who stabbed himself to death rather than be caught for a robbery he committed to provide for his unborn child. In heaven he is sentenced to years of purification fires, after which he may return to earth to perform one good deed.* Legend in 7 scenes and a prologue. 1 interior, 4 exteriors. 17 m., 5 f. (extras). Modern costumes. FRENCH, $1.00. Royalty $25.00.

LINDEN TREE, THE. J. B. Priestley. *The story of a college professor who feels that the time of want and unrest, the time of a peaceful revolution, demands the fulfillment of duties. It is not a time for defeatism, or a quick grab at superficial happiness.* Play in 2 acts. Interior. 4 m., 6 f. Modern costumes. FRENCH, $1.25. Royalty, $50.00.

LITTLE DOG LAUGHED, THE. Vera & Ken Tarpley. *Co-ed Laurie, amateur psychologist, discovers that psychoanalyzing the family can boomerang, with humorous results.* A comedy in three acts. Unique, single setting. 5 m., 5 f. (extras). Modern costumes, ROW, PETERSON, 85¢. Royalty for each performance, 15% of the gross receipts, with a maximum of $25.00, and no minimum.

LITTLE FOXES, THE. Lillian Hellman. *Prosperous, despotic Hubbard family schemes to steal $80,000 from ailing brother Horace with the help of his conniving wife, Regina.* Drama. Interior. 6 m., 4 f. Modern Southern costumes. Powerful. DRAMATISTS PLAY SERVICE, $1.00. Royalty, $25.00.

LITTLE MINISTER, THE. Roland Fernand (from the book by James Barrie). *Minister Gavin finally suc-*

ceeds in marrying the enticing Gypsy Babbie, leader of local revolts of poor weavers. Comedy in 3 acts. 1 interior. 5 m., 6 f. Scottish costumes, 19th century. DRAMATIC PUBLISHING Co., *90¢. Royalty, $25.00.*

LITTLE WOMEN. John Ravold (based on the novel by Louisa M. Alcott). *Famous story of a mother's love for her children, and their appreciation of it and her.* Drama in 3 acts. 1 interior. 4 m., 6 f. Victorian costumes. FRENCH, *75¢. Royalty, $10.00. (When ordering give dramatist's name).*

LO AND BEHOLD! John Patrick. *A cynical Nobel Prize winner has lived for many years on a meagre, unpalatable diet, to favor an ailing heart. He dies after one sumptuous meal, only to have his aesthete's heart plagued after his death by a procession of attractive but weird characters.* Comedy in 3 acts. Interior. 5 m., 3 f. Modern costumes. Amusing and not too difficult. FRENCH, *$1.00. Royalty, $50.00.*

LOST HORIZON. Anne Coulter Martens & Christopher Sergel (from novel by James Hilton). *Four people are kidnapped and brought to the exquisite but mysterious Utopia Shangri-La.* 3-act play. Interior. 7 m., 7 f. Modern and Tibetan costumes. DRAMATIC PUBLISHING Co., *90¢. Royalty, $25.00.*

LOVE IS TOO MUCH TROUBLE. Guernsey Le Pelley. *Financial and other troubles of adolescents, full of little intrigues and "scientific experiments".* Farce-comedy in 3 acts. 1 set: the campus hangout. 5 m., 9 f. Modern costumes. Row, PETERSON, *85¢. Royalty 20% of receipts, max. $25.00 per performance.*

LOVE OF DON PERLIMPLIN AND BELISA IN THE GARDEN, THE. Federico García Lorca (translated from the Spanish by Richard O'Connell & James Graham Lujan). *The story of Don Perlimpin's love for Belisa is ironic and beautiful.* Comedy. 3 interiors, 1 exterior. 1 m., 3 f., 2 sprites (m. or f.). Costumes, Spanish Court, 17th century. Witty and romantic satire. FRENCH, MSS. *Royalty, $35.00.*

LOVE YOUR NEIGHBOR. Albert Johnson. *Johnny Jones finally wins Tessy Vashki as his wife, at the "I do" stage of her wedding to another man. But this happens only after bee stings and a case of mistaken identity.* Farce-comedy in 3 acts. Interior. 8 m., 12 f. Modern costumes. Row, PETERSON, *85¢. Royalty, 20% of receipts; max. $25.00 per performance.*

LUCKY PEHR. August Strindberg (translated by Velma S. Howard). *Pehr, a young lad, runs away to see the world from which he has always been protected. An elf and a fairy each give him a parting gift, to bring luck on his journey. After several years of worldly living, he gladly returns to his old father, and finds Liza, his old sweetheart, awaiting him.* Allegory in 5 acts. 4 interiors, 3 exteriors. 36 m., 5 f. Costuming and staging picturesque and romantic. Not too difficult; may be cut for high school. *Royalty, $25.00 to* APPLETON-CENTURY-CROFTS.

LUTE SONG. Kao-Tong-Kai (adapted by Will Irwin). *A young scholar journeys to the capital to take examinations for the Imperial Service. He succeeds so well that he becomes Chief Magistrate of the Middle Kingdom, while his impoverished young bride and his parents await his news in vain.* Play in 3 acts. 1 basic set. 9 m., 6 f., extras as desired. Chinese costumes. Original version over 500 years old. DRAMATIC PUBLISHING Co., *90¢; Musical version, $1.00. Royalty on application.*

MADWOMAN OF CHAILLOT, THE. Jean Giraudoux (adapted by Maurice Valency). *The Madwoman of Chaillot foils the plans of a group* *of greedy prospectors to tear up Paris in search of oil.* Comedy in 3 acts. 1 interior, 1 exterior. 17 m., 8 f., extras. Modern Parisian costumes. A play of great charm, poetry, and popularity. DRAMATISTS PLAY SERVICE, $1.00. *Royalty, $50.00–$25.00.*

MAGISTRATE, THE. Arthur W. Pinero. *Mr. Posket, a magistrate, marries a widow with a son who she claims is fourteen, but who is really twenty; all goes well until a friend of Posket's from India returns to England and turns out to be the boy's godfather.* English society farce in 3 acts. 3 interiors. 12 m., 4 f. Modern British costumes. Amusing and effective if well done, requires rather advanced acting. *No royalty.*

MAGNIFICENT YANKEE, THE. Emmet Lavery. *The marriage that lasted 57 years—that of Justice Oliver Wendell Holmes and his wife, and the critical years between the administrations of Theodore Roosevelt and Franklin Delano Roosevelt.* Drama in 3 acts. Interior. 15 m., 2 f. Costumes, 1902–1933. A great piece of Americana. FRENCH, $1.00. *Royalty, $50.00.*

MAJOR BARBARA. G. Bernard Shaw. *Barbara, who has renounced her social position to become a Salvation Army major, refuses as "tainted money" the generous donations of Bodge, whiskey distiller, and Undershaft, her father, only to discover the army's views that money from whatever source is desirable. She is completely converted and marries a man who takes a position in her father's munitions factory.* Satiric comedy in 3 acts. 1 interior, 2 exteriors. 9 m., 6 f. Modern costumes brilliant and playable. Requires experienced actors. *Royalty, $25.00 to* FRENCH.

MAKROPOULOS SECRET, THE. Karel Čapek (adapted by Randal C. Burrell). *Emilia Marty, a beauti-*

ful singer, has, by the aid of the Makropoulos secret, lived for three hundred years; in a struggle over the possession of the secret, it is, with Emilia's consent, destroyed. Drama in 3 acts. 3 interiors. 8 m., 4 f. Unusual and interesting plot, swift in movement; for advanced amateurs. *Royalty on application to* BAKER.

MALE ANIMAL, THE. James Thurber & Elliott Nugent. *Tommy Turner insists on standing up for his rights and the four freedoms, at the risk of losing his wife and a comfortable teaching job at the University.* Comedy in 3 acts. Interior. 8 m., 5 f. Modern costumes. FRENCH, $1.00. *Royalty, $50.00.*

MAN AND SUPERMAN. G. Bernard Shaw. *Jack Tanner, who has been appointed Anne's guardian, discovers that she is interested in him romantically. He flies from her in his motor, but she follows and captures him.* Satiric comedy in 4 acts. 1 interior, 3 exteriors. 12 m., 5 f., extras. Modern costumes. Witty exposition of the "life force." Difficult staging; needs cutting; only for advanced amateurs. *Royalty, $25.00 to* FRENCH.

MAN FROM HOME, THE. Booth Tarkington & Harry Leon Wilson. *A contrast of the level-headed, matter-of-fact one-hundred-per-cent American with that type of pseudo-aristocrat which in the minds of some people characterizes old Europe. Done in a humorous vein.* Comedy in 4 acts. Interior. 13 m., 3 f. Modern costumes. An exceptionally fine play for high schools and Little Theaters. FRENCH, $1.00. *Royalty, $25.00.*

MAN WHO CAME TO DINNER, THE. Moss Hart & George S. Kaufman. *Portly Whiteside, a dinner guest of the Stanleys, slips on their doorstep and breaks his hip. The 6 weeks of confinement at their home prove* to be a series of tumultuous and bizarre happenings. Comedy. Interior. 15 m. (extras), 9 f. Modern costumes. DRAMATISTS PLAY SERVICE, $1.00. Royalty, $25.00.

MARY OF SCOTLAND. Maxwell Anderson. *The six years of Mary's life that began when she set foot on her unruly land as a queen, and ending with the sunset lowering on the barred window of her prison room in Carlisle Castle.* Drama in 3 acts. 4 interiors, 1 exterior. 22 m., 5 f., Elizabethan costumes. FRENCH, *$1.00.* ROYALTY, $25.00.

MEDEA. Robinson Jeffers. *The ambitious Jason forsakes Medea, his foreign wife, and takes a new bride for political advancement. On the day of her banishment, Medea succeeds in bringing death to the new young bride, and the most wanton horror to her husband, Jason.* Tragedy in 2 acts. Exterior. 5 m., 5 f., extras. Greek costumes. FRENCH, $1.00. Royalty, $50.00.

MEET CORLISS ARCHER. Christopher Sergel. *Corliss Archer's fake diary is the subject of much excitement and shock as Cousin Agnes becomes firmly convinced that the whole family is unbalanced and dangerous.* Comedy in 3 acts. Interior. 4 m., 8 f. Modern costumes. DRAMATIC PUBLISHING Co., 90¢. Royalty, $25.00.

MEET ME IN ST. LOUIS. Perry Clark (based on the novel by Sally Benson). *Four attractive sisters decide to run the family in general, and the romances of their only brother in particular.* Comedy in 3 acts. Interior. 7 m., 9 f. Early 20th-century costumes. Recommended highly for all groups. DRAMATIC PUBLISHING Co., 90¢. Royalty, $25.00.

MEMBER OF THE WEDDING, THE. Carson McCullers. *Perceptive portraits of a harum-scarum adolescent*

girl in Georgia, a Negro servant, and a busy little boy. Drama. 1 unit set. 6 m., 7 f. Modern Southern costumes. DRAMATISTS PLAY SERVICE, $2.75. Royalty, $50.00–$25.00.

MEN ARE LIKE STREET CARS. Christopher Sergel. *Maudie's education of her pretty but tongue-tied cousin, Joy, backfires to the point where Maudie must take drastic steps to safeguard her own interests in boy friends from Joy and her own sister Sylvia.* Comedy in 3 acts. Interior. 5 m., 10 f. Modern costumes. DRAMATIC PUBLISHING Co., 90¢. Royalty, $25.00.

MERCHANT OF YONKERS, THE. Thornton Wilder. *Horace Vandergelder, a 60-year old, successful, miserly merchant, decides to take unto himself a young wife. He enlists the help of a volatile lady of uncertain means who is planning to win the wealthy old man for herself.* Farce in 4 acts. 4 interiors. 9 m., 7 f. Costumes, 1890. Highly recommended for all groups. FRENCH, MSS. Royalty, $25.00.

MISTER ANGEL. Harry Segall. *The problems Item, a small girl angel, encounters in wanting to be born to a certain couple, who are too busy with the theater at the moment to consider such an event.* Comedy-fantasy. Interior. 5 m., 8 f. Modern costumes. DRAMATISTS PLAY SERVICE, $1.00. Royalty, $35.00–$25.00.

MISTER ROBERTS. Thomas Heggen & Joshua Logan. *The crew of a Navy cargo vessel rebels against the deadly boredom which is a part of the routine of war.* Drama. 3 interiors. 19 m., 1 f., extras. Costumes, World War II, U.S. Navy. DRAMATISTS PLAY SERVICE, $1.00. Royalty, $50.00–$25.00.

MONSIEUR BEAUCAIRE. Booth Tarkington (dramatized by Ethel H. Freeman). *Prince Louis Philippe of*

France goes to England incognito in search of romance, but becomes disillusioned and gladly returns home to marry his cousin, in obedience to his uncle, the King of France. Romantic comedy in 3 acts. 3 interiors, 1 exterior. 14 m., 7 f., extras. Costumes, about 1750. Colorful and romantic, popular with schools. BAKER, 75¢. Royalty, $10.00.

MOOR BORN. Dan Totheroh. *The theme is one of ironical sacrifice made by the three talented Brontë sisters, Emily, Charlotte and Anne, for their dissolute brother, Branwell, who has none of their native genius.* Drama in 5 scenes. Interior. 3 m., 5 f. Costumes, 1840–1850. FRENCH, $1.00. Royalty, $25.00.

MORNING'S AT SEVEN. Paul Osborn. *Myrtle has been waiting for fifteen years for Homer to ask her to marry him. When he still cannot break his home fireside bonds, she finally makes him propose, with an ingenious little secret.* Comedy in 3 acts. Exterior. 4 m., 5 f. Modern costumes. FRENCH, $1.00. Royalty, $25.00.

MOURNING BECOMES ELECTRA. Eugene O'Neill. *Follows the pattern of the* Oresteia *trilogy of Aeschylus, with a New England setting. Christine Mannon kills her husband upon his return from the Civil War. Her son kills her lover and virtually compels his mother to kill herself. Later he kills himself and leaves the Mannon mansion to his sister Lavinia.* Tragedy. Trilogy. Royalty, $75 for the group of three plays, to DRAMATISTS PLAY SERVICE.

MR. BARRY'S ETCHINGS. Walter Bullock & Daniel Archer. *Judson Barry perfects a $50 bill, and uses his counterfeit bills to rid his town of its corrupt political organization.* Comedy. Interior. 7 m., 6 f. Modern costumes. DRAMATISTS PLAY SERVICE, $1.00. Royalty, $25.00.

MR. PIM PASSES BY. A. A. Milne. *Mr. Pim's forgetfulness of names creates confusion, when he insists a woman's first husband, thought to be deceased, is alive.* Comedy in 3 acts. Interior. 3 m., 4 f. Modern costumes. FRENCH, $1.00. Royalty, $50.00.

MRS. McTHING. Mary Coyle Chase. *A witch's tricks convinces a mother to accept her little boy on his own terms and not to look down on other people.* Comic-fantasy. Interiors. 9 m., (1 child), 10 f., (1 child). Modern costumes. DRAMATISTS PLAY SERVICE, $1.00. Royalty, $50.00–$25.00.

MRS. MOONLIGHT. Benn W. Levy. *Mrs Moonlight, having been granted the magic wish that she will never grow old, finds the fulfillment displeasing to her husband. She disappears, to reappear in the second and third acts posing as different characters, unknown to her family, but constantly guiding their destiny.* Fantasy in 3 acts. 1 interior (furniture changes). 4 m., 4 f. Modern costumes. Unusual English play for advanced amateurs. FRENCH, $1.00. Royalty, $50.00.

MURDER IN THE CATHEDRAL. T. S. Eliot. *The martyrdom of Thomas Becket, archbishop, who, though tempted, refuses to seize temporal control of England.* Poetic drama in 2 acts. 3 interiors. 10 m., 9 f. Costumes, 1170. For advanced groups. FRENCH, $2.25. Royalty, $35.00.

MY HEART'S IN THE HIGHLANDS. William Saroyan. *Through his warm characters, the author dwells on themes of war and of love, of the place of money and of art in the world, of life and its wonders. The characters are the innocents of this world who long dimly for a beauty they but vaguely understand.* Fantasy. Simple sets. 13 m., 2 f., extras. Modern costumes. FRENCH, $1.00. Royalty, $25.00.

MY SISTER EILEEN. Joseph Fields & Jerome Chodorov (from the book by Ruth McKenney). *A 12-months' lease* on a Greenwich Village basement apartment by two girls is the beginning of a series of amusing and sometimes catastrophic events, culminating in their evacuation. Comedy. Interior. 21 m. (several minor bits), 6 f. Modern costumes. DRAMATISTS PLAY SERVICE, $1.00. Royalty, $25.00.

MY THREE ANGELS. Samuel & Bella Spewack. *Three convicts of French Guiana become the good angels of a harrassed household; all three are passionate believers in the "robinhood" of man.* Comedy. Interior. 7 m., 3 f. Modern costumes. DRAMATISTS PLAY SERVICE, $1.00. Royalty, $50.00–$25.00.

NATIVE SON. Paul Green & Richard Wright. *A rebellious Negro is victimized by a prejudiced society, driven to murder through fear, and pays for the crime in the electric chair.* Tragedy in 3 acts. 10 scenes. 17 m., 7 f. Modern costumes. FRENCH, MSS. Royalty, $50.00.

NIGHT MUST FALL. Emlyn Williams. *Dan, a completely selfish, self-centered psychopath with no feelings and a vast imagination, is a bellhop who has already murdered one woman and will soon murder another.* Melodrama in 3 acts. Interior. 4 m., 5 f. Modern costumes. Requires skillful acting. FRENCH, $1.00. Royalty, $25.00.

NINE GIRLS. Wilfred H. Pettitt. *A string of murders takes place in a mountain clubhouse, and each time one of the remaining girls confides in the wrong person with her theories about the killer. Finally, the murderess is caught.* Mystery-drama in a Prologue and 2 acts. Interior. 9 f. Modern costumes. DRAMATIC PUBLISHING CO., 90¢. Royalty, $25.00.

NO EXIT. Jean-Paul Sartre (adapted from the French by Paul Bowles). *Two women and one man are locked up together for eternity in one hideous room in hell. Ironically, the torture is not of rack and fire, but of the burning humiliation of each soul as it is stripped of its pretenses by the curious souls of the damned.* Fantasy in 2 acts. Interior. 2 m., 2 f. Modern costumes. For advanced groups. FRENCH, MSS. Royalty, $25.00.

NOAH. André Obey (adapted from the French by Arthur Wilmurt). *The biblical story of Noah, presented as the story of a kindly, simple old man who grows lonely in his faith, who pilots his craft safely to shore in the midst of doubts, and who is rudely deserted by the young folks the moment they touch foot to land.* Fantasy in 3 acts. 3 exteriors. 5 m., 4 f., extras. Biblical costumes. FRENCH, $1.00. Royalty, $25.00. Music, 60¢.

OF MICE AND MEN. John Steinbeck. *A tremendously moving drama built on a character study of two roving farmhands, one of whom, "with the strength of a gorilla and the mind of an untutored child," unwittingly murders a woman, and is killed by his friend to prevent his falling into the hands of the law.* Drama, 2 interiors, 1 exterior. 9 m., 1 f. Modern Western costumes. DRAMATISTS PLAY SERVICE, $1.00. Royalty, $25.00.

OF THEE I SING. George S. Kaufman & Morris Ryskind. Music by George Gershwin. Lyrics by Ira Gershwin. Pulitzer Prize, 1933. *John P. Wintergreen's campaign for President, and his triumphant election on the slogan "Put Love in the White House."* Glorious and highly amusing buffoonery. Musical play in 2 acts. Various simple interior and exterior scenes. 14 m., 5 f., extras. Modern costumes. FRENCH, *libretto, $1.00; Vocal score, $6.00. Information regarding royalty and music will be furnished on request.*

OLD ACQUAINTANCE. John van Druten. *Two women friends become closer, when the sweetheart of one marries the daughter of the other.*

Comedy. 2 interiors. 2 m., 5 f. Modern costumes. Gentle, sincere and understanding. Recommended for advanced amateurs. FRENCH, $1.00. Royalty, $35.00.

OLD MAID, THE. Zoë Akins (from the novelette by Edith Wharton). *A reconstruction of a picturesque bygone epoch of New York society, dealing with the long struggle to win the affection of a child who is the illegitimate daughter of an old maid.* Drama in 3 acts. 3 interiors. 5 m., 9 f. Early 19th-century costumes. For college groups. FRENCH, $1.00. Royalty, $25.00.

ON BORROWED TIME. Paul Osborn (from the novel by L. E. Watkins). *Death is chased up an apple-tree by a boy and his grandfather.* Fantasy. 11 m., 3 f. Modern costumes. DRAMATISTS PLAY SERVICE, $1.00. Royalty, $35.00–$25.00.

ONCE IN A LIFETIME. George S. Kaufman & Moss Hart. *Three down-and-out troupers from Hollywood try their luck with the newly invented talkies. The more they blunder, the more success they achieve, until the dumbest of them all becomes a god of the industry.* Satirical comedy in 3 acts. 5 interiors. 24 m., 14 f. Modern costumes. FRENCH, $1.00. Royalty, $50.00.

ONE FOOT IN HEAVEN. Anne Coulter Martens (from the novel by Hartzell Spence). *The struggle of Rev. Spence and his family in the dilapidated parsonage of their new parish.* Comedy in 3 acts. Interior. 8 m., 9 f. Modern costumes. DRAMATIC PUBLISHING CO., 90¢. Royalty, $25.00.

OUR HEARTS WERE YOUNG AND GAY. Jean Kerr (based on the book by Cornelia Otis Skinner, and Emily Kimbrough). *The sparkling and exuberant escapades of the two authors as girls on an uproarious and enchanting trip to Europe, as they "prove" how "mature and cosmopolitan" they can be.* Comedy in 3 acts. 1 unit set. 8 m., 9 f. Modern costumes, DRAMATIC PUBLISHING CO., 90¢. Royalty, $25.00.

OUR MISS BROOKS. Perry Clark (adapted from the original material material of R. J. Mann). *Miss Brooks is a most human and delightful English teacher, on whom the entire community depends.* Comedy in 3 acts. 1 interior. 5 m., 12 f. Modern costumes. Fast-paced action, humorous lines, hilarious situations, underlying sweetness. DRAMATIC PUBLISHING CO., 90¢. Royalty, $25.00.

OUR TOWN. Thornton Wilder. *The life of a New Hampshire village, with its humor, picturesqueness, and pathos, set against the background of centuries of time.* Drama in 3 acts. Bare stage. 17 m., 7 f., extras. Costumes, 1901. Deeply moving. FRENCH, $1.00. Royalty, $25.00.

OUTWARD BOUND. Sutton Vane. *A Group of oddly assorted characters are passengers on an ocean liner whose destination is unknown. Suddenly the bewildered and puzzled passengers realize that they are all dead and headed for Judgment Day.* Comedy-drama in 3 acts. Interior. 6 m., 3 f. Modern costumes. FRENCH, $1.25. Also in MSS. Royalty, $25.00.

PAOLO AND FRANCESCA. Stephen Phillips. *Giovanni, Tyrant of Rimini, marries Francesca, daughter of the Tyrant of Ravenna, only to find she is in love with his only brother, Paolo, whom he loves dearly. Paolo is to leave for the wars, but Giovanni, finding them together, kills them both.* Poetic tragedy in 4 acts. 4 interiors, 1 exterior. 7 m., 7 f., extras. Italian Renaissance costumes. Moving and dramatic tragedy. Royalty *on application to* FRENCH.

PASSING OF THE THIRD FLOOR BACK, THE. Jerome K. Jerome. *The household of a Bloomsbury lodging house is filled with unsavory charac-*

ters, until the third floor back is taken by a passer-by who influences all the boarders to lead better lives. Drama in 3 acts. Interior. 6 m., 6 f. Modern costumes. FRENCH, $1.25. Royalty, $25.00.

PATHS OF GLORY. Sidney Howard (from the novel by Humphrey Cobb). *How an otherwise brave general sacrifices some of the best men in his army, men who were given an impossible task and failed.* Play in 3 acts. 17 scenes, but can be set in unit stage. 44 m., 1 f. (Doubling possible). Military costumes, World War I. FRENCH, $1.00. Royalty, $25.00.

PATRIOTS, THE. Sidney Kingsley. *This beautiful tribute to the American spirit is a chronicle history of the important years in Jefferson's life.* Prologue & 3 acts. Seven interiors. 19 m., 5 f. Revolutionary war costumes. *Royalty, $25.00 to* DRAMATISTS PLAY SERVICE.

PEER GYNT. Henrik Ibsen (adapted by Paul Green). *Peer Gynt, a wild and imaginative mountain lad, whose roughness and lying offend people, realizes too late that nobody can exist alone.* Fantasy. Interiors and exteriors. 8 m., 12 f. 19th-century costumes. FRENCH, $2.50. Royalty, $35.00.

PERFECT ALIBI, THE. A. A. Milne. *Mr. Ludgrove is killed by two of his guests in full view of the audience. The murderers' alibis are perfect—almost.* Mystery in 3 acts. Interior. 3 m., 7 f. Modern costumes. FRENCH, $1.00. Royalty, $50.00.

PETRIFIED FOREST, THE. Robert E. Sherwood. *A party of gangsters confiscate the life insurance of Alan Squier, which a disillusioned sophisticate on his way to the Petrified Forest, i.e. self-destruction, has given Gaby, a waitress, so that she may go to Europe; then the gangsters accommodate Alan by killing him.*

Drama. Interior. 18 m., 3 f. Modern costumes. DRAMATISTS PLAY SERVICE, $1.00. Royalty, $25.00.

PHILADELPHIA STORY, THE. Philip Barry. *The inhibited romanticism of Tracy Lord, spoiled Philadelphia socialite, is awakened by her reunion with her divorced husband.* Comedy in 3 acts. Interior, exterior (Porch). 9 m., 6 f. Modern costumes. FRENCH, $1.00. Royalty, $50.00.

PICNIC. William Inge. *Into the congested, female surroundings, consisting of two women deserted by their husbands, the invalid mother of one of them, the two daughters of the other, and the boarder—a spinster school teacher, comes a young man whose animal vitality upsets the entire group.* Play. Unit setting. 4 m., 7 f. Modern costumes. DRAMATISTS PLAY SERVICE, $1.00. Royalty, $50.00–$25.00.

PILLARS OF SOCIETY, THE. Henrik Ibsen. (translated by William Archer). *Johan returns from exile where he had gone to cover up the wrongdoing of the now successful Bernick. On learning that Bernick has fastened another crime on him which will separate him from his sweetheart, Dina, Johan threatens to expose Bernick. Bernick plots his death, only to find that his own son is endangered. Bernick repents publicly and confesses.* Drama in 4 acts. 1 interior. 10 m., 9 f., extras. 19th-century costumes. A serious play, requiring excellent acting. BAKER, 75¢. No royalty.

PINK MAGIC. Merritt Stone & Floyd Crutchfield (based on the novel by Margaret Lee Runbeck). *A group of American tourists and their amusing experiences in Mexico City. There is an exotic background, "romance", and "dangerous" Latin-American males.* Comedy in 3 acts. Exterior. 7 m., 11 f. Modern costumes. FRENCH, $1.00. Royalty, $25.00.

PIPER, THE. Josephine Preston Peabody. *Dramatization of the Pied Piper story, with charming additions.* Poetic drama in 4 acts. 2 exteriors, 1 interior. 13 m., 6 f., 5 (or more) children. Medieval costumes. Literary and dramatic; difficult but possible for high school. FRENCH, MSS. Royalty, $25.00.

PLAYBOY OF THE WESTERN WORLD, THE. J. M. Synge. *A rollicking poetic comedy about a young man who thought he had murdered his father. He becomes the hero of the countryside, only to lose all when it is learned that his father is still alive.* Comedy in 3 acts. Interior. 7 m., 5 f., extras. Modern Irish costumes. FRENCH, $1.25. Royalty, $25.00.

PLAY'S THE THING, THE. Ferenc Molnár (adapted by P. G. Wodehouse). *Turai, a playwright, finds himself staying up all night writing a play to disguise the lovemaking of his prima donna into the text, to allay the suspicions of her fiancé who has overheard some dialogue not meant for his ears.* Comedy in 3 acts. Interior. 8 m., 1 f. Modern costumes. Sprightly. FRENCH, $1.00. Royalty, $50.00.

PLOUGH AND THE STARS, THE. Sean O'Casey. *The futile efforts of the leader of one of the Irish revolutions. He is finally killed and his wife goes mad after losing her unborn child.* Drama in 4 acts. 3 interiors, 1 exterior. 10 m., 5 f. Modern costumes. Gripping and difficult; for advanced groups. FRENCH, $1.25. Royalty, $25.00.

PRIDE AND PREJUDICE. Helen Jerome (from the novel by Jane Austen). *Mrs. Bennet's determination to get her daughters married. Especially daughter Elizabeth and her duel between her pride and her beloved's prejudice.* Comedy in 3 acts. 3 interiors. 10 m., 16 f. English costumes, 1796. FRENCH, $1.00. Royalty, $25.00. (*Mention name of author of this version.*)

PRIVATE LIVES. Noel Coward. *Two couples room in adjoining suites, both newlyweds. The husband of one and wife of the other were formerly married. After complications, verbal and physical fights, flight and pursuit to Paris, there is a final reshuffling, and the couple originally married and divorced is reunited.* Comedy in 3 acts. 2 interiors. 2 m., 3 f. Modern costumes. FRENCH, $1.25. Royalty, $50.00.

PROLOGUE TO GLORY. E. P. Conkle. *Young Abraham Lincoln, the poor, uneducated rail-splitter who was one of the "folks", and his attachment to young Ann Rutledge in his early twenties, when he was clerking in a store in New Salem.* Play in 8 scenes. 5 exteriors, 1 interior (used in 3 scenes). 14 m., 7 f., extras. American costumes, 1831. FRENCH, $1.00 in paper; $1.75 in cloth. Royalty, $25.00.

PYGMALION. G. Bernard Shaw. *Higgins, a crank on phonetics, enters into a bet with a friend that he can transform Eliza, a flower girl, into a duchess and pass her off at a court function. He succeeds, but complications arise when the affair is over and Eliza is no longer needed as a subject for experimentation.* English comedy in 5 acts. 1 exterior, 2 interiors. 5 m., 6 f., extras. Costumes, early 20th century. Difficult, possible for advanced amateurs. PENGUIN, 50¢. Royalty on application to FRENCH.

QUALITY STREET. J. M. Barrie. *Phoebe, one of several maiden women, and the only one who had not turned sour and officious, finally, after ten years, wins Valentine, the bachelor she had yearned for, as he returns from the Napoleonic Wars.* Comedy in 4 acts. 2 interiors. 6 m., 9 f., extras. Period costumes. Delightful. FRENCH, $1.00. Royalty, $35.00

JUNO AND THE PAYCOCK
Sean O'Casey

●

THE HOUSE OF BERNARDO ALBA
Federico García Lorca

WINTERSET
Maxwell Anderson

●

THE LADY'S NOT FOR BURNING
Christopher Fry

OUR TOWN
Thornton Wilder

•

THE CRUCIBLE
Arthur Miller

THE WIZARD OF OZ
Elizabeth Fuller Goodspeed

•

GREEN GROW THE LILACS
Lynn Riggs

first performance, $25.00 each subsequent performance.

QUEEN'S HUSBAND, THE. Robert Emmet Sherwood. *King Eric, who has always been ruled by his wife and the scheming statesmen, finally asserts himself and averts the marriage of his daughter, Anne, to a prince whom she does not love.* Comedy in 3 acts. 1 interior. 11 m., 4 f., extras. Royal court costumes. Excellent plot. Difficult to direct. LONGMANS, GREEN, 90¢. *Royalty, $25.00.*

RAIN. John Colton & Clemence Randolph (based on the short story by W. S. Maugham). *A missionary's attempt to reform a prostitute on a quarantined Pacific isle results in his suicide.* Drama in 3 acts. Interior. 10 m., 5 f. Modern costumes. FRENCH, $1.50. *Royalty, $50.00.*

RAMSHACKLE INN. George Batson. *An old maid librarian has saved her money for 20 years, in order to buy a hotel where she can meet interesting people. She purchases a strange tumble-down place near the ocean, and she gets what she bargains for—plus a good deal besides.* Melodramatic mystery-farce. 1 interior. 9 m., 6 f. Modern costumes. DRAMATISTS PLAY. SERVICE, $1.00. *Royalty, $25.00.*

RICHARD OF BORDEAUX. Gordon Daviot. *The story of Richard II is that of a man born before his time and not strong enough in self-mastery to be yet master of his time.* Historical drama in 2 acts and 12 scenes. 10 interiors, 1 exterior. 23 m., 6 f., extras. Costumes, time of Richard II. FRENCH, $1.25. *Royalty, $25.00.*

RING ROUND THE MOON. Jean Anouilh (adapted by Christopher Fry). *A fable about twin brothers and a beautiful, mysterious dancer-ballerina.* Comedy. 1 adjustable exterior. 6 m. (2 roles played by the same actor), 2 extras, 7 f. Modern costumes. DRAMATISTS PLAY SERVICE, $1.00. *Royalty, $50.00–$25.00.*

ROBE, THE. John McGreevey (from the novel by Lloyd C. Douglas). *The Robe of Christ, recently crucified by Marcellus, a young Roman officer, is instrumental in the latter's repentance and conversion.* Drama in 3 acts. Scene, in curtains, or as desired. 13 m., 9 f., extras. Early Christian and Roman costumes. DRAMATIC PUBLISHING CO., 90¢. *Royalty, $25.00.*

ROMANCE. Edward Sheldon. *To dissuade his grandson from marrying an actress, the Bishop of St. Giles' relates to the boy the story of his own youthful romance, which involved a beautiful opera singer. The effect on the grandson is to fix his determination to marry the actress.* Comedy in 3 acts. Interiors. 12 m., 9 f. Costumes, modern and 1870. Recommended for Little Theaters and colleges. FRENCH, MSS. *Royalty, $25.00.*

ROMANTIC AGE, THE. A. A. Milne. *Romantic Mélisande, dreaming of knights and dragons, is surprised to find that romance exists even in a stockbroker's heart.* Comedy in 3 acts. Interior, exterior. 5 m., 4 f. Modern costumes. FRENCH, $1.25. *Royalty, $50.00.*

ROMANTIC YOUNG LADY, THE. G. Martinez-Sierra (translated from the Spanish by Helen and Harley Granville-Barker). *A romantic young Spanish girl becomes interested in a strange young man whose hat blows into her room one stormy night. Later she visits the office of a popular novelist to get a job, and is indignant and disappointed to find out he is the strange young man; but his romantic self, like his novels, proves irresistible.* Comedy in 3 acts. 2 interiors. 6 m., 5 f. Modern Spanish costumes. Charming light play, not difficult, but requiring skillful playing. FRENCH, MSS. *Royalty, $50.00.*

ROOM FOR ONE MORE. William Davidson. *The Pumpkin Shell, a tiny summer cottage by the ocean, is the home of Poppy and Mother Rose,* *and innumerable homeless waifs. When tragedy strikes the cottage, and it is in danger of being sold, Jimmy John, one of the young unfortunates, comes to the rescue.* Comedy. 1 interior. 4 m., 8 f. Modern costumes. DRAMATIC PUBLISHING Co., 90¢. *Royalty, $25.00.*

ROPE (ROPE'S END). Patrick Hamilton. *For the mere sake of adventure, danger, and the "fun of the thing," Wyndham Brandon persuades his weak-minded friend to assist him in the murder of a fellow undergraduate, then invites guests to supper, using the wooden case in which they have hidden the body as a table.* Drama in 3 acts. Interior. 6 m., 2 f. Modern costumes. For advanced casts only. FRENCH, *$1.25. Royalty, $25.00.*

ROYAL FAMILY, THE. George S. Kaufman & Edna Ferber. *Three generations of Cavendishes, a great family of the American stage, under the rule of Fanny Cavendish, courageous, sharp-tongued, sarcastic.* Comedy in 3 acts. Interior. 11 m., 6 f. Modern costumes. FRENCH, *$1.00. Royalty, $35.00.*

R.U.R. Karel Čapek (English version by Paul Selver & Nigel Playfair). *The central office of the factory of Rossum's Universal Robots, on an island in our planet. The robots become humanized by secret formula, and overthrow mankind, until only one human is left. Finally, a man-robot and a woman-robot, with a bit of Adam and Eve in them, are about to start mankind afresh.* Fantastic melodrama in 3 acts and epilogue. 2 interiors (can be played in 1 set). 13 m., 4 f. Modern costumes. FRENCH, *$1.00. Royalty, $25.00.*

SABRINA FAIR. Samuel Taylor. *Modern Cinderella fable of the chauffeur's daughter who marries the son of her father's wealthy employer.* Romantic comedy. Exterior. 7 m., 7 f. Modern costumes. Wonderful character parts (e.g. the chauffeur who is a millionaire, too, but keeps his job because he wants to read on someone else's time). DRAMATISTS PLAY SERVICE, *$1.00. Royalty, $50.00–$25.00.*

SCARECROW, THE. Percy MacKaye. *Goody Rickby, a witch, with the help of Dickon, a familiar demon, "The Prince of Darkness," fashions a scarecrow to parody the emptiness of fashionable Massachusetts society in 1690. The scarecrow falls in love, and thereby gains a soul.* Fantastic melodrama in 4 acts. 2 interiors. 10 m., 6 f. Costumes, 17th century. Based on a story by Nathaniel Hawthorne. Difficult to stage and play, but interesting and worth-while. Demands a number of stage tricks. FRENCH, *$5.00. Royalty, $25.00.*

SEA GULL, THE. Anton Chekhov (translated by Stark Young). *Four unstable people become involved with each other, with tragic consequences.* Drama in 4 acts. 2 interiors. 2 exteriors. 8 m., 6 f. Costumes, about 1896. FRENCH, *$1.00. Royalty, $25.00.*

SECOND MAN, THE. S. N. Behrman. *Clark Storey is in the pleasant situation of being a novelist with whom two women are in love.* Comedy in 3 acts. Interior. 3 m., 2 f. Modern costumes. Clever and sophisticated. For advanced groups. FRENCH, *$1.00. Royalty, $50.00.*

SECOND THRESHOLD. Philip Barry (revised by Robert E. Sherwood). *The dilemma of an eminent public official who has reached the heights of achievement and devoted service, only to realize that he has lost all human contact with his family.* Drama. Interior. 4 m., 2 f. Modern costumes. DRAMATISTS PLAY SERVICE, *$1.00. Royalty, $50.00–$25.00.*

SERVANT IN THE HOUSE, THE. Charles Rann Kennedy. *Manson, embodying the spirit of Christ, enters a* *clergyman's home disguised as a butler, and transforms the family's conception of life.* Symbolic drama in 5 acts. 1 interior. 5 m., 2 f. Modern costumes. Difficult, but interesting and possible for advanced amateurs. FRENCH, *$1.00. Royalty, $25.00.*

SEVEN KEYS TO BALDPATE. George M. Cohan. *A writer goes to a mountain inn for a plot, and gets more than he bargained for.* Melodramatic farce in 3 acts. Interior. 9 m., 4 f. Modern costumes. Mystery, farce, and intrigue. FRENCH, *$1.00. Royalty, $25.00.*

SEVENTEEN. Booth Tarkington. *Silly Bill fell in love with Lola, the Baby-Talk Lady, a vapid if amiable little flirt.* Comedy of youth in 4 acts. Exterior, 2 interiors (can easily be arranged as one interior throughout). 8 m., 6 f. Modern costumes. Recommended for high school production. FRENCH, *$1.00. Royalty, $25.00.*

SEVENTEENTH SUMMER. Anne Coulter Martens (based on the book by Maureen Daly). *Several teen-age girls go through the sublime and the ridiculous emotions connected with first dates, while on summer vacations.* Comedy in 3 acts. Interior. 6 m., 7 f. Modern costumes. DRAMATIC PUBLISHING Co., *90¢. Royalty, $25.00.*

SHADOW AND SUBSTANCE. Paul Vincent Carroll. *The ramification of faith in the Catholic Church in Ireland, as experienced by a young girl, caretaker in the house of the canon.* Drama. Interior. 6 m., 4 f. Modern costumes. DRAMATISTS PLAY SERVICE, *$1.00. Royalty, $35.00–$25.00.*

SHOW-OFF, THE. George Kelly. *Aubrey Piper struggles to satisfy his enormous egotism and at the same time preserve his self-respect in the presence of discouraging obstacles.* Comedy in 3 acts. Interior. 6 m., 3 f. Modern costumes. FRENCH, *$1.00. Royalty, $50.00.*

SHRIKE, THE. Joseph Kramm. Pulitzer Prize, 1952. *The bitter story of Jim Downs who must make a compromise and choose the lesser of two evils. He chooses his evil wife over the asylum she has sent him to.* Drama. Interior. 17 m., 5 f. (some doubling possible). Modern costumes. DRAMATISTS PLAY SERVICE, *$1.00. Royalty, $50.00–$25.00.*

SHUBERT ALLEY. Mell Dinelli. *Episodes in the making of a theater star—Chris, whose opening night it is.* Prologue and seven scenes. Interior. 19 f. Modern costumes. Easy to produce because the various episodes can be rehearsed separately. BAKER, *85¢. Royalty, $25.00.*

SIGHT UNSEEN. Rosemary Foster & Warner Law. *Lady Judith Elliot inherits a capacious English manor house and three spirited ghosts.* Comedy in 3 acts. Interior. 6 m., 5 f. Modern costumes. FRENCH, *$1.00. Royalty, $25.00.*

SILVER BOX, THE. John Galsworthy. *A rich father saves his son from jail, while a poor man, whose crime was similar to that of the rich man, is sentenced to a year in prison.* Social drama in 3 acts. 3 interiors. 11 m., 7 f., extras. Modern costumes. Dramatic study of class injustice, possible for advanced amateurs, and worth playing. *Royalty, $25.00 to* French.

SILVER CORD, THE. Sidney Howard. *Left a widow at an early age, Mrs. Phelps works by means that are almost devilish to keep her two sons to herself. One of the sons escapes her domination, however.* Drama in 3 acts. 2 interiors. 2 m., 4 f. Modern costumes. FRENCH, *$1.00. Royalty, $25.00.*

SILVER WHISTLE, THE. Robert E. McEnroe. *A romantically minded tramp finds a birth certificate made out in the name of Oliver Erwenter, age 77, whom he then impersonates, and gets admitted on the basis of the* *certificate to an old-age home.* Comedy. 1 exterior. 10 m., 5 f. Modern costumes. DRAMATISTS PLAY SERVICE, *$1.00. Royalty, $50.00–$25.00.*

SKIN OF OUR TEETH, THE. Thornton Wilder. *Fantastic comedy, a tribute to the indestructability of the Antrobus family who have survived all sorts of plagues through the ages, by the skin of their teeth.* Fantasy in 3 acts. 1 interior, 1 exterior. 4 or 5 important male roles; 4 or 5 important female roles; many small parts and extras, doubling possible. Various costumes. FRENCH, *$1.00. Royalty, $50.00.*

SKY HIGH. Florence Ryerson & Alice D. G. Miller. *Bravery is learned by a group of fun-loving college students marooned at a skiing lodge who discover that the place is HQ for a group of spies.* Fast-moving comedy in 3 acts. Interior. 9 m., 5 f. Modern costumes. FRENCH, *$1.00. Royalty, $25.00.*

SMILIN' THROUGH. Allan Langdon Martin. *An old feud between the Carterets and the Maynes almost stops the marriage of two young lovers descended from the two feuding families.* Drama in 3 acts. 2 exteriors. 5 m., 5 f. Modern and 1870 costumes. FRENCH, *$1.00. Royalty, $35.00.*

SOLID GOLD CADILLAC, THE. Howard Teichmann & George S. Kaufman. *The wicked board of Directors of General Products is foiled with the help of a little old lady who owns $10.00 worth of stock and who cares.* Comedy. Stylized sets. 11 m., 6 f. Modern costumes. DRAMATISTS PLAY SERVICE, *$1.00. Royalty, $50.00–$25.00.*

SONG OF BERNADETTE, THE. Jean & Walter Kerr (from Franz Werfel's novel). *Day-dreaming Bernadette has a vision, and is disbelieved by the entire village. She enters the sisterhood, and finally the divinity of her*

vision is accepted. Play in 3 acts. Interiors, exteriors; a curtain set may be used. 7 m., 11 f., extras. Modern costumes. DRAMATIC PUBLISHING Co., *90¢. Royalty, $25.00.*

STAGE DOOR. Edna Ferber & George S. Kaufman. *A group of 16 young girls who have come to New York to study acting and find jobs, and what happens to each.* Comedy. Interior. 11 m., 21 f. Modern costumes. (Can be presented in a single setting. Directions on this, and instructions covering slight alterations rendering the play acceptable to high school audiences, sent free). DRAMATISTS PLAY SERVICE, *$1.00. Royalty, $25.00.*

STALAG 17. Donald Bevan & Edmund Trzcinski. *A group of American prisoners lodged in a German prison camp, trying to escape. The discovery of which among them is the German stooge, and the escape of one of them.* Comedy melodrama. Interior. 21 m. (no f.). Army costumes, World War II. Turbulent and gusty. DRAMATISTS PLAY SERVICE, *90¢. Royalty, $50.00–$25.00.*

STATE OF THE UNION. Howard Lindsay & Russel Crouse. *A successful businessman is urged to consider running for the Presidency while taking a cross-country tour to inspect his plants and to make speeches en route. He expresses some opinions that are too radical for the politicians who had urged him to run. At a final meeting with the politicians at his home, he gives up the idea because of his differences with them.* Satire on politics. 4 interiors (3 of which are essential). 11 m. (3 major roles), 6 f. (2 major roles) 3 nonspeaking m. Modern costumes. DRAMATISTS PLAY SERVICE, *$1.00. Royalty, $50.00–$25.00.*

STREET SCENE. Elmer Rice. Pulitzer Prize, 1929. *Mood picture; panorama of the comedy and tragedy of daily life played to the accompaniment of* *rumbling elevated trains and the tooting of whistles.* Drama in 3 acts. Exterior. 16 m., 11 f. Modern costumes. For advanced groups only. FRENCH, *$1.00. Royalty, $50.00.*

STREETCAR NAMED DESIRE, A. Tennessee Williams. *The superficiality and eventual madness of Blanche du Bois, whose life, undermined by romantic illusions, led her to reject reality.* Tragic and effective drama. Interior. 6 m., 6 f. (3 or 4 minor roles). Modern costumes. For advanced groups. DRAMATISTS PLAY SERVICE, *$1.00. Royalty, $50.00–$25.00.*

STRIFE. John Galsworthy. *Workmen of the Trenartha Tin Plate Works are striking. Roberts is the leader of the strikers; John Anthony is the chairman of the board of directors. After much suffering, they are both deposed by their followers and become broken men.* Social drama in 3 acts. 3 interiors, 1 exterior, 2 m., 7 f., boy, extras. Modern costumes, early 20th century. One of the most notable modern English plays; requires realistic treatment and skilled acting. *Royalty, $25.00 to* FRENCH.

SUMMER AND SMOKE. Tennessee Williams. *The love story of a somewhat puritanical young Southern girl and an unpuritanical young doctor. The latter realizes, years later, that the girl had been right, but time and circumstances won't let the two come together.* Drama. Simple unit set. 8 m., 6 f. Modern costumes. DRAMATISTS PLAY SERVICE, *$1.00. Fee for the use of music, $5.00 per performance. Royalty, $50.00–$25.00.*

SUSPECT. Edward Percy & Reginald Denham. *Enigmatic Mrs. Smith finds herself once again suspected of murder for which she had been tried years earlier, and discharged, the verdict being "not proven." Finally, she justifies herself and is acquitted.* Psychological drama. Interior. 4 m., 4 f. Modern costumes. Good for college groups. DRAMATISTS PLAY SERVICE, *$1.00. Royalty, $25.00.*

SWAN, THE. Ferenc Molnár (translated by Melville Baker). *Duty and love conflict when a young princess loses her heart to her brother's tutor, but realizes that she must make a marriage befitting her station.* Romantic comedy in 3 acts. 1 interior. 12 m., 8 f., extras. Court costumes. Imaginative and effective play, combining sentiment and comedy, possible for high schools. LONGMANS, GREEN, *$1.25. Royalty, $25.00.*

TEA AND SYMPATHY. Robert Anderson. *A sensitive boy who is ridiculed at boarding school for lack of manliness, tries to prove himself with the village strumpet. When this attempt fails because of his revulsion for her, he becomes desperate, until he finally finds solace and understanding from the schoolmaster's wife.* Drama in 3 acts. Composite interior. 9 m., 2 f. Modern costumes. For advanced groups. FRENCH, *$1.00. Production restricted. Royalty on application.*

TEAHOUSE OF THE AUGUST MOON, THE. John Patrick. *The problem of introducing democracy in Okinawa, handled in a delightful, comic manner.* Comedy in 3 acts. Settings in Okinawa. 18 m., 8 f., 3 children. Costumes of U. S. Army and native Okinawans. DRAMATISTS PLAY SERVICE, *$1.25. Royalty, when released, $50.00–$25.00.*

TEN LITTLE INDIANS. Agatha Christie. *Eight invited weekend guests and two house servants find themselves the subject of the nursery rhyme of the 10 little Indians.* Mystery-comedy in 3 acts. Interior. 8 m., 3 f. Modern costumes. Highly recommended for all groups. FRENCH, *$1.00. Royalty, $50.00.*

THERE SHALL BE NO NIGHT. Robert E. Sherwood. *The invasion of Finland by Russia, and the necessity for individual courage.* Drama. 3 interiors. 13 m., 4 f. (including 4 bit parts). Modern costumes. DRAMA-TISTS PLAY SERVICE, *$1.00. Royalty, $35.00–$25.00.*

THERE'S ALWAYS JULIET. John van Druten. *Leonora Perrycoste, a very attractive young English lady, meets Dwight Houston, a handsome American; they readily fall in love but are almost separated.* Comedy in 3 acts. Interior. 2 m., 2 f. Modern costumes. FRENCH, *$1.00. Royalty, $35.00.*

THEY KNEW WHAT THEY WANTED. Sidney Howard. *A genial Italian grape-grower accepts with philosophical equanimity his wife's return and the baby that arose from a love affair with an attractive young man.* Comedy-drama in 3 acts. Interior. 9 m., 4 f., extras. Modern costumes. For advanced casts. FRENCH, *$1.00. Royalty, $25.00.*

THIRTEENTH CHAIR, THE. Bayard Veiller. *A medium unmasks a clever murderer.* Mystery in 3 acts. Interior. 10 m., 7 f. Modern costumes. FRENCH, *$1.00. Royalty, $25.00.*

THREE SISTERS, THE. Anton Chekhov (translated by Stark Young). *Three sisters are stranded by their father's death in a provincial town and are longing to return to Moscow.* Drama in 4 acts. 2 interiors, exterior. 9 m., 5 f. Costumes, 1900. FRENCH, *$1.00. Royalty, $25.00.*

THUNDER ROCK. Robert Ardrey. *A lighthouse keeper finds his faith in mankind restored, and works to create a new order out of the chaos of the old.* Drama. Interior. 8 m., 3 f. Modern costumes. DRAMATISTS PLAY SERVICE, *$1.00. Royalty, $25.00.*

TIME OF YOUR LIFE. William Saroyan. *Joe's search for happiness and the answers to the far-reaching enigmas of life takes him to a waterfront saloon.* Comedy in 3 acts. 2 interiors. 18 m., 7 f. Modern costumes. FRENCH, *$1.00. Royalty, $35.00.*

TIME OUT FOR GINGER. Ronald Alexander. *Many delightful complications arise when a staid banker's daughter joins the football team of her high school.* Comedy. Interior. 5 m., 5 f. Modern costumes. DRAMATISTS PLAY SERVICE, *$1.00. Royalty, $50.00–$25.00.*

TO THE LADIES! George S. Kaufman & Marc Connelly. *Elsie succeeds in raising her young husband out of the mediocrity of his present existence as an average clerk reading success stories in the magazines.* Comedy in 3 acts. Interiors. 11 m., 3 f. Modern costumes. FRENCH, *$1.00. Royalty, $25.00.*

TOBIAS AND THE ANGEL. James Bridie. *A delightfully concocted dramatization of the Apochryphal Book of Tobit.* Romantic comedy in 3 acts. Interior, 3 exteriors. 4 m., 4 f. Biblical costumes. For advanced casts only. FRENCH, *$1.25. Royalty, $25.00.*

TOM SAWYER. Paul Kester (from the novel by Mark Twain). *The familiar epic of American boyhood.* Comedy in 3 acts. 2 interiors, 2 exteriors. 13 m., 8 f. Modern costumes. FRENCH, *$1.00. Royalty, $25.00.*

TOMORROW THE WORLD. James Gow & Arnaud d'Usseau. *The problem of rehabilitating children who are raised in totalitarian countries and who have been indoctrinated from birth with fascism is given in terms of a German lad who comes to America, after the war.* Melodrama in 3 acts. Interior. 6 m., 4 f. Modern costumes. FRENCH, MSS. *Royalty, $25.00.*

TONY DRAWS A HORSE. Lesley Storm. *Tony draws a horse on the wall outside his doctor-father's consulting room door. The drawing has repercussions within the whole family.* Comedy in 3 acts. 3 interiors. 7 m., 7 f. Modern costumes. FRENCH, *$1.25. Royalty, $25.00.*

TORCH-BEARERS, THE. George Kelly. *Fred Ritter, a sane and capable gentleman, has to resort to heroic methods to save Paula, his wife, from the idea that she is a great actress, which idea has been inculcated by Mrs. Pampinelli, the overpowering director of the local Little Theater.* American satire in 3 acts. 2 interiors. 6 m., 6 f. Modern costumes. Brilliant and classic satire on "Little Theater" movement. Very popular, not difficult. FRENCH, $1.00. Royalty, $50.00.

TOVARICH. Jacques Deval (translated by Robert E. Sherwood). *A tale of the impoverished White Russians in Paris at the time of the Bolshevik Revolution.* Comedy in 3 acts. 4 interiors. 8 m., 7 f. Modern costumes. FRENCH, $1.00. Royalty, $35.00.

TRUTH ABOUT BLAYDS, THE. A. A. Milne. *Just before his death, Oliver Blayds, great Victorian poet, confesses to his youngest daughter that he is a fraud.* Comedy in 3 acts. Interior. 4 m., 4 f. Modern costumes. FRENCH, $1.00. Royalty, $50.00.

TWO ON AN ISLAND. Elmer Rice. *The saga of a boy and girl in search of happiness and success in New York.* Drama. Exteriors and interiors. in Manhattan. Cast of 40, but only a few are important. Modern costumes. DRAMATISTS PLAY SERVICE, $1.00. Royalty, $35.00–$25.00.

UNCLE HARRY. Thomas Job. *A kindly and benevolent gentleman manages to arrange the murder of one disagreeable sister and the hanging of the other equally unpleasant one—and finds himself tortured to the point of confession . . . only to be unable to convince anyone that he is guilty.* Drama in 3 acts. 3 interiors. 9 m., 6 f. Costumes, about 1900. FRENCH, $1.00. Royalty, $50.00.

VALLEY FORGE. Maxwell Anderson. *General Washington takes heart from the courage and loyalty of his men,* at a time when the war seemed hopeless. Drama in 3 acts. 4 interiors. 32 m., 3 f., extras. Costumes, Colonial. FRENCH, MSS. Royalty, $25.00.

VELVET GLOVE, THE. Rosemary Casey. *A young history professor in a convent school for girls is about to be dismissed by the harsh Bishop for his modestly liberal views. A Monsignor and Mother Superior intercede for him.* Comedy in 3 acts. Interior. 5 m., 5 f. Modern and religious costumes. FRENCH, $1.00. Royalty, $50.00.

VENUS OBSERVED. Christopher Fry. *The aging Duke of Altair brings three of his ex-mistresses to his home in the intention of marrying one of them, but falls in love with the daughter of his secretary.* Poetic comedy. Interior, exterior. 7 m., 4 f. modern costumes. DRAMATISTS PLAY SERVICE, $1.00. Royalty, $50.00–$25.00.

VICAR OF WAKEFIELD, THE. Walter Kerr. *The Vicar and his family suddenly find themselves impoverished; and when, under the guise of benevolence, Squire Thornhill attempts to "help" them, chaos results.* Drama in 3 acts. Exterior. 12 m., 9 f. English costumes, 1766. FRENCH, 75¢. Royalty, $10.00.

VICTORIA REGINA. Laurence Housman. *A Biography of Queen Victoria in ten episodes.* BAKER, price per episode, 50¢. Royalty on application.

VOICE OF THE TURTLE, THE. John van Druten. *A charming young man and an equally attractive young woman gradually fall in love.* Comedy. Interior. 1 m., 2 f. Modern costumes. For advanced groups. DRAMATISTS PLAY SERVICE, $1.00. Royalty, $50.00–$25.00.

WATCH ON THE RHINE. Lillian Hellman. *A patriotic German sacrifices himself and his family to operate against the Nazis.* Drama. Interior. 6 m., (2 boys), 5 f. Modern costumes.

Royalty, $25.00 to DRAMATISTS PLAY SERVICE.

WE SHOOK THE FAMILY TREE. Perry Clark (based on the book by Hildegarde Dolson). *Hildegarde's efforts to round up a date for the big school dance cause merry pandemonium in the community and the family.* Comedy in 3 acts. 1 interior. 5 m., 7 f. Modern costumes. DRAMATIC PUBLISHING CO., 90¢. *Royalty, $25.00.*

WHAT A LIFE. Clifford Goldsmith. *Henry Aldrich struggles to keep out of trouble, and this is what involves him in one scrape after another, both serious and amusing.* Comedy. Interior. 8 m., 10 f., extras. Modern costumes. DRAMATISTS PLAY SERVICE, *$1.00 Royalty, $25.00.*

WHAT EVERY WOMAN KNOWS. J. M. Barrie. *John discovers that Maggie, his demure and modest wife, is the source and spirit of his success, and that he cannot do without her, despite an infatuation for a beautiful countess.* Comedy in 4 acts. 4 interiors. 7 m., 4 f., extras. Costumes, 1900. FRENCH, *$1.00. Royalty, $35.00–$25.00.*

WHITEHEADED BOY, THE. Lennox Robinson. *Twelve varied types that seem to characterize present-day Ireland.* Comedy in 3 acts. Interior. 5 m., 7 f. Modern costumes. FRENCH, *$1.00. Royalty, $50.00.*

WILLOW AND I, THE. John Patrick. *The tragic loves of two sisters for the same man.* Romantic drama. Interior. 5 m., 6 f. Costumes, 1900 and modern. DRAMATISTS PLAY SERVICE, *$1.00. Royalty, $25.00.*

WINGLESS VICTORY, THE. Maxwell Anderson. *A Malay woman kills herself and her two children when she finds her husband will not stand by her against the prejudice of his home town.* Tragedy. 2 interiors. 8 m., 8 f. Costumes, 1800. A deeply moving poetic tragedy. DRAMATISTS PLAY SERVICE, *$1.00. Royalty, $25.00.*

WINGS OVER EUROPE. Robert Nichols & Maurice Browne. *A scientist discovers the means of controlling the atom, but his discovery is misunderstood and he is shot.* Drama in 3 acts. Interior. 20 m. Modern costumes. FRENCH, *$1.00. Royalty, $25.00.*

WINSLOW BOY, THE. Terence Rattigan. *The incident of a youngster in an English Naval school who is expelled for alleged petty theft grows into a cause célèbre which nearly shakes the foundations of the government.* Drama. Interior. 7 m., 4 f. Modern costumes. DRAMATISTS PLAY SERVICE, *$1.00. Royalty, $50.00–$25.00.*

WINTERSET. Maxwell Anderson. *Mio, believing his father was innocent of the crime for which he was executed, pursues his long search for proof of his innocence.* Verse drama. 1 exterior, 1 interior. 16 m., 3 f. Modern costumes (bits and nonspeaking parts). DRAMATISTS PLAY SERVICE, *$1.00. Royalty, $25.00.*

WISTERIA TREES, THE. Joshua Logan (based on Chekhov's CHERRY ORCHARD). *The story of "progress" necessitating alteration in tradition and modification in the extravagances of life.* Drama. Interior. 8 m., 6 f. Southern costumes. DRAMATISTS PLAY SERVICE, MSS. *Royalty, $50.00–$25.00.*

WITNESS FOR THE PROSECUTION. Agatha Christie. *A highly suspenseful mystery of intricate and artfully woven plot.* Melodrama in 3 acts. 2 interiors. 17 m., 5 f., 8 nondescript. Modern costumes. FRENCH, *$1.00. Royalty on application.*

WIZARD OF OZ, THE. Elizabeth Fuller Goodspeed (based on the story by L. Frank Baum). *Dorothy finds herself in the land of the Munchkins, and must journey to see the Wizard of Oz. Her path takes her past fantastic places, and endears her to the Scarecrow, the Tin Woodman, and* *the Lion along the way. Each received his dearest wish after the long journey.* Fantasy in 3 acts. 3 interiors, 2 exteriors. 9 m., 5 f. (extras). Fantastic costumes. FRENCH, *$1.00. Royalty, $25.00.*

WOMEN, THE. Clare Boothe. *The efforts of a group of women to play their respective roles in an artificial society that consists of vain show, comedy, tragedy, hope, and disappointment.* Comedy. 11 interiors (several very simple). 35 f. (no m.). Modern costumes. DRAMATISTS PLAY SERVICE, *$1.00. Royalty, $25.00.*

WORLD WE LIVE IN, THE (THE INSECT COMEDY). Josef and Karel Capek (adapted and arranged by Owen Davis). *A philosopher's fantastic dream of the comedy and tragedy of the insect world, whose problems and affairs are uncomfortably like those of humans.* Comedy: Prelude, 3 acts, epilogue. 21 m., 9 f., (extras.) Modern and fantastic costumes, representing insects. FRENCH, *$1.00. Royalty, $25.00.*

YEARS AGO. Ruth Gordon. *The playwright's story of her determination to go on the stage, and how she ("Me" in the play") finally gets her parents' blessing on this venture.* Comedy. Interior. 4 m., 5 f. Modern costumes, early 20th century. DRAMATISTS PLAY SERVICE, *$1.00. Royalty, $35.00–$25.00. Piano and vocal music of the two songs necessary for the production of this play can be purchased from the* SERVICE *at 50¢. per song. Groups authorized to produce the play may have these free of charge.*

YELLOW JACKET, THE. George C. Hazelton & Benrimo. *Wu Hoo Git, the prince, survives a series of adventures, overcomes his enemies, and takes his rightful place as wearer of the royal yellow jacket.* Romantic comedy in 3 acts. 1 interior. 14 m., 12 f. Chinese costumes. Delightful play, done in Chinese manner. Rather

difficult. FRENCH, *$1.00. Royalty, $25.00. Music, $2.00.*

YOU AND I. Philip Barry. *A young man overcomes his pride by the realization of his limitations and the sacrifices to parental duty.* Recommended for high school production. Comedy in 3 acts. 2 interiors. 4 m., 3 f. Modern costumes. FRENCH, *$1.00. Royalty, $25.00.*

YOU CAN'T TAKE IT WITH YOU. Moss Hart & George S. Kaufman. *The Sycamores live an enchanted, if slightly strange life, built around the theory that life is a full-time thing, to be enjoyed to the utmost.* Comedy. Interior. 9 m., 7 f., 3 men extras. Modern costumes. DRAMATISTS PLAY SERVICE, *$1.00. Royalty, $25.00.*

YOU NEVER CAN TELL. G. Bernard Shaw. *The children of a "new woman" who has left her husband, the husband himself, and a struggling young dentist, become involved in complicated interrelations.* English comedy in 4 acts. 2 interiors, 1 exterior. 8 m., 4 f. Costumes, early 20th century. Brilliant comedy of witty talk, for advanced amateurs. *Royalty on application to* FRENCH.

YOUNG AND FAIR, THE. N. Richard Nash. *A timely comment on idealism and personal ethics, fighting compromise and deceit on a college campus, including religious bigotry.* Drama. 1 setting. 21 f. (no m.). Modern costumes. (Stage is divided into three sections, each of which is lighted in turn, while the others are in darkness). DRAMATISTS PLAY SERVICE, *$1.00. Royalty, $35.00–$25.00.*

YOUNGEST, THE. Philip Barry. *The youngest, a misunderstood and downtrodden youth, wants to write but his brothers and sister control the pursestrings and make life unpleasant for the youngest, until a stranger appears and changes matters.* Comedy in 3 acts. Interior, exterior. 4 m., 5 f. Modern costumes. FRENCH, *$1.00. Royalty, $25.00.*

YOUNG WOODLEY. John Van Dru ten. *Study in the character of an upright and delicate young man who suffers a guilt complex because he is attracted to the wife of his master at* *school.* Drama in 3 acts. 2 interiors. 7 m., 2 f. Modern costumes. Sophisticated. FRENCH, *$1.00. Royalty, $25.00.*

PART II

One-Act Plays

A ONE-ACT PLAY is a short play giving a single unified impression, tending to emphasize primarily either character, or plot, or atmosphere. It usually deals with a single incident, and contains one small group of characters.

It is often said that the one-act play is a new thing. This is not strictly true. In reality, it is as old or older than the longer form. The Greek tragedies are really one-act plays. So are early miracle plays—the acting-out by priests and choirboys of a simple Bible story for the uneducated congregation. Even after the longer form had become dominant, many hundreds of one-act plays were written and played in the theaters of England and continental Europe. In the nineteenth century, it was the custom to produce a short play as a preliminary to a longer one. These short plays were called *curtain raisers*. There is a sense, however, in which the one-act play is the product of our own period, almost of the last forty years. Before that time, the writing of one-act plays was rather accidental. Critics did not consider the one-act play worthy of serious study. It was in the same position as the short story before it had been developed and made a recognized form of art by Poe, Hawthorne, and the other pioneers. Now, however, all this has changed. Many of the best playwrights have produced them. Critics have begun to study them and to frame their fundamental principles. Many excellent one-act plays are at hand, and amateurs will find the production of them pleasant and profitable.

In many ways one-act plays are ideally suitable for amateurs. A bill of one-act plays usually gives a greater variety of characters, and a greater number of characters, than a single long play. They often furnish many more interesting problems in stagecraft. As a rule, in so far as the acting is concerned, they are apt to be easier to play effectively with inexperienced actors, for it is much easier to sustain a role effectively for thirty or forty minutes than it is to sustain one for an entire evening. They are more quickly prepared, too, and do not demand so many rehearsals from the same group of people. Finally, there is not the competition and the inevitable comparison with the professional stage. One-act plays can be novelties in a city or town with one or two stock companies and several theaters which offer Broadway plays. Even though most American audiences prefer the full evening play, it is decidedly worth-while for schools, colleges, and little theaters to help make the one-act play more popular with an occasional bill. One of the most serious problems of presenting a bill of one-act plays is that of stage setting. The backgrounds must therefore be kept simple; a cyclorama will do, with a few simple props, or, better still, an arena theater.

In preparing a bill of one-act plays, a certain balanced variety must be kept in mind. The plays must not be all of the same type or of the same mood. Three plays are usually enough for a full evening's entertainment, or four, at the most, if they are short. Three longer one-act plays are usually better than five or six shorter ones. Or, if one very short one is used, a longer one will balance the bill. In order to help producers, the playing time has been indicated in the list.

If there is a heavy play, a grim tragedy, for example, it is customary to have it come in the middle. The lightest, funniest play is usually placed at the end of the bill. For example, good bills would be a fantasy, a tragedy, a farce; or a melodrama, a drama, a light comedy.

Often it is amusing to group a bill of one-act plays about some idea or center. It might be possible to do three plays of the sea, or three Oriental plays, or three plays of rural life. In this case especially, care must be taken to see that there is variety in plot and action, if the atmosphere is similar.

SUMMARIES OF PLAYS

AFFECTED YOUNG LADIES, THE. Molière (translated by Barrett H. Clark). *Two young ladies are cured of their affectations by their two lovers who send their footmen to visit them in the guise of fine gentlemen.* Drawingroom. 3 m., 6 f., 5 extras. Costumes, 17th century. Famous comedy, possible all-girl cast. Plays 30 minutes. FRENCH, 50¢. No royalty.

AFTER THE TEMPEST. Geoffrey Tease. *The playwright's purpose is the portrayal of what the social metamorphosis coming with World War II and its aftermath, could be in Women's World.* Fantastic comedy. Veranda. 2 m., 3 f. Costumes, 20 years in the future. BAKER, 50¢. Royalty, $5.00.

ALL ON A SUMMER'S DAY. Florence Ryerson & Colin Clements. *Three maiden ladies sit in their garden sewing; each makes a wish which straightway comes true.* Fantastic comedy. A garden. 4 f. Crinoline period. Plays quaintly and pleasantly, if stylized. Plays 15 minutes. *Royalty, $5.00 to* FRENCH.

ALLISON'S LAD. Beulah M. Dix. *A young ne'er-do-well, captured by the Roundheads and sentenced to death, dies like a man under the influence of a noble Cavalier colonel who had loved his mother, Allison.* Drama.

Room in an inn. 6 m. Costumes, 1650. Strong little play, excellent for boys. Plays 30 minutes. *Royalty, $5.00 to* BAKER.

ANGELS DON'T MARRY. Florence Ryerson & Colin Clements. *Two people once married to each other and now divorced meet again and with the help of an old hotel-keeper decide to reunite.* Comedy. Interior. 1 m., 2 f. Modern costumes. Plays 35 minutes. FRENCH, 50¢. *Royalty, $5.00.*

ANNIVERSARY, THE. Anton Chekhov (translated by Constance Garnett) *Two emotional women enter and spoil a show-off presentation planned by the bank for its anniversary.* Russian farce-comedy. Pretentious office. 2 m., 2 f., extras. Costumes of 19th century in Russia. Excellent satire; good characters. Plays 15 minutes. *No royalty.*

ANTI-CLOCKWISE, Muriel & Sidney Box. *A woman is found dead, and her niece is accused of murdering her for the money she would inherit. The doctor proves that she is innocent. However, a flashback shows that the niece had tried to suffocate the aunt and failed, and that the aunt had died of a heart attack as a result of her rage.* Drama. Interior. 4 f. Modern costumes. Plays 30 minutes. FRENCH, 50¢. *Royalty, $5.00.*

ARIA DA CAPO. Edna St. Vincent Millay. *Under the prompting of Cothurnus, the muse of tragedy, two shepherds interrupt a harlequinade, innocently kill each other, and are again superseded by the harlequinade.* Poetic fantasy. A fantastic interior. 4 m., 1 f. Imaginative costumes. Original and imaginative satire on the futility of war. Requires skillful setting, directing, and acting. Plays 30 minutes. BAKER, 50¢. *Royalty, $15.00.*

ARTIST, THE. H. L. Mencken. *The spoken thoughts of a German pianist as he plays a recital, and the actions and reactions of his audience.* Farce. Auditorium. 5 m., 8 f., or more. Modern costumes. Leading actor must be a pianist. Easy to produce and amusing for musical clubs. Plays 25 minutes. *Royalty, $5.00 to* FRENCH.

AS GOOD AS GOLD. Lawrence Housman. *St. Francis of Assisi, in a quiet and humorous fashion, converts three robbers from their love of gold to the love of what is worth-while in life.* Fanciful morality. Wooded hillside. 7 m. Costumes of Middle Ages. Well written, not difficult. Plays 25 minutes. *Royalty, $5.00 to* FRENCH.

ASTONISHED HEART, THE. Noel Coward. *The story of a man who on his deathbed calls for an old girl friend. She enters his room and returns shortly to announce he has died, his last words being tender ones to his wife for whom he mistook the girlfriend.* Drama. Interior. 4 m., 3 f. Modern costumes. Plays 40 minutes. FRENCH, 50¢. *Royalty on application.*

BACK OF THE YARDS. Kenneth Sawyer Goodman. *A priest and a kindly sergeant get from a boy, wild but not bad, and the son of a widow, a confession of his part in a shooting.* Drama. Kitchen of a small flat. 3 m., 2 f. Modern costumes. Strong play of city-street problems. Plays 30 minutes. *No royalty.*

BEAUTY AND THE JACOBIN. Booth Tarkington. *Two women and one man are trying to escape from France during the Reign of Terror. They are tried before an agent of French Republic who finally, influenced by the woman, permits all three to escape.* Drama. An attic room. 3 m., 2 f. Costumes of French Revolution. Humorous and tense scene from the French Revolution. Not difficult with one good actor. Plays 80 minutes. *Royalty, $25.00 to* FRENCH.

BECAUSE IT'S JUNE. Babette Hughes. *About an earnest young*

college instructor showing how a girl manages to thaw the ice out of him and gets him to take her out for a canoe ride. Comedy. Interior. 2 m., 1 f. Modern costumes. BAKER, 50¢. *Royalty, $5.00.*

BEFORE BREAKFAST. Eugene O'Neill. *Dramatizes the last stages of a domestic struggle and the suicide of a husband off-stage.* A monologue —for an experienced actress. Interior. 1 f. Modern costumes. *Royalty, $5.00 to* DRAMATISTS PLAY SERVICE.

BEHIND THE LACE CURTAINS. Esther McCracken. *Two sisters late in life lose their property and valiantly try to keep up appearances.* Drama. Interior. 1 m., 3 f. Modern costumes. Plays 30 minutes. BAKER, 50¢. *Royalty, $5.00.*

BELLMAN OF MONS, THE. Dorothy Rose Googins. *For one hundred years the organ in Mons Cathedral has been silent because no one untouched by the world's selfishness has played it. The mayor declares one final trial day. The mysterious Bellman finds a ten-year old boy who is successful.* Fantasy, in 3 short acts. (1) Marketplace; (2) cottage interior. 8 m., 6 f., extras. Colorful and easy. French peasant costumes. Plays 30 minutes. BAKER, 35¢. *Royalty, $5.00.*

BENJAMIN FRANKLIN, JOURNEYMAN. Constance D'Arcy Mackay. *Benjamin Franklin at a tavern meets a young lady who is scornful of him because of his uncouth appearance, but his talk wins her over.* Comedy. Room in a tavern. 3 m., 2 f. 18th-century costumes. Not difficult, excellent for schools. Plays 20 minutes.

BEST THERE IS, THE. Marion Wefer. *Mr. Petersham, wealthy but forsaken, gives up his private room to a critically ill ward patient, Tessy's Pop. When Pop recovers miraculously, Tessy wants to thank Mr. Petersham who, unknown to her, is dying. She is embarrassed because she thinks* *that he already has "The best there is."* Drama. Hospital interior. 3 m., 4 f., extras. Modern costumes. About 25 minutes. Row, PETERSON, 50¢. *Royalty, $5.00.*

BIRTHDAY OF THE INFANTA, THE. Stuart Walker (dramatized from the story by Oscar Wilde). *The birthday surprise that most pleases the little Infanta is a little hunchback, who for the first times sees himself in a palace mirror, realizes that it is his ugliness that has amused people, and dies of a broken heart.* Drama. A palace room overlooking a garden. 5 m., 2 f. Spanish costumes of 16th century. Offers many interesting possibilities, yet is not too difficult. Plays 35 minutes. Touching drama. Also, in a different dramatization arranged by Vail Motter for 6 m., 2 f., and extras, LONGMANS, GREEN, 85¢. *Royalty, $10.00 if admission is charged; $5.00 if there is no charge.*

BLACKOUT MYSTERY, THE. James Reach. *A valuable diamond brooch disappears in a test blackout while it is being sold.* Mystery drama. Interior. 2 m., 3 f. Modern costumes. Plays 35 minutes. FRENCH, 50¢. *Royalty, $5.00.*

BLIND, THE. Maurice Maeterlinck. *Old Priest, having led the group of blind people out into the world, dies, leaving blind to mercy of elements.* Tragedy. Ancient forest. 7 m., 6 f. Imaginative costumes. Powerful, symbolic drama, only for skillful amateurs. Plays 35 minutes. *Royalty, $15.00 to* FRENCH.

BLUE TEAPOT, THE. Jean Lee Latham. *Pa and Ma Brown by their own example of a long and loving life together, reconcile the betrothed Jimmy and Cynthia, who have been quarrelling about the decoration of their new home without attempting to manage each other tactfully.* Comedy. Combination dining- and living-room of a farm house. 2 m., 2 f. Modern costumes. A sentimental folk play with appealing characters. Plays 25 minutes. DRAMATIC PUBLISHING CO., 50¢. *Royalty, $10.00 if admission is charged; $5.00 if there is no charge.*

BOOR, THE. Anton Chekhov (translated by Hjalmar Baukhage). *The charming widow Popoff has sworn to remain faithful to her dead husband the rest of her life, and to live in seclusion, but when the rude and boastful Lieutenant Smernoff forces his way in to collect a debt she changes her mind.* Farce. A Russian living-room. 2 m., 1 f., extras. Russian 19th-century costumes. Broad and amusing, for skilled players. Plays 25 minutes. FRENCH, 50¢. *No royalty.*

BOUND EAST FOR CARDIFF. Eugene O'Neill. *Yank and Driscoll, two rough sailors, make plans on the homeward voyage to leave the sea and settle down on a farm, but Yank, who is very ill, dies.* Tragedy. A forecastle. 11 m. Sailors' costumes. Little action, but very effective if well played; only for advanced amateurs. Plays 25 minutes. *Royalty, $5.00 to* DRAMATISTS PLAY SERVICE.

BOX AND COX. John M. Morton. *Sparkling farce about the housing shortage in the early days.* Farce. Interior. 2 m., 1 f. Modern costumes. Plays 35 minutes. FRENCH, 50¢. *No royalty.*

BOY COMES HOME, THE. A. A. Milne. *A domineering uncle insists that his nephew, who has just returned from the war, go into the jam business with him. In a dream he finds himself at the mercy of the nephew, and becomes very humble when he wakes, much to the surprise of the nephew.* Comedy. A living-room. 2 m., 3 f. Modern costumes. Clever and amusing, not difficult. Plays 35 minutes. FRENCH, 50¢. *Royalty, $10.00.*

BOY WHO DISCOVERED EASTER, THE. Elizabeth McFadden. *Dr.*

Dexter, who has no faith in God because his wife and crippled son died, regains faith through helping a poor crippled boy. Religious play, in 2 scenes. Doctor's study. 2 m., 2 f. Modern costumes. Excellent, may be made very effective. Plays 40 minutes. FRENCH, 50¢. *Royalty, $5.00.*

BOY WILL, THE. Robert Emmons Rogers. *Shakespeare leaves home to embark on a dramatic career.* Historical fantasy. Room in an inn. 3 m., 2 f. Elizabethan costumes. Charming imaginative little sketch, needs skilled playing. Plays 15 minutes. *No royalty.*

BRAINS, Martin Flavin. *A battle of wits between three scoundrelly sailors on a desert island, in which the brainiest wins and leaves the other two to perish.* Ironic comedy. Desert island. 3 m. Modern sailors' costumes. Powerful and well done, rather difficult. Plays 30 minutes. *Royalty, $5.00 to* FRENCH.

BREAD. Fred Eastman. *A mother and her two daughters skimp and save $100 to buy a piano only to find that the son, who yearns for spending money, has gambled it away.* Drama. Sitting-room in a farmhouse. 2 m., 4 f. Modern farm costumes. A plea for help for farmers, but at the same time dramatic and interesting. Plays 30 minutes. FRENCH, 50¢. *Royalty, $5.00.*

BRINK OF SILENCE, THE. E. E. Galbraith. *An Antarctic explorer, remaining in that region because he was supposed to have been lost, learns that his wife has remarried, meets his son, who has become an explorer, but the father is strong enough not to reveal his identity.* Drama. A cabin in the Antarctic. 4 m. Dramatic and effective. Costumes suitable for antarctic exploration. Plays 15 minutes. *No royalty.*

BUSHIDO. Takeda Idzumo (translated by M. C. Marcus). *A nobleman, de-*

voted to the interests of his over-lord's family, permits his own son to be slain in order to save the heir of his master. Tragedy. A Japanese schoolroom. 4 m., 3 f., 2 boys. Japanese classical costumes. A classic of the Japanese stage, powerful and moving; very difficult. Plays 35 minutes. *No royalty.*

CABBAGES. Edward Staadt. *Mrs. Grossmeier pays $2,000 to trace the family tree, and then pays another $2,000 to keep secret what she learns.* Comedy. Interior. 3 m., 4 f. Modern costumes. Plays 1 hour. FRENCH, 50¢ *Royalty, $5.00.*

CAMPBELL OF KILMHOR. A. J. Ferguson. *A Scotch Royalist peasant goes to his death rather than betray the hiding place of the fugitive king.* Tragedy. Interior of a cabin. 4 m., 4 f. Scottish costumes of mid-18th century. Dramatic, excellent roles. plays 35 minutes. FRENCH, 50¢. *Royalty, $5.00.*

CAN THE LEOPARD? M. E. Atkinson. *In order to make their up-to-date niece feel at home, the aunts exchange their sober attire for gaily-colored playsuits and practice the art of make-up and cigarette-smoking. The niece, in order to make her aunts feel at ease, has changed into a demure Quaker gown and eliminated all make-up.* Farce-comedy. Interior. 6 f. Modern costumes. Plays 30 minutes. BAKER, 50¢. *Royalty, $5.00.*

CASTLE OF MR. SIMPSON, THE. John Kirkpatrick. *A daughter tries to make her father's home his castle. She tries to get rid of her sister's boy friends and then discovers a boy friend for herself.* Farce. Interior. 4 m., 4 f. Modern costumes. Plays 30 minutes. FRENCH, 50¢. *Royalty, $5.00.*

CHINESE USURER IN HIS VILLAGE, THE. George Kuhung & Scott Farnworth. *With diabolical cleverness, the usurer Changsantze*

pits the brothers against one another. The retribution by the brothers resolves itself into an amusing and completely satisfactory finale. Comedy. Interior, exterior. Can be done without scenery. 6 m., 2 f. Chinese or modern costumes. Plays 35 minutes. FRENCH, 50¢. *Royalty, $5.00.*

CHRISTMAS AT HOME. Joseph Hayes. *Sentimental domestic comedy about the meaning of Christmas.* Comedy. Interior. 3 m., 4 f. Modern costumes. Plays 30 minutes. FRENCH, 50¢. *Royalty, $5.00.*

CHRISTMAS CAROL, THE. Charles Dickens (adapted by George M. Baker). *The well-known story of the conversion of Scrooge.* Comedy. An office. 4 m., 3 f., 2 children. 19th-century British costumes. May be arranged with music and tableaux. Plays 60 minutes. BAKER, 50¢. *No royalty.*

CHRISTMAS FOR THE DUCHESS. Evelyn Northrop. *Betty Rollins brings an English girl home from college for the Christmas vacation. She has given the girl such a build-up that the family believes her to be a duchess and plans to celebrate Christmas accordingly, to the disappointment of their English guest. However, tradition and happiness are restored.* Comedy. 45 minutes. Interior. 4 m., 7 f., and carolers. Modern costumes. BAKER, 40¢. *No royalty.*

CHURCH STREET. Lennox Robinson. *A dramatist goes back to his home town and recreates the tragedies he suspects are behind the smiles on the faces of his old friends. Truth proves more horrifying than fiction.* Melodrama. Interior, with various spotlighted insets. 1 m., 8 f. Modern Irish costumes. Plays 40 minutes. FRENCH, 75¢. *Royalty, $10.00.*

CINDERELLA MARRIED. Rachel Field. *A new version of an old romance, featuring Cinderella, Prince Charming, and the celebrated slip-*

pers of glass, which unfortunately she had outgrown. There are other domestic problems which she and the Prince eventually solve. Comedy. Interior. 2 m., 4 f. Fantastic costumes. Plays 40 minutes. FRENCH, 50¢. *Royalty,* $5.00.

CLOD, THE. Lewis Beach. *An uneducated country woman, a "clod," refuses to take sides in the Civil War, and then in a dramatic outburst explains her hatred for both sides.* Drama. A kitchen. 4 m., 1 f. Civil War costumes. A very actable thriller; needs capable actress. Plays 20 minutes. FRENCH, 50¢. *Royalty,* $10.00.

COLUMBINE. Reginald Arkell. *Two laborers are in a field at dusk, talking of fairies. Pierrot and Harlequin enter and contend for Columbine's love. Harlequin promises pleasure, Pierrot love. Pierrot wins.* Pierrot comedy. A field. 5 m., 1 f. Modern and fantastic costumes. Dainty, poetical fantasy, requires rather skilled and graceful acting. Plays 20 minutes. *Royalty,* $8.00 to FRENCH.

CONTRAST. Bessie P. Gephart. *An etching of three women of contrasting stations in life.* Comedy. Interior. 6 m., 5 f. Modern costumes. Plays 25 minutes. FRENCH, 50¢. *No Royalty.*

CUP OF TEA, A. Florence Ryerson. *A poet sends some sonnets to a married young woman. Her husband comes to shoot the poet. The wife straightens out the complications while serving tea.* Farce. Interior. 2 m., 2 f. Modern costumes. Plays 30 minutes. FRENCH, 50¢. *Royalty,* $5.00.

CURTAIN, THE. Hallie Flanagan Davis. *A fugitive from justice shows his daughter how through a series of lies he has wrecked his life, and makes her promise always to tell the truth. Her faith is tested when the police come to search for her father.* Drama. Interior. 4 m., 2 f. Modern costumes. Plays 30 minutes. FRENCH, 50¢. *Royalty,* $5.00.

DANSE MACABRE. Muriel & Sydney Box. *A sinister study of the inmates of a select home for elderly ladies.* Drama. Interior. 7 w. Modern costumes. Plays 30 minutes. BAKER, $1.00. *Royalty,* $5.00.

DARK LADY OF THE SONNETS. G. Bernard Shaw. *Shakespeare, coming to meet the Dark Lady, meets Queen Elizabeth, and seizes the opportunity to make love to her and to appeal to her for help for the theater.* Comedy. On terrace of palace. 2 m., 2 f. Elizabethan costumes. Clever and effective. Plays 20 minutes. *Royalty on application to* FRENCH.

DARKNESS FALLS ON LAUGHTER. Mary W. Howard. *Cassandra cannot save her beloved Troy from destruction even though Apollo woos her.* Fantasy. Exterior. 1 m., 6 w. Greek costumes. Plays 30 minutes. BAKER, 50¢. *Royalty,* $5.00.

DEVIL AND DANIEL WEBSTER, THE. Stephen Vincent Benét. *Daniel Webster, lawyer and orator extraordinaire, saves Jabez Stone, who has sold his soul to the Devil.* Comedy. Interior. 6 m. (12 jurymen), 1 f. (extras). New England 19th-century costumes. DRAMATISTS PLAY SERVICE, 50¢. *Royalty,* $5.00.

DEAR DEPARTED, THE. Stanley Houghton. *A family meets at the death of the grandfather, and proceeds to divide up his few possessions, but the old man is not really dead and appears on the scene.* Comedy. Sitting-room. 3 m., 3 f. Modern costumes. Effective if well played, not too difficult. Plays 30 minutes. FRENCH, 50¢. *Royalty,* $5.00.

DIABOLICAL CIRCLE, THE. Beulah Bomstead. *Cotton Mather of Colonial fame decides that his daughter should marry. He prefers one man; she another. Fortunately her choice proves himself to be more worthy.* Farce comedy. Living-room. 3 m.,

1 f. Puritan costumes. Very entertaining. Plays 30 minutes. *No royalty.*

DOLLAR, A. David Pinski. *A band of strolling players, without money, find a dollar and argue over it until it is lost to all of them.* Fantastic comedy. A forest glade. 5 m., 3 f. Modern costumes. May be made effective, needs skilled players. Plays 25 minutes. *Royalty, $5.00 to* FRENCH.

DOTS AND DASHES. Gordon Alderman. *Shows the growth of romance between two young people who meet from time to time in a bus terminal.* Comedy. Interior. 3 m., 4 f. Modern costumes. DRAMATISTS PLAY SERVICE, MSS. *Royalty, $5.00.*

DREAMY KID, THE. Eugene O'Neill. *A murderer, pursued by the police, goes to see his dying mother, and is captured.* Drama. Interior. 1 m., 3 f. Modern costumes of South. *Royalty, $5.00 to* DRAMATISTS PLAY SERVICE.

DUST OF THE ROAD, THE. Kenneth Sawyer Goodman. *A mysterious tramp-like character, who is wandering in expiation of a crime committed long ago, prevents a farmer from selling his soul for "thirty pieces of silver."* Drama. A living-room in a farmhouse. 3 m., 1 f. Modern costumes. Fine and unusual play, especially suited for Christmas. Plays 20 minutes. BANNER PLAY BUREAU, 50¢. *Royalty, $10.00 if admission is charged; $5.00 if no admission is charged.*

EL CRISTO. Margaret Larkin. *A colorful drama about a universal human struggle. The scene is laid on the Mexican border and has to do with the strange and interesting customs of a secret religious sect.* Drama. Interior. 4 m., 2 f. Costumes of Mexicans in Taos, N.M. Plays 20 minutes. FRENCH, 50¢. *Royalty, $10.00.*

ELDEST, THE. Edna Ferber. *The eldest sister is chained to her family and bed-ridden mother. She lives in the hope of reviving her romance, but the hope is lost when the man returns and falls in love with her younger sister.* Drama. Dining-room. 3 m., 4 f. Modern costumes. Well written serious play. Plays 30 minutes. *Royalty, $5.00 to* DRAMATISTS PLAY SERVICE.

ENCHANTED CHRISTMAS TREE, THE. Percival Wilde. *Ella and Josiah Benton, a self-centered couple who believe that children should be seen and not heard, order some "no-trespassing" signs to be placed about their property, but the expressman brings a Christmas tree by mistake. It turns out to be a magic tree, and in a dream the couple are surrounded by children who win them over.* Fantastic comedy. Living-room. 3 m. (or 1 m.), 1 f., 20 children. Modern costumes. Opportunity for Christmas music. Charmingly told story. Plays 45 minutes. BAKER, 50¢. *Royalty, $10.00.*

ENTER THE HERO. Theresa Helburn. *A sentimental girl invents a romance between herself and a boy who has been away for several years. When he returns, he has difficulty in extricating himself.* Comedy. A living-room. 1 m., 3 f. Modern costumes. Well written, easy to produce. FRENCH, 50¢. *Royalty, $10.00.*

EVENING CLOTHES. Zona Gale. *Inez and Peter want to marry before he goes out West, but Inez lacks a wedding dress. Grandma opens her old trunk, decks out all the village women, including Inez, and the gala occasion is a very merry one.* Comedy. Barn interior. 8 m., 8 f. Rural costumes. Simple, folk comedy, with occasional music. Plays 60 minutes. *Royalty, $10.00 to* BAKER.

EVENING DRESS INDISPENSABLE. Roland Pertwee. *A mother and daughter both find boy friends when the daughter refuses to go out and the mother and boy friend conspire to make her jealous.* Comedy. Interior. 2 m., 3 f. Modern costumes.

Plays 25 minutes. FRENCH, *50¢. Royalty, $10.00.*

EXCHANGE, THE. Althea Thurston. *The Judge, an exchanger of miseries, accepts pet miseries of Poor Man, Vain Woman, Rich Man, etc., giving each what he desires accompanied with some other misery. Each eventually comes back for his original misery, but the Judge is gone.* Fantasy in 2 scenes. Office. 4 m., 1 f. Fantastic costumes. Good characters, easy to produce. Plays 35 minutes. *Royalty, $10.00 to* BAKER.

FALCON, THE. Lord Tennyson. *Count Federigo, who has beggared himself in the vain attempt to win the love of the Lady Giovanna, kills his falcon for her, which moves her to confess her love.* Poetic drama. Room in a cottage (may be played in garden). 2 m., 2 f. Costumes, Italian, 15th century. Poetic dramatization of the old story, which can be made charming. Plays 25 minutes. *No royalty.*

FALL OF THE CITY, THE. Archibald MacLeish. *Poetic drama, originally written for radio, depicting the terror of the inhabitants of a city expecting an invading dictator momentarily.* Exterior. As many characters as desired. Modern costumes. *Royalty, $5.00 to* DRAMATISTS PLAY SERVICE.

FAME AND THE POET. Lord Dunsany. *The poet has an altar built to Fame in whom he believes. Just as he gives up hope of success and is about to tear down the altar Fame appears. Fame isn't the ideal goddess he expected and he decides he doesn't want her, but she announces that she has come to stay.* Satire. Exterior. 2 m., 1 f. Modern costumes. Easily acted, for mature players. Plays 20 minutes. *Royalty, $10.00 to* FRENCH.

FIFTEENTH CANDLE, THE. Rachel Field. *An Italian immigrant girl battles against her father's greed in order that her younger sister may continue her training in art.* Drama.

Basement kitchen-dining-living room. 2 m., 3 f. Modern costumes. Powerful, not too difficult. Plays 25 minutes. FRENCH, *50¢. Royalty, $5.00.*

FIGUREHEADS. Louise Saunders. *A pouty princess is reformed by a prince disguised as a fisherman.* Fantastic comedy. Room in a palace. 3 m., 2 f. Fantastic costumes. Charming and picturesque. Not too difficult. Plays 25 minutes. *Royalty, $10.00 if admission is charged; $5.00 if not, to* LONGMANS, GREEN.

FINDERS-KEEPERS. George Kelly. *A woman who has found some money makes little effort to trace the owner, but reacts in a different manner when she finds it has been stolen from her, and has cost her the respect of her husband.* American comedy. Living-room. 1 m., 2 f. Modern costumes. Effective and interesting; not difficult. Plays 40 minutes. FRENCH, *50¢. Royalty, $10.00.*

FINGER OF GOD, THE. Percival Wilde. *Strickland has made every preparation to commit a crime. At the last minute a girl appears to show him to himself as he really is.* Drama. Interior. 2 m., 1 f. Modern costumes. Plays 30 minutes. FRENCH, *50¢. Royalty, $10.00.*

FIRST DRESS SUIT, THE. Russell Medcraft. *The trials and tribulations of a young man and his first dress suit.* Comedy. Interior. 2 m., 2 f. Modern costumes. Plays 30 minutes. FRENCH, *50¢. Royalty, $10.00.*

FIVE MINUTES FROM THE STATION. Elaine Sterne Carrington. *Bert Adams, an ambitious young clerk, invites his boss to dine at his home against the wishes of his young wife, and a series of happy misfortunes causes the boss to promote him.* Comedy in 3 scenes, but not difficult to stage. (1) a corner in an office and (2) a telephone in a home, which are shown together; (3) a living-dining room. 2 m., 1 f. Modern costumes.

Amusing commonplace characters in an obvious plot. Plays 25 minutes.

FIXIN'S. Paul and Erma Green. *A young farm woman, whose ambitious, but hard and dull husband cannot understand her desire for a little of the beauty of life, for "fixin's," realizes the hopelessness of the situation and leaves him.* American drama. Room in a cabin. 2 m., 1 f. Farm costumes. Sincere and moving, for advanced amateurs. Plays 30 minutes. *Royalty, $5.00 to* FRENCH.

FLATTERING WORD, THE. George Kelly. *A famous actor breaks down the prejudices of people against the stage by flattering them into thinking they can act.* Satiric comedy. Living-room. 2 m., 3 f. Modern costumes. For advanced amateurs. Plays 30 minutes. FRENCH, 50¢. *Royalty, $10.00.*

FOURTEENTH GUEST, THE. Clyde Barrett. *While waiting for a lecturer the discovery is made that there are only thirteen guests at the luncheon. Humor of the play in the inviting and dropping out of guests which keeps the number at thirteen.* Comedy. Sitting-room. 16 f. Modern costumes. Good comedy. Plays 25 minutes. FRENCH, 50¢. *Royalty, $5.00.*

FUMED OAK. Noel Coward. *The story of how a henpecked husband finally gets enough money and courage to leave his wife, complaining mother-in-law, and his whining daughter.* Comedy. Interior. 1 m., 3 f. Modern costumes. Plays 40 minutes. FRENCH, 50¢. *Royalty on application.*

GAME OF CHESS, THE. Kenneth Sawyer Goodman. *A quick-witted Russian ruler tricks an assassin as though he were an opponent in a game of chess, and so saves his life.* Melodrama. Room in a palace. 4 m. Russian costumes, 19th century. One of the best thrillers, effective and picturesque. Not difficult. Plays 25 minutes. FRENCH, 50¢. *Royalty, $5.00*

if no admission is charged; $10.00 if admission is charged.

GAZING GLOBE, THE. Eugene Pillot. *The enchantment of the gazing globe causes Ohano to become dissatisfied with her life on the Island. Her lover, a successful hero, tired of the world, comes home from war and urges her to settle down. In his intensity he breaks the globe and she rushes to the sea to her death.* Tragedy. A garden. 1 m., 2 f. South Sea island costumes. Dramatic and effective. Plays 15 minutes. *Royalty, $5.00 to* FRENCH.

GAY NINETY. Florence Ryerson & Colin Clements. *A story about how a great-grandmother celebrates her birthday by going for an airplane ride, but not until after many complications.* Comedy. Interior. 8 f. Modern costumes. FRENCH, 50¢. *Royalty, $5.00.*

GHOST STORY, THE. Booth Tarkington. *George, home from college, wishes to be alone with Ann, and trying to frighten her friends away, tells a ghost story with an unexpected and startling result. All ends happily.* Comedy. Living-room. 5 m., 5 f. Modern costumes. Often played by high schools. Plays 40 minutes. FRENCH, 50¢. *Royalty, $10.00.*

GIFT, THE. Lucienne Glorieux. *A prisoner keeps his promise to his wife that he will be home for Christmas by breaking out of jail. He tries to keep it a secret from her, but she finds out and helps him escape on a ship to France.* Drama. Interior. 2 m., 2 f. Modern costumes. Plays 30 minutes. BAKER, 50¢. *Royalty, $5.00.*

GLORIA MUNDI. Patricia Brown. *A sort of parable of life, laid in a lunatic asylum, showing the courage necessary to face the bitter realities of life.* Fantastic drama. Interior 2 m., 4 f. Modern costumes. Plays 35 minutes. FRENCH, 50¢. *Royalty, $10.00.*

GOLDEN DOOM, THE. Lord Dunsany. *The prophets interpret the scribbling of a child on the king's gate as a symbol of doom. The king leaves his crown as an offering and it is picked up by a boy who had wished for a golden hoop.* Fantastic comedy. Outside gate and walls of a city. 9 m., 1 f. Fantastic costumes. Symbolic; beautiful and effective if properly staged. Plays 30 minutes. *Royalty, $10.00 to* FRENCH.

GOOD NEIGHBORS. James Reach. *A Women's Literary and Civic Club meets to hear a speech by a South American lady. Before the lecture, there is a business meeting at which is debated the momentous questions of what flowers to plant on the club grounds. The Señora finds herself involved, and draws an apt moral.* Comedy. Interior. 9 f., optional extras. Modern costumes. 30 minutes. FRENCH, *50¢. Royalty, $5.00.*

GOOD-BYE MISS LIZZIE BORDEN. Lillian de la Torre. *The story of the famous Borden murder case, and what happened to the two Borden sisters afterward.* Drama. Interior. 5 f. 19th-century costumes. Plays 35 minutes. BAKER, *50¢. Royalty, $5.00.*

GRAND CHAM'S DIAMOND. Allan Monkhouse. *Mrs. Perkin's humdrum existence promises to be broken when a diamond comes hurtling through her window, and she romantically plans a trip to South America. However, she reluctantly yields to honesty and her prospective son-in-law.* Comedy. Sitting-room. 3 m., 2 f. Modern costumes. Amusing and effective. Needs one skilled actress. Plays 30 minutes. *Royalty, $5.00 to* BAKER.

GRAY BREAD. Jean Lee Latham. *An old wise woman imparts some of her wisdom in living to one of her daughters.* Drama. Interior of a peasant cottage. 4 f. Modern costumes. 25 minutes. Row, PETERSON, *50¢. Royalty, $5.00.*

GREEN COAT. Alfred de Musset & Emile Augier. *A comic character sketch of the life of Bohemian artists in Paris.* Comedy. Interior. 3 m., 1 f. Mid-19th-century costumes. FRENCH, *50¢. No royalty.*

HANDS ACROSS THE SEA. Noel Coward. *A London social butterfly has a terrible time when she gets two Far-Eastern friends mixed up with some other Far-Eastern friends. But she finally straightens out the whole affair and everyone is happy.* Comedy. Interior. 6 m., 3 f. Modern costumes. Plays 30 minutes. FRENCH, *50¢. Royalty on application.*

HAPPY JOURNEY TO CAMDEN AND TRENTON, THE. Thornton Wilder. *The simple story of Pa and Ma who journey from Newark with their two children in the family car to visit their married daughter in Camden.* Character portraiture. Comedy. No scenery except four chairs and a cot. 3 m., 3 f. Modern costumes. 30 minutes. FRENCH, *50¢. Royalty, $10.00.*

HAPPY RETURNS. Essex Dane. *Mrs. Halliday gives a birthday party and receives only one gift which she likes. When she learns the donor and the reason for the gift, it reverts to its former owner.* Farce. Drawing-room. 10 f. Modern costumes. Hilarious action and good lines. Not difficult. Plays 40 minutes. BAKER, *50¢. Royalty, $5.00.*

HE CAME SEEING. Mary P. Hamlin. *A dramatic presentation of the story of a young man who comes under the personal influence of Christ and casts off his earlier belief in order to embrace Christianity.* Biblical drama. Interior. 3 m., 2 f. Biblical costumes. Plays 40 minutes. FRENCH, *50¢. Royalty, $5.00.*

HELLO, OUT THERE. William Saroyan. *Photo Finish, an itinerant gambler, is falsely accused of rape and meets his death in a small Texas town.* Drama. Interior (prison). 3

m., 2 f. Modern costumes. 30 minutes. FRENCH, 50¢. *Royalty, $10.00.*

HIGH WINDOW. Verne Powers. *A high window, overlooking a street, holds Walter Hodge in mental torment, and is the center of an enigma involving the recent death of his uncle, who fell from that window.* Melodrama in 1 act. Interior. 2 m., 3 f. Modern costumes. 28 minutes. ROW, PETERSON, 50¢. *Royalty, $5.00.*

HINT TO BRIDES, A. Kenyon Nicholson. *The idea is to have the bride's presents which are insured conveniently stolen. No harm is done to the presents, and there are practical difficulties in carrying out the author's hint.* Comedy. Interior. 2 m., 2 f. Modern costumes. Plays 35 minutes. FRENCH, 50¢. *Royalty, $5.00.*

HIS SAINTED GRANDMOTHER. Lord Dunsany. *Papa has been lecturing his daughter on her iniquities, and contrasting them with the virtues of his grandmother. She enters as a ghost and tells a thing or two of her unsaintly life, making her biggest point that her granddaughter should enjoy life to the full.* Comedy. Old-fashioned bedroom. 1 m., 3 f. Modern costumes. Light and trivial, but amusing. Plays 20 minutes. *Royalty, $10.00 to* FRENCH.

HOME OF THE FREE, THE. Elmer Rice. *A father refuses to let his son marry a certain girl on the grounds that the girl is his half-sister.* Comedy. Interior. 2 m., 2 f. Modern costumes. Plays 30 minutes. FRENCH, 50¢. *Royalty, $10.00.*

HOME TO MOTHER. Mary Lawrence. *A young wife goes home to mother when her husband forgets her birthday. After she leaves, her husband comes home to tell her that his boss is coming to dinner to see if he is the responsible person he should be for a new job. John winds up with three women masquerading as his wife,* when his real wife shows up. Farce. Interior. 2 m., 4 f. Modern costumes. Time 20 minutes. DRAMATIC PUBLISHING Co., 40¢. *No royalty.*

HOPE IS THE THING WITH FEATHERS. Richard Harrity. *A group of tramps and down-and-outs attempt to catch a duck on a lake in Central Park and cook it. Beneath the mere externals, there runs a savage and ironic commentary on mankind.* Comedy. Exterior. 9 m., no f. Modern costumes. DRAMATISTS PLAY SERVICE, $1.00. *Royalty, $5.00.*

HOPELESS PASSION OF MR. BUNYAN, THE. Lord Dunsany. *Bunyan is a clerk in Mr. Muffen's shop. Instead of working, he gazes at a wax figure in the window. The owner eventually tires of this and discharges him. Before leaving, he asks permission to say good-bye to the manikin. She replies to him and is also fired.* Comedy. Interior. 2 m., 1 f. Modern costumes. FRENCH, 50¢. *Royalty, $10.00.*

HOT LEMONADE. Florence Ryerson & Colin Clements. *A young wife plans to elope with her admirer. The young man becomes seasick and deserts her, but the husband appears and proves himself superior to the admirer.* Comedy. Steamship sitting-room. 3 m., 1 f. Modern costumes. Very amusing for adult groups. Plays 30 minutes. FRENCH, 50¢. *Royalty, $5.00.*

HOUR GLASS, THE. W. B. Yeats. *The Wise Man is confronted by an angel who tells him that ere the sands run through the hour glass he will die without hope of pardon unless within that time he finds one who believes in Heaven. He calls his pupils, his wife, and his servant, but all profess his teaching of denial. Finally, as sands run low he finds a Fool who believes.* Morality play, arranged in two versions, prose and verse. Bare room. 6 m., 2 f., 2 children. Imaginative costumes. High literary, pictorial, and dramatic quality. Not too difficult. Plays 30 minutes.

HOUR OF TRUTH (Formerly called CONFESSIONAL). **Percival Wilde.** *Roger Baldwin, an honest bank cashier, is offered a large bribe by the dishonest president of the bank, and his family urge him to accept, but finally his stubborness brings him due reward.* Drama. Cottage parlor. 3 m., 3 f. Modern costumes. Requires skillful acting. Plays 35 minutes. BAKER, *50¢. Royalty, $10.00.*

HOW HE LIED TO HER HUSBAND. G. Bernard Shaw. *A young man writes love poems to another man's wife which the husband finds. The poet, to get himself out of a difficult situation, says he could not love the wife, and the husband becomes incensed. At last the poet tells the truth, and all agree the poems are to be published.* English comedy. Drawing-room. 2 m., 1 f. Modern costumes. Clever turn to a trite situation. Plays 25 minutes. *Royalty, $10.00 to* FRENCH.

HUNGERERS, THE. William Saroyan. *In this symbolic fantasy, a writer dreams up four lonely people who are hungering for physical as well as spiritual nourishment. They reveal that the answer to death is an immortality based on love.* Drama. Interior. 3 m., 2 f. Modern costumes. FRENCH, *50¢. Royalty, $10.00.*

HYACINTH HALVEY. Lady Gregory. *Hyacinth, a weak-minded but virtuous youth, tired of the good reputation which follows him, tries to commit a crime but finds himself a hero.* Irish comedy. Outside rural post office. 3 m., 2 f. Irish costumes. Amusing play, not difficult. Plays 45 minutes. FRENCH, *50¢.. Royalty, $5.00.*

IDOLS. Phoebe M. Rees. *The plot is centered around the Reign of Terror in France. A mother maliciously attempts to denounce a daughter-in-law to the Tribunal. But her beloved son walks into the ingenious trap which was laid for his wife.* Drama. Interior. 6 f. 18th-century French costumes. Plays 30 minutes.* BAKER, *50¢. Royalty, $5.00.*

IF MEN PLAYED CARDS AS WOMEN DO. George S. Kaufman. *A group of men around a bridge table speak, behave, and think after the manner in which women are supposed to conduct their game.* Satirical comedy. Interior. 4 m. Modern costumes. Plays 30 minutes. FRENCH, *50¢. Royalty, $5.00.*

IF THE SHOE PINCHES. Babette Hughes. *Mrs. Pell, a silly divorcee, is trying on various pairs of shoes for size. Her sister, Laura, a business woman, is more sensible. Complications cause a postponement of their contemplated European trip, and may lead to the marriage of Mrs. Pell and the shoe salesman.* Interior. 4 f. Modern costumes. DRAMATISTS PLAY SERVICE, *50¢. Royalty, $5.00.*

ILE. Eugene O'Neill. *The wife of a whaling captain, driven almost mad by her loneliness, persuades her husband to start home without "ile." But a whale is sighted and he breaks his promise, determined not to go home until he is successful. This drives her to madness.* Tragedy. Cabin of a ship. 5 m., 1 f. Strong play; difficult roles. Plays 25 minutes. *Royalty, $5.00 to* DRAMATISTS PLAY SERVICE.

IN THE ZONE. Eugene O'Neill. *Smitty, a sailor, is under suspicion for his behavior. He is lashed to his bunk, and the others force open a box he had been safeguarding, only to find some letters from a girl who had broken her engagement to Smitty.* Drama. Interior. 9 m. Sailors' costumes. *Royalty, $5.00 to* DRAMATISTS PLAY SERVICE.

INTRUDER, THE. Maurice Maeterlinck. *The family thinks that the mother is recovering but Death, the Intruder, enters the home unfelt by*

all except the blind old grandfather.
Tragedy. Interior. 4 m., 3 f. Modern
and imaginative costumes. Melancholy and beautiful. Plays 20 minutes. *Royalty, $15.00 to* FRENCH.

JAZZ AND MINUET. Ruth Giorloff.
*Eleanor, a spoiled headstrong girl,
is waiting for her fiancé to take her
to a dance. When he cancels the date
because of a business engagement,
Eleanor calls another friend. While
waiting for him, she reads the diary
of her great aunt who never married
because her fiancé was killed in a
duel. Eleanor is chastened by this
experience, and when her fiancé appears makes up with him.* Comedy.
Living-room. 2 m., 3 f. Modern and
18th-century costumes. Good opportunity for acting and staging. Not
difficult. Plays 30 minutes. LONG-
MANS, GREEN, 65¢. *Royalty, $10.00.*

**JEPHTHAH'S DAUGHTER. Elma
Ehrlich Levinger.** *Jephthah has made
a covenant with God that if He will
give him victory he will sacrifice the
first person who meets him on his return. The first person is his daughter.
Jephthah wants to break his vow but
she makes him keep it.* Biblical
tragedy. Before Jephthah's house.
6 m., 5 f. Biblical costumes. Dramatic
and effective. Rather difficult. May
be presented with elaborate scenic
effects and augmented cast as a pageant play. As written, plays 25 minutes. *No royalty.*

**JEST OF HAHALABA, THE. Lord
Dunsany.** *With the help of an alchemist, Mr. Strangeways conjures
up the Spirit of Laughter, and requests a copy of the* London Times
*of the following year. Strangeways
enjoys reading about the rise in value
of his stocks, and other happenings,
but is shocked to death when he
reads about his death on January 1.*
Ironic play. Interior. 4 m. Modern
costumes. FRENCH, 50¢. *Royalty,
$10.00.*

**JINX FROM ALABAMA, THE. John
Kirkpatrick.** *The girl from Alabama
came to be a bridesmaid, but she, by
use of her Southern charms, almost
tears the house apart.* Comedy. Interior. 2 m., 6 f. Modern costumes.
Plays 30 minutes. FRENCH, 50¢. *Royalty, $5.00.*

JUDGE LYNCH. J. W. Rogers, Jr. *A
Negro who has killed a white man
known to have a quick temper, is
lynched, but his innocence is deftly
proven to the audience.* American
drama. Back porch of farmhouse. 2
m., 2 f. Modern costumes. Exceed-
ingly dramatic; difficult. Plays 20
minutes. FRENCH, 50¢. *Royalty,
$10.00.*

JUST NEIGHBORLY. Alexander Dean.
*A son who has been away for thirty
years writes that he is coming home.
A neighbor plants suspicion as to his
authenticity and he is driven from
home a second time although the
parents longed for his return.* American drama. Kitchen-sitting room. 2
m., 2 f. Modern costumes. Effective
study of New England life and character. Not too difficult to produce.
Plays 30 minutes. FRENCH, 50¢. *Royalty, $10.00.*

**KNAVE OF HEARTS, THE. Louise
Saunders.** *Violetta, the king's daughter, makes tarts to prove her fitness to
be a queen. They are a failure and
she thinks all is lost until the Knave
offers to substitute a tray of his wife's
tarts for those of Violetta.* Fantastic
comedy. Royal kitchen. 8 m., 2 f., 6
pages. Imaginative costumes. Pleasing fantasy, not difficult. Suitable for
all-girl cast. Plays 40 minutes. LONG-
MANS, GREEN, 65¢. *Royalty, $10.00.*

**LADY OF LARKSPUR LOTION,
THE. Tennessee Williams.** *Powerful
sketch about derelicts.* Interior. 1 m.,
2 f. *Royalty, $10.00 to* DRAMATISTS
PLAY SERVICE.

**LAND OF HEART'S DESIRE, THE.
W. B. Yeats.** *On the eve of May Day,*

Maire Bruin gives away food and fire to the fairies. A fairy child comes into the home, bids them hide the crucifix, enchants the people, and entices Maire's soul away. Poetic drama. Kitchen. 3 m., 3f. Irish peasant costumes. Beautiful but sad. Plays 30 minutes. FRENCH, 50¢. *No Royalty.*

LAST OF MY SOLID GOLD WATCHES, THE. Tennessee Williams. *Character sketch of a "drummer".* Interior. 3 m. Modern costumes. *Royalty, $10.00 to* DRAMATISTS PLAY SERVICE.

LAST OF THE LOWRIES, THE. Paul Green. *The patient mother of the Lowries (Croatan outlaws in the mountains of North Carolina), who has seen her husband and four sons killed by the sheriff, suffers the death of her youngest son, who kills himself to escape capture.* Tragedy. Kitchen. 1 m., 3 f. Rural costumes. Effective, not too difficult except dialect. Plays 30 minutes. FRENCH, 50¢. *Royalty, $5.00.*

LAST STRAW, THE. Bosworth Crocker. *Bauer, a good family man, misunderstood and hated by his neighbors, is arrested for killing a cat. Fined and disgraced, he has no more courage to face the neighborhood, and shoots himself.* Tragedy. Kitchen of a basement flat in New York City. 2 m., 1 f., 2 little boys. Modern costumes. Brief lines make the background lively and colorful, interesting contrast to the tragedy of the theme. Plays 20 minutes. *No royalty.*

LITTLE FATHER IN THE WILDERNESS, THE. Austin Strong & Lloyd Osborne. *Père Marlotte, missionary to America, is called with little ceremony before King Louis XV to settle a bet as to the height of Niagara Falls. When the great Frontenac arrives and kneels before Père Marlotte, the King, ashamed, makes the Father an Archbishop.* Historical drama. Antechamber at Versailles. 6 m., 1 f., many extras. French costumes, Louis XV period. Rich and colorful, excellent and worth doing. Plays 30 minutes. FRENCH, 50¢. *Royalty, $10.00.*

LITTLE MAN, THE. John Galsworthy. *A number of waiting passengers discuss philosophy of life. As they board the train the Little Man attempts to befriend a needy woman, takes her baby, leaving her on the platform. Others advise, but leave him when they suspect that the baby is ill. Little Man is arrested but vindicated.* Farcical Morality, in 3 scenes. (1) and (2) Two railway platforms; (3) interior of railway car. 9 m., 2 f. Modern costumes. A difficult little play, worthy of effort. Plays 40 minutes. *Royalty, $10.00 to* CURTIS BROWN, LTD.

LONESOME-LIKE. Harold Brighouse. *Sarah Ormerod, an old woman who is about to go to the poor house, is adopted as a mother by Sam Horrocks, a soft-hearted young man who is "lonesome like," having just been rejected by his sweetheart.* Comedy. Cottage interior. 2 m., 2 f. Modern British costumes. Excellent, with good parts. Plays 30 minutes. FRENCH, 50¢. *Royalty, $5.00.*

LONG VOYAGE HOME, THE. Eugene O'Neill. *Olson, one of a crew of sailors on shore leave, refuses to drink in order to be able to go home on his savings. He is drugged and robbed, then put on a ship bound on a long voyage.* Drama. Interior. 6 m., 3 f. Sailors' costumes. A fine ironic play. *Royalty, $5.00 to* DRAMATISTS PLAY SERVICE.

LORD'S PRAYER, THE. François Coppée. (translated by Mary Aldis). *Rose's brother, an Abbé, was killed by a soldier, but thinking of her love for her brother, she shelters and saves a soldier who is being sought.* Drama. Cottage room. 3 m., 3 f. French Revolution costumes. Easy, appealing plot of French Revolution. Plays 15 minutes. BAKER, 50¢. *Royalty, $3.00.*

LORD'S WILL, THE. Paul Green. *Lem Adams has only one purpose in life, to preach the gospel. He neglects his wife and child. The wife bears with him until the child dies from lack of medical care but then turns on him.* Tragedy. Kitchen-dining room. 1 m., 2 f. Modern costumes. Powerful little play, only for advanced amateurs. Plays 25 minutes. FRENCH, 50¢. *Royalty, $5.00.*

LOST SILK HAT, THE. Lord Dunsany. *A young man who has quarreled with his sweetheart and rushed out without his hat, attempts to send in for it a number of characters he meets in the street. Finally he goes back to get it himself, to the despair of a poet who forsees for him a smug and unromantic future.* Comedy. Outside a house. 5 m. Modern costumes. Subtle and effective little comedy; needs skillful playing and producing. Plays 25 minutes.

LUCK PIECE, THE. Percival Wilde. *Murder in a waterfront barroom late at night.* Drama. Interior. 5 m., 1 f. Modern costumes. Plays 30 minutes. BAKER, 50¢. *Royalty, $10.00.*

MAKER OF DREAMS, THE. Oliphant Down. *Pierrot is always seeking his ideal love, and finally, with the aid of the Maker of Dreams, finds her in Pierrette, who has long loved him secretly.* Fantastic comedy. Cottage room. 2 m., 1 f. Requires lightness of presentation. Pierrot needs good singing voice. Modern & Pierrot costumes. Plays 30 minutes. BAKER, 50¢. *Royalty, $8.00, payable to* FRENCH *or* BAKER.

MAN IN THE BOWLER HAT, THE. A. A. Milne. *John and Mary find themselves in the midst of an exciting adventure with thieves and detectives while the "man in the bowler hat" sits quietly in the corner; it turns out that he is the stage manager and the whole thing is a rehearsal.* Burlesque melodrama. Living-room. 5 m., 2 f. Modern costumes. Good

travesty, easy to play. Plays 30 minutes. FRENCH, 50¢. *Royalty, $10.00.*

MAN OF DESTINY, THE. G. Bernard Shaw. *A story of early campaigns of Napoleon. A message is lost and found through intrigue involving a lovely lady suspected as a spy.* Drama. Interior of Italian inn. 3 m., 1 f. French costumes of 19th century. Interesting, and effective if well played. Plays 30 minutes. *Royalty on application to* FRENCH.

MAN WHO MARRIED A DUMB WIFE. Anatole France. *A lawyer, Judge Leonard Botal, marries a young and charming wife who is dumb, has her cured by the learned doctors, finds her constant chatter drives him mad, and as a final resort permits himself to be made deaf to correct his error.* Medieval farce in 2 acts. Main room in Judge's house. 7 m., 2 f., extras. Medieval French costumes. A famous farce, full of satire and humor, which gives an opportunity for unique effects and setting. Not difficult. Plays 60 minutes. FRENCH, 85¢. *Royalty, $25.00.*

MANIKIN AND MINIKIN. Alfred Kreymborg. *Two bisque figures on a chime clock have a lovers' quarrel.* Fantasy. Parlor wall with mantel and clock. 1 m., 1 f. Imaginative costumes. Interesting to stage; good rhythmical prose. Plays 20 minutes. FRENCH, 50¢. *Royalty, $5.00.*

MARRIAGE HAS BEEN ARRANGED. A. Alfred Sutro. *A wealthy American proposes to an English debutante who despises his vulgarity and boastfulness. When he learns that she loves a penniless soldier, the millionaire generously promises to enrich the soldier so that a marriage can be arranged.* Comedy. Conservatory. 1 m., 1 f. Modern costumes. Clever dialogue. Plays 20 minutes. FRENCH, 50¢. *Royalty, $5.00.*

MARRIAGE PROPOSAL, THE. Anton Chekov (translated by Hjalmar Baukhage & Barrett H. Clark). *A* nervous and excitable man starts to propose to an attractive young woman but becomes involved in a quarrel over a boundary-line. Farce. Interior. 2 m., 1 f. Modern or Russian costumes. FRENCH, 50¢. No royalty.

MARRIED AT SUNRISE. John Kirkpatrick. A young soldier and his sweetheart decide to get married after he lies and tells her that his leave has been cancelled. She awakens his family to tell them the news, which is met with considerable excitement. Comedy. Interior. 2 m., 4 f. Modern costumes. Plays 35 minutes. FRENCH, 50¢. Royalty, $5.00.

MAYOR AND THE MANICURE, THE. George Ade. Just as Wallie Milford, son of the Mayor of Springfield, is returning from college and is about to marry a society girl, Genevieve Le Clair appears before the Mayor and claims that Wallie should marry her. The Mayor, by the clever use of a dummy phone, shows Genevieve to be a blackmailer. Drama. Mayor's private office. 2 m., 2 f. Modern costumes. Excellent for adult amateurs. Plays 30 minutes. FRENCH, 50¢. Royalty, $5.00.

MINNIE FIELD. E. P. Conkle. The life history of a poor Midwestern farm woman who lies dead in the next room. DRAMA. Interior. 5 m. Modern costumes. FRENCH, 50¢ Royalty, $5.00.

MINUET, A. Louis N. Parker. A marquis and marquise, long separated and estranged, meet in prison on the eve of his execution, and reunited, go bravely out together to the guillotine. French Revolution drama in verse. Gaoler's living-room. 2 m., 1 f. Costumes of French Revolution. Delicate and charming, needs skilled playing. Plays 15 minutes. FRENCH, 50¢. Royalty, $10.00.

MONKEY'S PAW, THE. W. W. Jacobs & Louis N. Parker. A monkey's paw, said to have magic properties, brings tragic fulfilment of its owner's three wishes. Melodrama. 40 minutes. Interior. 4 m., 1 f. Modern costumes. A suspenseful thriller. FRENCH, 50¢. Royalty, $10.00.

MOON OF THE CARIBBEES, THE. Eugene O'Neill. A dramatic episode in the life of a group of sailors as their ship docks in a Caribbean port. Drama. Ship's deck. 17 m., 4 f. Sailors' costumes. DRAMATISTS PLAY SERVICE. Royalty on application to DRAMATISTS PLAY SERVICE.

MOONSHINE. Arthur Hopkins. A revenue officer is captured by a moonshiner who has been "laying" for him, but talks his way to an escape. Melodrama. Cabin interior. 2 m. Modern costumes. Interesting, not difficult. Plays 20 minutes. FRENCH, 50¢. Royalty, $5.00.

MOONY'S KID DON'T CRY. Tennessee Williams. Short play about a worker, his wife and child. Interior. 1 m., 1 f. Modern costumes. Plays 30 minutes. DRAMATISTS PLAY SERVICE, 90¢. Royalty, $10.00.

NEIGHBORS, THE. Zona Gale. A friendless child is cared for by "The Neighbors" in a small town. Comedy. Interior. 2 m., 6 f. Modern costumes. 1 hour. FRENCH, 50¢. Royalty, $10.00–$5.00.

NIGHT AT AN INN, A. Lord Dunsany. An Eastern idol visits retribution on a set of thieves who have stolen his ruby eye. Tense melodrama. Interior. 8 m. Modern costumes. 30 minutes. FRENCH, 50¢. Royalty, $10.00.

OF TIME AND THE BLIZZARD. John Kirkpatrick. Reminiscenses, about the famous blizzard of '88 begin a chain reaction of events which make a visiting English author believe that he may be in a madhouse. Farce. Interior. 3 m., 4 f. Modern costumes. Plays 30 minutes. FRENCH, 50¢. Royalty, $5.00.

OLD LADY SHOWS HER MEDALS, THE. J. M. Barrie. *Mrs. Dowey is entertaining three other charwomen at tea; they are all proud of their sons in the army (1914–1918). Mrs. Dowey had no son, and so "adopts" from the newspaper a Kenneth Dowey, private in the army, and mothers him while he's on leave. She becomes highly attached to him. He doesn't return.* Play. Interior. 2 m., 4 f. Modern costumes. FRENCH, 50¢. *Royalty, $10.00.*

OVERTONES. Alice Gerstenberg. *Harriet and Margaret, two cultured women, engage in a conversation; but their thoughts, which differ radically, are spoken by their primitive selves, Hetty and Maggie.* Satiric fantasy. Living-room. 4 f. Sophisticated satire, with unusual effects. Plays 25 minutes. FRENCH, $1.00. *Royalty, $25.00.*

PEARLS. Dan Totheroh. *Tad is accused of stealing a valuable string of pearls from the store in which he works. Tad gives his sister a string of pearls for her birthday. Suspicion and suspense develop quickly but Tad is exonerated.* Drama. Interior. 2 m., 2 f. Modern costumes. FRENCH, 50¢. *Royalty, $5.00.*

PIPE OF PEACE. Margaret Cameron. *Gladys exchanges her husband's meerschaum pipe for a chair which proves to be only a reproduction. The pipe is finally recovered and peace re-established after Gladys has confessed.* Comedy. Dining-room. 1 m., 2 f. Modern costumes. Excellent light comedy. Interesting and human. Plays 25 minutes. *No royalty.*

PLAYGOERS. Arthur Wing Pinero. *A young mistress of a London household decides to favor her servants with a visit to the theatre. The disputes that ensue wind up in all of the domestics giving notice.* Satirical comedy. Interior. 2 m., 6 f. Modern costumes. Plays 25 minutes. FRENCH, 50¢. *Royalty, $5.00.*

POOR AUBREY. George Kelly. *Aubrey, practically living on charity, insists upon getting himself and wife into trouble by bragging in order to impress people.* Comedy. Sitting-room. 1 m., 3 f. Modern costumes. Amusing, needs one good actor. Plays 40 minutes. BAKER, 50¢. *Royalty, $10.00.*

POST OFFICE, THE. Rabindranath Tagore. *A sick child, kept indoors because of illness, experiences the romance of the out-of-doors as he watches the King's post office being built.* Drama in two scenes. (1) Living-room; (2) child's bedroom. 9 m., 1 f. Modern costumes. Poetic and symbolic play, requiring subtle and sympathetic interpretation. Plays 60 minutes. *Royalty* on application to PERFORMING RIGHT SOCIETY, Ltd.

PRINCESS MARRIES THE PAGE, THE. Edna St. Vincent Millay. *A page who breaks in on the privacy of a princess in her tower turns out to be the son of a neighboring ruler.* Verse play. Interior. A tower room. 6 m., 1 f. Imaginative costumes. Plays 40 minutes. Music by Deems Taylor. BAKER, 50¢. *Royalty, $10.00.*

PROMISED ONE, THE. Martha Bayle Shanon. *A pageant of the First Christmas, for production in a church auditorium, with Bible readings and street-scenes in Bethlehem.* 6 m., 3 f., 2 children, angels, shepherds, choir, and a group of travelers. Biblical costumes. About 30 minutes. ROW, PETERSON, 50¢. *No royalty if 8 copies are purchased.*

PURPLE DOORKNOB, THE. Walter Prichard Eaton. *A charming young actress succeeds in getting an old, bed-ridden woman to sell her an antique by performing for her and with her, in the old lady's bedroom.* Comedy. Simple, old-fashioned interior (bedroom). 3 f. Modern costumes. 25 minutes. FRENCH, 50¢. *Royalty, $5.00.*

"Q." Stephen Leacock & Basil McDonald Hastings. *A young man in* *need of cash, disguised as a spiritual-istic medium, dupes a superstitious victim.* Farce. Living-room. 3 m., 1 f. Modern costumes. Amusing and easy to stage effectively. Plays 25 minutes. FRENCH, 50¢. *Royalty, $5.00.*

QUARE MEDICINE. Paul Green. *An itinerant quack doctor comes to a house where a father and son are ruled by the wife of the latter, and accidentally, with his "quare medicine," causes the husband to win the upper hand.* Comedy. Sitting-bed-room. 3 m., 1 f. Modern costumes. Well-written and entertaining play for advanced amateurs. Plays 25 minutes. *Royalty on application to* FRENCH.

QUEEN'S ENEMIES, THE. Lord Dunsany. *An Egyptian Queen has invited her enemies to a banquet in a chamber below the temple. Her guests are suspicious, but they are gradually won over. The Queen leaves them and floods the chamber, destroying her enemies.* Drama. Interior. 9 m., 2 f. Ancient Egyptian costumes. Plays 30 minutes. FRENCH, 50¢. *Royalty, $10.00.*

QUIET, PLEASE. Howard Buermann. *Two brothers who are feuding have drawn a chalk line down the middle of their cabin. When an overnight visitor, Catherine, comes, they stop the feud temporarily. They are rec-onciled when she leaves, but start quarreling all over again when they try to recall what the original feud was about.* Comedy. Interior. 3 m., 4 f. Modern costumes. DRAMATISTS PLAY SERVICE, 40¢. *Royalty, $5.00.*

RECTOR, THE. Rachel Crothers. *The trials of the rector of a small country church. The rector feels it is time for him to marry and consults Margaret Norton, the clearest head of any of his congregation. Margaret loves him, but when she realizes that he loves another woman, she advises him to marry her.* Comedy. Interior. 1 m., 6 f. Modern costumes. Plays 35 minutes. FRENCH, 50¢. *No royalty.*

RED CARNATIONS. Glenn Hughes. *She had met "him" at a masked ball, where they had arranged to meet again in the park, he wearing an identifying red carnation. Her father comes to chaperone, also wearing a red carnation. The ensuing complica-tions end happily.* Comedy. Bench in a park. 2 m., 1 f. Modern costumes. Simple and entertaining. Plays 25 minutes. FRENCH, 50¢. *Royalty, $5.00.*

RED ROSES. William de Lisle. *She is lying dead, and mourning at her bed-side are Donald, her husband, Alma, her best friend, Martha, her sister, and Mr. Fosdick, her father-in-law. In the midst of their grieving, He, the man who carries the light, appears; He offers to bring She back to life.* Drama. Interior. 7 m., 3 f. Modern costumes. FRENCH, 50¢. *Royalty, $5.00.*

REHEARSAL. Christopher Morley. *Six schoolgirls rehearse an Irish peasant play.* Comedy. Interior. 6 f. Modern costumes. Plays 20–25 minutes. LONGMANS, GREEN, 75¢. *Royalty, $10.00 with admission, $5.00 with-out.*

RIDERS TO THE SEA. J. M. Synge. *The mother of a fisherman buries her last son, drowned at sea.* Drama. Interior. 1 m., 3 f. (extras). Costumes, Irish peasant. The most impressive of the Synge one-acters. Plays 20 minutes. FRENCH, 50¢. *Royalty, $10.00.*

RISING OF THE MOON, THE. Lady Gregory. *A homeless individual is escaping from the law when he falls in with a sergeant of police on the lookout for him. The individual gains the other man's sympathies to such an extent that he is assisted to escape from the law.* Comedy in 1 act. Ex-terior. 4 m. Irish costumes. Plays 20 minutes. FRENCH, 50¢. *Royalty, $5.00.*

ROBIN-A-TIPTOE. Bernard Merivale. *A tea shop is the headquarters for a country house robbery. A valiant old grandmother suspects the crook and fouls her plans.* Drama. Interior. 7 f. Modern costumes. Plays 30 minutes. BAKER, *50¢. Royalty, $5.00.*

ROMANCE OF THE WILLOW PATTERN. Ethel Van der Veer. *The characters from a willow pattern plate descend from heaven to re-enact the scenes of their love and betrothal and their attempted escape from the irate Mandarin's garden across the fatal bridge.* Fantasy. Settings in Chinese manner. 3 m., 1 f. and incense-bearer. Prologue and 7 scenes. Chinese costumes. Plays 30 minutes. FRENCH, *50¢. Royalty, $5.00.*

ROMANCERS, THE. Edmond Rostand (translated by Barrett H. Clark). *The story of two sentimental youngsters who rebel against their parents' wishes for them to marry.* Romantic comedy. Exterior. 5 m., 1 f. Fantastic costumes. Plays 40 minutes. FRENCH, *50¢. No royalty.*

ST. MICHAEL COMES TO SHEPHERD'S BUSH. James Parish. *From a shattered cathedral window, Eustace picked up two bits of glass as souvenirs, never suspecting one was from the spearhead of St. Michael—the other from the tail of the devil. While the devil is trying his wiles, he is, according to tradition, transfixed by St. Michael's spearhead.* Fantastic comedy. Interior. 3 m., 1 f. Modern and medieval costumes. Plays 30 minutes. BAKER, *50¢. Royalty, $5.00.*

SEQUEL, THE. Percival Wilde. *What happens to a couple in a play after the curtain falls on a happy ending?* Comedy. Interior. 3 m., 1 f. Modern costumes. Plays 30 minutes. BAKER, *50¢. Royalty, $10.00.*

SEVEN WOMEN. J. M. Barrie. *Bachelor Captain Rattray meets a woman by whom he is fascinated at a party given by his friend, who told him he had invited seven women. Rattray learns that the woman he met, whom he cannot classify as a type, is all seven women.* Comedy in one act, 30 minutes. Interior. 2 m., 3 f., Modern and naval costumes. FRENCH, *50¢. Royalty, $10.00.*

SHALL WE JOIN THE LADIES? J. M. Barrie. *Thirteen well-to-do people attend a dinner-party at which their host unmasks them and implicates them in the murder of his brother at Monte Carlo several years before.* Mystery in 1 act. Interior. 8 m., 8 f. Modern costumes. Absorbing. Plays 45 minutes. FRENCH, *50¢. Royalty, $10.00.*

SHAM. Frank G. Tompkins. *A young couple find a burglar in their home. They have the usual reactions which he forestalls by showing that because of his reputation as a connoisseur, if he did NOT take anything, the neighbors would realize that everything in the apartment was imitation.* Satire. Living-room. 3 m., 1 f. Modern costumes. Excellent plot and characterizations. Plays 25 minutes. BAKER, *50¢. Royalty, $5.00.*

SLAVE WITH TWO FACES, THE. Mary Carolyn Davies. *Life is shown as a slave who will do your bidding if you are not afraid, but becomes a cruel tyrant to all who show fear.* Fantasy. A wood. 4 m., 3 f., extras. Modern and fantastic costumes. Serious fantasy, for advanced amateurs. Plays 30 minutes. FRENCH, *50¢. Royalty, $5.00.*

SLEEPING DOGS. John Kirkpatrick. *A magazine editor takes a nation-wide poll on "Are you happy with your husband?" and gets into trouble with the next-door neighbors.* Comedy. Interior. 2 m., 3 f. Modern costumes. Plays 30 minutes. FRENCH, *50¢. Royalty, $5.00.*

SO WONDERFUL (IN WHITE). M. Richard Nusbaum. *Margaret Shipman, a nurse in training in a metropolitan hospital, brings to her calling bright hope and idealism. The many heartbreaks and conflicts between personal interest and duty make this good drama.* Drama. Interior, in hospital. 9 f. Hospital costumes. Plays 30 minutes. FRENCH, 50¢. *Royalty,* $5.00.

SORRY, WRONG NUMBER. Lucille Fletcher. *A mystery thriller, the tale of a neurotic invalid, whose only contact with the outside world is her phone.* Drama. Interior. 3 m., 4 f. (1 woman commands the stage throughout). Modern costumes. Plays 30 minutes. DRAMATISTS PLAY SERVICE, $1.00. *Royalty,* $10.00.

SPARKIN'. E. P. Conkle. *Orry, a timid young man, comes to a farm kitchen to woo Lillie, but his shyness almost defeats him. Granny intercedes for him after many hilarious episodes occur.* Folk comedy. Interior. 1 m., 3 f. Modern costumes. Plays 25 minutes. FRENCH, 50¢. *Royalty,* $5.00.

SPREADING THE NEWS. Lady Gregory. *An innocent argument between two men grows, through gossip, into a story of murder and infidelity. When the "murdered" man appears, the gossips are confounded.* Comedy. Outskirts of a fair. 7 m., 3 f. Irish peasant costumes. Easy to do and always popular. Plays 25 minutes. FRENCH, 50¢. *Royalty,* $5.00.

STILL ALARM, THE. George S. Kaufman. *Two actors are trapped in a hotel room when a fire breaks out. They ignore it in the best drawing-room manner and go placidly about their work. Two firemen enter, one with a violin case. The musical firefighter cannot find any time to practice and so takes this opportunity. While the hotel burns, he calmly goes into "Keep the Home Fires Burning."* Satirical comedy. Interior. 5 m. Modern and firemen's costumes. Plays 15 minutes. FRENCH, 50¢. *Royalty,* $5.00.

STRANGEST FEELING, THE. John Kirkpatrick. *Father hears a great deal from his wife and two daughters about intuition. After a humorous adventure with a dancing teacher, the daughters return. The younger one, using her intuition, finds her way out of a dilemma.* Comedy. Interior. 2 m., 4 f. Modern costumes. Plays 35 minutes. FRENCH, 50¢. *Royalty,* $5.00.

SUBMERGED. H. Stuart Cottman & LeVergne Shaw. *An officer and five men are trapped at the bottom of the ocean in a submarine, and one man must sacrifice his life to attract the notice of searching parties.* Tragedy. 1 interior. 6 m. Naval costumes. Plays 25 minutes. Row, PETERSON, 50¢. *Royality,* $5.00.

SUBWAY CIRCUS. William Saroyan. *A series of sketches unified in mood, dramatizing the dreams of ordinary people riding on a subway train.* Fantasy. Simple sets. Flexible cast of men and women. Modern costumes. Plays 45 minutes. FRENCH, 50¢. *Royalty,* $10.00.

SUGAR AND SPICE. Florence Ryerson & Colin Clements. *When a girl friend straight from France steals Jane's boy friend, she learns that more flies are caught with sugar than vinegar.* Comedy. Interior. 2 m., 3 f. Modern costumes. Plays 40 minutes. FRENCH, 50¢. *Royalty,* $5.00.

SUPPRESSED DESIRES. George Cook & Susan Glaspell. *Henrietta's obsession with psychoanalysis leads to a weird interpretation of a dream, and nearly to a divorce before the absurdity is realized.* Satire. Studio apartment. 1 m., 2 f. Modern costumes. A very amusing and effective travesty on misapplied Freudian psychology. Plays 40 minutes. BAKER, 50¢. *Royalty,* $10.00.

TEA-POT ON THE ROCKS, THE. John Kirkpatrick. *A young lady puts her career of running a tearoom ahead of marriage, thus making her boy friend hope and pray for the tearoom to fail. He has his chance to make it fail, but his good sportsmanship saves the day.* Comedy. Interior.

3 m., 3 f. Modern costumes. Plays 40 minutes. FRENCH, 50¢. Royalty, $5.00.

TERRIBLE MEEK, THE. Charles Rann Kennedy. *The revelation in dramatic form of the effect of the Crucifixion on a Roman captain, a soldier, and an Unknown Woman.* Religious drama. Exterior. Roman costumes. 2 m., 1 f. Plays 50 minutes. FRENCH, 50¢. No royalty.

THIS PROPERTY IS CONDEMNED. Tennessee Williams. Dramatic dialogue. Exterior. 1 boy, 1 girl. Modern costumes. Plays 30 minutes. *Royalty, $10.00 to* DRAMATISTS PLAY SERVICE.

TRAVELLERS, THE. Booth Tarkington. *An American family, travelling in Sicily, spends a terrifying night in an apparently mysterious hotel. Morning brings the logical explanation that sinister remarks were only Sicilian pleasantries.* Farce. Hotel bedroom. 7 m., 4 f. Modern costumes. Excellent play, easy to produce. Plays 35 minutes. FRENCH, 50¢. Royalty, $10.00.

TRIFLES. Susan Glaspell. *The wife of a strangled farmer is under arrest on suspicion. While officers and neighbors are searching the old farmhouse for evidence, two women friends discover a slain canary and a broken cage, evidences of the husband's unremitting cruelty and clues by which she can be proven guilty.* Drama. Kitchen. 3 m., 2 f. Rural costumes. Unusually powerful and effective; needs two good actresses. Plays 40 minutes. BAKER, 50¢. Royalty, $10.00.

TRYSTING PLACE, THE. Booth Tarkington. *Four couples simultaneously carry on a rendezvous in the same hotel lounge, but the situation is humorously complicated before each man meets his proper partner.* Comedy. Lounge of a summer hotel. 4 m., 3 f. Modern costumes. Excellent farce with clever dialogue. Plays 45 minutes. *Royalty, $10.00 to* BAKER.

TWELVE-POUND LOOK, THE. J. M. Barrie. *The typist Sir Harry Simms hires to answer the congratulatory messages on his knighthood turns out to be his former wife, Kate.* Comedy. Interior. 2 m., 2 f. Modern costumes. 30 minutes. FRENCH, 50¢. Royalty, $10.00.

TWILIGHT SAINT, THE. Stark Young. *St. Francis of Assisi shows young Guido, the poet, that simple love and sacrifice are better than fame.* Poetic drama. Simple room. 2 m., 2 f. Costumes, 13th century. Beautiful poetic incident treated with artistic skill. Only for advanced players. Plays 25 minutes. FRENCH, 50¢. Royalty, $5.00.

TWO CROOKS AND A LADY. Eugene Pillot. *A crippled old lady, unable to move from her chair, outwits two crooks, one of whom is her maid, and saves her pearls.* Melodrama. Library. 3 m., 3 f. Modern costumes. Exceptionally clever, easy to produce. Plays 30 minutes. FRENCH, 50¢. Royalty, $10.00.

TWO SLATTERNS AND A KING. Edna St. Vincent Millay. *The king who vows to marry the tidiest maid in his kingdom, by chance happens upon Tidy when for once she is slovenly and upon Slut when she is tidy. He marries Slut and discovers his mistake too late.* Fantasy. Drapes. 2 m., 2 f. Imaginative costumes. Amusing if properly produced. Opportunity for interesting staging. Plays 10 minutes. *Royalty, $10.00 to* BAKER.

VALIANT, THE. Holworthy Hall & Robert Middlemass. *A young murderer conceals his identity, even from the long-unseen sister who has come to see if he is her brother, and goes bravely to his death, allowing his family to think he died nobly in France.* Drama. Warden's office. 5 m., 1 f. Modern costumes. Powerful, impressive, and fine. Plays 25 minutes. LONGMANS, GREEN, 65¢. Royalty, $10.00.

WAYS AND MEANS. Noel Coward. *In a bedroom in Mrs. Lloyd Ransome's fabulous Villa Zephyre on the fashionable Côte d'Azur are heiress Stella Cartright and her gambling husband, Tony. They are broke although for a time it appears that they may split the proceeds of a robbery by a chauffeur. He, in turn, robs them and thus saves their honor.* Comedy. Interior of hotel bedroom on French Côte d'Azur. 5 m., 4 f. Modern costumes. Plays 40 minutes. FRENCH, 50¢. Royalty on application.

WEAK SPOT, THE. George Kelly. *Husband and wife are quarreling. She spills salt and predicts bad news. He laughs it off. Jenny, a pedlar woman, tells the wife's fortune and predicts that there will be news of the husband's death from heart trouble. A message comes from a hospital saying that a friend who borrowed Mr. West's raincoat has died. Mr. West is won over to superstition. He spills the salt and dashes it over his left shoulder.* Comedy. Interior. 1 m., 2 f. Modern costumes. Plays 25 minutes. FRENCH, 50¢. Royalty, $10.00.

WEDDING, A. John Kirkpatrick. *A bridegroom is looking for his collar button. The best man complains because the bride's aunt is trying to run things. Mishaps and misunderstandings occur and the wedding almost doesn't take place; but the bride and groom are reconciled in time.* Comedy. Interior. Modern costumes. 4 m., 3 f. Plays 35 minutes. FRENCH, 50¢. Royalty, $5.00.

WEDDING PRESENT, THE. William Carson. *A couple of honeymooners make frantic efforts to remember which of their wedding presents was the gift of the friend who is coming to visit them, but are saved by the fact that he, too, has forgotten.* Comedy. Living-room. 2 m., 1 f. Modern

costumes. Light, amusing, and easy to produce. Plays 25 minutes. BAKER, 50¢. *Royalty free with purchase of three copies.*

WHAT NEVER DIES. Percival Wilde. *Two charwomen aid a third whose son gambles away her money.* Drama. Interior. 1 m., 3 f. Modern costumes. Plays 40 minutes. BAKER, 50¢. Royalty, $10.00.

WHEN THE WHIRLWIND BLOWS. Essex Dane. *An aristocratic woman, delivering a list of suspected workmen's names to the government, exposes her former maid as the murderess of a peasant's son.* Drama. Rough room. 3 f. Costumes of Russian Revolution. Excellent, easy to stage. Plays 30 minutes. BAKER, 50¢. Royalty, $5.00.

WHERE THE CROSS IS MADE. Eugene O'Neill. *An old sea captain, who has years before committed a crime in connection with a treasure hunt, is seen going mad when shadows from the past come to haunt him.* Drama. Interior. 6 m., 1 f. Modern costumes. Plays 40 minutes. *Royalty, $5.00 to* DRAMATISTS PLAY SERVICE.

WHITE IRIS. Roberta Shannon. *A study of contrast between the personality of a sister who has everything and that of a sister who has nothing.* Drama. Interior of 1894. 4 f. Costumes, 19th century. Plays 30 minutes. BAKER, $1.00. Royalty, $5.00.

WHY THE CHIMES RANG. Elizabeth McFadden. *The divine beauty of charity.* Fantasy. 3 m., 1 f., extras. Imaginative costumes. Plays 40 minutes. FRENCH, 50¢. Royalty, $5.00.

WILL, THE. James M. Barrie. *Mr. and Mrs. Ross, young lovers, make their tiny bequests. Mr. Ross, the magnate, disagrees with his imperious wife years later over the changes; and lastly, Sir Philip Ross, bereft of heirs, realizes too late what his greed has* *cost.* Drama in 3 scenes. Lawyer's office, in 3 different years. 4 m., 1 f. Modern costumes. A fine serious little play, with difficult characterizations. Excellent for advanced amateurs. Plays 30 minutes. BAKER, 50¢. *Royalty, $10.00.*

WILL O' THE WISP. Doris F. Halman. *A waif is befriended by a country woman who used to house a poet in the summer. The poet's wife, a worldly woman, comes for a stay, reveals that she has prevented the poet's writing, and causes the waif to lead the poet's wife to death in the sea.* Fantasy. Farmhouse interior. 4 f. Modern costumes. Poetic quality; dramatic, effective, difficult. Plays 25 minutes. BAKER, 50¢. *Royalty, $10.00 if admission is charged; $5.00 if none is charged.*

WOMAN'S PRIVILEGE, A. Marrijane & Joseph Hayes. *When the woman of the house begins to see a psychiatrist, she almost breaks up her marriage.* Comedy. Interior. 2 m., 2 f. Modern costumes. Plays 35 minutes. FRENCH, 50¢. *Royalty, $5.00.*

WONDER HAT, THE. Kenneth Sawyer Goodman & Ben Hecht. *An old huckster sells a wonder hat to Harlequin, which makes him invisible, and thus causes unexpected complication in his affair with Columbine, who has bought a slipper with mysterious powers from the same source.* Comedy. A formal garden. 3 m., 2 f. Imaginative costumes. An unusual and satiric Harlequinade, which may be made amusing. Plays 30 minutes. FRENCH, 50¢. *Royalty, $10.00 if admission is charged; $5.00 if no admission is charged.*

WORKHOUSE WARD, THE. Lady Gregory. *Two men in a workhouse ward quarrel all the time. The sister of one comes to take him away but he refuses to leave without his mate. She goes in disgust and they continue their happy quarrel.* Comedy. Workhouse ward. 2 m., 1 f. Irish costumes.

Lively and amusing. Easy except for Irish dialect. Plays 15 minutes. FRENCH, 50¢. *Royalty, $5.00.*

WURZEL-FLUMMERY. A. A. Milne. *Meriton, a leading Liberal politician, jeers at Crashaw, the leading Conservative and the father of the girl he loves, because, to gain a rich legacy, he contemplates changing his name to "Wurzel-Flummery." Meriton changes his manner and his mind when the same offer is made to him.* Comedy. Interior. 3 m., 2 f. Modern costumes. Plays 30 minutes. FRENCH, 50¢. *Royalty, $10.00. Also in 2-act form for 4 m., 3 f. Same cost and royalty.*

YES MEANS NO. Howard Emmett Rogers (added dialogue by Helen & Nolan Leary). *Dad promises Ted $100 every time he says "No" during lunch hour, to teach him to be less easy with giving credit to customers. Ted nearly ruins Dad's business by overeagerness to say "No."* Farce. 1 interior. 3 m., 2 f. Modern costumes. DRAMATISTS PLAY SERVICE, 40¢. *Royalty, $5.00.*

YOUTH MUST BE SERVED. Harriet Ford. *Silas Holt, a stubborn farmer, is determined that his son shall become a farmer, but his son's sweetheart and mother, by pretending horror and fear, arrange things so that he shall be an airman.* Comedy. Farm living-room. 3 m., 2 f. Rural costumes. Amusing, suitable for high school or college. Plays 20 minutes. *Royalty, $5.00 to* FRENCH.

ZONE POLICE, THE. Richard Harding Davis. *By a clever trick, Lieutenant Standish of the Zone Police forces Major Aintree to swear off drinking by making him believe he has shot a man during one of his drunken rages.* Drama. Military headquarters. 4 m. Military costumes. Easy to produce. Very good for men. Plays 30 minutes. FRENCH, 50¢. *Royalty, $5.00.*

PART III

Television Plays

NOTE: Television plays are usually designed to fit, with commercials and announcements, into time slots of one hour, a half-hour, or fifteen minutes. Accordingly the indicated length of the plays below includes the entire program. A one-hour play normally runs about fifty minutes, a half-hour play twenty-four minutes, and a fifteen-minute play about thirteen minutes or less.

SUMMARIES OF PLAYS

ALMANAC OF LIBERTY, AN. Reginald Rose. *John Carter has been beaten by a gang. On the anniversary of the approval of the Bill of Rights by Congress, everyone assembles at the Ridgeville Town Hall at 10:24 for an unknown reason. Out of the silence grows a revelation of antagonism toward Carter, who had said some unpopular things. Some come to Carter's support, and all realize they have violated the Bill of Rights.* Documentary. Interior Town Hall, street corner. 15 m., 7 f., 1 boy, 1 girl, extras. Modern costumes. One hour.

BACHELOR PARTY, THE. Paddy Chayefsky. *Charley, with his wife pregnant, is bored. A bachelor party for a groom in his office provides the illusion of freedom. But the married men become more bored than ever by the monotony of bar after bar, the fascinating bachelor seems hectic,* and the groom becomes so drunk he almost calls off his wedding. Charlie is glad to come home. Drama. One-and-a-half room apartment, apartment kitchen, interior of subway car, office, interior of restaurant, phone booth, bar, Village night club, 8th Ave. bar, 7 m., 4 f. Modern costumes. One hour.

BIG DEAL, THE. Paddy Chayefsky. *Joe Manx, once a successful builder, lives on dreams of recouping his fortune. He tries to borrow $4000 to buy marshland to build houses, but no-nobody will lend it to him. Harry Gerber offers him a job as building inspector at $3600 per year, and he rejects it. Joe asks his daughter to lend him the $5000 which she had inherited and on which she expects to marry a doctor who has not finished his education. When she agrees, Joe crumples and decides to take the job.* Drama. Interior restaurant, interior another restaurant, apartment hall-way, Manx's living room, bedroom, and dining-room, interior of construction shack, Gerber's living-room, daughter's bedroom. 9 m., 2 f. Modern costumes. Moving, with excellent characterizations and surprise ending. One hour.

BILLY ADAMS, AMERICAN. Theodore W. Case. *Krueger, a German, who has a serious heart condition wants his son Willi to have the advantages of America. He teaches Willi perfect colloquial English, and they stow away on a ship. In New York both are caught, but Krueger has a fatal heart attack and a reporter, inspired by the father's faith, guarantees the publicity which will secure an act of Congress to admit Billy.* Drama. Hamburg park, Krueger's living-room, pier, sickbay on the ship, the ship's deck, immigration office. 10 m., 3 f., 1 boy. Modern costumes. Powerful. Half-hour.

CRIME IN THE STREETS. Reginald Rose. *Frankie is the leader of a gang of toughs. His father had abandoned the family, his mother works hard, and his little brother Richie gets all the attention. Ben, a social worker, tries to gain their confidence. The gang plans to kill McAllister, who informed on a member. Ben tells Frankie he needs love. At the moment of the "killing," Richie intervenes, and Frankie's tough front breaks.* Drama. Fire escape, Frankie's apartment, Baby's store, the street, the alley. 4 m., 1 f., 7 boys. Modern costumes. Tense, but in excellent taste. One hour.

DANCERS, THE. Horton Foote. *Horace comes to visit his sister who is determined to make a success of him. However, he does not dance well. He is repulsed by Emily, but makes a friend of Mary Catherine, and they give each other the confidence necessary to become accomplished dancers.* Comedy. Drug store, the Stanley living-room, the Crawford living-room, Mary Catherine's cottage and yard. 3 m., 7 f. Modern costumes. Sensitive picture of teen-age loneliness. One hour. *For amateur rights, apply to* DRAMATISTS PLAY SERVICE. *For all other rights, apply to* LUCY KROLL AGENCY, 119 W. 57th St., New York, 19.

DANIEL WEBSTER. Hector Chevigny. *Daniel Webster, abetted by his wife, is anxious for the Presidency. However, he goes to England to see about a vital treaty at convention time, and Harrison and Tyler are nominated. Harrison dies and Tyler, vetoing the Bank Bill, is read out of the party. The cabinet, except for Webster, resigns. Webster sacrifices himself for the treaty, losing financial backing and his chance for the Presidency.* Drama. Webster's dining-room, Clay's Senate office, Webster's library, a ship's cabin, Inauguration, the President's office, Caroline's bedroom. 11 m., 1 f. Costumes of 1840's. One hour. *All rights reserved by the author.*

DEATH OF THE OLD MAN, THE. Horton Foote. *The Old Man is dying. After helping everyone, he has nothing to leave his spinster daughter Rosa and an old Negro servant. He lies powerless as he watches how his sons try to evade responsibility, but is gratified to see Cousin Lyd offer his daughter and servant a home.* Drama. Bedroom. 4 m., 3 f. 19th-century costumes. Half-hour. Beautiful pathos. *For amateur performance, apply to* DRAMATISTS PLAY SERVICE. *For all other rights, apply to* LUCY KROLL AGENCY, 119 W. 57th St., New York 19.

ERNIE BARGER IS FIFTY. Tad Mosel. *Ernie Barger leaves his ailing wife alone to go to his son's graduation. His son shows he no longer needs him, and goes off to be married. His business partner tells him he has not kept up to date, and approves designs without him. He breaks down, to find solace in his* *wife's love.* Drama. Office interior, Barger bedroom, outside college building, "The Central" Bar, Barger living-room. 7 m., 2 f. Modern costumes. Effective. One hour. *All rights reserved by the author.*

HAVEN, THE. Tad Mosel. *Howie is restless about his family life, and tries to break the monotony by selling his lakeside summer cabin at the lake. He is unsuccessful, and his wife promises him to change her ways if they can return there. When they arrive, she finds the cabin cleaner than she left it, and other evidence tells her Howie had been there that winter with another woman. Howie tells her that the woman killed herself because he still loved his wife. They are reconciled.* Drama. Living-room of town house, exterior of cottage, interior of cottage. 3 m., 1 f., 1 boy, 1 girl. Modern costumes. Excellent characterizations, and good suspense. One hour.

HOLIDAY SONG. Paddy Chayefsky. *A Jewish cantor, oppressed by the evils of the world, loses faith in God. His friends send him to see Rabbi Marcus. Both times he is put on the wrong subway train by a mysterious guard. First he meets a despairing Dutch girl, and the second time he meets her lost husband. He reunites them. Thus he finds renewed faith and a husband for his unwed niece.* Comedy-drama. Living-room, bedroom, subway platform, interior of subway car, hallway, girl's room, Rabbi's study, synagogue corridor, synagogue interior. 7 m., 4 f. Rabbi's and modern costumes. Moving. Excellent characterizations and dialogue. One hour.

IMPERSONATION. Anne Howard Bailey. *Pete, who has fled the prison farm, leaps aboard a streamlined train, only to be convinced by a lovely girl that it is better to face the music and then make his own opportunities. She is handcuffed, a smuggler.* Comedy. Side of brick warehouse, rear platform of a streamlined train, interior of club car, interior of roomette. 4 m., 1 f., and other passengers. Modern costumes. 15 minutes.

INN, THE. Roger Garis. *Bill Guernsey stops for the night at an inn at Hormuth. He is mistaken for Bassick, who escaped a lynching for killing Chester's sister four years before. He is beaten, thrown into jail. Only Marcia, niece of the innkeeper, believes in him. When the mob again storms the jail, Bill refuses to run, but faces them, wins a ten-minute delay, and breaks Chester down so that he confesses he killed his sister because she disgraced the family.* Drama. Highway sign, exterior of inn, lobby of inn, small bedroom, garage, taxi office, drugstore fountain, jail cell, exterior of jail. 14 m., 3 f., and men in the mob. Prison garb and modern costumes. One hour. Tense.

MAN ON THE MOUNTAINTOP. Robert Alan Aurthur. *A child prodigy who felt like a freak is reclaimed by a girl who has patience and loves him, although she cannot secure reconciliation with his father, who never forgave him for the death of his mother in childbirth.* Drama. Horace's bedroom, Blake's living-room, hall, cafeteria, back row in a movie theatre. 5 m., 2 f. Modern costumes. One hour. *All rights reserved by the author.*

MARTY. Paddy Chayefsky. *Marty, a butcher, 36, is lonely and unmarried, though everyone plagues him to get married. His cousins ask his mother to take his aunt, with whom they cannot get along, into his house, and she agrees. They suggest Marty go to the Waverly Ballroom where he meets a plain girl. They like each other and, despite his aunt's and mother's selfish fears and his friends' disapproval, Marty decides to marry her.* Drama. Butcher shop, Marty's dining-room, kitchen, living-room, and bedroom, Waverly Ballroom, fire escape, foyer and living-room of Virginia's apartment, exterior of church. 7 m., 7 f. Butcher uniform and modern costumes. Moving, with excellent characterizations. One hour.

MIDNIGHT CALLER, THE. Horton Foote. *Helen Crews and Harvey Weems had been in love, but their mothers prevented their marriage. Harvey took to drink and Helen moved into Mrs. Crawford's boarding house. Mr. Johnson is the lone male there, and he and Helen are attracted to each other. Harvey, drunk, comes repeatedly at night, calling Helen, and she cannot calm him. Eventually she goes off to marry Mr. Johnson, and Harvey is put into jail.* Drama. Crawford living-room, Helen's room, front porch of the house. 2 m., 5 f. Modern costumes. One hour. *For all rights, apply to* LUCY KROLL AGENCY, 119 W. 57th St., New York 19.

MOTHER, THE. Paddy Chayefsky. *An elderly mother, who had lost her husband a month before, is desperate for something to do. Her daughter wants to take her into her home and prevent the mother from working because she is not well, but the mother persists, although she loses every job she gets.* Drama. Mother's living-room, daughter's bedroom, mother's kitchen, park bench, factory, factory office, daughter's hallway, interior of subway car, child's bedroom. 2 m., 8 f. Modern costumes. One hour. Sympathetic treatment of the problems of the aged, with excellent dialogue.

MY LOST SAINTS. Tad Mosel. *Kate has been a happy maid to the Hallets for eighteen years, idolizing them. Her mother loses her farm and stops in to see her on her way to Minneapolis. She falls and stays in bed unnecessarily for weeks, trying to get Kate to go with her and disorganizing the house. Eventually Mr. Hallet objects. When Mama gets Kate to agree to leave with her, she gets "well" in ten minutes. Kate is disil-* *lusioned, sends Mama to Minneapolis, and stays with the Hallets.* Drama. Kitchen, Hallets' bedroom, living-room, Kate's bedroom, dining-room. 1 m., 3 f., 1 girl. Modern costumes. One hour. Sensitive character portrayal.

ONE IN TWELVE. John Latham. *Bert Lewis was foreman of a jury which decided the accused was guilty of murder. One juror says there was undue pressure which forced him to change his dissenting vote. It is grounds for a new trial. The play shows how jurors are selected, the problems jurors face in the jury room, and highlights democratic responsibility.* Documentary. Courtroom, cleaning and dyeing store, county clerk's office, jury room. 4 m., 2 f., and other jurors. Modern costumes. Half-hour.

OTHER PEOPLE'S HOUSES. Tad Mosel. *Dad is senile and causes Rena and Ralph so much trouble they decide to ask Rena's sister Inez to put him in an old people's home. Inez objects, but cannot bring about a solution, so that she, who never intended to do anything to hurt anyone, must be unkind to her own father. After she takes him to the home, she notices that Rena has grown in independence and industry.* Drama. Porch of a small house, living-room, dining-room, kitchen, interior of a bus terminal. 3 m., 2 f. Modern costumes. One hour. *All rights reserved by the author.*

PRINTER'S MEASURE. Paddy Chayefsky. *Mr. Healy takes pride in his craft of hand-setting type and tries to inspire a boy in his shop. When the boss brings in a linotype machine, Healy is afraid of being fired and attempts to smash the machine. The boy, whose father has just died, decides there is more of a future in learning linotype operation. Healy retires.* Drama. Exterior of print shop, interior of print shop, cafeteria, bar, Healy's living-room, boy's living-room, printers' union headquarters, Healy's bedroom. 11 m., 6 f., 3 boys, 1 girl. Modern costumes.

REMARKABLE INCIDENT AT CARSON CORNERS, THE. Reginald Rose. *The children put Mr. Kovalsky, the janitor of their school, on trial for the murder of a boy who fell to his death when the fire escape railing gave way. Eventually, the entire town is proved to be responsible.* Drama. Exterior of school, schoolroom, fire escape, cellar and basement workshop, living-room, interior of drugstore. 8 m., 6 f., 6 boys, 2 girls. Modern costumes. Remarkable suspense; good for adult or high school performance. One hour.

SHE WALKS IN BEAUTY. James Truex. *Prim Miss Ingersoll reports a student, Hawkins, to the principal for writing a love poem to Miss Riley. The principal has done the same thing. But Miss Riley is going to marry the chemistry teacher and retire.* Comedy. Principal's office. 1 m., 2 f., 1 boy. Modern costumes. Fifteen-minute program. *For permission apply to* BLANCHE GAINES, 350 W. 57th St., New York, 16.

STAR IN THE SUMMER NIGHT. Tad Mosel. *Miss Girard, 68, once a star of musical comedy, loses her job and tries to secure friends by giving away her possessions. She has no money and her friend and maid leave her. When she is near the breaking point, she tells a policeman she still has her last job. He takes her there and she is reinstated at half salary and under humiliating conditions.* Drama. Nightclub, alley behind the club, delicatessen, Miss Girard's living room and bedroom. 9 m., 4 f. Modern costumes. Effective. *All rights reserved by the author.*

STAR-MINDED. Kenneth T. Parker. *Mrs. Benton neglects her husband while she is president of the Glenn Sherman Fan Club. In desperation, Mr. Benton goes to see a columnist, who promises to cure Mrs. Benton by arranging for her to have dinner with the movie idol. When Mr. Benton encourages his wife, she becomes ashamed and gives up both the dinner and fan club.* Domestic comedy. Living room, kitchen, small room at newspaper office. 1 m., 3 f., voice. Modern costumes. Plays half an hour. *Amateur royalty, $5.00, payable to* NORTHWESTERN PRESS. *For other rights, apply to* NORTHWESTERN PRESS.

TEARS OF MY SISTER, THE. Horton Foote. *Cecilia is upset by the nightly weeping of her lovely sister. Bessie, 18, is being persuaded by her mother to marry Stacy, 34, who is wealthy, although Bessie loves Syd Davis. Bessie yields to her mother's importunities.* Drama. Porch of an old Victorian house, Bessie and Cecilia's bedroom. 2 m., 4 f. Victorian costumes. Sensitivity redeems a trite plot. Half-hour. For all rights, apply to LUCY KROLL AGENCY, 119 W. 57th St., New York, 19.

THUNDER ON SYCAMORE STREET. Reginald Rose. *All Sycamore St. is incensed when Joe Blake, an ex-convict (he had killed a man in an automobile accident), moves into their street. They march on his house, tell him to get out, and are near a riot. Joe stands up to them and is finally joined by Arthur, who is usually meek. The mob becomes ashamed and disperses.* Drama. Exteriors and foyers and living-rooms of three houses. 6 m., 6 f., 1 boy. Modern costumes. A powerful story of prejudice and mob violence. One hour.

TRIP TO BOUNTIFUL, THE. Horton Foote. *Old Mrs. Watts lives with her browbeaten son and his wife who cares only about Mrs. Watt's pension check. Mrs. Watts wants only to see her old home at Bountiful before she dies. After several vain attempts, she manages to escape pursuit. At Harrison, her son orders her detained by the sheriff, but she is able to persuade* him to take her to Bountiful, where a few minutes gives her the peace she needs. Drama. Apartment living-room, railroad ticket booth, bus station, interior of bus, interior of bus station, front of ramshackle house. 7 m., 3 f. Modern costumes. Pathos, together with sensitive characterizations, makes the play noteworthy. One hour. *For amateur rights, apply to* DRAMATISTS PLAY SERVICE. *For all other rights, apply to* LUCY KROLL AGENCY, 119 W. 57th St., New York 19.

TWELVE ANGRY MEN. Reginald Rose. *All the men in the jury are for the conviction of a man who is the member of a minority group, with one exception. Eventually he is able to interpret the evidence in such a way that he proves the accused is innocent. This, and despite the overwhelming prejudice of some of the jurors, results in exoneration.* Drama. Jury room, jury box. 14 m. Modern costumes. A powerful play, with a great deal of tension, since rewritten for the stage and screen. One hour.

VISIT TO A SMALL PLANET. Gore Vidal. *Kreton, who comes from the future and another planet, lands on earth and secretly assumes power over it. Just as he is about to entertain himself with a war, a compatriot comes to take him back.* Fantasy. Living-room, outside the house, study, bedroom. 8 m., 2 f. Modern costumes. One hour. *All rights reserved by the author.*

WAITING PLACE, THE. Tad Mosel. *A 14-year-old motherless girl, who is enamoured of her father and has a mind filled with adolescent fancies, uses a lonely ravine as her refuge. Her father cannot understand her, misses her mother, but finds himself attracted to the woman who does his housework. To destroy this attachment the girl remains in the ravine a whole evening, and when her father does not come for her, she is forced to see things in their proper perspective and to approve her father's forthcoming marriage.* Drama. Outside the ruin of a brick building in the wooded ravine, farmhouse kitchen, the yard outside the kitchen door. 1 m., 2 f., 1 boy, 1 girl. Modern costumes. One hour. *All rights reserved by the author.*

YOUNG LADY OF PROPERTY, A. Horton Foote. *Wilma, 15, was willed a house orally by her mother. At first Wilma and her friend Arabella want to go to Hollywood, but a visit to her house convinces her that life in it would be preferable. She discovers that her father is going to marry Mrs. Leighton and sell the house. She gets Mrs. Leighton to intervene and becomes reconciled to the marriage. Arabella convinces her that it is not the house which is important, but the life in it.* Drama. Post Office interior and exterior, kitchen, front porch and yard of a Victorian cottage. 3 m., 6 f. One hour. Fine portrait of an adolescent girl. *For amateur rights, consult* DRAMATISTS PLAY SERVICE. *For all other rights, apply to* LUCY KROLL AGENCY, 119 W. 57th St., New York 19.

PART IV

Guidance and Mental Health Plays

WITHIN THE past few years, a number of organizations and publishing firms have made available special dramatic materials for guidance and mental health purposes and programs.

The major object of these plays is to present real-life problems—personal, social, family, school, career, etc.—that will stimulate audience discussion after the performance. Members in the audience can see themselves, their children, or their students, in the play's characters, and through this identification they may be encouraged to present their own views on the problems raised in the play or in the discussion. By sharing ideas with others, seeing how others react to these problems, they may gain insight into their own problems and acquire a greater understanding of how to help others to work out their problems in a satisfactory manner.

Although the plays are under different classifications, mental health plays, socio-guidramas, and guidance plays, there are several common characteristics for all:

1. Each play is intended to provoke a discussion, and, therefore, a discussion period should follow the presentation. The discussion leader should be guidance-mental health oriented and be familiar with the techniques for effective group discussion procedures.

2. For each play there is a discussion guide available to suggest possible ideas for the leader.

3. Producing these particular plays is relatively simple. No scenery is required for presentation. A stage manager can come before the audience to describe the settings and time sequences in the play. No difficult costumes —all modern dress—and a minimum of properties simplify production demands.

4. The play can be presented in a rather small area, either on a stage or in a classroom.

5. Each play lends itself to a reading, although this is less effective than the actual presentation.

6. The plays would be of interest to parents, teachers, students, but care should be taken in the selection of an appropriate play for a given audience. Since the plays are based on problem themes, one should choose a play based on a problem of interest and concern within that community.

7. All of the plays have been presented before a large number of audiences with a high degree of success.

The major firms that are now making this material available are: (1) The NATIONAL ASSOCIATION FOR MENTAL HEALTH, 10 Columbus Circle, New York 19, New York, and MENTAL HEALTH MATERIALS CENTER, 1790 Broadway, New York 19, New York, distributors of the plays for mental health education, written by Norah Stirling, and produced by the American Theatre Wing Community Plays; (2) OCCU-PRESS, 489 Fifth Avenue, New York 17, New York, publishers of socio-guidramas, edited by Dr. Sarah Splaver; (3) WHITESIDE, Inc., 425 Fourth Avenue, New York 16, New York, publishers of the guidance plays by Dr. M. Jerry Weiss.

PLAYS FOR MENTAL HEALTH EDUCATION:
SUMMARIES

AND YOU NEVER KNOW. Norah Stirling. *A series of minor crises arising from a 12-year-old's jealousy of her sister. Mother, father and a daughter gain a clearer understanding of their feelings about one another by talking them over openly for the first time.* Living-room. 1 m., 2 f. Plays 30 minutes. Modern costumes. *Producing packet, $4.50 (includes a discussion guide by Dr. Nina Ridenour). Single script copy for review, $1.00. Royalty on application to* AMERICAN THEATRE WING, INC.

CASE OF THE MISSING HANDSHAKE, THE. Norah Stirling. *Valerie, a 10-year-old, is rude and impetuous around the house, and well-mannered and considerate outside. She presents a problem to her parents when the camp counselor comes to the house to interview the parents*

and child. Living-room. 1 m., 3 f. Modern costumes. Plays 30 minutes. *Producing packet, $4.50 (includes a discussion guide by Dr. Nina Ridenour). Single script copy, $1.00. Royalty, on application to* AMERICAN THEATRE WING, INC.

FRESH, VARIABLE WINDS. Norah Stirling. *Tucky Simmons, age 10, gets into trouble with an older group because his father has not given him the attention he needs.* Living-room. 2 m., 3 f. Plays 30 minutes. Modern costumes. *Producing packet, $4.50 (includes a discussion guide by Lawrence K. Frank). Single script copy for review, $1.00. Royalty on application to* AMERICAN THEATRE WING, INC.

HIGH PRESSURE AREA. Norah Stirling. *Sally Wickham and her friend decide to go to a party out at a road-*

house with some older men. Sally's parents object to her going out with men, and, because of their attitude, Sally decides, her girl friend also, not to go to the roadhouse with the men. Living-room. 1 m. 3 f. Modern costumes. Plays 30 minutes. *Producing packet, $4.50* (includes a discussion guide by Lawrence K. Frank). *Single script copy, $1.00. Royalty on application to* AMERICAN THEATRE WING, INC.

INS AND OUTS, THE. Norah Stirling. *Action centers around an incident in the lives of five boys and girls in high school involving the "ins" (those who belong to a group) with an "out" (who tries to belong but is excluded).* Interior. 3 m., 2 f. Modern costumes. Plays 20 minutes. *Producing packet, $2.00* (includes a discussion guide by Lawrence K. Frank). *Single script copy for review, $1.00. Royalty on application to* AMERICAN THEATRE WING, INC.

RANDOM TARGET. Norah Stirling. *Nick Stewart, age 11, is the cause of concern to his parents because he, to them for no reason at all, damaged a smaller child's bike and beat the child up. Action centers around a crucial moment in the lives of parents who come to realize that their son's aggression results from his buried resentments against them. The play demonstrates that youngsters need to express their feelings of anger and hostility and not run away from them, if they are to develop into mature adults prepared to meet life's challenges.* Living-room. 2 m., 2 f. Modern costumes. Plays 30 minutes. *Producing packet, $5.00* (includes a discussion guide by Dr. Nina Ridenour). *Single script copy for review, $1.00. Royalty on application to* AMERICAN THEATRE WING, INC.

ROOM UPSTAIRS, THE. Norah Stirling. *A daughter's resentment of her mother's forgetfulness, messiness, attitude of "martyrdom" and "living in the past" is effectively portrayed in a* series of household incidents. On the other hand, a grandmother's resentment on being treated like a child and having no place of her own—except "the room upstairs"—is demonstrated with telling effect. The incidents show that old people and young people can live together without friction, given honesty, patience and sympathy on both sides. Living-room. 1 m., 3 f. Modern costumes. Plays 30 minutes. *Producing packet, $5.00* (includes a discussion guide by Dr. Nina Ridenour). *Performing rights in New York City and within a radius of 50 miles reserved for the professional casts of the* AMERICAN THEATRE WING COMMUNITY PLAYS. *Single script copy for review, $1.00. Royalty on application to* AMERICAN THEATRE WING, INC.

SCATTERED SHOWERS. Norah Stirling. *Three mothers are in the park with their children; the play shows how their preschool youngsters act in a crisis when each child has been reared according to a different method of discipline.* A park bench. 3 f. Modern costumes. Plays 30 minutes. *Producing packet, $4.50* (includes a discussion guide by Lawrence K. Frank). *Single script copy for review, $1.00. Royalty on application to* AMERICAN THEATRE WING, INC.

TOMORROW IS A DAY. Norah Stirling. *Irene's 15-year-old daughter, Louise, lacks self-confidence, and Irene becomes concerned about it and talks it over with her neighbor. She recalls troublesome incidents of the past, and realizes how often she and others have acted in a way that disheartened the daughter. The mother determines to use the many tomorrows to balance out the old discouraging experiences with more day-by-day encouragement at home.* Interior. 1 m., 7 f. Modern costumes. Plays 30 minutes. *Producing packet, $5.00* (includes a discussion guide by Dr. Nina Ridenour). *Performing rights in New York City and within* *a radius of 50 miles reserved for the professional casts of the* AMERICAN THEATRE WING COMMUNITY PLAYS. *Single script copy for review, $1.00. Royalty on application to* AMERICAN THEATRE WING, INC.

WHAT DID I DO? Norah Stirling. *Ethel Harris is an extremely conscientious mother. She is pretty much overwhelmed when her husband becomes quite sick and her daughter gets into trouble in an act of vandalism. The play provides provocative material for discussing how parents feel about their influence on their children and how they can achieve a healthy balance in assuming enough, but not too much responsibility for shaping their children's personalities.* Living-room. 3 f. (1 off-stage voice). Modern costumes. Plays 30 minutes. *Producing packet, $5.00* (includes a discussion guide by Dr. Nina Ridenour). *Performing rights in New York City and within a radius of 50 miles reserved for the professional casts of the* AMERICAN THEATRE WING COMMUNITY PLAYS. *Single script copy for review, $1.25. Royalty on application to* AMERICAN THEATRE WING, INC.

SOCIO-GUIDRAMAS: SUMMARIES

"A" IS FOR BROTHER. Sarah Splaver. *Joe, an athletic student, is not spending enough time studying, according to his older brother, Jim, who is a serious student, but not athletic. There is friction in the family because of this.* Guidance counselor's office, dining-room. 4 m. 1 f. Modern costumes. Plays 10 minutes. (Brief discussion guide). OCCU-PRESS, 50¢. *No royalty.*

AFTER HIGH SCHOOL—WHAT? Sarah Splaver. *John's father wants him to go into his business, but John wants to be a teacher. Trouble results, and John's father refuses to pay his way through college.* Guidance counselor's office, living-room. 2 m., 2 f. Modern costumes. Plays 10 minutes. (Brief discussion guide). OCCU-PRESS, 50¢. *No royalty.*

BOTTLE OF TROUBLE. Robert M. Goldenson. *Tom Strand's father finds a half empty bottle of liquor in the car after Tom had the car out, and he becomes upset about it and lectures Tom on the foolishness of drinking just because someone else does.* Guidance counselor's office, dining-room. 4 m., 1 f. Modern costumes. Plays 10 minutes. (Brief discussion guide). OCCU-PRESS, 50¢. *No royalty.*

"BUT DAD, EVERYBODY DRIVES!" Jane Krumacher. *Jerry and his friend want to use Jerry's father's car to go to a high school prom, and his father and mother won't let them use it.* Guidance counselor's office, living-room. 4 m. 1 f. Modern costumes. Plays 10 minutes. (Brief discussion guide). OCCU-PRESS, 50¢. *No royalty.*

CAREER CHOICE—WHEN? William H. Atkins. *Joe, a ninth-grader, does not yet know what he wants to do with his life, and his parents are becoming concerned about it.* Guidance counselor's office, living-room. 3 m., 1 f. Modern costumes. Plays 10 minutes. (Brief discussion guide). OCCU-PRESS, 50¢. *No royalty.*

CONFIDENCE — ZERO. Milton Schwebel. *Martin, because of his mother's demands and bossiness in general, lacks confidence to the extent that he is unable to take part in* *the school debating team.* Guidance counselor's office, living-room. 4 m., 2 f. Modern costumes. Plays 10 minutes. (Brief discussion guide). Occu-Press, 50¢. *No royalty.*

"DO'S" AND "DON'TS" ON DATES. **Robert M. Goldenson.** *Nancy and her friend and two boys are talking about what to do on a date, and Nancy objects to petting as a necessity. Later, when talking to the guidance counselor, she is sorry she spoke up and said what she did.* Guidance counselor's office, booth, next to window, in Sam's Snackery. 2 m., 3 f. Modern costumes. Plays 10 minutes. (Brief discussion guide). Occu-Press, 50¢. *No royalty.*

"EVERY KID'S GOT ONE!" **Sarah Splaver.** *Nickey's parents and his classmate's parents debate on how much to give a child.* Guidance counselor's office, porch of Nickey's home. 4 m., 3 f. Modern costumes. Plays 10 minutes. (Brief discussion guide). Occu-Press, 50¢. *No royalty.*

"GRANNY, THIS ISN'T 1890." **Velma D. Hayden.** *Linda, a high school junior, is going to model an off-the-shoulder evening gown in a fashion show, and Mrs. Lewis, her grandmother, who lives at Linda's house, thinks it is indecent.* Guidance counselor's office, living-room of Linda's home. 1 m., 4 f. Modern costumes. Plays 10 minutes. (Brief discussion guide). Occu-Press, 50¢. *No royalty.*

HIGH SCHOOL WEDDING BELLE. **Sarah Splaver.** *Ronald, 20 years old, and Grace, almost 18, want to get married, and her parents think they are too young.* Guidance counselor's office, living-room. 2 m. 3 f. Modern costumes. Plays 10 minutes. (Brief discussion guide). Occu-Press, 50¢. *No royalty.*

I.Q. HIGH—AMBITION LOW. **Jane Krumacher.** *Mr. and Mrs. Rogers are worried about their son because he has not been getting good grades in school and he does have the ability. Mrs. Rogers goes to the guidance counselor to seek advice.* Guidance counselor's office, living-room. 2 m., 2 f. Modern costumes. Plays 10 minutes. (Brief discussion guide). Occu-Press, 50¢. *No royalty.*

JILL AND PERRY GO MILITARY. **Sarah Splaver.** *Perry Meyers, a high school senior, wants to enlist in the army four months before graduation, and his friends try to dissuade him, but to no avail.* Front entrance to high school building, lowest step of broad stairway leading to front entrance of high school. 5 m., 1 f. Modern costumes. Plays 10 minutes. (Brief discussion guide). Occu-Press, 50¢. *No royalty.*

LATE DATE. Sarah Splaver. *Betty, a high school student, gets into trouble with her father because he thinks she is getting in too late from her dates. Her father makes a scene in front of her and her date.* Guidance counselor's office, hallway of Betty's home. 2 m., 3 f. Modern costumes. Plays 10 minutes. (Brief discussion guide). Occu-Press, 50¢. *No royalty.*

LOOK WHO'S SMOKING! Jane Krumacher. *Chuck Campbell talks his cousin into smoking a cigarette, and just as she is about to light it, her mother, who disapproves of smoking, sees her and scolds her, because of the sociological aspects, rather than the medical aspects.* Guidance counselor's office, front porch of home of Jean's aunt. 2 m., 5 f. Modern costumes. Plays 10 minutes. (Brief discussion guide). Occu-Press, 50¢. *No royalty.*

MA AND SUE ON A JOB INTERVIEW. Sarah Splaver. *When Sue, a high school student, goes to apply for a part-time job, her mother goes along, and as a result she gets the job rather than Sue, much to Sue's dismay.* Guidance counselor's office, kitchen, interviewer's office. 3 m., 3 f.

Modern costumes. Plays 10 minutes. (Brief discussion guide). OCCU-PRESS, 50¢. *No royalty.*

MIKE, THE MECHANIC. Sarah Splaver. *Mike, a person talented mechanically wishes to enter the radio and TV field as a repairman, and his mother strongly objects because of the sociological aspects of being a repairman.* Guidance counselor's office, living-room. 3 m., 1 f. Modern costumes. Plays 10 minutes. (Brief discussion guide). OCCU-PRESS, 50¢. *No royalty.*

PARENTS CAN BE PROBLEMS. Willa Norris & Buford Stefflre. *Bill, a high school junior, wishes to have the family car, and his mother speaks up and says she wants the car to buy a new dress for a party. His father objects to her buying the dress because he is trying to save for Bill's college education. An argument develops, and Bill is put in an awkward position as they try to force him to take sides.* Guidance counselor's office, living-room. 3 m., 1 f. Modern costumes. Plays 10 minutes. (Brief discussion guide). OCCU-PRESS, 50¢. *No royalty.*

SHALL WE GO STEADY? Gertrude Forrester. *Ann and Bob tell Ann's parents that they are going steady, and Mr. Stewart objects. Ann then goes to the guidance counselor and discusses the pros and cons of going steady.* Guidance counselor's office, living-room. 3 m., 4 f. Modern costumes. Plays 10 minutes. (Brief discussion guide). OCCU-PRESS, 50¢. *No royalty.*

TELEPHONITIS. Willa Norris & Buford Stefflre. *Jan, a high school sophomore, monopolizes the telephone to the dissatisfaction of her parents. Her parents crack down and forbid her to use the telephone for one month; Jan complains about this to the guidance counselor.* Guidance counselor's office, living-room. 1 m.,

4 f. Modern costumes. Plays 10 minutes. (Brief discussion guide). OCCU-PRESS, 50¢. *No royalty.*

TIMID TEEN. Willa Norris & Buford Stefflre. *David Sanders, a high school sophomore, is somewhat shy. When he is asked to come to a party, his parents answer for him.* Guidance counselor's office, living-room. 4 m., 1 f. Modern cotumes. Plays 10 minutes. (Brief discussion guide). OCCU-PRESS, 50¢. *No royalty.*

TOO YOUNG TO DATE. Willa Norris & Buford Stefflre. *Kathy, a ninth-grader, turns down a date with a 15-year-old because he is too young, and she accepts a date with a senior. Her parents think he is too old for her and tell him that he can't date her.* Guidance counselor's office, living-room. 4 m., 3 f. Modern costumes. Plays 10 minutes. (Brief discussion guide). OCCU-PRESS, 50¢. *No royalty.*

TRUST—ABSENT. Sara Splaver. *Fred Bailey, a high school student, 15 years old, seeks advice from the guidance counselor about the lack of trust his parents have in him.* Guidance counselor's office, kitchen. 4 m., 2 f. Modern costumes. (Brief discussion guide). Plays 10 minutes. OCCU-PRESS, 50¢. *No royalty.*

WHO'S DELINQUENT? David Goodman. *Tommy Gordon, age 13, is brought into court by a neighbor because he had splashed red paint on her garage. He was provoked by the neighbor. Tommy's father, who has a temper, thinks that Tommy has a temper, and Tommy's mother thinks that Tommy's actions are harmless.* Guidance counselor's office, living-room. 4 m., 1 f. Modern costumes. Plays 10 minutes. (Brief discussion guide). OCCU-PRESS, 50¢. *No royalty.*

YOUR FRIENDS—WHO CHOOSES THEM? Velma D. Hayden. *Brenda Williams, a popular student, has chosen to go to the dance with an*

ambitious and likable mechanic's son. Mrs. Williams wishes that she had chosen to go with a son of wealthy and prominent parents.

Guidance counselor's office, living-room. 2 m., 4 f. Modern costumes. Plays 10 minutes. (Brief discussion guide). OCCU-PRESS, 50¢. *No royalty.*

GUIDANCE PLAYS: SUMMARIES

ACTOR, THE. M. Jerry Weiss. *Fred thinks he has the talent and wants to go on to study acting as a career. Fred's father, opposed to his son's vocational choice, forces him to switch to a course in business. Fred fails because of his disinterest in this vocational area.* Living-room. 2 m., 3 f. Modern costumes. Plays 30 minutes. *No royalty.*

DEBBY'S DILEMMA. M. Jerry Weiss. *Debby, an overprotected child, goes away from home to attend college. There she faces the problem of social adjustment away from Mother.* Dean's office, dormitory room, campus bench. 2 m., 5 f. Modern costumes. Plays 30 minutes. *No royalty.*

GREETINGS FROM . . . M. Jerry Weiss. *Many of Fred's friends have decided to quit high school and enlist in the armed services. Fred wants to join them. His parents are opposed.* Kitchen, two tables in a drug store, living-room. 6 m., 4 f. Modern costumes. Plays 35 minutes. *No royalty.*

HER BIG CRUSH. M. Jerry Weiss. *Ann, a 15-year-old, tells her parents that she is going to go steady with*

Jim Mandell, a new boy in town, who kept her out too late once before. Ann uses the excuse, "Anybody who is ANY BODY goes steady!" Living-room. 3 m., 3 f. Modern costumes. Plays 30 minutes. *No royalty.*

MONEY TALKS. M. Jerry Weiss. *Nick is not happy in having to ask his mother or sister for spending money, particularly when it comes to having enough cash on hand to date Ann. Too, several of his friends have quit school and been able to get jobs. Nick can't find a part-time job, and although his mother is totally against the idea, Nick decides to quit school one year before graduation.* Outside school building, two tables in drug store, kitchen. 5 m., 4 f. Modern costumes. Plays 30 minutes. *No royalty.*

PARENTS ARE PEOPLE. M. Jerry Weiss. *When Carol, the baby-sitter for the evening, accepts a last-minute date, and decides to leave two young boys alone for "just a little while," and trouble ensues, her parents begin to wonder what they have done in raising Carol to cause her to "neglect her responsibilities."* Living-room. 4 m., 3 f. Modern costumes. Plays 30 minutes. *No royalty.*

PART V

Anthologies
of Long and Short Plays

NOTE: The numbers of the anthologies below are for cross-reference from the Index of Plays. No price has been indicated because some of the books listed are out of print and the prices on many others change rapidly. The Committee thought it best to have readers direct their inquiries directly to the publishers for the availability and prices of these books. Most of the out-of-print books will be found in school, college, and public libraries; or can be readily obtained from the larger out-of-print bookstores.

1. ADAMS, John Quincy, *Chief Pre-Shakespearean Dramas* (Houghton Mifflin, 1924).

The Wordless Alleluia Sequence, The Quem-Quaeritis Trope, The Easter Sepulchre, Semi-Dramatic Trope, Sepulchrum (The Visit of the Marys), Sepulchrum (The Visit of the Marys, & the Race of Peter & John), Sepulchrum (The Visit of the Marys, The Race of Peter & John, & The Appearance to Mary Magdalene), Peregrini, Pastores, Magi, Herodes, Prophetae, Conversio Beati Pauli Apostoli, Ludus Super Iconia Sancti Nicolai, Tres Clerici Adeodatus, The Sepulchre, The Wayfarers, The Shepherds Banns (N. Towne), The Fall of Lucifer, The Creation of Eve, with the Expelling of Adam and Eve out of Paradise. The Killing of Abel, Noah, The Deluge, The Sacrifice of Isaac, Pharaoh, The Prophets, The Salutation and Conception, The Birth of Jesus, The Shepherds, The Magi, Herod, and the Slaughter of the Innocents, Christ's Ministry, The Betraying of Christ. The Trial of Christ, The Harrowing of Hell, The Resurrection of Christ, The Judgment Day, Dux Moraud, The Conversion of St. Paul, Mary Magdalene, The Play of the Sacrament, The Castle of Perseverance, Everyman, Mankind, Wyt and Science, Robin Hood and the Sheriff of Nottingham, Robin Hood and the Friar, Shetland Sword Dance, Oxfordshire St. George Play, Leicestershire St. George Play, The Revesby Sword Play, The Playe Called the Foure PP, A Merry Play between Johan Johan the Husbande, Tyb his Wyfe and Syr Johan the Preest, The Play of the Wether, Roister Doister, Gammer Gurton's Needle, Gorboduc; or Ferrex & Perrex, Supposes, Damon and Pithias, Campaspe, Cambises, The Famous Victories of Henry the Fifth, George a Greene, the Pinner of Wakefield.

2. ANSORGE, Elizabeth Frances and Others, *Prose and Poetry for Appreciation* (Singer, 1942).

They Fly Through the Air, Spreading the News, The American Way, Never Come Monday, Cartwheel.

3. ASHTON, John William, *Types of English Drama* (Macmillan, 1940).
Abraham and Melchizedek and Lot, with the Sacrifice of Isaac, A Blot in the 'Scutcheon, The Way of the World, Everyman, The Beggar's Opera, Friar Bacon and Friar Bungay, A Woman Killed with Kindness, The Alchemist, Edward II, Anna Christie, The Critic, The Importance of Being Earnest.

4. ATKINSON, Brooks, *New Voices in the American Theatre* (Modern Library, 1955).
A Streetcar Named Desire, Death of a Salesman, Come Back, Little Sheba, The Seven Year Itch, Tea and Sympathy, The Caine Mutiny Court-Martial.

5. AYLIFF, H. K., *Malvern Festival Plays* (London, Heath Cranton, 1933).
The Conversion of St. Paul, All for Love, The Fair Maid of the West, The Dancing Girl, The Love-Chase, Gammer Gurton's Needle.

6. BAKER, George P., *Harvard Plays*, Vol. I (Brentano, 1918).
Three Pills in a Bottle, The Good Men Do, Two Crooks and a Lady, Free Speech.

7. BAKER, George P., *Harvard Plays*, Vol. II (Brentano, 1920).
The Florist Shop, The Bank Account, The Rescue, America Passes By.

8. BAKER, George P., *Harvard Plays*, Vol. III (Brentano, 1922).
Garafelia's Husband, The Four-Flushers, The Harbor of Lost Ships, Scales and the Sword.

9. BAKER, George P., *Harvard Plays*, Vol. IV (Brentano, 1923).
The Playroom, The Flitch of Bacon, Cooks and Cardinals, Torches.

10. BAKER, George P., *Yale One-Act Plays* (French, 1930).
The Mistress, Hans Bulow's Last Puppet, Immersion, Yella, Minnie Field, "L."

11. BAKSHY, Alexander, Translator, *Soviet Scene* (Yale University Press, 1946).
Far Taiga, The Square of Flowers, Twelve Months, The Chimes of the Kremlin, Father Unknown, Lyubov Yarovaya.

12. BARNES, John R. and Others, *Prose and Poetry of the World* (Singer, 1941).
Medea, A Doll's House, Where the Cross Is Made, The Wandering Scholar from Paradise, Riders to the Sea.

13. BARNOUW, Erik, *Radio Drama in Action* (Rinehart, 1945).
Columbus Day, Will This Earth Hold?, The Battle of the Warsaw Ghetto, Mr. Ledford and the TVA, Open Letter on Race Hatred, Button Woods, The Last Day of the War, A Child Is Born, The Halls of Congress, Radioman Jack Cooper, Concerning the Red Army, Inside a Kid's Head, London by Clipper, Japanese-Americans, The Lonesome Train, The Boise, Grandpa and the Statue, Booker T. Washington in Atlanta, North Atlantic Testament, Typhus, Pacific Task Force, Against the Storm, The Negro Domestic, Japan's Advance Base: The Bonin Islands, The House I Live In.

14. BARRIE, James Matthew, *Plays* (Scribner, 1952).
Peter Pan; or, the Boy Who Would Not Grow Up, Quality Street, The Admirable Crichton, Alice-Sit-by-the-Fire, What Every Woman Knows, A Kiss for Cinderella, Dear Brutus, Mary Rose, Pantaloon, Half an Hour, Seven Women,

Old Friends, Rosalind, The Will, The Twelve-Pound Look, The New Word, A Well-Remembered Voice, Barbara's Wedding, The Old Lady Shows Her Medals, Shall We Join the Ladies?

15. BASKERVILL, Charles Read, HELTZEL, Virgil B., and NETHERCOT, Arthur H., *Elizabethan and Stuart Plays* (Holt, 1934).

Arden of Feversham, Attowell's Jig, The Knight of the Burning Pestle, The Maid's Tragedy, Philaster, Bussy d'Ambois, The Honest Whore, Part I, The Shoemakers' Holiday, The Faithful Shepherdess, The Broken Heart, Perkin Warbeck, The Witch of Edmonton, Supposes, Friar Bacon and Friar Bungay, George a Greene, A Woman Killed with Kindness, The Alchemist, Every Man in His Humor, The Hue and Cry after Cupid, The Sad Shepherd, Sejanus, His Fall, Volpone, The Spanish Tragedy, Endymion, Doctor Faustus, Edward II, Tamburlaine, Part I, The Malcontent, The Maid of Honor, A New Way to Pay Old Debts, A Trick to Catch the Old One, The Changeling, Mucedorus, Gorboduc, The Arraignment of Paris, The Old Wives' Tale, Cambises, The Cardinal, The Lady of Pleasure, Gammer Gurton's Needle, Ralph Roister Doister, The Dutchess of Malfi.

16. BENÉT, Stephen Vincent, *We Stand United and Other Radio Scripts* (Rhinehart, 1944).

Dear Adolf-Letters 1–6, Thanksgiving Day—1941, A Time to Reap, They Burned the Books, The Undefended Border, Listen to the People, A Child Is Born, Your Army, Toward the Century of Modern Man—Prayer.

17. BENTLEY, Eric, *From the Modern Repertoire,* Series I (University of Denver Press, 1949).

Fantasio, Danton's Death, La Parisienne, Round Dance, The Snob, Sweeney Agonistes, The Threepenny Opera, The Love of Don Perlimplin and Belisa in the Garden, The Infernal Machine, A Full Moon in March.

18. BENTLEY, Eric, *From the Modern Repertoire,* Series II (Indiana University Press, 1952).

Jest, Satire Irony and Deeper Significance, Easy Money, The Epidemic, The Marquis of Keith, Him, Venus and Adonis, Electra, The King and the Duke, The Dark Tower, Galileo.

19. BENTLEY, Eric, *From the Modern Repertoire,* Series III (Indiana University Press, 1956).

Leonce and Lena, A Door Should Be Either Open or Shut, Thérèse Raquin, The Magistrate, Anatole, Dr. Knock, Saint Joan of the Stockyards, Intimate Relations, Cecile; or, the School for Fathers, The Cretan Woman.

20. BENTLEY, Gerald Eades, *The Development of English Drama* (Appleton-Century-Crofts, 1950).

The Deluge or Noah's Flood, Abraham & Isaac, The Second Shepherds' Play, The Summoning of Everyman, Friar Bacon and Friar Bungay, Doctor Faustus, The Shoemakers' Holiday, The Knight of the Burning Pestle, The Alchemist, The White Devil, The Wild-Goose Chase, 'Tis Pity She's a Whore, The Indian Queen, All for Love, or the World Well Lost, Love for Love, The Way of the World, The London Merchant, The West Indian, She Stoops to Conquer, The School for Scandal, London Assurance, Lady Windermere's Fan, The Second Mrs. Tanqueray.

21. BIERSTADT, Edward Hale, *Three Plays of the Argentine* (Duffield, 1920).

Santos Vega, Juan Moreira, The Witches' Mountain.

22. BLACKIE, John Stuart, Translator, *The Lyrical Dramas of Aeschylus* (London, Dent, 1906; Everyman's Library).

Agamemnon, Choephorae; or, The Libation Bearers, The Eumenides, Prometheus Bound, The Suppliants, The Seven against Thebes, The Persians.

23. BLAIR, Walter and GERBER, John C., *Better Reading*, Vol. 2 (Scott, Foresman, 1949).

The Swan Song, A Night at an Inn, Hedda Gabler, Tartuffe, Anna Christie, Oedipus the King.

24. BLAIR, Walter, HORNBERGER, Theodore, and RANDALL, Stewart, *The Literature of the United States*, 2 vols. (Scott, Foresman, 1946–47).

Uncle Tom's Cabin; or Life among the Lowly, The New York Idea, The Hairy Ape, The Contrast.

25. BOAS, Frederick Samuel, *Five Pre-Shakespearean Comedies* (Oxford University Press, 1934).

Supposes, The Four PP, Fulgens and Lucrece, Gammer Gurton's Needle, Ralph Roister Doister.

26. BOYD, James, *The Free Company Presents* (Dodd, Mead, 1942).

The People with Light Coming Out of Them, The Mole on Lincoln's Cheek, An American Crusader, One More Free Man, Freedom's a Hard-bought Thing, His Honor, the Mayor, A Start in Life, The States Talking, The Miracle of the Danube, "Above Suspicion."

27. BROOKE, Charles Frederick Tucker, and PARADISE, Nathaniel Burton, *English Drama, 1580–1642* (Heath, 1933).

The Knight of the Burning Pestle, The Maid's Tragedy, Philaster, Bussy d'Ambois, Eastward Ho!, The Shoemakers' Holiday, The Island Princess, Beggar's Bush, The Broken Heart, Friar Bacon and Friar Bungay, A Woman Killed with Kindness, The Alchemist, Epicoene; or, the Silent Woman, Every Man in His Humor, The Gipsies Metamorphosed, Volpone; or, the Fox, The Spanish Tragedy, Endymion, Doctor Faustus, Edward II, The Jew of Malta, Tamburlaine, Part I, The Malcontent, A New Way to Pay Old Debts, A Game at Chess, The Changeling, The Arraignment of Paris, The Old Wives Tale, The Cardinal, The Duchess of Malfi.

28. BROOKS, Cleanth, PURSER, John Thibaut, and WARREN, Robert Penn, *An Approach to Literature*, 3rd ed. (Appleton-Century-Crofts, 1952).
Murder in the Cathedral, Hedda Gabler, The Circle, All My Sons, Antony and Cleopatra.

29. BROWN, Leonard Stanley, WAITE, Harlow O., and ATKINSON, Benjamin P., *Literature for Our Time* (Holt, 1947).

Winterset, The Philadelphia Story, Biography, R.U.R., We Hold These Truths, The Fall of the City, The Hairy Ape.

30. BROWN, Leonard Stanley and PERRIN, Porter, *A Quarto of Modern Literature* (Scribner, 1935).

Dear Brutus, Justice, The Silver Cord, In the Zone.

31. BROWN, Leonard Stanley and PERRIN, Porter Gale, *A Quarto of Modern Literature*, 3rd ed. (Scribner, 1950).

Loyalties, The Madwoman of Chaillot, The Silver Cord, Death of a Salesman, The Emperor Jones, Abe Lincoln in Illinois.

32. Buck, Philo M. Jr., *An Anthology of World Literature* (Macmillan, 1934).

Agamemnon, Prometheus Bound, The Frogs, Iphigenia at Aulis, Faust, Parts I and II, The Sunken Bell, Maria Magdalena, An Enemy of the People, Shakuntala, The Misanthrope, Tartuffe, Electra, Athaliah, Antigone, Oedipus the King.

33. Buck, Philo M., Jr. and Alberson, Hazel Stewart, *An Anthology of World Literature*, 3rd ed. (Macmillan, 1951).

Agamemnon, Prometheus Bound, The Frogs, The Book of Job, Iphigenia at Aulis, Medea, Faust, The Sunken Bell, Maria Magdalena, An Enemy of the People, Shakuntala, Aulularia, Athaliah, Antigone, Oedipus the King.

34. Buck, Philo M. Jr., Gassner, John, and Alberson, H. S., *A Treasury of the Theatre*, Vol. II (Dryden-Simon & Schuster, 1940).

Maria Magdalena, Faust, Part I, The Way of the World, Phaedra, The Misanthrope, Volpone, Hamlet, Everyman, Abraham and Isaac, Shakuntala, Job, The Menaechmi, Lysistrata, Electra, Antigone, Agamemnon, The Duchess of Malfi.

35. Campbell, Oscar James, Van Gundy, Justine, and Shrodes, Caroline, *Patterns for Living* (Macmillan, 1940).

Winterset, Shadow and Substance, Mr. Pim Passes By, No More Peace!

36. Campbell, Oscar James, Van Gundy, Justine, and Shrodes, Caroline, *Patterns for Living*, Alternate ed., Vol. I (Macmillan, 1943).

R.U.R., Claudia.

37. Campbell, Oscar James, Van Gundy, Justine, and Shrodes, Caroline, *Patterns for Living*, Alternate ed., Vol. II (Macmillan, 1943).

Winterset, Watch on the Rhine.

38. Canfield, Curtis, *Plays of Changing Ireland* (Macmillan, 1936).

The Old Lady Says "No!," Mr. Jiggins of Jigginstown, Yahoo, Youth's the Season, Bridge Head, Church Street, The New Gossoon, The Words upon the Windowpane.

39. Canfield, Curtis, *Plays of the Irish Renaissance, 1880–1930* (Ives Washburn, 1929).

On Baile's Strand, The Jealousy of Emer, Deirdre, Hyacinth Halvey, The Twisting of the Rope, The Dandy Dolls, Riders to the Sea, The Land, Birthright, The Singer, Maeve, Juno and the Paycock, The Big House.

40. Carpenter, Bruce, *A Book of Dramas* (Prentice-Hall, 1929).

Agamemnon, Oedipus, The Trojan Women, Phaedra, Riders to the Sea, The Misanthrope, Love for Love, The Second Man, The Farce of the Worthy Master Pierre Patelin, The Importance of Being Earnest, A Minuet, Hedda Gabler, The Cherry Orchard, The Cricket on the Hearth, Miss Julia, The Intruder, Beggar on Horseback, The Green Goddess, Hernani.

41. Carpenter, Bruce, *A Book of Dramas*, Rev. ed. (Prentice-Hall, 1949).

Agamemnon, The Second Man, The Cherry Orchard, Love for Love, The Trojan Women, Hedda Gabler, Beggar on Horseback, The Intruder, The Misanthrope, The Long Voyage Home, Phaedra, Cyrano de Bergerac, Oedipus, King of Thebes, Riders to the Sea, The Importance of Being Earnest.

42. Cassidy, Frederic G., *Modern American Plays* (Longmans, Green, 1949).

Abe Lincoln in Illinois, Watch on the Rhine, Anna Christie, Winterset, Life with Father, Waiting for Lefty.

43. CAWLEY, A. C., *Everyman and Medieval Miracle Plays* (London, Dent, 1957; Everyman's Library).

The Creation, and the Fall of Lucifer, The Creation of Adam and Eve, The Fall of Man, Cain and Abel, Noah's Flood, Abraham and Isaac, The Annunciation, The Second Shepherds' Pageant, Herod the Great, The Woman Taken in Adultery, The Crucifixion, The Harrowing of Hell, The Resurrection, The Judgment, Everyman, The Death of Pilate.

44. CERF, Bennett and CARTMELL, Van H., *The Most Successful Plays of the American Stage* (Garden City Publishing Co., 1944).

Uncle Tom's Cabin, East Lynne, The Two Orphans, The Old Homestead, Rip Van Winkle, The Man from Home, Lightnin', Peg O' My Heart, Abie's Irish Rose, Tobacco Road, Life with Father, The Bat, Arsenic and Old Lace, Oklahoma.

45. CERF, Bennett and CARTMELL, Van H., *Sixteen Famous American Plays,* (Garden City Publishing Co., 1941).

They Knew What They Wanted, The Front Page, The Green Pastures, Biography, Ah, Wilderness!, The Petrified Forest, Waiting for Lefty, Dead End, Boy Meets Girl, The Women, Having Wonderful Time, Our Town, The Little Foxes, The Man Who Came to Dinner, The Time of Your Life, Life with Father.

46. CERF, Bennett and CARTMELL, Van H., *Sixteen Famous British Plays* (Garden City Publishing Co., 1942).

The Green Goddess, What Every Woman Knows, Milestones, The Barretts of Wimpole Street, Cavalcade, Loyalties, Victoria Regina, The Circle, Mr. Pim Passes By, The Second Mrs. Tanqueray, Dangerous Corner, The Green Bay Tree, Journey's End, Outward Bound, The Importance of Being Earnest, The Corn Is Green.

47. CERF, Bennett and CARTMELL, Van H., *Sixteen Famous European Plays* (Garden City Publishing Co., 1943).

The Wild Duck, The Weavers, The Sea Gull, The Lower Depths, The Dybbuk, Cyrano de Bergerac, Tovarich, Amphitryon, The Cradle Song, Six Characters in Search of an Author, Anatol, R.U.R., Liliom, Grand Hotel, The Playboy of the Western World, Shadow and Substance.

48. CERF, Bennett and CARTMELL, Van H., *Thirteen Famous Plays of Crime and Detection* (Blakiston, 1946).

Sherlock Holmes, Within the Law, Seven Keys to Baldpate, On Trial, Under Cover, The Thirteenth Chair, The Cat and the Canary, The Bat, Broadway, Payment Deferred, Kind Lady, Night Must Fall, Angel Street.

49. CERF, Bennett and CARTMELL, Van H., *Thirty Famous One-Act Plays* (Garden City Publishing Co., 1943; Modern Library, 1949).

The Man Who Married a Dumb Wife, Miss Julie, Salomé, The Rising of the Moon, The Boor, The Twelve-Pound Look, The Green Cockatoo, A Miracle of St. Antony, The Monkey's Paw, The Little Man, Riders to the Sea, A Sunny Morning, A Night at an Inn, The Dear Departed, The Drums of Oude, Helena's Husband, Suppressed Desires, The Game of Chess, Lithuania, The Valiant, In the Zone, If Men Played Cards as Women Do, Another Way Out, The Clod, Aria da Capo, Overtones, Fumed Oak, Waiting for Lefty, Hello Out There, Bury the Dead.

50. CHANDLER, Frank Wadleigh and CORDELL, Richard Albert, *Twentieth Century Plays* (Nelson, 1934).

Dona Clarines, And So Ad Infinitum, The Miracle at Verdun, The Green Pastures, Private Lives, As Husbands Go, John Ferguson, The Last of the De Mullins, Dolly Reforming Herself, The Coward, The Breadwinner, The Swan, Marco Millions, The Thunderbolt, Each in His Own Way, Street Scene, The Far-off Hills, Journey's End, The Live Corpse, What Price Glory.

51. CHANDLER, Frank Wadleigh and CORDELL, Richard Albert, *Twentieth Century Plays*, Rev. ed. (Nelson, 1939).

Dona Clarines, Winterset, Rain from Heaven, And So Ad Infinitum, The Miracle at Verdun, The Green Pastures, Private Lives, John Ferguson, The Last of the De Mullins, The Silver Cord, Dolly Reforming Herself, Beggar on Horseback, The Coward, The Breadwinner, The Swan, Anna Christie, The Thunderbolt, Each in His Own Way, Street Scene, The Far-off Hills, Journey's End, The Live Corpse.

52. CHANDLER, Frank Wadleigh and CORDELL, Richard Albert, *Twentieth Century Plays, British,* Rev. and Enl. (Nelson, 1941).

The Admirable Crichton, Private Lives, John Ferguson, The Silver Box, The Last of the De Mullins, Dolly Reforming Herself, The Breadwinner, The Thunderbolt, The Far-off Hills, Journey's End.

53. CHAPMAN, John, *The Best Plays of 1949–1950* (Dodd, Mead, 1950). *See also entries, 212–214, 238–269, 414.*

The Cocktail Party, The Member of the Wedding, The Innocents, Lost in the Stars, Come Back, Little Sheba, The Happy Time, The Wisteria Trees, I Know My Love, The Enchanted, Clutterbuck.

54. CHAPMAN, John, *The Best Plays of 1950–1951* (Dodd, Mead, 1951).

Bell, Book and Candle, Guys and Dolls, The Country Girl, The Second Threshold, Affairs of State, Darkness at Noon, The Rose Tattoo, The Autumn Garden, Season in the Sun, Billy Budd.

55. CHAPMAN, John, *The Best Plays of 1951–1952* (Dodd, Mead, 1952).

Mrs. McThing, I Am a Camera, Point of No Return, Barefoot in Athens, The Fourposter, The Shrike, Jane, Venus Observed, Gigi, Remains to Be Seen.

56. CHAYEFSKY, Paddy, *Television Plays* (Simon & Schuster, 1955).

Holiday Song, Printer's Measure, The Big Deal, Marty, The Mother, The Bachelor.

57. CHEKHOV, Anton, *Best Plays,* translated by Stark Young (Modern Library, 1956).

The Sea Gull, Uncle Vanya, The Three Sisters, The Cherry Orchard.

58. CHEKHOV, Anton, *Plays,* translated by Constance Garnett (Modern Library, 1930).

The Sea Gull, The Cherry Orchard, The Three Sisters, Uncle Vanya, The Anniversary, On the High Road, The Wedding.

59. CHILD, Clarence Griffin, *The Second Shepherds' Play, Everyman and Other Early Plays* (Houghton Mifflin, 1910).

The Brome Abraham and Isaac, Everyman, The Oxfordshire St. George Play, The Quem Quaeritis, Robin Hood and the Friar, Robin Hood and the Knight, Robin Hood and the Potter, The Second Shepherds' Play.

60. CHURCH, Virginia Woodson, *Curtain!* (Harper, 1932).

The Great Adventure, What Men Live By, The Lost Silk Hat, The Man Who Died at Twelve O'Clock, Napoleon Crossing the Rockies, Aria da Capo, The Great Broxopp, Good Theatre, Wings over Europe, The Emperor Jones, The Angel on the Ship.

61. CLARK, Barrett H., *Representative One-Act Plays by British and Irish Authors* (Little, Brown, 1921).

The Widow of Wasdale Head, The Goal, Salome, The Man in the Stalls, 'Op-o'-Me-Thumb, The Impertinence of the Creature, The Stepmother, Rococo, James and John, The Snow Man, Fancy Free, Lonesome-Like, Miss Tassey, Makeshifts, The Maker of Dreams, The Land of Heart's Desire, Riders to the Sea, Spreading the News, The Magnanimous Lover, The Golden Doom.

62. CLARK, Barrett H., and COOK, Thomas R., *One-Act Plays* (Heath, 1929).

Sparkin', The Kelly Kid, Knives from Syria, Ile, Saved, The Resignation of Bill Synder, The No 'Count Boy, The Organ, Bargains in Cathay, Money, Backstage, The Song of Solomon.

63. CLARK, Barrett H. and DAVENPORT, William H., *Nine Modern American Plays* (Appleton-Century-Crofts, 1951).

The Hairy Ape, Street Scene, Green Grow the Lilacs, High Tor, Stage Door, You Can't Take It with You, Abe Lincoln in Illinois, The Glass Menagerie, Command Decision.

64. CLARK, Barrett H., *World Drama,* Vol. I (Appleton-Century, 1933).

Abstraction, Adam, The Clouds, The Maid's Tragedy, The Chalk Circle, Fair Ladies at a Game of Poem-cards, Alcestis, Everyman, The Farce of the Worthy Master Pierre Patelin, The Beaux' Stratagem, She Stoops to Conquer, A Woman Killed with Kindness, Every Man in His Humour, Sakoontala, The Tragical History of Dr. Faustus, The Captives, The Play of St. George, The Wandering Scholar from Paradise, Nakamitsu, The Second Shepherds' Play, Medea, The School for Scandal, Antigone, Phormio, The Wise Virgins and the Foolish Virgins.

65. CLARK, Barrett H. *World Drama,* Vol. II (Appleton-Century, 1933).

Prometheus Bound, Saul, M. Poirier's Son-in-Law, The Barber of Seville, Bilora, The Constant Prince, The Cave of Salamanca, The Cid, The Demi-Monde, Egmont, The Fan, Jeppe of the Hill, Hernani, A Doll's House, Miss Sara Sampson, The Cit Turned Gentlemen, The Thunderstorm, Berenice, The Portrait, William Tell, The King, The Greatest Alcalde.

66. CLARK, Barrett H., and NICHOLSON, Kenyon, *The American Scene* (Appleton, 1930).

Greasy Luck, Bound East for Cardiff, Chuck, The Quarry, Blood o' Kings, The Last Straw, Money, No Cause for Complaint, Wanderlust, The Girl in the Coffin, Town, The No 'Count Boy, 'Lijah, The Tie that Binds, Bumblepuppy, The Medicine Show, The Cow with Wings, The Trysting Place, The Eldest, The Feast of the Holy Innocents, The Barbarians, Bread, Trifles, Minnie Field, The Cajun, Addio, The Resignation of Bill Snyder, Reckless, Across the Border, The Organ, Last Day for Grouse, The End of the Trail, Day's End, Good Vintage.

67. CLARK, David Lee, GATES, William Bryan, and LEISY, Ernest Erwin, *The Voices of England and America,* Vol. I (Nelson, 1939).

All for Love, Everyman, The Beaux' Stratagem, Every Man in His Humour, The Tragical History of Doctor Faustus, Comus, The Second Shepherds' Play, The Rivals.

68. CLARK, David Lee, GATES, William Bryan, and LEISY, Ernest Erwin, *The Voices of England and America*, Vol. II (Nelson, 1939).
The Emperor Jones, The Second Mrs. Tanqueray.

69. CLARK, William Smith, II, *Chief Patterns of World Drama* (Houghton Mifflin, 1946).
Prometheus Bound, Mary of Scotland, The Birds, The Admirable Crichton, The Maid's Tragedy, The Life of the Insects, The Sea Gull, The Shoemakers' Holiday, Alcestis, The Man of Mode; or Sir Fopling Flutter, The Silver Box, The Inspector-General, Roll Sweet Chariot, Maria Magdalena, Hedda Gabler, Epicoene; or, The Silent Woman, The Troublesome Reign and Lamentable Death of Edward the Second, The Miser, The Hairy Ape, Naked, The Pot of Gold, Andromache, The Second Shepherds' Play, Nice Wanton, The School for Scandal, Electra, The Playboy of the Western World, Phormio, The Star of Seville.

70. CLEMENTS, Colin Campbell, *Sea-Plays* (Dodd, Mead, 1925).
The Ship Comes In, The Brink of Silence, Just Two Men, The Magic Sea-Shell, The Outside, The Rusty Door, Second Best, Sintram of Skagerrak, Will-o'-the-Wisp, The Wondership.

71. COFFMAN, George R., *A Book of Modern Plays* (Scott, Foresman, 1925).
Caste, Milestones, Riders to the Sea, Workhouse Ward, Where the Cross Is Made, Enemy of the People, Romancers.

72. COFFMAN, George R., *Five Significant English Plays* (Nelson, 1930).
The Shoemakers' Holiday, Dr. Faustus, The Second Mrs. Tanqueray, The School for Scandal, The Conscious Lovers.

73. COHEN, Helen Louise, *Longer Plays by American Authors* (Harcourt, Brace, 1922).
Beau Brummel, Copperhead, Dulcy, Intimate Strangers.

74. COHEN, Helen Louise, *Milestones of the Drama* (Harcourt, Brace, 1940).
Everyman, A Doll's House, Doctor Faustus, The Emperor Jones, Cyrano de Bergerac, The School for Scandal, Oedipus, King of Thebes.

75. COHEN, Helen Louise, *One-Act Plays by Modern Authors* (Harcourt, Brace, 1921).
Beauty and the Jacobin, Pierrot of the Minute, Maker of Dreams, Gettysburg, Wurzel-Flummery, Maid of France, Spreading the News, Welsh Honeymoon, Boy Will, Riders to the Sea, Night at an Inn, Twilight Saint, Masque of Two Strangers, Intruder, Fortune and Men's Eyes, Little Man.

76. COHEN, Helen Louise, *More One-Act Plays by Modern Authors* (Harcourt, Brace, 1927).
Night of "Mr. H.," Last of the Lowries, Hearts Enduring, Pearls, Dear Departed, Poor House, The Siege, Change-House, Little Father of the Wilderness, The Artist, Good Theatre, Carved Woman, Where the Cross Is Made, A Way Out.

77. CONGREVE, William, *The Comedies of William Congreve,* edited by Norman Marshall (London, Lehman, 1948).

The Old Bachelor, The Double-Dealer, Love for Love, The Way of the World.

78. CONKLE, E. P., *Crick Bottom Plays* (French, 1928).

Minnie Field, Sparkin', Warter-Wucks, 'lection, Things Is That-a-Way.

79. COOK, George C. and SHAY, Frank, *Provincetown Plays* (Appleton, 1921).

Suppressed Desires, Aria da Capo, Cocaine, Night, Enemies, The Angel Intrudes, Bound East for Cardiff, The Widow's Veil, The String of the Samisen, Not Smart.

80. COOPER, Charles W., *Preface to Drama* (Ronald, 1955).

Fumed Oak, H.M.S. Pinafore, "A Good Lesson!," Hedda Gabler, Life with Father, The Crucible, The Ridiculous Precieuses, The Long Voyage Home, Othello, Candida, Antigone, The Happy Journey to Trenton and Camden, The Glass Menagerie.

81. CORDELL, Kathryn (Coe) and CORDELL, William Howard, *The Pulitzer Prize Plays*, New ed. (Random House, 1938).

Both Your Houses, The Green Pastures, Icebound, Miss Lulu Bett, Alison's House, In Abraham's Bosom, You Can't Take It with You, They Knew What They Wanted, Hell-Bent fer Heaven, Of Thee I Sing, Craig's Wife, Men in White, Anna Christie, Beyond the Horizon, Strange Interlude, Street Scene, Idiot's Delight, Why Marry?

82. CORDELL, Richard A., *Representative Modern Plays: British and American, from Robertson to O'Neill* (Nelson, 1929).

Caste, Sweethearts, A Woman of No Importance, Mrs. Dane's Defense, Iris, The Great Adventure, A Bill of Divorcement, The Circle, Success, Juno and the Paycock, The Climbers, The College Widow, Expressing Willie, Hell-Bent fer Heaven, Beggar on Horseback, Diff'rent.

83. CORDELL, Richard A., *Twentieth Century Plays, American*, 3rd ed. (Ronald, 1947).

Anna Christie, Abe Lincoln in Illinois, Street Scene, The Green Pastures, The Silver Cord, The Little Foxes, Winterset, The Late George Apley.

84. CORDELL, Richard A., *Twentieth Century Plays, British, American, Continental*, 3rd ed. (Ronald, 1947).

Winterset, The Admirable Crichton, R.U.R., The Silver Box, The Little Foxes, The Circle, The Late George Apley, Anna Christie, Street Scene, Cyrano de Bergerac, Abe Lincoln in Illinois.

85. CORNEILLE, Pierre and RACINE, Jean, *Six Plays by Corneille and Racine*, translated by Paul Landis and Robert Henderson (Modern Library, 1931).

By Corneille: The Cid, Cinna.

By Racine: Andromache, Britannicus, Phaedra, Athalaiah.

86. CORWIN, Norman, *Thirteen by Corwin* (Holt, 1942).

The Odyssey of Runyon Jones, Radio Primer, They Fly through the Air with the Greatest of Ease, The Plot to Overthrow Christmas, Daybreak, Old Salt, A Soliloquy to Balance the Diet, Ann Rutledge, Seems Radio is Here to Stay, Tim at Twenty, My Client Curley, Appointment, The Oracle of Philadelphi.

87. CORWIN, Norman, *More by Corwin* (Holt, 1944).

Mary and the Fairy, Coomer, We Hold These Truths, Descent of the Gods, The Long Name None Could Spell, Good Heavens, Psalm for a Dark Year, A Man

with a Platform, Samson, Anatomy of Sound, Excerpts from "This Is War,"
Murder in Studio One, Between Americans, A Moment of the Nation's Time,
Double Concerto, Program to Be Opened in a Hundred Years.

88. CORWIN, Norman, *Untitled and Other Radio Dramas* (Holt, 1947).

The Undecided Molecule, Untitled, El Capitan and the Corporal, Savage En-
counter, London by Clipper, Home Is Where You Hang Your Helmet, An
Anglo-American Angle, Clipper Home, You Can Dream, Inc., The Moat Farm
Murder, N.Y.: A Tapestry for Radio, Tel Aviv, Moscow, There Will Be Time
Later, On a Note of Triumph, 14 August, Set Your Clock at U235, Critical
Reception.

89. CROSS, Ethan Allen, *World Literature* (American Book, 1935).

Prometheus Bound, Richelieu; or the Conspiracy, Iphigenia in Aulis, The Silver
Box, The Master Builder, The Miser, Menaechmi; or, the Twin Brothers,
Medea, Antony and Cleopatra, Antigone, Andria.

90. CROSS, Tom Peete and SLOVER, Clark H., *Heath Readings in the Literature
of Europe* (Heath, 1933).

The Play of Adam, Prometheus Bound, The Birds, Le Cid, Faust, Part I, A
Curious Mishap, Ghosts, Minna von Barnhelm, The Misanthrope, The Captives,
Medea, The Star of Seville.

91. CUBETA, Paul M., *Modern Drama for Analysis* (William Sloane, 1950).

The Glass Menagerie, The Cherry Orchard, Juno and the Paycock, The Skin
of Our Teeth, Watch on the Rhine, The Wild Duck, The Playboy of the
Western World, The Emperor Jones.

92. DAVENPORT, William H., WIMBERLY, Lowry C. and SHAW, Harry, *Dominant
Types in British and American Literature*, Vol. I (Harper, 1949).

Winterset, The Twelve-Pound Look, The Hairy Ape, The Adding Machine,
The Second Shepherds' Play, King Henry the Fourth, The School for Scandal,
Riders to the Sea, Lady Windermere's Fan.

93. DEAN, Leonard Fellow, *Elizabethan Drama* (Prentice-Hall, 1950).

Doctor Faustus, Henry IV, Part I, King Lear, The Duchess of Malfi.

94. DEAN, Leonard Fellow, *Nine Great Plays from Aeschylus to Eliot* (Harcourt,
Brace, 1950).

Agamemnon, The Cherry Orchard, The Way of the World, Murder in the
Cathedral, The Wild Duck, Volpone; or, The Fox, The Misanthrope, The
Emperor Jones, King Oedipus.

95. DEKKER, Thomas, *Dramatic Works*, edited by Fredson Bowers, Vol. I (Cambridge [Eng.] University Press, 1953).

Sir Thomas More, The Shoemakers' Holiday, Old Fortunatus, Patient Grissil,
Satiromastix, Sir Thomas Wyatt.

96. DEKKER, Thomas, *Dramatic Works*, edited by Fredson Bowers, Vol. II (Cambridge [Eng.] University Press, 1953).

The Honest Whore, Part I, The Honest Whore, Part 2, The Magnificent Entertainment Given to King James, Westward Ho, Northward Ho, The Whore of
Babylon.

97. DEMILLE, Alban Bertram, *Three English Comedies* (Allyn and Bacon, 1924).
She Stoops to Conquer, The Rivals, The School for Scandal.

98. DICKINSON, Thomas H., *Chief Contemporary Dramatists*, 1st Series (Houghton Mifflin, 1915).

Lady Windermere's Fan, Second Mrs. Tanqueray, Michael and His Lost Angel, Strife, Madras House, Hour Glass, Riders to the Sea, Rising of the Moon, The Truth, The Great Divide, The Witching Hour, Scarecrow, The Weavers, Vale of Content, Red Robe, Know Thyself, Pelléas and Mélisande, Beyond Human Power, The Father, the Cherry Orchard.

99. DICKINSON, Thomas H., *Chief Contemporary Dramatists*, 2nd Series (Houghton Mifflin, 1921).

Milestones, Our Betters, Abraham Lincoln, Mixed Marriage, King Argimenes and the Unknown Warrior, The Easiest Way, The Piper, The Yellow Jacket, A Loving Wife, Cyrano de Bergerac, Pasteur, Moral, Living Hours, The Concert. Gioconda, Bonds of Interest, The Lower Depths, Tragedy of Love.

100. DICKINSON, Thomas H., *Chief Contemporary Dramatists*, 3rd Series (Houghton Mifflin, 1930).

The Emperor Jones, In Abraham's Bosom, The Silver Cord, The Dover Road, Juno and the Paycock, Such Is Life, From Morn to Midnight, Electra, The Steamship Tenacity, Time Is a Dream, Naked, The Love of Three Kings, Malvaloca, A Lily among Thorns, He Who Gets Slapped, The Theatre of the Soul, Liliom, R.U.R., The Dybbuk, Eyvind of the Hills.

101. DICKINSON, Thomas H., and CRAWFORD, Jack, *Contemporary Plays* (Houghton Mifflin, 1925).

Hindle Wakes, Paolo and Francesca, The Circle, Chains, Rutherford and Son, Oliver Cromwell, John Glayde's Honor, The Voysey Inheritance, The Cassilis Engagement, The Mollusc, Icebound, The Hairy Ape, The Unchastened Woman, Kindling, The Adding Machine, Mary the Third.

102. DICKINSON, Thomas H., *Continental Plays*, Vol. I (Houghton Mifflin, 1935).

The Power of Darkness, Pelléas and Mélisande, The Weavers, Light-O'-Love, Francesca da Rimini, The Cherry Orchard, A Bright Morning, Liliom, The Tidings Brought to Mary, R. U. R.

103. DICKINSON, Thomas H., *Continental Plays*, Vol. II (Houghton Mifflin, 1935).

The Great Galeoto, Erdgeist, Cyrano de Bergerac, The Red Robe, The Lower Depths, A Dream Play, The Life of Man, The Coral, Six Characters in Search of an Author, L'Invitation Au Voyage.

104. DOBRÉE, Bonamy, *Five Restoration Tragedies* (Oxford University Press, 1928; World's Classics).

All for Love, Venice Preserv'd Oroonoko, The Fair Penitant, Cato.

105. DOWNER, Alan S., *The Art of the Play* (Holt, 1955).

Prometheus Bound, The Sea Gull, Ghosts, Doctor Faustus, Tartuffe, The Emperor Jones, Antony and Cleopatra, Fuente Ovejuna.

106. DUCKWORTH, George Eckel, *The Complete Roman Drama*, Vol. I (Random House, 1942).

Amphitryon, The Braggart Warrior, The Captives, The Carthaginian, Casina, The Casket, The Comedy of Asses. Curculio, Epidicus, The Girl from Persia, The Haunted House, The Merchant, The Pot of Gold, Pseudolus, The Rope.

107. DUCKWORTH, George Eckel, *The Complete Roman Drama*, Vol. II (Random House, 1942).

Stichus, The Three-Penny Day, Truculentus, The Twin Menaechmi, The Two Bacchides, Querolus, Agamemnon, Hercules on Oeta, Mad Hercules, Medea, Octavia, Oedipus, Phaedra, The Phoenecian Women, Thyestes, The Trojan Women, The Brothers, The Eunuch, The Mother-in-Law, Phormio, The Self-Tormentor, The Woman of Andros.

108. DUNN, Esther Cloudman, *Eight Famous Elizabethan Plays* (Modern Library, 1932).

The Tragical History of Doctor Faustus, The Shoemakers' Holiday, A Woman Killed with Kindness, Volpone, The Maid's Tragedy, The Duchess of Malfi, A New Way to Pay Old Debts, 'Tis Pity She's a Whore.

109. DUNSANY, Lord, *Five Plays* (Little, Brown, 1914).

The Gods of the Mountain, The Golden Doom, King Argimenes and the Unknown Warrior, The Glittering Gate, The Lost Silk Hat.

110. DUNSANY, Lord, *Seven Modern Comedies* (Putnam, 1928).

Atalanta in Wimbledon, The Raffle, The Journey of the Soul, In Holy Russia, His Sainted Grandmother, The Hopeless Passion of Mr. Bunyon, The Jest of Hahalaba.

111. DURHAM, Willard Higley and DOBBS, John W., *British and American Plays, 1830–1945* (Oxford University Press, 1947).

Winterset, The Admirable Crichton, Richelieu, Shadow and Substance, The Green Pastures, John Ferguson, Strife, An Enemy of the People, The Liars, Of Thee I Sing, The Circle, Juno and the Paycock, Waiting for Lefty, The Great God Brown, The Second Mrs. Tanqueray, The Adding Machine, Caste, There Shall Be No Night, The Playboy of the Western World, Cathleen ni Houlihan.

112. EATON, Walter Prichard, *Twelve One-Act Plays* (Longmans, Green, 1926).

The Valiant, Romance of the Willow Pattern, The Grill, The Last Straw, Thank You, Doctor, Copy, The Trap, Good Medicine, God Winks, A Woman of Character, Jazz and Minuet, The Most Foolish Virgin.

113. EDADES, Jean and FOSDICK, Carolyn F., *Drama of the East and West* (Manila, Bookman, 1956).

A Sunny Morning, The Cherry Orchard, Medea, Forever, A Doll's House, A Portrait of the Artist as Filipino, Shakuntala, The Misanthrope, Sabina, Other Tomorrows, The Menaechmi, Romeo and Juliet, Bury the Dead, Mir-i-nisa, The Sorrows of Han, Educating Josefina, The Importance of Being Earnest, Our Town, The Corn Is Green.

114. ELIOT, Charles W., *Harvard Classics*, 50 Vols. (Collier, 1909–1910). Numbers in parentheses refer to volumes.

Agamemnon(8), The Furies(8), The Libation-Bearers(8), Prometheus Bound (8), The Frogs (8), Philaster (47), A Blot in the 'Scutcheon (18), Manfred (18), Life Is a Dream (26), Polyeucte (26), The Shoemakers' Holiday(47), All for Love; or, The World Well Lost(18), The Bacchae(8), Hippolytus(8), Egmont(19), Faust,Pt.I(19), She Stoops to Conquer(18), The Alchemist(47), Minna von Barnhelm; or, The Soldier's Fortune(26), Doctor Faustus(19), Edward the Second(46), A New Way to Pay Old Debts(47), Comus(4), Samson Agonistes(4), Tartuffe; or The Hypocrite (26), Phaedra(26), Wilhelm Tell(26), The Tempest(46), The Tragedy of Hamlet, Prince of Denmark(46), The Tragedy of King Lear(46), The

Tragedy of Macbeth(46), The Cenci(18), The School for Scandal(18), Antigone(8), Oedipus the King(8), The Duchess of Malfi(47).

115. ELIOT, Samuel A. Jr., *Little Theatre Classics*, Vol. III (Little, Brown, 1921).
Bushido, The Old Wife's Tale, Pericles, The Duchess of Pavy.

116. EVERETT, Edwin Mallard, Brown, Calvin S., and WADE, John D., *Masterworks of World Literature*, Vol. I, (Dryden, 1947).
Medea, Antigone, Oedipus the King.

117. EVERETT, Edwin Mallard, Brown, Calvin S., and WADE, John D., *Masterworks of World Literature*, Vol. II (Dryden, 1947).
Faust, Part I, An Enemy of the People, Tartuffe, Phaedra, Romeo and Juliet.

118. FARQUHAR, George, *The Complete Works of George Farquhar*, edited by Charles Stonehill, Vol. I (London, Nonesuch, 1930).
Love in a Bottle, The Constant Couple, Sir Harry Wildair, The Inconstant, The Twin-Rivals.

119. FARQUHAR, George, *The Complete Works of George Farquhar*, edited by Charles Stonehill, Vol. II (London, Nonesuch, 1930).
The Stage Coach, The Recruiting Officer, The Beaux' Stratagem, The Adventures of Covent-Garden.

120. FEIGENBAUM, Lawrence, *Radio and Television Plays* (Globe, 1956).
Plays from Radio: Sorry, Wrong Number, The Melody Man, The Word, A Medal for Miss Walker. *Plays from Television:* She Walks in Beauty, One in Twelve, U.F.O., Daniel Webster.

121. FINCH, Robert, *Plays of the American West* (Greenberg, 1947).
Miracle at Dublin Gulch, The Desert Shall Rejoice, The Old Grad, Summer Comes to the Diamond O, Murder in the Snow, From Paradise to Butte, Western Night, Goodbye to the Lazy K, Johnny, Ghost Town, Rodeo, The Return, Gone Today, Near Closing Time, The Day They All Come Back.

122. FITTS, Dudley, Translator, *Greek Plays in Modern Translation* (Dial, 1947).
Agamemnon, Eumenides, Prometheus Bound, Alcestis, Hippolytus, Medea, The Trojan Women, Antigone, Electra, King Oedipus, Oedipus at Colonus.

123. FITTS, Dudley, Translator, *Six Greek Plays in Modern Translation* (Dryden, 1955).
Agamemnon, Choephoroe, Eumenides, The Birds, Andromache, Philoctetes.

124. FLAVIN, Martin, *Brains and Other One-Act Plays* (French, 1926).
Brains, Casualties, An Emergency Case, The Blind Man, A Question of Principle, Caleb Stone's Death Watch.

125. FOOTE, Horton, *Harrison, Texas: Eight Television Plays* (Harcourt, Brace 1956).
A Young Lady of Property, John Turner Davis, The Tears of My Sister, The Death of the Old Man, Expectant Relations, The Midnight Caller, The Dancers, The Trip to Bountiful.

126. FREIER, Robert, Lazarus, ARNOLD Leslie, and POTELL, Herbert, *Adventures in Modern Literature*, (4th ed. Harcourt, Brace, 1956).
Trifles, The End of the Beginning, Caesar and Cleopatra, Journey's End.

127. **FULTON**, Albert Rondthaler, *Drama and Theatre, Illustrated by Seven Modern Plays* (Holt, 1946).
A Well-Remembered Voice, Blithe Spirit, Roger Bloomer, Beyond the Horizon, The Second Mrs. Tanqueray, Street Scene, Our Town.

128. **GALBRAITH**, Esther R., *Plays Without Footlights* (Harcourt, Brace, 1945).
Journey to Jerusalem, Papa Is All, This Bull Ate Nutmeg, Flittermouse, The Bishop's Candlesticks, Tails Up, The People with Light Coming out of Them, Fun after Supper, The Master Salesman. The Happy Journey to Trenton and Camden.

129. **GALSWORTHY**, John, *Plays* (Scribner, 1928).
The Silver Box, Joy, Strife, The Eldest Son, Justice, The Little Dream, The Pigeon, The Fugitive, The Mob, A Bit o' Love, The Foundation, The Skin Game, A Family Man, Loyalties, Windows, The Forest, Old English, The Show, Escape, (*Six Short Plays*): The First and Last, The Little Man, Hall-Marked, Deceit, The Sun, Punch and Go.

130. **GASSNER**, John, *Twenty Best Plays of the Modern American Theatre*, 1st Series (Crown, 1939).
Idiot's Delight, Of Mice and Men, Golden Boy, The Women, End of Summer, Green Pastures, Dead End, Yes, My Darling Daughter, The Fall of the City, Boy Meets Girl, Winterset, The Children's Hour, Johnny Johnson, Tobacco Road, Bury the Dead, You Can't Take It with You, Stage Door, Animal Kingdom, Three Men on a Horse, High Tor.

131. **GASSNER**, John, *Best Plays of Modern American Theatre*, 2nd Series (Crown, 1947).
The Glass Menagerie, The Time of Your Life, I Remember Mama, Life with Father, Born Yesterday, The Voice of the Turtle, The Male Animal, The Man Who Came to Dinner, Dream Girl, The Philadephia Story, Arsenic and Old Lace, The Hasty Heart, Home of the Brave, Tomorrow the World, Watch on the Rhine, The Patriots, Abe Lincoln in Illinois.

132. **GASSNER**, John, *Best Plays of the Modern American Theatre*, 3rd Series (Crown, 1952).
Death of a Salesman, Medea, Detective Story, A Streetcar Named Desire, Billy Budd, The Member of the Wedding, State of the Union, The Autumn Garden, The Iceman Cometh, Bell, Book and Candle, Mister Roberts, Anne of the Thousand Days, Come Back, Little Sheba, All My Sons, Darkness at Noon, The Moon Is Blue, Summer and Smoke.

133. **GASSNER**, John, *Twenty-Five Best Plays of the Modern American Theatre* (Crown, 1949).
The Hairy Ape, Desire under the Elms, What Price Glory?, They Knew What They Wanted, Beggar on Horseback, Craig's Wife, Broadway, Paris Bound, The Road to Rome, The Second Man, Saturday's Children, Porgy, The Front Page, Machinal, Gods of Lightning, Street Scene, Strictly Dishonorable, Berkeley Square, The Clod, Trifles, Ile, Aria da Capo, Poor Aubrey, White Dresses, Minnie Field.

134. **GASSNER**, John, *A Treasury of the Theatre*, Rev. ed. for Colleges (Simon & Schuster, 1950).
Elizabeth the Queen, The Admirable Crichton, The Vultures, The Private Life of the Master Race, R.U.R., The Cherry Orchard, The Green Pastures.

Blithe Spirit, Escape, Blood Wedding, The Lower Depths, The Workhouse Ward, The Weavers, The Little Foxes, Ghosts, Hedda Gabler, The Intruder, The Circle, Death of a Salesman, Liliom, The Plough and the Stars, Golden Boy, Anna Christie, The Hairy Ape, Six Characters in Search of an Author, Cyrano de Bergerac, My Heart's in the Highlands, The Flies, Candida, Journey's End, What Price Glory?, The Father, There Are Crimes and Crimes, Riders to the Sea, The Power of Darkness, The Tenor, The Importance of Being Earnest, Our Town, The Glass Menagerie.

135. GASSNER, John, *Twenty Best European Plays on the American Stage* (Crown, 1957).

Tiger at the Gates, The Lark, A Month in the Country, My Three Angels, Ondine, The Madwoman of Chaillot, No Exit, Jacobowsky and the Colonel, The Sea Gull, Noah, Volpone, The Late Christopher Bean, The Play's the Thing, As You Desire Me, The Good Hope, The World We Live in (The Insect Comedy), The Dybbuk, From Morn to Midnight, The Passion Flower, Redemption.

136. GAVER, Jack, *Critics' Choice* (Hawthorn, 1955).

High Tor, Winterset, Watch on the Rhine, Picnic, Darkness at Noon, The Patriots, The Member of the Wedding, All My Sons, Death of a Salesman, The Teahouse of the August Moon, The Time of Your Life, Of Mice and Men, I Am a Camera, Cat on a Hot Tin Roof, The Glass Menagerie, A Streetcar Named Desire.

137. GAYLEY, Charles Mills, *Representative English Comedies*, Vol. I (Macmillan, 1903).

Play of the Wether, Mery Play between Johan, Johan, Tyb his Wyfe and Sir John the Priest, Roister Doister, Gammer Gurton's Needle, Alexander and Campaspe, The Old Wives' Tale, Honourable Historie of Friar Bacon, The Two Angry Women of Abington.

138. GAYLEY, Charles Mills, *Representative English Comedies*, Vol. II (Macmillan, 1912).

Every Man in His Humour, The Silent Woman, The Alchemist, Eastward Hoe!, The Merry Devil of Edmonton.

139. GAYLEY, Charles Mills, *Representative English Comedies*, Vol. III (Macmillan, 1914).

The Shoemakers' Holiday, The Spanish Gipsie, Rule a Wife and Have a Wife, A New Way to Pay Old Debts, The Antipodes, The Royall Master.

140. GAYLEY, Charles Mills, *Representative English Comedies*, Vol. IV (Macmillan, 1936).

Cutter of Coleman-Street, The Spanish Fryar, The Plain-Dealer, The Provok'd Wife, The Way of the World, The Recruiting Officer.

141. GERSTENBERG, Alice, *Ten One-Act Plays* (Brentano, 1928).

He Said and She Said, Overtones, The Unseen, The Buffer, Attuned, The Pot Boiler, Hearts, Beyond, Fourteen, The Illuminati in Drama Libre.

142. GOLDBERG, Isaac, Translator, *Plays of the Italian Theatre* (Luce, 1921).

The Sparrow, Gastone the Animal Tamer, Water upon Fire, Sicilian Limes, The Wolf-Hunt.

143. GOLDSTONE, George A., *One-Act Plays* (Allyn and Bacon, 1926).
The Diabolical Circle, Figureheads, The Romancers, The King's English, The Lost Silk Hat, The Thrice-Promised Bride, The Boor, The Unseen, Sham, Confessional, Dust of the Road, Ile, The God of Quiet, The White Hawk, The Workhouse Ward.

144. GOODMAN, Kenneth Sawyer, *Quick Curtains* (Stage Guild, 1915).
Dust of the Road, The Game of Chess, Barbara, Ephraim and the Winged Bear, Back of the Yards, Dancing Dolls, A Man Can Only Do His Best.

145. GORDON, Dudley, KING, Vernon R. and LYMAN, William W., *Today's Literature* (American Book, 1935).
Lars Killed His Son, Amaco, Youth Must Be Served, The Silver Box, In Abraham's Bosom, The Workhouse Ward, Moonshine, No More Frontier, Where the Cross Is Made, Knives from Syria.

146. GOSSE, Edmund W., *Restoration Plays from Dryden to Farquhar* (London, Dent, 1929).
The Way of the World, All for Love, The Beaux' Stratagem, Venice Preserved, The Provok'd Wife, The Country Wife.

147. Gow, J. Rodger and HANLON, Helen J., *Five Broadway Plays* (Harper, 1948).
Abe Lincoln in Illinois, High Tor, Junior Miss, On Borrowed Time, The Barretts of Wimpole Street.

148. GREBANIER, Bernard D. N., MIDDLEBROOK, Samuel, THOMPSON, Stith, and WATT, William, *English Literature and Its Backgrounds*, Rev. ed., Vol. I (Dryden, 1949).
Abraham and Isaac, The Way of the World, The Shoemakers' Holiday, Everyman, The Tragical History of Doctor Faustus, Samson Agonistes, The Misanthrope, Othello, The School for Scandal, Oedipus the King.

149. GREBANIER, Bernard D. N., MIDDLEBROOK, Samuel, THOMPSON, Stith, and WATT, William, *English Literature and Its Backgrounds*, Rev. ed., Vol. II (Dryden, 1949).
In a Balcony, The Playboy of the Western World, The Importance of Being Earnest, The Corn Is Green.

150. GREEN, Paul, *The House of Connelly and Other Plays* (French, 1931).
The House of Connelly, Potter's Field, Tread the Green Grass.

151. GREEN, Paul, *In the Valley and Other One-Act Plays* (French, 1928).
In the Valley, No 'Count Boy, In Aunt Mahaly's Cabin, Man on the House, Supper for the Dead, Quare Medicine, The Goodbye, The Picnic, Unto Such Glory, A Saturday Night, Man Who Died at Twelve O'Clock.

152. GREEN, Paul, *The Lord's Will and Other Carolina Plays* (Holt, 1925).
The Lord's Will, Blackbeard, Old Wash Lucas: the Miser, The No 'Count Boy, The Old Man of Edmonton, The Last of the Lowries.

153. GREGORY, Lady, *Seven Short Plays* (Dublin, Maunsel, 1909).
Spreading the News, Hyacinth Halvey, The Rising of the Moon, The Jackdaw, The Workhouse Ward, The Travelling Man, The Gaol Gate.

154. GRENE, David, Translator, *Three Greek Tragedies* (University of Chicago Press, 1942).
Prometheus Bound, Hippolytus, Oedipus the King.

155. GRIFFITH, Francis J. and MERSAND, Joseph, *Modern One-Act Plays* (Harcourt, Brace, 1950).

The Will, The Doctor from Dunmore, The Adventures of Mr. Bean, A Sunny Morning, The Happy Journey to Trenton and Camden, God and Texas, Franklin and the King, The Stolen Prince, The Golden Doom, The Other Side, The Far-Distant Shore, Finders-Keepers, Emergency, Stand By!, The Bottle Imp, My Client Curley, The Nosebag.

156. GRIFFITH, Francis J. and MERSAND, Joseph, *One-Act Plays for Today* (Globe, 1945).

The Farce of the Worthy Master Pierre Patelin, Fright, The Gooseberry Mandarin, The No 'Count Boy, The Boy: What Will He Become?, Blood of the Martyrs, Movie Mother, Dark Glasses, Cartwheel, Meridian 7-1212, Air Raid, The End of the Trail, The Curtain.

157. GUERNEY, Bernard Guilbert, Translator, *A Treasury of Russian Literature* (Vanguard, 1943).

The Three Sisters, The Inspector General, The Lowest Depths.

158. GUINAGH, Kevin and DORJAHN, Alfred Paul, *Latin Literature in Translation* (Longmans, Green, 1942).

The Menaechmi, The Rudens; or The Rope, The Adelphi; or The Brothers, The Phormio.

159. HALLINE, Allan Gates, *American Plays* (American Book, 1935).

Superstition, You and I, The Gladiator, Francesca da Rimini, Horizon, Icebound, André, The Field God, The Henrietta, The Danites in the Sierras, The New York Idea, Madame Sand, Fashion, The Great God Brown, The Bucktails; or, Americans in England; The Contrast, Bianca Visconti.

160. HAMILTON, Edith, Translator, *Three Greek Plays* (Norton, 1937).

Agamemnon, Prometheus Bound, The Trojan Women.

161. HAMPDEN, John, *Eighteenth-Century Plays* (London, Dent, 1928).

Cato, The Clandestine Marriage, The West Indian, The Tragedy of Tragedies; or, Tom Thumb the Great, The Beggar's Opera, The London Merchant; or, George Barnwell, Jane Shore.

162. HAMPDEN, John, *Four Modern Plays* (Nelson, 1931).

The Man of Ideas, The Spinsters of Lushe, The Theatre, Wayside War.

163. HAMPDEN, John, *Ten Modern Plays* (Nelson, 1928).

Thirty Minutes in a Street, The House with the Twisty Windows, Columbine, Moonshine, The New Wing at Elsinore, Mrs. Adis, Tickless Time, X = O: A Night of the Trojan War, Elizabeth Refuses, Brother Wolf.

164. HARRIS, Brice, *Restoration Plays* (Modern Library, 1956).

The Way of the World, All for Love, The Man of Mode, The Beaux' Stratagem, Venice Preserved, The Relapse, The Rehearsal, The Country Wife.

165. HARRISON, G. B., *Major British Writers*, Vol. I (Harcourt, Brace, 1954).

Hamlet, King Henry IV, Part I, The Tempest.

166. HARTLEY, Lodwick Charles and LADU, Arthur Irish, *Patterns in Modern Drama* (Prentice-Hall, 1948).

Uncle Vanya, The Pigeon, The Little Foxes, An Enemy of the People, Craig's Wife, The Emperor Jones, The Male Animal.

167. HATCHER, Harlan Henthorne, *Modern American Dramas* (Harcourt, Brace, 1941).
Winterset, Dodsworth, The Adding Machine, A Passenger to Bali, Abe Lincoln in Illinois, Our Town, Awake and Sing, Beyond the Horizon.

168. HATCHER, Harlan Henthorne, *Modern American Dramas,* New Ed. (Harcourt, Brace, 1949).
Winterset, Mister Roberts, All My Sons, The Emperor Jones, The Adding Machine, The Time of Your Life, Abe Lincoln in Illinois, The Glass Menagerie.

169. HATCHER, Harlan Henthorne, *Modern British Dramas* (Harcourt, Brace, 1941).
If, Justice, The Constant Wife, The Conquering Hero, The Informer, Mid-Channel, The Playboy of the Western World.

170. HATCHER, Harlan Henthorne, *Modern Continental Dramas* (Harcourt, Brace, 1941).
The Cherry Orchard, The Tidings Brought to Mary, The Lower Depths, Hannele, Hedda Gabler, Squaring the Circle, Time Is a Dream, Pelléas and Mélisande, The Cradle Song, Liliom, As You Desire Me, Cyrano de Bergerac, The Ghost Sonata, Miss Julia, Transfiguration, R.U.R.

171. HATCHER, Harlan Henthorne, *Modern Dramas,* Shorter ed. (Harcourt, Brace, 1944).
Winterset, R.U.R., The Cherry Orchard, Justice, Watch on Rhine, Hedda Gabler, The Informer, Beyond the Horizon, Abe Lincoln in Illinois.

172. HATCHER, Harlan Henthorne, *Modern Dramas,* New Shorter ed. (Harcourt, Brace, 1948).
Winterset, R.U.R., Justice, The Little Foxes, Hedda Gabler, Squaring the Circle, The Circle, Beyond the Horizon, Abe Lincoln in Illinois.

173. HIBBARD, Clarence Addison, *Writers of the Western World* (Houghton Mifflin, 1942).
Agamemnon, The Frogs, Medea, The Theatre of the Soul, Faust, Part I, The Master Builder, The Misanthrope, The Hairy Ape, Phaedra, King Lear, Antigone.

174. HILDRETH, William Henry and DUMBLE, Wilson Randle, *Five Contemporary American Plays* (Harper, 1939).
Winterset, Of Thee I Sing, Waiting for Lefty, Ah, Wilderness!, Idiot's Delight.

175. HOUSTON, Percy Hazen and SMITH, Robert Metcalf, *Types of World Literature* (Doubleday, Doran, 1930).
Agamemnon, The Birds, Hippolytus, Everyman, A Doll's House, The Misanthrope, The Captives, Athaliah, As You Like It, King Lear, The Rivals, Antigone, The Importance of Being Earnest.

176. HOWARD, Edwin Johnson, *Ten Elizabethan Plays* (Nelson, 1931).
The Knight of the Burning Pestle, Philaster, The Shoemakers' Holiday, The Honorable History of Friar Bacon and Friar Bungay, The Alchemist, The Spanish Tragedy, Tamburlaine the Great, The Tragical History of Doctor Faustus, A New Way to Pay Old Debts, The Duchess of Malfi.

177. HOWE, George and HARRER, Gustave Adolphus, Translators, *Greek Literature in Translation* (Harper, 1924).

Agamemnon, The Clouds, The Frogs, Alcestis, Medea, The Arbitration, Oedipus the King.

178. HUBBELL, Jay B., and BEATY, John O., *An Introduction to Drama* (Macmillan, 1927).

Antigone, Menaechmi, Three Miracle Plays, Faustus, Tartuffe, Iolanthe, A Doll's House, Lady Windermere's Fan, The Second Mrs. Tanqueray, Cyrano de Bergerac, The Assumption of Hannele, The Goal, Land of Heart's Desire, Riders to the Sea, A Night at an Inn, Intruder, The Boor, Overtones, Trifles, Peggy, The Emperor Jones, Volpone.

179. HUDSON, Arthur Palmer, HURLEY, Leonard Buswell, and CLARK, Joseph Deadrick, *Nelson's College Caravan*, Vol. II (Nelson, 1936).

Unto Such Glory, Marco Millions, Cyrano de Bergerac, Journey's End, Antigone.

180. HUGHES, Glenn, *Short Plays for Modern Players* (Appleton, 1931).

The Ambush, Uncle Jimmy, The Man with the Iron Jaw, What Never Dies, The Calf That Laid the Golden Eggs, A Small Down Payment, Under the Oak, Three Cans of Beans, A Duel about Nothing, Five Minutes from the Station, Gilt-Edged, Really My Dear.

181. HUGHES, Leo and SCOUTEN A. H., *Ten English Farces* (University of Texas Press, 1948).

The Emperor of the Moon, The Bilker Bilk'd, Hob; or, The Country Wake, No Song-No Supper, Appearance Is against Them, The Devil to Pay; or, The Wives Metamorphosed, The Cobbler of Preston, The Anatomist; or, The Sham Doctor, The Brave Irishman, A Duke and No Duke.

182. INGLIS, Rewey Belle, GEHLMAN, John, BOWMAN, Mary Rives, and FOERSTER, Norman, *Adventures in American Literature*, 3rd ed. (Harcourt, Brace, 1941).

Textiles, Where the Cross Is Made, Our Town.

183. INGLIS, Rewey Belle, COOPER, Alice Cecilia, OPPENHEIMER, Celia, and BENÉT, William Rose, *Adventures in English Literature*, 4th ed. (Harcourt, Brace, 1946).

The Old Lady Shows Her Medals, Strife, Macbeth, Riders to the Sea.

184. INGLIS, Rewey Belle and STEWART, William Kilbourne, *Adventures in World Literature* (Harcourt, Brace, 1936).

No Smoking, The Bird-Catcher in Hell, An Enemy of the People, The Physician in Spite of Himself, The Horse Thief, Antigone.

185. ISAACS, Edith J. R., *Plays of American Life and Fantasy* (Coward-McCann, 1929).

Moonshine, The Dreamy Kid, Bumblepuppy, Blockade, The End of the Trail, Charivari, Kills-with-Her-Man, Brother Bill, Rapunzel, The No 'Count Boy, Rose Windows, Spring Sluicing, Zombi, The Portrait of Tiero, Trap Doors, The Queen of Sheba, The Autocrat of the Coffee-Stall, The Gooseberry Mandarin.

186. JAGENDORF, Moritz, *Twenty Non-Royalty Mystery Plays* (Greenberg, 1945).

Mystery at the Depot, The Rime of the Ancient Mariner, The Late Mr. Scarface, Terrible Night, The Shadow of Screecham Isle, Her Highness, the Cook, Heavenly Mystery, Snowbound, Mysterious-Yellow Moon, Clear-Silver Moon, Fog on the Bay, The Great Meatloaf Mystery, Shadow-een, It's about

Time, End of the Rainbow, His Wonders to Perform, False Alarm!, Cheating Cheaters, Ghost to Ghost, The Family Tree, The Mummy's Foot.

187. JOHNSON, Theodore, *Miniature Plays for Stage and Study* (Baker, 1930).
Bargains, Dispatch Goes Home, Early Frost, The Fifth Commandment, The Final Refuge, La Carota, For Distinguished Service, The Lost Saint, Love and Lather, The Singapore Spider, The Greek Vase.

188. JOHNSON, Theodore, *Plays in Miniature* (Baker, 1928).
The Baggage, It Sometimes Happens, Catherine Parr or Alexander's Horse, Wrong Numbers, Square Pegs, At the Sign of the Cleft Heart, Fleurette and Company, The Umbrella Duologue, On the Way Home, Outwitted, Confessions.

189. JOHNSON, Theodore, *More Plays in Miniature* (Baker, 1932).
His Only Way, Spring, Famine and the Ghost, Xanthippe and Socrates, The Other Voice, Secrets of the Heart, The Drawback, The Marriage of Dotty, Double Dummy, A Vicious Circle, Yes and No, Come Here, At the Ferry, Au Revoir, Just Advertise, The Wooden Leg.

190. JOHNSON, Theodore, *Ten Fantasies for Stage and Study* (Baker, 1932).
The Apothecary, The Crown of St. Felice, The Golden Arrow, In Arcady, Is Romance Dead?, The Man of the Moment, The Passing of Galatea, St. Anselm Only Carved One Soul, Twilight of the Moon, The Workers at the Looms.

191. JOHNSON, Theodore and PHILLIPS, Leroy, *Types of Dramatic Composition* (Baker, 1927).
The Kelly Kid, The Dweller in the Darkness, Wanderlust, Grandma Pulls the String, Cabbages and Kings, A Fool of a Man, Dawn, Bethlehem, Maurice's Own Idea, The Crumbs that Fall, 'Lijah, Meredew's Right Hand, Trifles, Peggy, Uncle Jimmy, The Closet, The Killer, The Lean Years, Pierrot, Before the Seven Doors, Daggers and Diamonds.

192. KATZIN, Winifred, *Eight European Plays* (Brentano, 1927).
Glamour, Martine, The Nüremberg Egg, The Fire at the Opera House, Madame Legros, The Stairs, A Place in the World, Uncle's Been Dreaming.

193. KAUFMAN, William I., *The Best Television Plays of the Year* (Merlin, 1950).
The Nantucket Legend, No Shoes, Zone of Quiet, The Door, Operation Coral, The Goldbergs, Something in the Wind, The Julian Houseman Story, Battle Bismarck.

194. KAUFMAN, William I., *The Best Television Plays, 1950–1951* (Merlin, 1952).
The Pharmacist's Mate, The Night They Made a Bum out of Helen Hayes, The Kathryn Steffan Story, The Rocking Horse, Vincent Van Gogh, Borderline of Fear, The Goldbergs, The Lottery.

195. KAUFMAN, William I., *The Best Television Plays*, Vol. III (Merlin, 1954).
A Seacoast in Bohemia, One in Twelve, Daniel Webster, Johnny Pickup, Ashes in the Wind, The Happy Housewife, Rescue.

196. KAUFMAN, William I., *Best Television Plays, 1957* (Harcourt, Brace, 1957).
Requiem for A Heavyweight, Cracker Money, The Five-Dollar Bill, The Trial of Poznan, Survival, Lee at Gettysburg, Thank You, Edmondo.

197. KELLY, George Edward, *The Flattering Word, and Other One-Act Plays* (Little, Brown, 1925).
The Flattering Word, Smarty's Party, The Weak Spot, Poor Aubrey.

198. KETCHUM, Roland and GILLIS, Adolph, *Three Masters of English Drama* (Dodd, Mead, 1934).
All for Love, Julius Caesar, Caesar and Cleopatra.

199. KEYES, Rowena Keith and ROTH, Helen M., *Comparative Comedies Present and Past* (Noble and Noble, 1935).
Holiday, The Goose Hangs High, She Stoops to Conquer, The Rivals.

200. KNICKERBOCKER, Edwin Van B., *Short Plays* (Holt, 1931).
The Florist Shop, The Game of Chess, The Man Who Married a Dumb Wife, Two Crooks and a Lady, Torches, Poor Maddalena, A Wedding, The Valiant, The Gods of the Mountain, Pryamus and Thisbe, On Vengeance Height, The Noble Lord, Allison's Lad, The Stepmother, Where the Cross Is Made, Ulysses.

201. KNICKERBOCKER, Edwin Van B., *Twelve Plays* (Holt, 1924).
Where but in America, The Forfeit, Poor Maddalena, Playing with Fire, Stepmother, On Vengeance Height, Marriage Proposal, Pipe of Peace, Enter the Hero, Pot Boiler, Over the Hills, Game of Chess.

202. KOCH, Frederick H., *Carolina Folk Plays,* 1st Series (Holt, 1922).
When Witches Ride, Peggy, Dod Gad Ye Both, Off Nags Head, The Last of the Lowries.

203. KOCH, Frederick H., *Carolina Folk Plays,* 2nd Series (Holt, 1926).
Trista, The Return of Buck Gavin, Gaius and Gaius, Jr., Fixin's, The Beaded Buckle.

204. KOCH, Frederick H., *Carolina Folk Plays,* 3rd Series (Holt, 1928).
The Scuffletown Outlaws, Job's Kinfolks, In Dixon's Kitchen, A Shotgun Splicin', Lighted Candles, Quare Medicine.

205. KOCH, Frederick H., *Carolina Folk Comedies,* 4th Series of *Carolina Folk Plays* (Holt, 1931).
Cloey, Magnolia's Man, Companion-Mate Maggie, Ever' Snitch, Agatha, Dog-Wood Bushes, The Lie, The New Moon.

206. KOZLENKO, William, *The Best Short Plays of the Social Theatre* (Random House, 1939).
The Dog beneath the Skin, Plant in the Sun, The Cradle Will Rock, Hymn to the Rising Sun, This Earth of Ours, Private Hicks, Waiting for Lefty, Bury the Dead, Give All Thy Terrors to the Wind, Running Dogs.

207. KOZLENKO, William, *One-Hundred Non-Royalty, One Act Plays* (Greenburg, 1940).
Women in Council, Do unto Others, And No Birds Sing, Title Go, The Long Retreat, Second Honeymoon, Goodbye to the Lazy K, Death Comes to My Friends, The Man in the Fur Cap, Best Friend Graduates, Mildred Is My Name, The Fallen Bough, Who Stand and Wait, Escape, Day for Truants, Souls at Sea, Calling Mr. and Mrs. America, Lo, the Gaunt Wolf, Library Open Hours, Indian Summer, The Other Mother, The Darkest Night, In the Merry Month of May, The Jeweled Toad, The Master's Touch, The Last One, The Third Plate, Jade, Even Exchange, Saturday Supplement, Mind over

Matter, Primary Day, Quarantine, Bitter Wine, The Parrot, An Empty Gesture, The First Margaret, Morgan's Raid, Phoebe Louise, Pierrot, Poltram, Jilted, Company House, The Byronic, Escape by Moonlight, Night Call, Progress in the Air, The Bird on Nellie's Hat, Rehearsal, The Desire of All Nations— Egypt, Babylon, Greece, The World, The Nativity, Halves!, Unto Bethlehem, Oh, Say, Can You Sing!, Too Many Hands on a Watch, Youth Adds a Dash of Pepper, Low Bridge, The Ghost of Green Mansion, Yesterday's Rations, David, Sixteen, Fortune Is a Cowboy, Mama Goes to the Convention, This Lad George, Virginia Creeper, Vacation Memories, The Kingdom of Happiness, Our Country, The Floating Branch, Tempest over a Tea-Cup, The Pied Piper of Healthy Town, Danger over Dumpling, Zelda, The Elves and the Shoemaker, The Fate of Greedy Gus, The Gift Perfect, King Cole's Court, Rainbow Gold, The Truth Fairy and the Magic Ink, Exit the Queen, Marybell, The Discovery of America, Red Riding Hood, Flopodopolus, Bumpingjump Steps into Legend, The Easter Rabbit, Hansel and Gretel, A Christmas Miracle, Where the Cross Was Made, The Declaration of Independence, The Winning of Ohio, Braddock's Defeat, The Luck of Roaring Camp, The Autocrat of the Breakfast Table, The Fall of the House of Usher, The Legend of Sleepy Hollow, When Lincoln Came to Pittsburgh, Typee.

208. KOZLENKO, William, *One Hundred Non-Royalty Radio Plays* (Greenberg, 1949).

A Special Announcement, Two Bottles of Relish, Luck, The Pussycat and the Expert Plumber Who Was a Man, Red Head Baker, All You Need Is One Good Break, A Matter of Life and Death, Moon Watch, Arena, The League of Animals, Royal March, Three Strikes You're Out, The "Americas" Cup, Sherril, Boy Waiting, The Man Who Broke Bingo, The Long Hour, Telegram from Heaven, John Wiffle Concentrates, Back to 1960!, Prague Is Quiet, Derricks on a Hill, Frontier Fighters, I Wyatt Erp, II Wild Bill Hickok, The Rebel Saint, Unidentified, The University Today, Virginia's Letter to Santa Claus, Widows Shouldn't Weep, Hunk Is a Punk, Alabama Fables, The Black Death, Panic in Salem, A Blot on the Landscape, High Water, Unfinished Symphony, The Girl from Kavalla, The Past Is Present, Banting: Discoverer of Insulin, What's in a Word?, The Rights of Man, 1.The Exile, 2.Racial Freedom, 3.Cultural Freedom, 4.The Right to Organize, Independence Hall, And the Gods Play, William Ireland's Confession, Mount Vernon Interlude, The Devil's Flower, The Last Word, The Odyssey of Homer, The Affidavit, Gardenias: Ten Cents, Revolt In Orthoepy, The Christmas Story, The Story of Silent Night, My Mother, These Honored Dead, Give Me Wings, Brother, His Name Shall Be: Remember, Dvorak's Song of the New World, Ask Aunt Mary, Facing Westward, Delayed Glory, Going Home, This Obscene Pomp, The Ladder under the Maple Tree, What We Defend, The March on Chumley Hollow, Nancy Clare, The Soldiers of Fortune, Speak o' the Devil, Even the Blind, The Lion Roars, Legend of Dust, The Magic Git-Flip, Cask of Amontillado, What Time Is It?, Handsome Is, Peace on Earth, The Old Oaken Bucket, The Key, Story in Dogtown Common, Visitation, What Men Live By, Murder among Psychologists, Who Called You Here, Away from It All, Henry Hudson, What's Your Name, Dear?, Prometheus in Granada, The Bottle Imp, The Comeback, The Silver Coronet, $100,000 for a Wife, The Quality of Mercy.

209. KOZLENKO, William, *Twenty-Five Non-Royalty One-Act American Comedies* (Greenberg, 1943).

From Paradise to Butte, Cupid's Bow, The Reign of Minnie Belle, The More the Merrier, The Man of the House, Freedom's Bird, The Package for

Ponsonby, Man of Arts, Bargain Rack, Over Fourteen and Single, Mary's Cerise Heart, Yankee Nickels, Two Birds with One Stone, Quimby Comes Across, For Better or Worse, Keep Me a Woman Grown, Triflin', Jennie Knows, Moonlight to Match, What's in a Name?, Outbound for Romance, For a Rainy Day, Annie's Man, Remember Your Diaphragm, Psychologically Speaking.

210. KREYMBORG, Alfred, *Poetic Drama* (Modern Age Books, 1941).
Agamemnon, Oedipus Coloneus, Ion, The Acharnians, The Chalk Circle, Nakamitsu, Adam, Abraham, Melchisedec and Isaac, The Second Shepherds' Play, Everyman, The Wandering Scholar from Paradise, Tamburlaine the Great, Part I, Measure for Measure, Volpone or the Fox, A New Way to Pay Old Debts, The White Devil, The Sheep Well, Cinna, Athaliah, The Misanthrope, Torquato Tasso, The Death of Wallenstein, The Cenci, The White Saviour, The Last Night of Don Juan, The King's Threshold, Gruach, The Dog beneath the Skin, The Death of Eve, Aria da Capo, Hole in the Wall, The Fall of the City, Shenandoah.

211. KREYMBORG, Alfred, *Puppet Plays* (London, Secker, 1923).
When the Willow Nods, Blue and Green, Manikin and Minikin, Jack's House, Lima Beans, People Who Die, Pianissimo.

212. KRONENBERGER, Louis, *The Best Plays of 1952–1953* (Dodd, Mead, 1953). *See also entries 52–53, 238–269, 414.*
Dial M for Murder, Picnic, The Love of Four Colonels, Time of the Cuckoo, Wonderful Town, Climate of Eden, My Three Angels, The Emperor's Clothes, The Crucible, Bernadine.

213. KRONENBERGER, Louis, *The Best Plays of 1953–1954* (Dodd, Mead, 1954).
The Caine Mutiny Court-Martial, In the Summer House, The Confidential Clerk, Take a Giant Step, The Teahouse of the August Moon, The Immoralist, Tea and Sympathy, The Girl on the Via Flaminia, The Golden Apple, The Magic and the Loss.

214. KRONENBERGER, Louis, *The Best Plays of 1954–1955* (Dodd, Mead, 1955).
The Boy Friend, The Living Room, Bad Seed, Witness for the Prosecution, The Flowering Peach, The Desperate Hours, The Dark Is Light Enough, Bus Stop, Cat on a Hot Tin Roof, Inherit the Wind.

215. LANDIS, Paul, *Four Famous Greek Plays* (Modern Library, 1929).
Medea, Oedipus, The Frogs, Agamemnon.

216. LASS, A. H., McGILL, E. L., and AXELROD, Donald, *Plays from Radio* (Houghton Mifflin, 1948).
Sorry, Wrong Number, My Client Curley, The Signal Man, The Ghost of Benjamin Sweet, The Test, The Clinic, A Trip to Czardis, One Special for Doc, Read Death, One More Free Man, Grandpa and the Statue, Little Johnny Appleseed, The Devil and Daniel Webster, Many a Watchful Night.

217. LAUGHLIN, James, *New Directions in Prose and Poetry*, 12 vols. (New Directions, 1936–1950). Numbers in parentheses refer to year of publication.
Mother Courage(41), Woyzeck(50), Les Maries de la Tour Eiffel(37), In the Frame of Don Cristobal(44), The Tower of Babel(40), The Case of Astrolabe(44), A Play about Joseph Smith, Jr.(44), No Strings Attached(44), Iphigenia at Aulis(44), Phaedra(44), Paris and Helen(41), Appolinaris(42),

Daniel Webster, Eighteen in America(37), Dos Ranchos; or, The Purification (44), Trial Horse No. 1: Mary Loves (42), Salome's Head (44), The Fourth Room(44).

218. LAW, Frederick Houk, *Modern Plays, Short and Long* (Century, 1924).
The Green Goddess, What Men Live By, Masks, Just Neighborly, Iolanthe, Bushido, Benjamin Franklin, Journeyman, Off Nags Head, The Pioneers, The Maid Who Wouldn't Be Proper, Rip Van Winkle.

219. LE GALLIENNE, Eva, *Eva Le Gallienne's Civic Repertory Plays* (Norton, 1928).
Three Sisters, La Locandiera, Hedda Gabler, $2 \times 2 = 5$.

220. LEONARD, Sterling Andrus, *The Atlantic Book of Modern Plays* (Atlantic Monthly Press, 1921).
The Philosopher of Butterbiggens, Spreading the News, The Beggar and the King, Tides, Ile, Campbell of Kilmhor, The Sun, The Knave of Hearts, Fame and the Poet, The Captain of the Gate, Gettysburg, Lonesome-Like, Riders to the Sea, The Land of Heart's Desire, The Riding to Lithend.

221. LEVERTON, Garrett Hasty, *Plays for the College Theater* (French, 1932).
The York Nativity, The Summoning of Everyman, The Portrait, Gammer Gurton's Needle, The Rehearsal, The Doctor in Spite of Himself, Patrie!, Belle Lamar, The Wild Duck, Cyrano de Bergerac, The Green Cockatoo, The Man Who Married a Dumb Wife, Springtime for Henry, A Kiss in Xanadu, Lima Beans, A Christmas Carol, The Two Shepherds, The Butter-and-Egg Man, Houseparty, The Moon of the Caribbees, The Drums of Oude, The Lord's Will, "L," Liliom, Green Grow the Lilacs, Hotel Universe, Michel Auclair, Low Bridge.

222. LEWIS, B. Roland, *Contemporary One-Act Plays* (Scribner, 1922).
The Twelve-Pound Look, Tradition, The Exchange, Sam Average, Hyacinth Halvey, The Gazing Globe, The Boor, The Last Straw, Manikin and Minikin, White Dresses, Moonshine, Modesty, The Deacon's Hat, Where but in America, A Dollar, The Diabolical Circle, The Far-Away Princess, The Stronger.

223. LEWIS, B. Roland, *University of Utah Plays* (Baker, 1928).
The Exchange, The Gray Switch, The Boomer, Sara, the Turkey Girl, And the Devil Laughs, A Man of Temperament.

224. LIEDER, Paul Robert, LOVETT, Robert Morss, and ROOT, Robert Kilburn, *British Drama* (Houghton Mifflin, 1929).
Philaster; or, Love Lies A-Bleeding, The Brome Abraham and Isaac, The Way of the World, All for Love; or, The World Well Lost, Everyman, The Alchemist, The Tragical History of Dr. Faustus, The Second Shepherds' Play, The School for Scandal, Lady Windermere's Fan.

225. LIEDER, Paul Robert, LOVETT, Robert Morss, and ROOT, Robert Kilburn, *British Prose and Poetry*, Vol. I, Rev. ed. (Houghton Mifflin, 1938).
All for Love, Volpone, Dr. Faustus, Second Shepherds' Play, The School for Scandal.

226. LIEDER, Paul Robert, LOVETT, Robert Morss, and ROOT, Robert Kilburn, *British Prose and Poetry*, Vol. II, Rev. ed. (Houghton Mifflin, 1938).
The Playboy of the Western World, Lady Windermere's Fan.

227. LOCKE, Alain Le Roy and MONTGOMERY, Gregory, *Plays of Negro Life* (Harper, 1927).

Sahdji, an African Ballet, Rackey, The Death Dance, In Abraham's Bosom, The No 'Count Boy, White Dresses, Plumes, 'Cruiter, The Dreamy Kid, The Emperor Jones, The Broken Banjo, The Flight of the Natives, Judge Lynch, The Starter, Balo, The Danse Calinda, Granny Maumee, The Rider of Dreams, The Bird Child, Sugar Cane.

228. LOCKE, Louis Glenn, GIBSON, William M., and ARMS, George, *Introduction to Literature*, Readings for Liberal Education, Vol. II (Rinehart, 1948).

Alcestis, Doctor Faustus, The Emperor Jones, The Male Animal.

229. LOOMIS, Roger Sherman and CLARK, Donald Leman, *Modern English Readings* (Farrar and Rinehart, 1934).

Success Story, The Moon of the Caribbees, The Importance of Being Earnest.

230. LOOMIS, Roger Sherman and CLARK, Donald Leman, *Modern English Readings*, 3rd ed. (Farrar and Rinehart, 1939).

Both Your Houses, The Green Pastures, The Fall of the City, Beyond the Horizon, Riders to the Sea.

231. LOOMIS, Roger Sherman and CLARK, Donald Leman, *Modern English Readings*, 4th ed. (Farrar and Rinehart, 1942).

The Green Pastures, You Can't Take It with You, The Fall of the City, Beyond the Horizon, Riders to the Sea.

232. LOOMIS, Roger Sherman and CLARK, Donald Leman, *Modern English Readings*, 5th ed. (Rinehart, 1946).

The Green Pastures, Good Heavens, You Can't Take It with You, The Fall of the City, Beyond the Horizon, Riders to the Sea.

233. LOOMIS, Roger Sherman and WELLS, Henry Willis, *Representative Medieval and Tudor Plays*, Translated and Modernized (Sheed & Ward, 1942).

John, Tyb, and Sir John, The Pardoner and the Friar, The Miracle of Saint Nicholas and the Image, The Miracle of the Blind Man and the Cripple, The Miracle of Saint Nicholas and the School Boys, The Miracle of Saint Nicholas and the Virgins, The Mystery of the Redemption, The Second Shepherds' Play, The Summoning of Everyman.

234. LORCA, García Federico, *Three Tragedies*, translated by Richard L. O'Connell and James Graham Luján (New Directions, 1946).

Blood Wedding, Yerma, House of Bernarda Alba.

235. LUCAS, Harriet Marcelia and others, *Prose and Poetry for Appreciation*, 4th ed. (Singer, 1950).

The Odyssey of Runyon Jones, The Mikado, Trifles, Abe Lincoln in Illinois.

236. LYONS, Eugene, *Six Soviet Plays* (Houghton Mifflin, 1934).

Fear, Days of the Turbins, Inga, Squaring the Circle, Bread, Tempo.

237. MACKAY, Constance D'Arcy, *Patriotic Plays and Pageants for Young People* (Holt, 1912).

Abraham Lincoln: Rail-Splitter, Benjamin Franklin: Journeyman, The Boston Tea Party, Daniel Boone: Patriot, George Washington's Fortune, In Witchcraft Days, Merrymount, Princess Pocahontas.

238. MANTLE, Burns and SHERWOOD, Garrison, *Best Plays of 1899–1909* (Dodd, Mead, 1944). *See also entries 53–55, 212–214, 414.*

Barbara Frietchie, The Climbers, If I Were King, The Darling of the Gods, The County Chairman, Leah Kleschna, The Squaw Man, The Great Divide, The Witching Hour, The Man from Home.

239. MANTLE, Burns and SHERWOOD, Garrison P., *The Best Plays of 1909–1919* (Dodd, Mead, 1933).

The Easiest Way, Mrs. Bumpstead-Leigh, Disraeli, Romance, Seven Keys to Baldpate, On Trial, The Unchastened Woman, Good Gracious Annabelle, Why Marry?, John Ferguson.

240. MANTLE, Burns, *Best Plays of 1919–1920* (Small, Maynard, 1920).

Abraham Lincoln, Beyond the Horizon, The Famous Mrs. Fair, Wedding Bells, The Jest, Jane Clegg, Declassee, Mama's Affair, Adam and Eva, Clarence.

241. MANTLE, Burns, *Best Plays of 1920–1921* (Small, Maynard, 1921).

Deburau, The First Year, Enter Madame, The Green Goddess, Liliom, Mary Rose, Nice People, The Bad Man, The Emperor Jones, The Skin Game.

242. MANTLE, Burns, *The Best Plays of 1921–1922* (Small, Maynard, 1922).

Anna Christie, A Bill of Divorcement, Dulcy, He Who Gets Slapped, Six Cylinder Love, The Hero, The Dover Road, Ambush, The Circle, The Nest.

243. MANTLE, Burns, *The Best Plays of 1922–1923* (Small, Maynard, 1923).

Rain, You and I, Loyalties, Icebound, Why Not?, The Fool, Merton of the Movies, The Old Soak, R.U.R., Mary the Third.

244. MANTLE, Burns, *The Best Plays of 1923–1924* (Small, Maynard, 1924).

The Show Off, Hell-Bent fer Heaven, The Swan, Outward Bound, The Goose Hangs High, Beggar on Horseback, The Changelings, Sun-up, Chicken Feed, Tarnish.

245. MANTLE, Burns, *The Best Plays of 1924–1925* (Small, Maynard, 1925).

What Price Glory, They Knew What They Wanted, Desire under the Elms, The Firebrand, Dancing Mothers, Mrs. Partridge Presents, The Fall Guy, The Youngest, Minick, Wild Birds.

246. MANTLE, Burns, *The Best Plays of 1925–1926* (Dodd, Mead, 1926).

Craig's Wife, The Great God Brown, The Green Hat, The Dybbuk, The Enemy, The Last of Mrs. Cheyney, The Bride of the Lamb, Young Woodley, The Butter and Egg Man, The Wisdom Tooth.

247. MANTLE, Burns, *The Best Plays of 1926–1927* (Dodd, Mead, 1927).

Broadway, Saturday's Children, Chicago, The Constant Wife, The Road to Rome, The Play's the Thing, The Silver Cord, The Cradle Song, Daisy Mayme, In Abraham's Bosom.

248. MANTLE, Burns, *The Best Plays of 1927–1928* (Dodd, Mead, 1928).

Strange Interlude, The Royal Family, Burlesque, Coquette, Behold the Bridegroom, Porgy, Paris Bound, Escape, The Racket, The Plough and the Stars.

249. MANTLE, Burns, *The Best Plays of 1928–1929* (Dodd, Mead, 1929).

Street Scene, Journey's End, Wings over Europe, Holiday, The Front Page, Let Us Be Gay, Machinal, Little Accident, Gypsy, The Kingdom of God.

250. MANTLE, Burns, *The Best Plays of 1929–1930* (Dodd, Mead, 1930).
The Green Pastures, The Criminal Code, Berkeley Square, Strictly Dishonorable, The Last Mile, The First Mrs. Fraser, June Moon, Michael and Mary, Death Takes a Holiday, Rebound.

251. MANTLE, Burns, *The Best Plays of 1930–1931* (Dodd, Mead, 1931).
Elizabeth the Queen, Tomorrow and Tomorrow, Once in a Lifetime, Green Grow the Lilacs, As Husbands Go, Alison's House, Five-Star Final, Overture, The Barretts of Wimpole Street, Grand Hotel.

252. MANTLE, Burns, *The Best Plays of 1931–1932* (Dodd, Mead, 1932).
Of Thee I Sing, Mourning Becomes Electra, Reunion in Vienna, The House of Connelly, The Animal Kingdom, The Left Bank, Brief Moment, Another Language, The Devil Passes, Cynara.

253. MANTLE, Burns, *The Best Plays of 1932–1933* (Dodd, Mead, 1933).
Both Your Houses, Dinner at Eight, When Ladies Meet, Design for Living, Biography, Alien Corn, The Late Christopher Bean, We, The People, Pigeons and People, One Sunday Afternoon.

254. MANTLE, Burns, *The Best Plays of 1933–1934* (Dodd, Mead, 1934).
Mary of Scotland, Men in White, Dodsworth, Ah, Wilderness!, They Shall Not Die, Her Master's Voice, No More Ladies, Wednesday's Child, The Shining Hour, The Green Bay Tree.

255. MANTLE, Burns, *Best Plays of 1934–1935* (Dodd, Mead, 1935).
The Children's Hour, Valley Forge, The Petrified Forest, The Old Maid, Accent on Youth, Merrily We Roll Along, Awake and Sing, The Farmer Takes a Wife, Lost Horizons, The Distaff Side.

256. MANTLE, Burns, *Best Plays of 1935–1936* (Dodd, Mead, 1936).
Winterset, Idiot's Delight, End of Summer, First Lady, Victoria Regina, Boy Meets Girl, Dead End, Call It a Day, Ethan Frome, Pride and Prejudice.

257. MANTLE, Burns, *The Best Plays of 1936–1937* (Dodd, Mead, 1937).
High Tor, You Can't Take It with You, Johnny Johnson, Daughters of Atreus, Stage Door, The Women, St. Helena, Yes, My Darling Daughter, Excursion, Tovarich.

258. MANTLE, Burns, *The Best Plays of 1937–1938* (Dodd, Mead, 1938).
Of Mice and Men, Our Town, Shadow and Substance, On Borrowed Time, The Star Wagon, Susan and God, Prologue to Glory, Amphitryon, Golden Boy, What a Life.

259. MANTLE, Burns, *The Best Plays of 1938–1939* (Dodd, Mead, 1939).
Abe Lincoln in Illinois, The Little Foxes, Rocket to the Moon, The American Way, No Time for Comedy, The Philadelphia Story, The White Steed, Here Come the Clowns, Family Portrait, Kiss the Boys Good-bye.

260. MANTLE, Burns, *The Best Plays of 1939–1940* (Dodd, Mead, 1940).
There Shall Be No Night, Key Largo, The World We Make, Life with Father, The Man Who Came to Dinner, The Male Animal, The Time of Your Life, Skylark, Margin for Error, Morning's at Seven.

261. MANTLE, Burns, *The Best Plays of 1940–1941* (Dodd, Mead, 1941).
Native Son, Watch on the Rhine, The Corn Is Green, Lady in the Dark, Arsenic

and Old Lace, My Sister Eileen, Flight to the West, Claudia, Mr. & Mrs. North, George Washington Slept Here.

262. MANTLE, Burns, *The Best Plays of 1941–1942* (Dodd, Mead, 1942).

In Time to Come, The Moon Is Down, Blithe Spirit, Junior Miss, Candle in the Wind, Letters to Lucerne, Jason, Angel Street, Uncle Harry, Hope for a Harvest.

263. MANTLE, Burns, *Best Plays of 1942–1943* (Dodd, Mead ,1943).

The Patriots, The Eve of St. Mark, The Skin of Our Teeth, Winter Soldiers, Tomorrow the World, Harriet, The Doughgirls, The Damask Cheek, Kiss and Tell, Oklahoma.

264. MANTLE, Burns, *Best Plays of 1943–1944* (Dodd, Mead, 1944).

Winged Victory, The Searching Wind, The Voice of the Turtle, Decision, Over Twenty-One, Outrageous Fortune, Jacobowsky and the Colonel, Storm Operation, Pick-Up Girl, The Innocent Voyage.

265. MANTLE, Burns, *Best Plays of 1944–1945* (Dodd, Mead, 1945).

A Bell for Adano, I Remember Mama, The Hasty Heart, The Glass Menagerie, Harvey, The Late George Apley, Soldier's Wife, Anna Lucasta, Foolish Notion, Dear Ruth.

266. MANTLE, Burns, *Best Plays of 1945–1946* (Dodd, Mead, 1946).

State of the Union, Home of the Brave, Deep Are the Roots, The Magnificent Yankee, Antigone, O Mistress Mine, Born Yesterday, Dream Girl, The Rugged Path.

267. MANTLE, Burns, *Best Plays of 1946–1947* (Dodd, Mead, 1947).

All My Sons, The Iceman Cometh, Joan of Lorraine, Another Part of the Forest, Years Ago, John Loves Mary, The Fatal Weakness, The Story of Mary Suratt, Christopher Blake, Brigadoon.

268. MANTLE, Burns, *Best Plays of 1947–1948* (Dodd, Mead, 1948).

A Streetcar Named Desire, Mister Roberts, Command Decision, The Winslow Boy, The Heiress, Allegro, Eastward In Eden, Skipper Next to God, An Inspector Calls, Me and Molly.

269. MANTLE, Burns, *Best Plays of 1948–1949* (Dodd, Mead, 1949).

Death of a Salesman, Anne of the Thousand Days, The Madwoman of Chaillot, Detective Story, Edward, My Son, Life with Mother, Light Up the Sky, The Silver Whistle, Two Blind Mice, Good-bye, My Fancy.

270. MANTLE, Burns and GASSNER, John, *A Treasury of the Theatre,* Rev. and Adapted for Colleges by Philo M. Buck, Jr., John Gassner, and H. S. Alberson, Vol. I (Simon & Schuster, 1940).

Elizabeth the Queen, What Price Glory?, The Cherry Orchard, The Green Pastures, Escape, The Lower Depths, The Weavers, Hedda Gabler, Liliom, Awake and Sing, Anna Christie, Six Characters in Search of an Author, Cyrano de Bergerac, Candida, Journey's End, The Father, Riders to the Sea, The Importance of Being Earnest.

271. MANTLE, Burns and GASSNER, John, *A Treasury of the Theatre,* Rev. and Adapted for Colleges by Philo M. Buck, Jr., John Gassner, and H. S. Alberson, Vol. II (Simon & Schuster, 1940).

Abraham and Isaac, Agamemnon, Lysistrata, The Way of the World, **Electra,** Everyman, Faust, Part I, Maria Magdalena, Job, Volpone, Shakuntala, The Misanthrope, The Menaechmi, Phaedra, Hamlet, Antigone, The Duchess of Malfi.

272. MANTLE, Burns and GASSNER, John, *A Treasury of the Theatre,* 3rd ed. (Simon & Schuster, 1955).

Of Thee I Sing, The Green Pastures, Elizabeth the Queen, What Price Glory?, Anna Christie, Journey's End, Candida, Escape, Riders to the Sea, The Importance of Being Earnest, Six Characters in Search of an Author, Liliom, Cyrano de Bergerac, The Lower Depths, The Cherry Orchard, The Weavers, The Father, Hedda Gabler, The Cenci, Faust; Part I, The Way of the World, Phaedra, The Misanthrope, The Duchess of Malfi, Volpone, Hamlet, Everyman, Sotoba Komachi, A Noh Play, Job, Lysistrata, Electra, Antigone, Agamemnon, Shakuntala.

273. MARKS, Jeanette, *The Merry Merry Cuckoo and Other Welsh Plays* (Appleton, 1927).

The Merry Merry Cuckoo, The Deacon's Hat, Welsh Honeymoon, A Tress of Hair, Love Letters, Steppin' Westward, Look to the End.

274. MARRIOTT, J. W., *The Best One-Act Plays of 1931* (London, Harrap, 1932).

Mrs. Noah Gives the Sign, Women Do Things like That, Vindication, Poet's Corner, Smoke-Screens, The Bride, The Hoose o' the Hill, The Annual Jumble Sale, Exit, Shanghai, The Perfect Marriage, Back Home.

275. MARRIOTT, J. W., *Great Modern British Plays* (London, Harrap, 1929).

Milestones, Caste, Trelawny of the "Wells," The Liars, Pygmalion and Galatea, The Virgin Goddess, The Walls of Jericho, Hobson's Choice, The Return of the Prodigal, The New Morality, The Circle, A Bill of Divorcement, At Mrs. Beam's, The Man with a Load of Mischief, The White Chateau, The Likes of Her, The Young Idea, Strife, Outward Bound.

276. MARRIOTT, J. W., *One-Act Plays of Today,* 1st Series (London, Harrap, 1924; Dodd, Mead, 1929).

Boy Comes Home, Followers, The Stepmother, The Maker of Dreams, The Little Man, A Night at an Inn, Campbell of Kilmhor, The Grand Cham's Diamond, Thread o' Scarlet, Becky Sharp, X=O: A Night of the Trojan War.

277. MARRIOTT, J. W., *One-Act Plays of Today,* 2nd Series (London, Harrap, 1925; Dodd, Mead, 1929).

Riders to the Sea, Waterloo, It's the Poor That 'Elps the Poor, A Marriage Has Been Arranged, Lonesome-Like, The Rising of the Moon, The King's Waistcoat, The Dear Departed, 'Op-o'-Me-Thumb, The Monkey's Paw, Night Watches, The Child in Flanders.

278. MARRIOTT, J. W., *One-Act Plays of Today,* 3rd Series, (London, Harrap, 1926).

The Dumb and the Blind, How the Weather Is Made, The Golden Doom, Rory Aforesaid, The Master of the House, Friends, Mimi, The Bishop's Candlesticks, Between the Soup and the Savory, Master Wayfarer, The Pot of Broth, A King's Hard Bargain.

279. MARRIOTT, J. W., *One-Act Plays of Today,* 4th Series, (London, Harrap, 1928).

The Prince Who Was a Piper, Square Pegs, The Man in the Bowler Hat, The Betrayal, The Flight of the Queen, St. Simeon Stylites, The Patchwork Quilt, Five Birds in a Cage, Paddly Pools, The Poacher, The Constant Lover.

280. MARRIOTT, J. W., *One-Act Plays of Today*, 5th Series (London, Harrap, 1931).

The Stoker, Birds of a Feather, The Invisible Duke, Old Boyhood, The Spartan Girl, The King of Barvender, The Lovely Miracle, The Mousetrap, The Scarecrow, The Pathfinder, Aucassin and Nicolette.

281. MASSEY, Vincent, *Canadian Plays from Hart House Theatre*, Vol. I (Toronto, Macmillan, 1926).

Three Weddings of a Hunchback, The Translation of John Snaith, Balm, Brothers in Arms, The Weather Breeder, The Second Lie, The Point of View, Pierre.

282. MASSEY, Vincent, *Canadian Plays From Hart House Theatre*, Vol. II (Toronto, Macmillan, 1927).

The God of Gods, The Freedom of Jean Guichet, Trespassers.

283. MATTHEWS, Brander, *The Chief European Dramatists* (Houghton Mifflin, 1916).

Agamemnon, Oedipus the King, Medea, The Frogs, The Captives, Phormio, The Star of Seville, Life Is a Dream, The Cid, Tartuffe, Phaedra, The Barber of Seville, Hernani, The Son-in-Law of M. Poirier, The Outer Edge of Society, The Mistress of the Inn, Minna von Barnhelm, Goetz von Berlichingen, William Tell, Rasmus Montanus, A Doll's House.

284. MATTHEWS, Brander and LEIDER, Paul R., *The Chief British Dramatists* (Houghton Mifflin, 1924).

Every Man in His Humor, A Woman Killed with Kindness, Philaster, The Duchess of Malfi, A New Way to Pay Old Debts, The Plain Dealer, All for Love, The Brome Abraham and Isaac, The Second Shepherds' Play, Ralph Roister Doister, The Spanish Tragedy, The Troublesome Reign and Lamentable Death of Edward II, Venice Preserved, The Provoked Wife, The Way of the World, The Beaux' Stratagem, She Stoops to Conquer, The School for Scandal, Richelieu, London Assurance, Caste, Pygmalion and Galatea, Lady Windermere's Fan, The Second Mrs. Tanqueray, The Liars.

285. MAYORGA, Margaret, *Best One-Act Plays of 1937* (Dodd, Mead, 1938).

A Husband for Breakfast, Soldadera, Devil Take a Whittler, The Foundling, If the Shoe Pinches, Twenty-Five Cents, The Maker of Laws, Tobacco Alley, This Earth Is Ours, Debt Takes a Holiday, The Fall of the City, Goodnight Please!.

286. MAYORGA, Margaret, *The Best One-Act Plays of 1938* (Dodd, Mead, 1939).

Mañana Bandits, Farewell to Love, The Feast of Ortolans, Hawk A-Flyin', Ballad of Youth, Never No Third Degree, Cloud over Breakshin, Alma Mater, Dust, Resurrection Ezra, This Is Villa, Goodnight, Caroline.

287. MAYORGA, Margaret, *Best One-Act Plays of 1939* (Dodd, Mead, 1940).

Air Raid, A World Elsewhere, That's Hollywood, Gold Is Where You Don't Find It, The Hungerers, The Captains and the Kings, Hospital Scene, Haunted Water, The Devil Is a Good Man, One-Car Wedding, Of Time and the Blizzard, Days End.

288. MAYORGA, Margaret, *Best Plays of 1940* (Dodd, Mead, 1941).

Mr. F, Moony's Kid Don't Cry, Summer Comes to the Diamond O, Subway Circus, Rainbows in Heaven, According to Law, Farmer Brown's Pig, Danbury Fair, Sleeping Dogs, Parting at Imsdorf.

289. MAYORGA, Margaret, *The Best One-Act Plays of 1941* (Dodd, Mead, 1942).

The States Talking, Until Charlot Comes Home, All-American Ape, Equinox, The Lady of Larkspur Lotion, The Miracle of the Danube, The Love of Annuziata, The Doctor from Dunmore, Hello Out There, It's Fun to Be Free.

290. MAYORGA, Margaret, *The Best One-Act Plays of 1942* (Dodd, Mead, 1943).

The Last of My Solid Gold Watches, House Divided, The Courting of Marie Jenvrin, City Symphony, The Strangest Feeling, We Refuse to Die, We Hold These Truths, Memo to Berchtesgaden, They Burned the Books, So Long, Son.

291. MAYORGA, Margaret, *The Best One-Act Plays of 1943* (Dodd, Mead, 1944).

Letter to Jackie, God and Texas, Quiet-Facing the Park, A Tribute to Gallantry, Where E'er We Go, Mid-Passage, The Death of Aunt Aggie, Murder Is Fun!, They Asked for It, Journey for an Unknown Soldier, The Bridegroom Waits.

292. MAYORGA, Margaret, *The Best One-Act Plays of 1944* (Dodd, Mead, 1945).

The Picnic, It Ain't Brooklyn, District of Columbia, That They May Win, Miracle on the Pullman, Concerning the Red Army, Ship Ahoy!!, On the Way Home, Strange Rain, 27 Wagons Full of Cotton, The Admiral.

293. MAYORGA, Margaret, *The Best One-Act Plays of 1945* (Dodd, Mead, 1946).

Atomic Bombs, A Note of Triumph, The Face, To the American People, A Bunyan Yard, Summer Fury, The Devil's Foot, The Unsatisfactory Supper, The Fisherman, Silver Nails, The Far-Distant Shore.

294. MAYORGA, Margaret, *The Best One-Act Plays of 1946–1947* (Dodd, Mead, 1947).

How They Knocked the Devil out of Uncle Ezra, Freight, Making the Bear, Transition in India, Skeletons, Bride-Ship, The Lord and Hawksaw Sadie (Play with Music), Open Secret, The Soldier Who Became a Great Dane, The Eagle (television script).

295. MAYORGA, Margaret, *Best One-Act Plays 1947–1948* (Dodd, Mead, 1948).

On This Green Bank, The Sunny Side of the Atom, Suffer the Little Children, Who Are the Weavers, A Woman's Privilege, Frankie and Albert, Easter Eve, Through a Glass, Darkly, The Meadow, Before the Bullfight.

296. MAYORGA, Margaret, *The Best One-Act Plays of 1949–1950* (Dodd, Mead, 1950).

Doctor Faustus Lights the Lights, The Camel and I, August Heat, Going Home, The Beast, Day before Yesterday, Exodus, Period House, Fantasia on an Old Familiar Theme, The Long Fall.

297. MAYORGA, Margaret, *The Best One-Act Plays of 1951–1952* (Dodd, Mead, 1952).

The Least One, Paradise Inn, In Darkness, Hugh of the Glen and His Clogs Are All One, The Shadow of the Cathedral, Tour of Duty, Glory Day, The Safecracker's Pride, The Happy Housewife, Sun Deck.

298. MAYORGA, Margaret, *The Best Short Plays of 1952–1953* (Dodd, Mead, 1953).

Innermost I Land, The Beams of Our House, Dope, Tunnel of Love, A Trap
Is a Small Place, Arbie, the Bug Boy, The Youngest Shall Ask, Incident at a
Grave, The Changeling, The Imploring Flame.

299. MAYORGA, Margaret, *The Best Short Plays of 1953–1954* (Dodd, Mead,
1954).
The Little Flaw of Ernesto Lippi, Telling of the North Star, John Turner
Davis, A Remittance from Spain, Salt for Savor, The Forgotten Land, A
World in Your Ear, Another Summer, Karma, The Wishful Taw.

300. MAYORGA, Margaret, *The Best Short Plays of 1954–1955* (Dodd, Mead,
1955).
The Conqueror, Song for a Hero, Brewsie and Willie, Rouge Atomique, Half-
Hour, Please, The Return of Chandra, Next-to-Last Rites, The Island, A Medal
for Julien, A Cabin by the Lake.

301. MAYORGA, Margaret, *The Best Short Plays of 1955–1956* (Beacon, 1956).
Once a Thief, This Music Crept by Me upon the Waters, Something Un-
spoken, Five Days, The High School, Hangs over Thy Head, Dino, Let There
Be Farce, Three People, Blue Concerto.

302. MAYORGA, Margaret, *The Best Short Plays*, 20th Anniversary ed. (Beacon,
1957).
In the Zone, In Abraham's Bosom, The Fall of the City, Devil Take a
Whittler, The Man with the Heart in the Highlands, The Miracle of the
Danube, Summer Fury, The Fisherman, The Soldier Who Became a Great
Dane, Frankie and Albert, Through a Glass, Darkly, The Long Fall, Fortunata
Writes a Letter, The Triumph of the Egg, A Trap Is a Small Place, Brewsie
and Willie, 27 Wagons Full of Cotton, The Stallion.

303. MAYORGA, Margaret G., *Representative One-Act Plays by American Authors*
(Little, Brown, 1919).
Sam Average, Six Who Pass While the Lentils Boil, Voices, Merry Merry
Cuckoo, Sintram of Skagerrak, Will-o'-the-Wisp, Beyond, A Good Woman,
Funiculi Funicula, Hunger, In the Zone, The Brink of Silence, Allison's Lad,
Mrs. Pat and the Law, Lima Beans, The Wonder Hat, Suppressed Desires,
Where but in America, A Question of Morality, Martha's Mourning, Ryland,
The Last Straw, Hattie, Dregs.

304. MAYORGA, Margaret, *Representative One-Act Plays by American Authors*
Rev. ed. (Little, Brown, 1937).
Sam Average, A Good Woman, Pawns, The Merry Merry Cuckoo, Ryland,
The Clod, Will o' the Wisp, Six Who Pass While the Lentils Boil, In the Zone,
Suppressed Desires, The Last Straw, The Wonder Hat, Tuning In, Sintram of
Skagerrak, The Robbery, Poor Aubrey, Good Vintage, Unto Such Glory,
Sparkin', Reckless, The Terrible Meek, The Last Mile, Lawd, Does You Unda-
stan'?, Till the Day I Die, America, America.

305. MCCLINTOCK, Marshall, *The Nobel Prize Treasury* (Doubleday, 1948).
His Widow's Husband, Between the Battles, The Street Singer, The Sunken
Bell, Interior, Desire under the Elms, Our Lord of the Ships, The Land of
Heart's Desire.

306. MCDERMOTT, John Francis, *Modern Plays* (Harcourt, Brace, 1932).
R.U.R., They Knew What They Wanted, Hell-Bent fer Heaven, A Doll's
House, The Circle, Mr. Pim Passes By, The Emperor Jones.

307. McGRAW, H. Ward, *Prose and Poetry of America* (Singer, 1934).
Nathan Hale, Trifles, Moonshine.

308. McGRAW, H. Ward, *Prose and Poetry for Appreciation* (Singer, 1934).
A Night at an Inn, The Rising of the Moon, The Grand Cham's Diamond, Monsieur Beaucaire.

309. McGRAW, H. Ward, *Prose and Poetry of England* (Singer, 1934).
The Lost Silk Hat, She Stoops to Conquer, Macbeth.

310. McILWRAITH, Archibald Kennedy, *Five Elizabethan Comedies* (London, Oxford University Press, 1934; World's Classics).
The Shoemakers' Holiday, Friar Bacon and Friar Bungay, Campaspe, The Merry Devil of Edmonton, The Old Wives' Tale.

311. McILWRAITH, Archibald Kennedy, *Five Elizabethan Tragedies* (London, Oxford University Press, 1938; World's Classics).
Arden of Feversham, A Woman Killed with Kindness, The Spanish Tragedy, Gorboduc, Thyestes.

312. MacMILLAN, Dougald and JONES, Howard Mumford, *Plays of the Restoration and Eighteenth Century* (Holt, 1931).
Cato, Love's Last Shift, The Clandestine Marriage, The Way of the World, The West Indian, The Siege of Rhodes, Part I, All for Love, The Indian Queen, The Man of Mode, The Beaux' Stratagem, The Beggar's Opera, She Stoops to Conquer, Douglas, False Delicacy, The Stranger, The Rival Queens, The London Merchant, Venice Preserv'd, The Fair Penitent, The Squire of Alsatia, The School for Scandal, The Conscious Lovers, The Relapse, The Rehearsal.

313. MENDENHALL, John Cooper, *English Literature, 1650–1800* (Lippincott, 1940).
The Way of the World, Aureng-Zebe, Venice Preserv'd.

314. MILLER, Helen Louise, *Gold Medal Plays for Holidays* (Plays, Inc., 1958).
The Greedy Goblin, A School for Scaring, The Mystery of Turkey-Lurkey, Strictly Puritan, Thanks to Butter-fingers, Mr. Snow White's Thanksgiving, Mary's Invitation, Turning the Tables, The Miraculous Tea Party, The Forgotten Hero, Vicky Gets the Vote, The Christmas Umbrella, Softy the Snowman, The Birds' Christmas Carol, The Santa Claus Twins, The Christmas Runaways, Santa Claus for President, Mystery at Knob Creek Farm, Melody for Lincoln, The Tree of Hearts, Crosspatch and Cupid, The Washington Shilling, Dolly Saves the Day, Washington's Leading Lady, Bunnies and Bonnets, The Bashful Bunny, Mother's Fairy Godmother, The Magic Carpetsweeper, Lacey's Last Garland, The Talking Flag.

315. MILLER, Helen Louise, *On Stage for Teen-Agers* (Plays, Inc., 1948).
Party Line, Pin-Up Pals, What's Cookin'?, Snoop's Scoop, Cupid on the Loose, Homework, Band Aid, Doctor's Daughter, Say It with Flowers, Papa Pepper's Bombshell, Horrors, Incorporated, The Rummage Rumpus, The Soft Hearted Ghost, Thanksgiving Beats the Dutch, Angel Child, Home for Christmas, The Missing Link, Miss Loneyheart, The Washingtons Slept Here, Nothing to Wear. A Surprise for Mother.

316. MILLETT, Fred Benjamin, *Reading Drama* (Harper, 1950).
The Will, Beyond the Horizon, A Farewell Supper, Riders to the Sea, The Long Christmas Dinner, Cathleen ni Houlihan.

317. MILLETT, Fred Benjamin and BENTLEY, Gerald Eades, *The Play's the Thing* (Appleton-Century, 1936).
The Return of Peter Grimm, Uncle Vanya, Chester Play of the Deluge, Love for Love, The West Indian, All for Love, Hippolytus, Hyacinth Halvey, Ned McCobb's Daughter, Ghosts, Interior, Doctor Faustus, The Misanthrope, The Hairy Ape, The Haunted House, Phaedra, Cyrano de Bergerac, Antony and Cleopatra, Twelfth Night, Oedipus, King of Thebes, The Drums of Oude.

318. MILTON, John, *The Portable Milton,* edited by Douglas Bush (Viking, 1949).
Contains *Comus.*

319. MOLIÈRE, *Comedies,* translated by H. Baker & J. Miller, Vol. I (London, Dent; New York, Dutton; Everyman's Library, 1943).
The Blunderer; or, the Counter-Plots, The Amorous Quarrel, The Miser, The Romantic Ladies, The School for Husbands, The School for Wives, The School for Wives Criticised, The Impromptu of Versailles, The Man-Hater, The Mock-Doctor.

320. MOLIÈRE, *Comedies,* translated by H. Baker & J. Miller, Vol. II (London, Dent; New York, Dutton; Everyman's Library, 1943).
Don Juan; or, the Feast of the Statue, Love's the Best Doctor, Tartuffe; or, the Imposter, Squire Lubberly, George Dandin; or the Husband Defeated, The Cit Turned Gentleman, The Impertinents, The Learnèd Ladies, The Cheats of Scapin, The Hypochondriack.

321. MOLIÈRE, *Eight Plays,* translated by Morris Bishop (Modern Library, 1957).
The Precious Damsels, The School for Wives, The Critique of the School for Wives, The Versailles Impromptu, Tartuffe, The Misanthrope, The Physician in Spite of Himself, The Would-Be Gentleman.

322. MOLIÈRE, *Five Plays,* translated by John Wood (Penguin, 1953).
The Would-Be Gentleman, That Scoundrel Scapin, The Miser, Love's the Best Doctor, Don Juan; or, the Statue at the Feast.

323. MOORE, Cecil A., *Famous Plays of the Restoration and Eighteenth Century* (Modern Library, 1933).
The Country Wife, All for Love; or, The World Well Lost, Venice Preserv'd; or, A Plot Discover'd, Love for Love, The Provok'd Wife, The Way of the World, The Beaux' Stratagem, The Beggar's Opera, The Clandestine Marriage, She Stoops to Conquer; or, The Mistakes of a Night, The Rivals, The School for Scandal.

324. MOORE, John Robert, *Representative English Dramas* (Ginn, 1929).
All for Love, Everyman, She Stoops to Conquer, The Tragical History of Doctor Faustus, The School for Scandal, Lady Windermere's Fan.

325. MORGAN, Arthur Eustace, *English Plays, 1660–1820* (Harper, 1935).
Cato, Luke the Labourer, The Clandestine Marriage, The Way of the World, The West Indian, All for Love; or, the World Well Lost, Almanzor and Almahide; or, the Conquest of Granada by the Spaniards, The Man of Mode; or, Sir Fopling Flutter, The Beaux' Stratagem, The Mayor of Garret, The Beggar's Opera, She Stoops to Conquer; or, the Mistakes of a Night, The

Suspicious Husband, Douglas, The London Merchant, Speed the Plough, All in the Wrong, Venice Preserv'd; or, a Plot Discover'd, The Dramatist; or, Stop Him Who Can!, Bury-Fair, The Rivals, The Conscious Lovers, High Life Below the Stairs, The Relapse; or, Virtue in Danger, The Plain-Dealer.

326. MOSEL, Tad, *Other People's Houses* (Simon & Schuster, 1956).

The Waiting Place, Stars in the Summer Night, Other People's Houses, My Lost Saints, The Lawn Party, The Haven, Ernie Barger Is Fifty.

327. MOSES, Montrose Jonas, *British Plays from the Restoration to 1820* (Little, Brown, 1929).

The Rehearsal, The Spanish Fryar: or the Double Discovery, The Man of Mode; or, Sir Fopling Flutter, The Plain-Dealer, The Way of the World, The Provok'd Wife, Venice Preserv'd; or, A Plot Discover'd, The Careless Husband, The Conscious Lovers, Jane Shore, The Beaux' Stratagem, The Beggar's Opera, Douglas, She Stoops to Conquer; or, The Mistakes of a Night, The Fashionable Lover, The Clandestine Marriage, The School for Scandal, The Cenci.

328. MOSES, Montrose Jonas and CAMPBELL, Oscar J., *Dramas of Modernism* (Little, Brown, 1941).

The Cherry Orchard, Night's Lodging (The Lower Depths), He Who Gets Slapped, From Morn to Midnight, The Machine-Wreckers, The Dream Doctor, Right You Are (If You Think So), Adam the Creator, Liliom, There Are Crimes and Crimes, The Circle, The Truth about Blayds, Wings over Europe, Craig's Wife, The Silver Cord, Desire under the Elms, Idiot's Delight, Winterset, Shadow and Substance, Golden Boy.

329. MOSES, Montrose Jonas and KRUTCH, Joseph Wood, *Representative American Dramas* (Little, Brown, 1941).

A Texas Steer, The Girl of the Golden West, The Witching Hour, The City, The Scarecrow, The Piper, Mrs. Bumpstead-Leigh, It Pays to Advertise, The Famous Mrs. Fair, The Emperor Jones, Nice People, The Detour, Dulcy, The Adding Machine, The Show-Off, Lucky Sam McCarver, The Second Man, Holiday, The Green Pastures, Awake and Sing, The Petrified Forest, The Masque of Kings.

330. MOSES, Montrose Jonas, *Representative British Dramas, Victorian and Modern,* New rev. ed. (Little, Brown, 1931).

London Assurance, A Blot in the 'Scutcheon, Richelieu; or, The Conspiracy, Easy Virtue, A Bill of Divorcement, The Gods of the Mountain, The Silver Box, H. M. S. Pinafore; or, The Lass That Loved a Sailor, The Madras House, The Workhouse Ward, The Cassilis Engagement, Black-Ey'd Susan; or, All in the Downs, The Masqueraders, Virginius, Our Betters, First Blood, At Mrs. Beam's, The Gay Lord Quex, Caste, Riders to the Sea, The Ticket-of-Leave Man, The Importance of Being Earnest, Cathleen ni Houlihan.

331. MOSES, Montrose Jonas, *Representative Continental Dramas* (Little, Brown, 1924).

The Wild Duck, The Lonely Way, The Fires of St. John, The Sunken Bell, The Seagull, The Life of Man, The Daughter of Jorio, Like Falling Leaves, The World and His Wife, The Bonds of Interest, Cyrano de Bergerac, The Vultures, Lovers, Monna Vanna, The Dawn.

332. MOSES, Montrose Jonas, *Representative One-Act Plays by Continental Authors* (Little, Brown, 1922).

Countess Mizzie, Death and the Fool, The Blind, The Birthday Party, The
Woman Who Was Acquitted, Five Little Dramas, Francoise's Luck, Morituri:
Theias, The Court Singer, Sacred Ground, An Incident, A Merry Death, By
Their Words Ye Shall Know Them, The Lover, Simoom.

333. MOSES, Montrose Jonas, *Representative Plays by American Dramatists, 1765–
1819*, Vol. I (Dutton, 1918).
The Prince of Parthia, Ponteach, The Group, The Battle of Bunker Hill, The
Fall of British Tyranny, The Politician Out-Witted, The Contrast, André, The
Indian Princess, She Would Be a Soldier.

334. MOSES, Montrose Jonas, *Representative Plays by American Dramatists, 1815–
1858*, Vol. II (Dutton, 1921).
Fashionable Follies, Brutus, Sertorius, Tortesa, The People's Lawyer, Jack
Cade, Fashion, Uncle Tom's Cabin, Self, Horseshoe Robinson.

335. MOSES, Montrose Jonas, *Representative Plays by American Dramatists, 1856–
1911*, Vol. III (Dutton, 1925).
Rip Van Winkle, Francesca da Rimini, Love in '76, Paul Kauvar, Shenandoah,
In Mizzoura, The Moth and the Flame, The New York Idea, The Easiest Way,
The Return of Peter Grimm.

336. MURPHY, Charles T., GUINAGH, Kevin, and OATES, Whitney J., Translators,
Greek and Roman Classics in Translation (Longmans, Green, 1947).
Prometheus Bound, The Clouds, Hippolytus, Oedipus the King.

337. MURRAY, Gilbert and Others, Translators, *Ten Greek Plays* (Oxford University Press, 1930).
Agamemnon, The Choephoroe, The Eumenides, The Frogs, Plautus, the God
of Riches, Electra, Iphigenia in Tauris, Medea, Antigone, Oedipus, King of
Thebes.

338. NAGELBERG, Munjou Moses, *Drama in Our Time* (Harcourt, Brace, 1948).
One-third of a Nation, R.U.R., El Capitan and the Corporal, Watch on the
Rhine, Yellow Jack, The Human Comedy, Abe Lincoln in Illinois, Our Town.

339. NATHAN, George Jean, *The Critics Prize Plays,* (World Publishing Co., 1945).
High Tor, Of Mice and Men, Watch on the Rhine, The Patriots, The Time
of Your Life, Winterset.

340. NATHAN, George Jean, *Five Great Modern Irish Plays* (Modern Library,
1941).
Shadow and Substance, Spreading the News, Juno and the Paycock, The
Playboy of the Western World, Riders to the Sea.

341. NATHAN, George Jean, *World's Great Plays* (World Publishing Co., 1944).
Lysistrata, The Cherry Orchard, Faust, The Master Builder, The Plough and
the Stars, The Emperor Jones, Cyrano de Bergerac.

342. NEILSON, W. A., *Chief Elizabethan Dramatists* (Houghton Mifflin, 1939).
Endymion, The Old Wives' Tale, The Honorable History of Friar Bacon and
Friar Bungay, Tamburlaine Part I, Doctor Faustus, The Jew of Malta, Trouble-
some Reign of Edward the Second, The Spanish Tragedy, Bussy D'Ambois,
Every Man in His Humor, Sejanus, Volpone, The Alchemist, The Shoemakers'
Holiday, The Honest Whore I and II, The Malcontent, A Woman Killed with
Kindness, The Knight of the Burning Pestle, Philaster, The Maid's Tragedy,

The Faithful Shepherdess, The Wild Goose Chase, The Duchess of Malfi, A Trick to Catch the Old One, The Changeling, A New Way to Pay Old Debts, The Broken Heart, The Lady of Pleasure, The Cardinal.

343. NELSON, John Herbert and CARGILL, Oscar, *Contemporary Trends: American Literature since 1900*, Rev. ed. (Macmillan, 1949).

Winterset, The Fall of the City, Bound East for Cardiff, Lazarus Laughed.

344. NETTLETON, George Henry and CASE, Arthur Ellicott, *British Dramatists from Dryden to Sheridan* (Houghton Mifflin, 1939).

Cato, The Rehearsal, The Careless Husband, The Jealous Wife, The Way of the World, The West Indian, All for Love; or, The World Well Lost, The Conquest of Granada by the Spaniards, Part I, The Man of Mode; or, Sir Fopling Flutter, The Beaux' Stratagem, Tom Thumb, The Lying Valet, The Beggar's Opera, She Stoops to Conquer, Douglas, The London Merchant, Venice Preserv'd, The Tragedy of Jane Shore, The Critic; or, A Tragedy Rehearsed, The Rivals, The School for Scandal, The Conscious Lovers, The Relapse; or, Virtue in Danger, The Plain Dealer.

345. NICHOLSON, Kenyon, *The Appleton Book of Short Plays*, 1st Series (Appleton, 1926).

The Managers, Finders-Keepers, Apartments to Let, One Egg, The End of the Trail, George Washington at the Delaware, Society Notes, Social Balance, The Wedding Dress, When the Clock Strikes, Pierrot's Mother, The Ghost Story.

346. NICHOLSON, Kenyon, *The Appleton Book of Short Plays,* 2nd Series (Appleton, 1927).

The Eldest, Post Mortems, Samson à La Mode, The Warrior's Husband, Ambush, The Melancholy Dame, A Cup of Tea, Gas Air and Earl, Appearances, 'Twas Ever Thus, Prince Gabby, Delilah.

347. NICOLL, Allardyce, *Lesser English Comedies of the Eighteenth Century* (London, Oxford University Press, 1927; World's Classics).

The Jealous Wife, Every One Has His Fault, Speed the Plough, The Way to Keep Him, The Dramatist.

348. NOYES, George Rapall, *Masterpieces of the Russian Drama* (Appleton-Century, 1933).

Professor Storitsyn, The Cherry Orchard, The Young Hopeful, The Inspector, Down and Out, Wit Works Woe, Mystery-Bouffe, The Poor Bride, A Bitter Fate, The Death of Ivan the Terrible, The Power of Darkness, A Month in the Country.

349. OATES, Whitney Jennings and O'NEILL, Eugene Gladstone, Jr., Translators, *The Complete Greek Drama*, Vol. I (Random House, 1938).

Agamemnon, The Choephori, The Eumenides, The Persians, Prometheus Bound, The Seven against Thebes, The Suppliants, Alcestis, Andromache, The Heracleidae, Heracles, Hippolytus, Ion, Iphigenia in Tauris, Medea, The Suppliants, The Trojan Women, Ajax, Antigone, Electra, Oedipus at Colonus, Oedipus the King, Philoctetes, The Trachiniae, Hecuba.

350. OATES, Whitney Jennings and O'NEILL, Eugene Gladstone, Jr., Translators, *The Complete Greek Drama*, Vol. II (Random House, 1938).

The Acharnians, The Birds, The Clouds, The Ecclesiazusae, The Frogs, The Knights, Lysistrata, Peace, Plutus, Thesmophoriazusae, The Wasps, The

Bacchae, The Cyclops, Electra, Helen, Iphigenia in Aulis, Orestes, The Phoenissae, Rhesus, The Arbitration, The Girl from Samos, The Shearing of Glycera.

351. OBOLER, Arch and LONGSTREET, Stephan, *Free World Theatre* (Random House, 1944).
The People March, Your Day Is Coming, Rip Van Dinkel of Nuremberg, I Have No Prayer, White House Kitchen, Music for Freedom, The Fountain of Dancing Children, Night Flight, Fiesta, U.S.S. Middletown, China to America, Last Will and Testament of Tom Smith, My Mothers Never Weep, Something About Joe, Man with a Beard, General Armchair, The Second Battle of Warsaw, In Memory of a Hero, V-Day.

352. OBOLER, Arch, *Ivory Tower and Other Radio Plays* (William Targ, 1940).
Ivory Tower, Alter Ego, The Ugliest Man in the World.

353. OBOLER, Arch, *Plays for Americans* (Rinehart, 1942).
Letter at Midnight, Hate, Ghost Story, Chicago, Germany, Paul Reverski, Memo to Berchtesgaden, Adolph and Mrs. Runyon, Miracle in 3B, The Welburns—A Confidential Report, Blood Story, Execution, The Last in the World, Johnny Quinn, U.S.N.

354. OLFSON, Lewy, *Radio Plays from Shakespeare* (Plays, Inc., 1958).
A Midsummer Night's Dream, The Taming of the Shrew, Much Ado About Nothing, As You Like It, The Tempest, Romeo and Juliet, Julius Caesar, Hamlet, King Lear, Macbeth.

355. OLIPHANT, Ernest Henry Clark, *Elizabethan Dramatists Other Than Shakespeare* (Prentice-Hall, 1931).
Arden of Feversham, The Knight of the Burning Pestle, The Maid's Tragedy, Philaster, A Jovial Crew, The Honest Whore, Part II, The Merry Devil of Edmonton, The Broken Heart, Friar Bacon and Friar Bungay, A Woman Killed with Kindness, The Alchemist, Bartholomew Fair, Volpone, Eastward Hoe!, The Spanish Tragedy, Campaspe, Edward II, Doctor Faustus, A New Way to Pay Old Debts, Women, Beware Women, The Changeling, Comus, The Old Wives' Tale, The Two Angry Women at Abington, A Fair Quarrel, The Traitor, The Revenger's Tragedy, The Duchess of Malfi, The White Devil, A Yorkshire Tragedy.

356. O'NEILL, Eugene Gladstone, *The Long Voyage Home: Seven Plays of the Sea* (Random House, 1946).
The Moon of the Caribbees, Bound East for Cardiff, The Long Voyage Home, In the Zone, Ile, The Rope, Where the Cross Is Made.

357. O'NEILL, Eugene Gladstone, *Nine Plays*, edited by Saxe Commins (Random House, 1954).
Strange Interlude, Mourning Becomes Electra, The Emperor Jones, Desire under the Elms, The Hairy Ape, All God's Chillun Got Wings, The Great God Brown, Marco Millions, Lazarus Laughed.

358. O'NEILL, Eugene Gladstone, *The Plays of Eugene O'Neill*, Vol. I, (Random House, 1951).
Strange Interlude, Desire under the Elms, Lazarus Laughed, The Fountain, The Moon of the Caribbees, Bound East for Cardiff, The Rope, The Dreamy Kid, Before Breakfast.

359. O'Neill, Eugene Gladstone, *The Plays of Eugene O'Neill*, Vol. II, (Random House, 1951).

Ah, Wilderness! All God's Chillun Got Wings, Marco Millions, Welded, Diff'rent, Gold.

360. O'Neill, Eugene Gladstone, *The Plays of Eugene O'Neill*, Vol. III, (Random House, 1951).

Anna Christie, Beyond the Horizon, The Emperor Jones, The Hairy Ape, The Great God Brown, The Straw, Dynamo, Days without End, The Iceman Cometh.

361. Parker, Kenneth T., *Parker's Television Plays* (Northwestern Press, 1954).

A Cup of Tea, Shall We Dance?, Voice of the Machines, Star Minded, Within the Family, Cry on My Shoulder, Stand Up to Death, Double Identity.

362. Parks, Edd Winfield and Beaty, Richard Croom, *The English Drama: An Anthology, 900–1642* (Norton, 1935).

Abraham and Isaac, Philaster; or, Love Lies A-Bleeding, The Vision of the Twelve Goddesses, The Shoemakers' Holiday, Everyman, Two Noble Kinsmen, 'Tis a Pity She's a Whore, The Honorable History of Friar Bacon and Friar Bungay, A Merry Play between John John the Husband, A Woman Killed with Kindness, Every Man in His Humour, Oberon, the Fairy Prince, Sejanus, His Fall, Volpone; or, the Fox, The Spanish Tragedy, Endymion, Edward II, The Jew of Malta, The Tragical History of Dr. Faustus, A New Way to Pay Old Debts, Comus, Oxfordshire St. George Play, The Old Wives' Tale, The Miles Gloriosus, The Quem Queritis, Robin Hood and the Friar, The Second Shepherds' Play, Thyestes, Shetland Sword Dance, The Cardinal, The Lady of May, Ralph Roister Doister, The White Devil.

363. Parry, W. Dyfed, *Old Plays for Modern Players*, (London, Arnold, 1930).

Abraham and Isaac, The Four P's, The Play of the Weather, Volpone; or, the Fox, Noah's Flood, The Old Wives' Tale, The Shepherds' Play.

364. Pence, Raymond Woodbury, *Dramas by Present-Day Writers* (Scribner, 1927).

The Slave with Two Faces, Cophetua, Loyalties, Trifles, Spreading the News, A Love Passage, The Goal, Counsel Retained, Thursday Evening, Ile, A Marriage Has Been Arranged, Confessional, Milestones, Merton of the Movies, Monsieur Beaucaire.

365. Quinn, Arthur H., *Contemporary American Plays* (Scribner, 1923).

Why Marry, The Emperor Jones, Nice People, The Hero, To the Ladies.

366. Quinn, Arthur H., *Representative American Plays* (Century 1917).

Superstition, Madame Butterfly, The Broker of Bogotá, Francesca da Rimini, The Octoroon; or, Life in Louisiana, He and She, Pocahontas, or, The Settlers of Virginia, André, Her Great Match, Secret Service, The Prince of Parthia, Shenandoah, Leonora; or, the World's Own, The Scarecrow, Hazel Kirke, The New York Idea, The Faith Healer, Charles the Second, Rip Van Winkle, Fashion, The Boss, The Triumph at Plattsburg, The Witching Hour, The Contrast, Tortesa the Usurer.

367. Quinn, Arthur H., *Representative American Plays, 1767–1923*, 3rd ed. (Century, 1925).

Superstition, Madame Butterfly, The Broker of Bogotá, Francesca da Rimini, The Octoroon; or, Life in Louisiana, He and She, Pocahontas; or, The Settlers of Virginia, André, Her Great Match, Secret Service, The Prince of Parthia, Shenandoah, Leonora; or, The World's Own, The Scarecrow, Hazel Kirke, The New York Idea, The Faith Healer, Beyond the Horizon, Charles the Second, Rip Van Winkle, Fashion, The Boss, The Triumph at Plattsburg, The Witching Hour, The Contrast, Sun-up, Tortesa the Usurer.

368. QUINN, Arthur H., *Representative American Plays, 1767–1923*, 4th ed. (Century, 1930).

The Prince of Parthia, The Contrast, André, Superstition, Charles the Second, The Triumph at Plattsburg, Pocahontas; or, The Settlers of Virginia, The Broker of Bogatá, Tortesa the Usurer, Fashion, Francesca da Rimini, Leonora, The Octoroon, Rip Van Winkle, Hazel Kirke, Shenandoah, Secret Service, Madame Butterfly, Her Great Match, The New York Idea, The Witching Hour, The Faith Healer, The Scarecrow, The Boss, He and She, Beyond the Horizon, The Silver Cord.

369. QUINN, Arthur H., *Representative American Plays: from 1767 to the Present Day*, 6th ed. (Appleton-Century, 1936).

Winterset, Superstition, Paris Bound, Madame Butterfly, The Broker of Bogotá, Francesca da Rimini, The Octoroon; or, Life in Louisiana, He and She, Pocahontas; or, The Settlers of Virginia, André, The Girl with the Green Eyes, Secret Service, The Prince of Parthia, Margaret Fleming, Shenandoah, The Silver Cord, The Scarecrow, Hazel Kirke, The New York Idea, The Faith Healer, Beyond the Horizon, Charles the Second, Rip Van Winkle, Fashion, The Boss, The Witching Hour, The Contrast, Sun-up, Tortesa the Usurer.

370. QUINN, Arthur H., *Representative American Plays: from 1767 to the Present Day*, 7th ed. (Appleton-Century-Crofts, 1953).

The Prince of Parthia, The Contrast, André, Superstition, Charles the Second, Pocahontas; or, The Settlers of Virginia, The Broker of Bogotá, Tortesa the Usurer, Fashion, Francesca da Rimini, The Octoroon; or, Life in Louisiana, Rip Van Winkle, Hazel Kirke, Shenandoah, Margaret Fleming, Secret Service, Madame Butterfly, The Girl with the Green Eyes, The New York Idea, The Witching Hour, The Faith Healer, The Scarecrow, The Boss, He and She, Beyond the Horizon, Sun-up, The Silver Cord, Paris Bound, Winterset, Command Decision, South Pacific.

371. RHYS, Ernest, *Everyman and Other Interludes* (London, Dent, 1909; Everyman's Library).

Everyman, The Deluge, Abraham, Melchisedec, and Isaac, The Wakefield Second Shepherds' Play, The Coventry Nativity Play, The Wakefield Miracle-Play of the Crucifixion, The Cornish Mystery-Play of the Three Maries, The Mystery of Mary Magdalene and the Apostles, The Wakefield Pageant and the Harrowing of Hell, God's Promises.

372. RHYS, Ernest, *Everyman, with Other Interludes, including Eight Miracle Plays* (London, Dent, 1926; Everyman's Library).

Abraham, Melchisedec, and Isaac, God's Promises, The Crucifixion, The Deluge, Everyman, The Harrowing of Hell, Mary Magdalene, Pageant of Shearmen and Taylors, St. George and the Dragon, Second Shepherds' Play, The Three Maries.

373. RICKABY, Franz, *Dakota Playmaker Plays*, First Series (Baker, 1923).

The Diabolical Circle, John Bargrave, Gentleman, Another Man's Place, Dowry and Romance.

374. ROBBINS, Harry Wolcott and COLEMAN, William Harold, *Western World Literature* (Macmillan, 1938).
Agamemnon, The Frogs, Keep Your Own Secret, Iphigenia at Aulis, Everyman, Faust, Part I, Ghosts, The Misanthrope, Beyond the Horizon, The Captives, Phaedra, King Lear, The Rivals.

375. ROBERTS, Carl Eric Bechhofer, Translator, *Five Russian Plays, with One from the Ukrainian* (Dutton, 1916).
The Jubilee, The Wedding, The Beautiful Despot, A Merry Death, The Babylonian Captivity, The Choice of a Tutor.

376. ROBERTS, Edward Barry, *Television Writing and Selling* (The Writer, 1954).
The Inn, Impersonation, Best Trip Ever.

377. ROBINSON, Charles Alexander, Jr., *An Anthology of Greek Drama* (Rinehart, 1949).
Agamemnon, Lysistrata, Hippolytus, Medea, Antigone, Oedipus the King.

378. ROBINSON, Donald Ray, *The Harvard Dramatic Club Miracle Plays* (French, 1928).
The Pageant of the Shearmen and the Tailors: The Coventry Play, The Towneley Play. The Nativity: The Chantilly Play, The Benediktbeuren Play. The Wisemen: The Spanish Play, The Provençal Play, The Hessian Christmas Play, The Maastricht Play. The Star: The Bilsen Play, The Umbrian Play.

379. ROCKWELL, Ethel, *Wisconsin Rural Plays* (Dramatic Publishing Co., 1931).
Goose Money, Dreams, King Row, Sons of Soil, Short Cut.

380. ROHAN, Pierre de, *Federal Theatre Plays* (Random House, 1938).
One-Third of a Nation, Prologue to Glory, Haiti, Power, A Living Newspaper, Spirochete, Triple A Plowed Under.

381. ROLFE, Franklin Prescott, DAVENPORT, William H., and BOWERMAN, Paul, *The Modern Omnibus* (Harcourt, Brace, 1946).
Key Largo, Of Thee I Sing, The Male Animal, Abe Lincoln in Illinois.

382. ROSE, Reginald, *Six Television Plays* (Simon & Schuster, 1956).
The Remarkable Incident at Carson Corners, Thunder on Sycamore Street, Twelve Angry Men, An Almanac of Liberty, Crime in the Streets, The Incredible World of Horace Ford.

383. ROWE, Kenneth Thorpe, *University of Michigan Plays*, Vol. I (George Wahr, 1929).
Outside This Room, Passion's Progress, My Man, The Joiners, Puppet.

384. ROWE, Kenneth Thorpe, *University of Michigan Plays*, Vol. II (George Wahr, 1930).
Lassitude, The Day's Work, Three-a-Day, Many Happy Returns, Wives-in-Law, They Too.

385. ROWELL, George, *Nineteenth-Century Plays* (Oxford 1953; World's Classics).
Black-Ey'd Susan, Money, Masks and Faces, The Colleen Bawn, Lady Audley's Secret, The Ticket-of-Leave Man, Caste, Two Roses, The Bells, A Pair of Spectacles.

386. RUBENSTEIN, H. F., *Great English Plays* (Harper, 1928).
A Wakefield Nativity, Everyman, John Tyb and the Curate, The Spanish Tragedy, The Old Wives' Tale, Doctor Faustus, Edward the Second, The Shoemakers' Holiday, A Yorkshire Tragedy, The Silent Woman, Eastward Ho!, The Maid's Tragedy, The Chances, The Bondmen, A New Way to Pay Old Debts, The White Devil, 'Tis a Pity She's a Whore, Venice Preserv'd, The Provok'd Wife, The Way of the World, The Recruiting Officer, She Stoops to Conquer, The School for Scandal, Society, Judah, Lady Windermere's Fan.

387. RYERSON, Florence and CLEMENTS, Colin, *All on a Summer's Day and Six Other Short Plays* (French, 1928).
All on a Summer's Day, On the Lot, Men Folk, Storm, Letters, A Romantic Interval, Love Is like That.

388. RYLANDS, George Humphrey W., *Elizabethan Tragedy* (London, Bell, 1933).
Bussy d'Ambois, 'Tis a Pity She's a Whore, A Woman Killed with Kindness, Tamburlaine the Great; Part I, The Revenger's Tragedy, The White Devil.

389. SARTRE, Jean Paul, *The Flies and In Camera*, translated by Stuart Gilbert (London, Hamilton, 1946).
The Flies, In Camera (No Exit, in American translation).

390. SAUNDERS, Louise, *Magic Lanterns* (Scribner, 1923).
Figureheads, Our Kind, Poor Maddalena, See-Saw, King and Commoner.

391. SAYLER, Oliver M. *The Eleonora Duse Series of Plays* (Brentano, 1923).
The Dead City, Thy Will Be Done, Ghosts, The Lady from the Sea, The Closed Door.

392. SAYLER, Oliver M., *Moscow Art Theatre Series of Russian Plays* (Brentano, 1923).
The Cherry Orchard, The Three Sisters, Uncle Vanya, The Lower Depths, Tsar Fyodor Ivanovitch.

393. SAYLER, Oliver M., *Moscow Art Theatre Series of Russian Plays*. 2nd Series (Brentano, 1923).
Ivanoff, The Brothers Karamazoff, The Mistress of the Inn, An Enemy of the People, Enough Stupidity in Every Wise Man.

394. SCHELLING, Felix Emmanuel, *Typical Elizabethan Plays* (Harper, 1926).
The Maid's Tragedy, Philaster; or, Love Lies A-Bleeding, Eastward Ho!, The Pleasant Comedy of Old Fortunatus, Rule a Wife and Have a Wife, The Chronical History of Perkin Warbeck, a Strange Truth, A Pleasant Conceited Comedy, A Woman Killed with Kindness, The Hue and Cry after Cupid, The Sad Shepherd, Volpone; or, the Fox, The Lamentable and True Tragedy of Master Arden of Feversham in Kent, Endymion, the Man in the Moon, The Tragical History of Doctor Faustus, The Troublesome Reign and Lamentable Death of Edward II, A New Way to Pay Old Debts, The Changeling, Sir Thomas More, The Return from Parnassus; or, The Scourge of Simony, Part II, The Lady of Pleasure, The Tragedy of the Duchess of Malfi.

395. SCHWEIKERT, H. C., *Early English Plays* (Harcourt, Brace, 1928).
Quem Quaeritis, Banns, The Fall of Lucifer, Noah, Abraham and Isaac, The Second Sheperds' Play, The Judgment Day, Everyman, Robin Hood and the Friar, Saint George and the Dragon, Ralph Roister Doister, Gorboduc, Endymion, The Old Wives' Tale, The Honorable History of Friar Bacon and Friar

Bungay, The Spanish Tragedy, Tamburlaine the Great, The Tragical History of Dr. Faustus, Every Man in His Humor, The Shoemakers' Holiday.

396. SEBOYER, Gerald Edwin and BROSIUS, Rudolph, *Readings in European Literature* (Crofts, 1928).

Prometheus Bound, The Frogs, Medea, Ghosts, The High-Brow Ladies, The Crock of Gold, Phaedra, Antigone, Andria; the Fair Andrian.

397. SELDES, George S. and Gilbert, Translators, *Plays of the Moscow Art Theatre Musical Studio* (Brentano, 1925).

Lysistrata, The Daughter of Madame Angot, Carmencita and the Soldier, La Perichole, Love and Death.

398. SETTEL, Irving, *Top TV Shows of the Year, 1954–1955* (Hastings House, 1955).

Toys and Science, A Letter to the Boss, Report on Senator Joseph McCarthy, Arthritis and Rheumatism, Elisha and the Long Knives, Native Dancer, The Thinking Heart, Camel News Caravan, What's My Line?, Governor Herman Talmadge of Georgia, Conquest of Pain, The Home Show.

399. SHAFER, Robert, *From Beowulf to Thomas Hardy*, Vol. I, New ed., (Doubleday, 1939).

The Shoemakers' Holiday, All for Love; or The World Well Lost, Everyman, The Tragical History of Doctor Faustus, The Second Shepherds' Play.

400. SHAFER, Robert, *From Beowulf to Thomas Hardy*, Vol. II, New ed. (Doubleday, 1939).

The Rivals, The Importance of Being Earnest.

401. SHAW, Bernard, *Selected Plays*, Vol. I (Dodd, Mead, 1948).

The Doctor's Dilemma, Pygmalion, Major Barbara, Heartbreak House, Captain Brassbound's Conversion, The Man of Destiny, Androcles and the Lion.

402. SHAW, Bernard, *Selected Plays*, Vol. II (Dodd, Mead, 1948).

Back to Methuselah, Saint Joan, John Bull's Other Island, You Never Can Tell, In Good King Charles's Golden Days.

403. SHAW, Bernard, *Selected Plays*, Vol. III (Dodd, Mead, 1948).

Mrs. Warren's Profession, Arms and the Man, Candida, The Devil's Disciple, Caesar and Cleopatra, Man and Superman, Fanny's First Play, The Dark Lady of the Sonnets.

404. SHAW, Bernard, *Selected Plays*, Vol. IV (Dodd, Mead, 1957).

Misalliance, The Apple Cart, Getting Married, Widowers' Houses, Great Catherine, Too True to Be Good, The Millionairess.

405. SHAY, Frank, *The Appleton Book of Christmas Plays* (Appleton, 1929).

Dust of the Road, The Littlest Shepherd, Christmas Eve, A Christmas Tale, A Modern Viking, The Boy on the Meadow, Exile, The Enchanted Christmas Tree, The Duquesne Christmas Mystery, A Christmas Carol, The Seven Gifts.

406. SHAY, Frank, *The Appleton Book of Holiday Plays* (Appleton, 1930).

The Pie and the Tart, Lee the Virginian, Child of the Frontier, Young Washington at Mt. Vernon, Two Blind Men and a Donkey, Washington and Betsy Ross, Some There Are Who Remember, For God and Spain, Two Plum Puddings, Columbine Madonna.

407. SHAY, Frank and LOVING, Pierre, *Fifty Contemporary One-Act Plays* (Appleton, 1920).

Madonna Dianora, Literature, The Intruder, Interlude, Autumn Fires, M. Lamblin, Françoise' Luck, Altruism, The Tenor, A Good Woman, The Little Stone House, Mary's Wedding, The Pierrot of the Minute, The Subjection of Kezia, The Constant Lover, The Judgment of Indra, The Workhouse Ward, Louise, The Grandmother, The Rights of the Soul, Love of One's Neighbor, The Boor, His Widow's Husband, A Sunny Morning, The Creditor, Brothers, In the Morgue, The Baby Carriage, A Death in Fever Flat, The Slave with Two Faces, The Slump, Mansions, Trifles, The Pot Boiler, Enter the Hero, The Shepherd in the Distance, Boccaccio's Untold Tale, Another Way Out, Aria da Capo, Helena's Husband, The Shadowed Star, Ile, The Nursery Maid of Heaven, Three Travelers Watch a Sunrise, Sham, The Medicine Show, For All Time, The Finger of God, Night, Forgotten Souls.

408. SHAY, Frank, *Fifty More Contemporary One-Act Plays* (Appleton, 1928).

Liars, Marthe, Faithful Admirer, A Morality Play for the Leisured Class, Winter's Night, Death Says It Isn't So, Orlando Furioso, The Duchess Says Her Prayers, Across the Border, Mountain Laurel, A Lady and the Law, The Weather Breeder, Whose Money?, Winners All, Two Passengers for Chelsea, The Home for the Friendly, Bumbo the Clown, The Vanishing Princess, The Death of Nero, Quare Medicine, Juliet and Romeo, Jack and Jill and a Friend, The Demands of Society, Creeds, The Unruly Member, A Leap-Year Bride, Pottery, The Liar and the Unicorn, The Eve in Evelyn, A Comedy of Danger, Blue Blood, Don Juan's Christmas Eve, The Threshold, The Avenue, The Razor, The Marriage of Little Eva, The Birdcatcher, The Moon of the Caribbees, Wind o' the Moors, Escape, Brothers, The Chip Woman's Fortune, The Veil, Bumblepuppy, The Third Angle, Moral Courage, The Giant's Stair, The Dance Below, A Budapest Salesman Should Not Read French Illustrated Magazines, The Letters.

409. SHAY, Frank, *Plays for Strolling Mummers* (Appleton, 1926).

Dancing Dolls, Inside Stuff, Great Moments, The Flirtation, All on a Summer's Day, My Tailor, A Course in Piracy, Creatures of Impulse.

410. SHAY, Frank, *Treasury of Plays for Men* (Little, Brown, 1932).

Four Who Were Blind, The Devil's Gold, Blood o' Kings, It Isn't Done, Outclassed, The Hand of Siva, Action!, The Alchemist, The Silent Waiter, Vote the New Moon, The Stick-Up, The Accomplice, The Judgment of Indra, The Beggar and the King, Just Two Men, Freedom, Release, The Rusty Door, The Gold Circle, Three Wishes, In Front of Potter's.

411. SHAY, Frank, *Treasury of Plays for Women* (Little, Brown, 1922).

The Siege, Columbine, The Lost Pleiad, The China Pig, A Patroness, Ever Young, For Distinguished Service, Rocking Chairs, Manikin and Minikin, The Death of Tintagiles, The Conflict, The Lamp and the Bell, Rehearsal, Before Breakfast, My Lady Dreams, Blackberryin', The Stronger Woman, Motherly Love.

412. SHAY, Frank, *Twenty Contemporary One-Act Plays, American* (Appleton, 1922).

Mirage, Napoleon's Barber, Goat Alley, Sweet and Twenty, Tickless Time, The Hero of Santa Maria, All Gummed Up, Thompson's Luck, Fata Deorum, Pearl of Dawn, Finders-Keepers, Solomon's Song, Matinata, The Conflict, Two

Slatterns and a King, Thursday Evening, The Dreamy Kid, Forbidden Fruit, Jezebel, Sir David Wears a Crown.

413. SHAY, Frank, *Twenty-Five Short Plays, International* (Appleton, 1925).

The Accomplice, The Festival of Bacchus, Interior, Chintamani, The Witness, Pyentsa, Brother in Arms, The Thrice-Promised Bride, When Love Dies, Eyes That Cannot See, Pan in Pimlico, Pierre Patelin, Jubilee, The Bridegroom, The Marriage, A Snowy Night, The Cherry-Blossom River, The Sentence of Death, In Confidence, On the Highway, The Street Singer, The Disenchanted, Poverty, Joe, The Shunamite.

414. SHERWOOD, Garrison, and CHAPMAN, John, *Best Plays of 1894–1899* (Dodd, Mead, 1955). *See also entries 53–55, 212–214, 238–269, 414.*

Rebellious Susan, Heart of Maryland, Secret Service, The Little Minister, Trelawny of the Wells.

415. SMITH, Alice M., *Short Plays by Representative Authors* (Macmillan, 1922).

The Hraun Farm, The Merry Merry Cuckoo, The Locked Chest, The Post Office, Six Who Pass While the Lentils Boil, The Silver Lining, By Ourselves, The Rider of Dreams, Spreading the News, The Swan Song, The Man on the Kerb, The Shadowed Star.

416. SMITH, Betty, *Twenty Prize-Winning Non-Royalty One-Act Plays* (Greenberg, 1943).

According to Law, Western Night, Give Us Time to Sing, Franklin and the King, To the Lovely Margaret, These Doggone Elections, The Feast of Ortolans, Comin' for to Carry, The Ring for General Macías, Exclusive Model, Short-Tail Boy, Mañana Bandits, Ring Once for Central, There's a Nation, Fires at Valley Forge, Her Husband's Consent, Danbury Fair, Casualty South of Manila, Pot Luck, The Levite.

417. SMITH, Milton, *Short Plays of Various Types* (Bobbs-Merrill, 1924).

The Dark of the Dawn, The Maker of Dreams, A Night at an Inn, The Brink of Silence, The Rising of the Moon, The Silver Lining, The Turtle Dove, The Romancers, Pyramus and Thisbe, A Comedie Royall, The Falcon, Where but in America.

418. SMITH, Robert M., *Types of Domestic Tragedy*, Vol. I, World Drama Series (Prentice-Hall, 1928).

A Woman Killed with Kindness, George Barnwell, Maria Magdalena, The Father, Hedda Gabler, Gioconda, Mid-Channel.

419. SMITH, Robert M., *Types of Farce Comedy*, Vol. II, World Drama Series (Prentice-Hall, 1928).

The Frogs, The Menaechmi, The Taming of the Shrew, The Doctor in Spite of Himself, The Beggar's Opera, Patience, The Magistrate, The Importance of Being Earnest, The Man Who Married a Dumb Wife.

420. SMITH, Robert M., *Types of Historical Drama*, Vol. III, World Drama Series (Prentice-Hall, 1928).

Henry IV; Part I, William Tell, Prince of Homburg, Agnes Bernauer, Becket, The Pretenders.

421. SMITH, Robert M., *Types of Philosophic Drama*, Vol. IV, World Drama Series (Prentice-Hall, 1928).

Book of Job. Prometheus Bound, Everyman, Faustus, Samson Agonistes, Manfred, Prometheus Unbound, The Life of Man.

422. SMITH, Robert M., *Types of Romantic Drama*, Vol. V, World Drama Series (Prentice-Hall, 1928).

Romeo and Juliet, The Cid, All for Love, Pelléas and Mélisande, Cyrano de Bergerac, Paolo and Francesca, Sappho.

423. SMITH, Robert M., *Types of Social Comedy*, Vol. VI, World Drama Series (Prentice-Hall, 1928).

A New Way to Pay Old Debts, Tartuffe, The Way of the World, She Stoops to Conquer, The School for Scandal, Lady Windermere's Fan, The Gay Lord Quex, Our Betters.

424. SMITH, Robert M., *Types of World Tragedy*, Vol. VII, World Drama Series (Prentice-Hall, 1928).

Oedipus Rex, Medea, Phaedra, Othello, The Cenci, Ghosts, The Weavers, The Lower Depths.

425. SNYDER, Franklyn Bliss and MARTIN, Robert Grant, *A Book of English Literature*, Vol. I, 4th ed. (Macmillan, 1942).

Abraham and Isaac, All for Love, Everyman, Doctor Faustus, Noah's Flood, The Rivals.

426. SNYDER, Franklin Bliss and MARTIN, Robert Grant, *A Book of English Literature*, Vol. II (Macmillan, 1943).

Loyalties, Juno and the Paycock.

427. SPENCER, Hazelton, *Elizabethan Plays* (Little, Brown, 1933).

The Knight of the Burning Pestle, The Maid's Tragedy, Philaster; or, Love Lies A-Bleeding, Bussy d'Ambois, Eastward Ho!, The Honest Whore, The Shoemakers' Holiday, The Wild-Goose Chase, The Broken Heart, The Honourable History of Friar Bacon and Friar Bungay, A Woman Killed with Kindness, The Alchemist, Bartholomew Fair, Every Man in His Humour, Volpone; or, The Fox, The Spanish Tragedy, Endymion, The Jew of Malta, Tamburlaine, Part I, The Tragical History of Doctor Faustus, The Troublesome Reign and Lamentable Death of Edward II, The Malcontent, A New Way to Pay Old Debts, A Trick to Catch the Old One, The Changeling, The Lady of Pleasure, The White Devil.

428. STAUFFER, Ruth Matilda, *The Progress of Drama through the Centuries* (Macmillan, 1927).

The Lady of Lyons; or, Love and Pride, The Constant Prince, Polyeucte, The Trojan Women, Everyman, The Truth, She Stoops to Conquer, An Enemy of the People, Epicoene; or The Silent Woman, Doctor Faustus, L'Avare, Aulularia; or, The Pot of Gold, Berenice, William Tell, The Second Shepherds' Play, Hamlet, The School for Scandal, Antigone.

429. STEEVES, Harrison R., *Plays from the Modern Theatre* (Heath, 1931).

Ghosts, The Second Mrs. Tanqueray, The Beaver Coat, The Importance of Being Earnest, Lovers, The Cherry Orchard, Intermezzo, Liliom, The Great God Brown.

430. STEVENS, David Harrison, *Types of English Drama, 1660–1780* (Ginn, 1923).

Cato, The Rehearsal, Love for Love, The Way of the World, All for Love; or, The World Well Lost, Aureng-Zebe, The Man of Mode; or, Sir Fopling

Flutter, The Beaux' Stratagem, The Tragedy of Tragedies; or, The Life and Death of Tom Thumb the Great, The Beggar's Opera, The Good-Natured Man, She Stoops to Conquer, Douglas, The London Merchant, Venice Preserved; or, a Plot Discovered, Jane Shore, Bury Fair, The Critic, The Duenna, The Rivals, The School for Scandal, The Conscious Lovers.

431. Sutro, Alfred, *Five Little Plays* (Brentano's, 1912).
The Man in the Stalls, A Marriage Has Been Arranged, The Man on the Kerb, The Open Door, The Bracelet.

432. Tatlock, John, S. P. and Martin, Robert G., *Representative English Plays*, 2nd ed. (Appleton-Century-Crofts, 1938).
Noah's Flood, Abraham and Isaac, The Second Shepherds' Play, Everyman, Mother Bombie, The Troublesome Reign and Lamentable Death of Edward II, The Shoemakers' Holiday, A Woman Killed with Kindness, Philaster, The Alchemist, The Duchess of Malfi, The Wild-Goose Chase, The Changeling, Almanzor and Almahide, Venice Preserv'd, The Way of the World, Cato, The Conscious Lovers, The Tragedy of Tragedies, The London Merchant, She Stoops to Conquer, The School for Scandal, The Cenci, The Lady of Lyons, Caste, Lady Windermere's Fan, The Second Mrs. Tanqueray.

433. Taylor, Joseph Richard, *European and Asiatic Plays* (Expression, 1936).
The Frogs, Life Is a Dream, The Cid, The Shoemakers' Holiday, The Cormorant Fisher, The Bird Catcher in Hell, Medea, Everyman, The Four P's, Dulcitus, Shakuntala, A New Way to Pay Old Debts, The Menaechmi, Gorboduc, Atsumori, The Second Shepherds' Play, Medea, The Comedy of Errors, The Traitor, The Sorrows of Han, Ralph Roister Doister.

434. Taylor, W. D., *Eighteenth-Century Comedy* (Oxford, 1929).
The Beaux' Stratagem, The Conscious Lovers, The Beggar's Opera, The Tragedy of Tragedies, She Stoops to Conquer.

435. Thomas, Charles Swain, *Atlantic Book of Junior Plays* (Atlantic Monthly Press, 1924).
What Men Live By, Kinfolk of Robin Hood, Nerves, The Violin-Maker of Cremona, The Dyspeptic Ogre, The Fifteenth Candle, The Bellman of Mons, A Marriage Proposal, Jephtha's Daughter, A Minuet, The Play of Saint George, The Birthday of the Infanta, The Christmas Guest.

436. Thomas, Russell Brown, *Plays and the Theatre* (Little, Brown, 1937).
Elizabeth the Queen, The Barretts of Wimpole Street, An Enemy of the People, Poor Aubrey, Master Pierre Patelin, The Miser, Box and Cox, In the Zone, Romeo and Juliet, The School for Scandal, Antigone, The Giant's Stair.

437. Thompson, Stith, *Our Heritage of World Literature* (Dryden, 1938).
Agamemnon, The Frogs, The Cherry Orchard, Alcestis, Faust, Part I, A Doll's House, The Miser, The Captives, Phaedra, Hamlet, Antigone, The Importance of Being Earnest.

438. Tickner, Frederick James, *Restoration Dramatists* (London, Nelson, 1930).
Aureng-Zebe, The Beaux' Stratagem, Venice Preserv'd, A Journey to London.

439. Tucker, S. Marion, *Modern American and British Plays* (Harper, 1931).
The Circle, The Field God, Granite, The Great God Brown, The Hero, Hindle Wakes, Hobson's Choice, The Importance of Being Earnest, In a Garden, John Ferguson, The King's Henchman, The King's Jewry, Madame Sand,

Mary the Third, Rain, Saturday's Children, The Silver Cord, Sun-up, Thunderbolt, To the Ladies, The Truth about Blayds, The Vortex, Waste.

440. TUCKER, S. Marion, *Modern Continental Plays* (Harper, 1929).
He Who Gets Slapped, La Malquerida, Beyond Our Power, Phantasms, False Gods, R.U.R., The Tidings Brought to Mary, Francesca da Rimini, Electra, The Lower Depths, The Rats, The Coral, Gas I and II, Pelléas and Mélisande, Liliom, Cyrano de Bergerac, Light-o'-Love, Comrades, The Cherry Orchard, S.S.Tenacity, Such Is Life.

441. TUCKER, S. Marion, *Modern Plays* (Macmillan, 1932).
Mary the Third, The Ivory Door, Hell-Bent fer Heaven, Milestones, The Emperor Jones.

442. TUCKER, S. Marion, *Twelve One-Act Plays for Study and Production* (Ginn, 1929).
The Trysting Place, A Night at an Inn, Thursday Evening, Confessional, The Hundredth Trick, The Aulis Difficulty, A Minuet, Where the Cross Is Made, The Workhouse Ward, Moonshine, Back of the Yards, The Grand Cham's Diamond.

443. TUCKER, S. Marion, *Twenty-Five Modern Plays* (Harper, 1931).
The Circle, The Cherry Orchard, Comrades, The Coral, Cyrano De Bergerac, The Field God, Francesca da Rimini, The Great God Brown, He Who Gets Slapped, The Importance of Being Earnest, In a Garden, John Ferguson, La Malquerida, Light-o'-Love, Liliom, Mary the Third, Pélleas and Mélisande, The Rats, R.U.R., The Silver Cord, Sun-up, S.S. Tenacity, The Thunderbolt, The Truth about Blayds, The Vortex.

444. TUCKER, S. Marion and DOWNER, Alan S., *Twenty-Five Modern Plays*, Rev. ed. (Harper, 1948).
He Who Gets Slapped, The Ascent of F6, La Malquerida, R.U.R., The Cherry Orchard, The Infernal Machine, John Ferguson, The Lower Depths, The Field God, Command Decision, The Rats, The Silver Cord, Rosmersholm, The Coral, Gas I, Gas II, Pelléas and Mélisande, Liliom, The Plough and the Stars, The Great God Brown, The Thunderbolt, Roadside, Cyrano de Bergerac, Light-o'-Love, Comrades, Riders to the Sea, The Importance of Being Earnest.

445. TUPPER, Frederick and TUPPER, James W., *Representative English Dramas from Dryden to Sheridan*, New and enl. ed. (Oxford University Press, 1934).
Cato, Love's Last Shift, The Way of the World, All for Love, The Conquest of Granada, The Man of Mode, The Beaux' Stratagem, Tom Thumb the Great, The Beggar's Opera, She Stoops to Conquer, The London Merchant, Venice Preserv'd, The Tragedy of Jane Shore, The Rivals, The School for Scandal, The Conscious Lovers, The Relapse, The Country Wife.

446. TURRELL, Charles Alfred, Translator, *Contemporary Spanish Dramatists* (Badger, 1919).
The Women's Town, Juan José, The Claws, When The Roses Bloom Again, Electra, The Passing of the Magi.

447. UHLER, John E., *The Best Eighteenth-Century Comedies* (Crofts, 1930).
Beaux' Stratagem, Beggar's Opera, She Stoops to Conquer, The Rivals, The School for Scandal.

448. VIDAL, Gore, *Best Television Plays* (Ballantine, 1956).
The Mother, Thunder on Sycamore Street, Man in the Mountaintop, A Young Lady of Property, The Strike, The Rabbit Trap, Visit to a Small Planet.

449. VOADEN, Herman Arthur, *Four Good Plays to Read and Act* (Toronto, Longmans, Green, 1944).
Cavalcade, Pride and Prejudice, The Fall of the City, My Heart's in the Highlands.

450. WALKER, Stuart, *Portmanteau Adaptations* (Appleton, 1921).
Gammer Gurton's Needle, The Birthday of the Infanta, Sir David Wears a Crown, Nellijumbo.

451. WALKER, Stuart, *Portmanteau Plays* (Appleton, 1917).
The Trimplet, Nevertheless, The Medicine Show, Six Who Pass While the Lentils Boil.

452. WALL, Vincent and McCORMICK, James Patton, *Seven Plays of the Modern Theatre* (American Book, 1950).
The Hairy Ape, Blithe Spirit, The Glass Menagerie, Winterset, Hedda Gabler, The Circle, Uncle Vanya.

453. WALLEY, Harold Reinoehl, *The Book of the Play* (Scribner, 1950).
The Sea Gull, The Way of the World, An Enemy of the People, The Misanthrope, Desire under the Elms, Phaedra, Cyrano de Bergerac, The Tragedy of Hamlet, Prince of Denmark, Twelfth Night; or, What You Will, Oedipus the King, The Dream Play, The Playboy of the Western World.

454. WALLEY, Harold Reinoehl and WILSON, John Harold, *Early Seventeenth-Century Plays,* 1600–1642. (Harcourt, Brace, 1930).
A King or No King, A Mad Couple Well Matched, The Revenge of Bussy D'Ambois, Eastward Ho!, Love and Honor, The Honest Whore, Part I, The Wild-Goose Chase, 'Tis a Pity She's a Whore, A Woman Killed with Kindness Volpone; or, the Fox, The Dutch Courtesan, A New Way to Pay Old Debts, A Chaste Maid in Cheapside, The Cardinal, The White Devil.

455. WARNOCK, Robert and ANDERSON, George K., *The World in Literature,* Vol. I (Scott, Foresman, 1950).
Agamemnon, The Clouds, Hippolytus, Shakuntala, Oedipus the King.

456. WARNOCK, Robert and ANDERSON, George K., *The World in Literature,* Vol. II (Scott, Foresman, 1950).
Hamlet, Prince of Denmark, The Sheep Well.

457. WATSON, Ernest Bradlee, and PRESSEY, Benfield, *Contemporary Drama,* Vol. I, *American Plays* (Scribner, 1931).
The New York Idea, The Emperor Jones, Processional, Beggar on Horseback, The Silver Cord.

458. WATSON, Ernest Bradlee, and PRESSEY, Benfield, *Contemporary Drama,* Vol. II, *English and Irish Plays* (Scribner, 1931).
Riders to the Sea, Hyacinth Halvey, What Every Woman Knows, Mid-Channel, The Glittering Gate, Justice.

459. WATSON, Ernest Bradlee, and PRESSEY, Benfield, *Contemporary Drama,* Vol. III, *English and Irish Plays* (Scribner, 1931).
Mr. Pim Passes By, The Circle, Loyalties, Dear Brutus, Juno and the Paycock.

460. WATSON, Ernest Bradlee, and PRESSEY, Benfield, *Contemporary Drama,* Vol. IV, *European Plays* (Scribner, 1931).
A Doll's House, The Vultures, The Fossils, The Beaver Coat, Light-o'-Love.

461. WATSON, Ernest Bradlee, and PRESSEY, Benfield, *Contemporary Drama,* Vol. V, *European Plays* (Scribner, 1931).
Hedda Gabler, Pelléas and Mélisande, Magda, Cyrano de Bergerac, Uncle Vanya.

462. WATSON, Ernest Bradlee, and PRESSEY, Benfield, *Contemporary Drama,* Vol. VI, *European Plays* (Scribner, 1931).
The Sea Gull, The Lower Depths, Francesca da Rimini, The Dream Play, The Passion Flower.

463. WATSON, Ernest Bradlee, and PRESSEY, Benfield, *Contemporary Drama,* Vol. VII, *European Plays* (Scribner, 1931).
The Cherry Orchard, He Who Gets Slapped, Man and the Masses, R.U.R., Henry IV.

464. WATSON, Ernest Bradlee and PRESSEY, Benfield, *Contemporary Drama: European, English and Irish* (Scribner, 1941).
Elizabeth the Queen, He Who Gets Slapped, Dear Brutus, What Every Woman Knows, Hotel Universe, The Passion Flower, R.U.R., The Cherry Orchard, Uncle Vanya, The Fossils, The Glittering Gate, Justice, Loyalties, Night's Lodging; or, the Lower Depths, Hyacinth Halvey, The Beaver Coat, The Silver Cord, A Doll's House, Hedda Gabler, Beggar on Horseback, Processional, Pelléas and Mélisande, The Circle, Mr. Pim Passes By, Juno and the Paycock, The Emperor Jones, The Hairy Ape, Mid-Channel, Henry IV, Street Scene, Cyrano de Bergerac, Light-o'-love, Abe Lincoln in Illinois, The Dream Play, Magda, Riders to the Sea, Man and the Masses.

465. WATSON, Ernest Bradlee and PRESSEY, Benfield, *Contemporary Drama: Eleven Plays* (Scribner, 1956).
Pygmalion, The Green Pastures, The Happy Journey to Trenton and Camden, Ways and Means, Hello Out There, Antigone, The Glass Menagerie, The Madwoman of Chaillot, Another Part of the Forest, Death of a Salesman, Venus Observed.

466. WATT, Homer Andrew and CARGILL, Oscar, *College Reader* (Prentice-Hall, 1948).
End of Summer, Radio Primer, Strife, Spreading the News.

467. WATT, Homer Andrew and MUNN, James Buell, *Ideas and Forms in English and American Literature,* Vol. II (Scott, Foresman, 1932).
Hyacinth Halvey, The Dover Road, Gammer Gurton's Needle, The Second Mrs. Tanqueray, The School for Scandal, Riders to the Sea, The Duchess of Malfi, The Land of Heart's Desire.

468. WEATHERLEY, Edward Howell, MOFFETT, Harold Y., PROUTY, Charles T., and NOYES, Henry H. *The English Heritage,* Vol. I (Ginn, 1945).
Everyman, The Beaux' Stratagem, The Tragical History of Doctor Faustus, Noah's Flood, The Rivals.

469. WEATHERLEY, Edward Howell, MOFFETT, Harold Y., PROUTY, Charles T., and NOYES, Henry H. *The English Heritage,* Vol. II (Ginn, 1945).
The Twelve-Pound Look, Riders to the Sea.

470. WEATHERLEY, Edward H., WAGENER, A. Pelzer, ZEYDEL, Edwin H., and YARMOLINSKY, Avrahm, *The Heritage of European Literature,* Vol. I (Ginn, 1948).

Agamemnon, Electra, Oedipus the King, Phormio, The King the Greatest Alcalde.

471. WEATHERLEY, Edward H., WAGENER, A. Pelzer, ZEYDEL, Edwin H., and YARMOLINSKY, Avrahm, *The Heritage of European Literature,* Vol. II (Ginn, 1949).

The Cherry Orchard, Faust, Part I, The Wild Duck, Tartuffe; or, The Imposter, The Physician in Spite of Himself, Phaedra, William Tell.

472. WEBBER, J. P., and WEBSTER, H. H., *One-Act Plays for Secondary Schools* (Houghton Mifflin, 1923).

Boy Comes Home, Followers, Sunny Morning, Falcon, Coming of Fair Annie, Romancers, Lord's Prayer, Cottage on the Moor, Solemn Pride, X = O: A Night of the Trojan War, Rising of the Moon, Nevertheless, Manikin and Minikin, Beau of Bath, Unseen Host, Shoes That Danced, Columbine.

473. WEBBER, J. P., and WEBSTER, H. H., *Short Plays for Junior and Senior High Schools* (Houghton Mifflin, 1925).

Prince of Stamboul, Toy Shop, Stolen Prince, End of the Rainbow, Princess on the Road, "Good Night Babette!", To Dust Returning, Travelling Man, Shuttin' o' the Door, Wraggle-Taggle Gypsies, Pyramus and Thisbe, Miss Burney at Court, John Silver Off Duty, Little Boy Out of the Wood, Legend of St. Dorothy, In the Good Green Wood, Lion's Whelp, Benjamin Franklin: Journeyman, Boston Tea Party, Little King.

474. WEBBER, J. P., and WEBSTER, H. H., *Typical Plays for Secondary Schools* (Houghton Mifflin, 1929).

The Rehearsal, A Mistake at the Manor, The Prince of Court Painters, Frances and Francis, Augustus in Search of a Father, Pharaoh's Daughter, The Thrice-Promised Bride, The Copper Pot, Sweethearts, The Gibson Upright, The Dragon.

475. WEISER, Norman S., *The Writer's Radio Theatre, 1941* (Harper, 1941).

We Hold These Truths, Stronghold of the Buccaneers, Millions for Defense, The Welburns—Confidential Report, Native Land, The Precious Freedom, Welcome to Glory, Thanks to Mr. Shakespeare, Splash of Water, The Hollywood Doctor.

476. WHEELER, Charles B., *Six Plays by Contemporaries of Shakespeare* (Oxford University Press, 1928; World's Classics).

Philaster, The Shoemakers' Holiday, A New Way to Pay Old Debts, The Duchess of Malfi, The White Devil, The Knight of the Burning Pestle.

477. WHITMAN, Charles Huntington, *Representative Modern Dramas* (Macmillan, 1936).

Elizabeth the Queen, Hotel Universe, Biography, The Bonds of Interest, The Red Robe, The Cherry Orchard, Strife, The Lower Depths, In Abraham's Bosom, The Weavers, The Silver Cord, The Wild Duck, Pelléas and Mélisande, Our Betters, Liliom, Juno and the Paycock, The Hairy Ape, Mid-Channel, Six Characters in Search of an Author, Cyrano de Bergerac, The Lonely Way, The Father, Riders to the Sea, The Importance of Being Earnest.

478. WHITMAN, Charles Huntington, *Seven Contemporary Plays* (Houghton Mifflin, 1931).
The Cherry Orchard, Strife, The Sunken Bell, An Enemy of the People, Beyond the Horizon, Cyrano de Bergerac, Riders to the Sea.

479. WILDER, Thornton, *The Angel That Troubled The Waters and Other Plays* (Coward-McCann, 1928).
Nascunter Poetae, Proserpina and the Devil, Fanny Otcott, Brother Fire, The Penny That Beauty Spent, The Angel on the Ship, The Message and Jehanne, Childe Roland to the Dark Tower Came, Centaurs, Leviathan, And the Sea Shall Give up Its Dead, Now the Servant's Name Was Malchus, Mozart and the Gray Stewart, Hast Thou Considered My Servant Job?, The Flight into Egypt, The Angel That Troubled the Waters.

480. WILDER, Thornton, *The Long Christmas Dinner & Other Plays in One Act* (Coward-McCann, 1931).
The Long Christmas Dinner, Queens of France, Pullman Car Hiawatha, Love, and How to Cure It, Such things Only Happen in Books, The Happy Journey to Trenton and Camden.

481. WILLIAMS, Tennessee, *American Blues* (Dramatists Play Service, 1948).
Moony's Kid Don't Cry, The Dark Room, The Case of the Crushed Petunias, The Long Stay Cut Short; or, the Unsatisfactory Supper, Ten Blocks on the Camino Real.

482. WILLIAMS, Tennessee, *Twenty Seven Wagons Full of Cotton, and Other One-Act Plays* (New Directions, 1953).
This Property Is Condemned, The Purification, The Last of My Solid Gold Watches, Auto-da-Fé, The Strangest Kind of Romance, 27 Wagons Full of Cotton, The Lady of Larkspur Lotion, Hello from Bertha, Portrait of a Madonna, Lord Byron's Love Letters, The Long Goodbye, Something Unspoken, Talk To Me like the Rain, and Let Me Listen.

483. WISHENGRAD, Morton, *The Eternal Light* (Crown, 1947).
The Tender Grass, Moses Mendelssohn, The Battle of the Warsaw Ghetto, The Parable of Reb Yisrael, Thomas Kennedy, A Pity for the Living, A Sound of Music, A Rhode Island Refuge, Schecter, The Black Death, The Microscope and the Prayer Shawl, They Knocked the Devil out of Uncle Ezra, Hunger, A Chassidic Tale, A Second Exodus, The Death of Akiba, The Day of the Shadow, The Broken Sabbath of Rabbi Asher Brandeis, My Father's Talis, The Ransom of Rabbi Moir, My Cousin Aveigdor, Rabbi Israel Salenter, My Favorite Assassin, For a Suit of New Clothes, The Lantern in the Inferno.

484. WOODS, George B., WATT, Homer A., and ANDERSON, George K., *The Literature of England*, Vol. I (Scott, Foresman, 1936).
The Shoemakers' Holiday, The Tragical History of Doctor Faustus, The Second Shepherds' Play, The Rivals.

485. WOODS, George B., WATT, Homer A., and ANDERSON, George K., *The Literature of England*, Vol. II (Scott, Foresman, 1936).
Strife, The Importance of Being Earnest.

486. WYLIE, Max, *Best Broadcasts of 1938–1939* (Whittlesey House, 1939).
Surprise for the Boys, A Trip to Czardis, Blood of the Martyrs, The Lighthouse Keepers, The Story of John Milton, The Nuremberg Stove, New Horizons,

Alice in Wonderland, The Twilight Shore, Peter Stuyvesant, The Eddie Doll Case, The Steel Worker, Expert Opinion, Sandhogs, No Help Wanted, We Become a Nation, Seems Radio Is Here to Stay, Air Raid, The Trojan Women.

487. WYLIE, Max, *Best Broadcasts of 1939–1940* (Whittlesey House, 1940).
My Client, Curley, In the Fog, The Dark Valley, For-Richer-For-Richer, This Lonely Heart, The Clinic.

488. WYLIE, Max, *Best Broadcasts of 1940–1941* (Whittlesey House, 1941).
We Hold These Truths, An American Crusader, Maudie's Diary, Honest Abe, Roadside, And Six Came Back, The Little Wife, Elementals.

489. YEATS, William Butler, *Plays in Prose and Verse* (Macmillan, 1922).
Cathleen ni Houlihan, The Pot of Broth, The Hour-Glass (in prose), The King's Threshold, On Baile's Strand, The Shadowy Waters, Deirdre, The Unicorn from the Stars, The Green Helmet, The Hour-Glass (in verse), The Player-Queen.

490. ZACHAR, Irwin J., and KIMBALL, Rodney A., *Plays As Experience* (Odyssey, 1944).
Three's a Crowd, A Night at an Inn, The Boor, Last of the Lowries, Spreading the News, Western Night, Bread, The Fifteenth Candle, The Devil and Daniel Webster, The Valiant, Haven of the Spirit, We'd Never Be Happy Otherwise, Pawns. Suffer Little Children.

The following anthologies for which no editor is given are listed alphabetically by title.

491. *All American University One-Act Plays* (Eldridge, 1931).
Barbara Celebrates, The Easy Way, The Family, A Half Hour Reformation, The Higher Command, If Lacking Only Truth, LeDonne, Lita's Man, Puppets, The Scientist, Two Pairs of Spectacles.

492. *Book of Make-Believe, The,* (Allyn and Bacon, 1932).
Told in a Chinese Garden, Robin Hood in Sherwood, The Romancers, The Finger of God, The Farce of the Worthy Master Pierre Patelin, Dust of the Rood, The Thrice-Promised Bride, The Man Who Married a Dumb Wife, The White Hawk, The Lost Silk Hat, Sham, The Boor, The God of Quiet, The Merchant of Venice.

493. *Eleven Short Biblical Plays* (Longmans Green, 1929).
Betrayal, Cleopas, The Door, Elisha, For His Name's Sake, The Friend of Potiphar's Wife, The Gift of Jehovah, The Light upon the Way, Maundy Thursday, The Third Shepherd's Play, The Woman from Nod.

494. *Embassy Successes*, Vol. I (London, Sampson, Low, Marston, 1946).
Father Malachy's Miracle, Worm's Eye View, Zoo in Silesia.

495. *Embassy Successes*, Vol. II (London, Sampson, Low, Marston, 1946).
National Velvet, Skipper Next to God, No Room at the Inn.

496. *Embassy Successes*, Vol. III (London, Sampson, Low, Marston, 1948).
Peace Comes to Peckham, Away from It All, "Let My People Go."

497. *Famous Plays of Today* (London, Gollancz, 1929).
The Lady with the Lamp, Such Men Are Dangerous, Many Waters, Mrs. Moonlight, Journey's End, Young Woodley.

498. *Famous Plays of 1931* (London, Gollancz, 1932).
Autumn Crocus, The Barretts of Wimpole Street, To See Ourselves, The Improper Duchess, After All, London Wall.

499. *Famous Plays of 1932* (London, Gollancz, 1932).
The Rose without a Thorn, Once in a Lifetime, Musical Chairs, See Naples and Die, Somebody Knows, There's Always Juliet.

500. *Famous Plays of 1933* (London, Gollancz, 1933).
Alien Corn, Of Thee I Sing, Richard of Bordeaux, The Late Christopher Bean.

501. *Famous Plays of 1932–1933* (London, Gollancz, 1933).
Strange Orchestra, Service, Miracle at Verdun, Counsellor-at-Law, Behold We Live, Children in Uniform.

502. *Famous Plays of 1933–1934* (London, Gollancz, 1934).
The Laughing Woman, The Wind and the Rain, Clive of India, Reunion in Vienna, Sixteen, The Distaff Side.

503. *Famous Plays of 1934* (London, Gollancz, 1934).
Touch Wood, Queen of Scots, Old Folks at Home, Family Affairs, Men in White, The Maitlands.

504. *Famous Plays of 1934–1935* (London, Gollancz, 1935).
The Old Ladies, The Dominant Sex, Viceroy Sarah, Lovers' Leap, Frolic Wind, Flowers of the Forest.

505. *Famous Plays of 1935* (London, Gollancz, 1935).
Grief Goes Over, Accent on Youth, Close Quarters (*Attentat*), The Mask of Virtue, Youth at the Helm, Night Must Fall.

506. *Famous Plays of 1935–1936* (London, Gollancz, 1936).
After October, Call It a Day, Katie Roche, Red Night, Awake and Sing, St. Helena.

507. *Famous Plays of 1936* (London, Gollancz, 1936).
The Two Bouquets, Till the Day I Die, Parnell, Professor Bernhardi, Bury the Dead, Boy Meets Girl.

508. *Famous Plays of 1937* (London, Gollancz, 1937).
The Women, In Theatre Street, People in Love, Judgment Day, Busman's Honeymoon, A Month in the Country.

509. *Famous Plays of 1938–1939* (London, Gollancz, 1939).
To Love and to Cherish, Harvest in the North, Glorious Morning, Six Men of Dorset, Golden Boy, The Zeal of Thy House.

510. *International Modern Plays* (London, Dent, 1950; Everyman's Library).
The Life of the Insects, The Mask and the Face, The Infernal Machine, Hannele, Lady Julie.

511. *Minor Elizabethan Drama*, Vol. I (London, Dent, 1939; Everyman's Library).
Arden of Feversham, The Spanish Tragedy, Gorboduc, David and Bethsabe, Cambyses.

512. *Minor Elizabethan Drama*, Vol. II (London, Dent, 1939; Everyman's Library).

Friar Bacon and Friar Bungay, James the Fourth, Endimion, The Old Wives'
Tale, Ralph Roister Doister.

513. *Modern Plays* (London, Dent, 1937; Everyman's Library).
Milestones, Hay Fever, For Services Rendered, The Dover Road, Journey's
End.

514. *My Best Play* (London, Faber & Faber, 1934).
The Venetian, Hay Fever, Granite, The Circle, Success, The Rumour, The
Whiteheaded Boy, After All.

515. *New Plays for Women and Girls* (French, 1932).
O Bright Flame Lifted, For the Love of Michael, The First White Woman,
Green Eyes from Romany, I Know George Washington, The Night-Club Girl,
Mrs. Leicester's School, Uplifting Sadie, One of Those Days, Lady Luck, Let
It Burn, I'm Not Complaining, The Wish Shop, Lavender and Red Pepper,
The Clouds.

516. *One-Act Plays for Stage and Study*, 1st Series (French, 1924).
The Man Upstairs, The Mayor and the Manicure, The Red Owl, The Rector,
A Flower of Yeddo, Deceivers, The Girl, Peace Manoeuvres, Moonshine, The
Dying Wife, The Little Father of the Wilderness, The Robbery, Such a
Charming Young Man, Judge Lynch, The Widow of Wasdale Head, Dolly's
Little Bills, The Man in the Bowler Hat, Lonesome-Like, Hanging and Wiv-
ing, 'Op-o-Me-Thumb, Phipps, Spreading the News, A Minuet, The Ghost
of Jerry Bundler, Wealth and Wisdom.

517. *One-Act Plays for Stage and Study*, 2nd Series (French, 1925).
The Drums of Oude, Young America, The Prairie Doll, The Passing of Chow-
Chow, The Dickey Bird, Meet the Missus, The Same Old Thing, Red Carna-
tions, Saved, The Man Who Died at Twelve O'Clock, Among Thieves, A
Question of Principle, And There Was Light, The Corsican Lieutenant, On
the Race Course, The Black Bottle, The Knife, Claude, The Idealist, At the
Telephone, The Host.

518. *One-Act Plays for Stage and Study*, 3rd Series (French, 1927).
One of Those Things, Napoleon Crossing the Rockies, Jane, Jean and John,
Knives from Syria, The Kite, The Eligible Mr. Bangs, The Londonderry Air,
Changing Places, The Sundial, Youth Must Be Served, Papers, The Voice of
the Snake, Unto Such Glory, Mary Means What She Says, Dave, The Cob-
bler's Den, Cupid in Clapham, When Did They Meet Again?, Duetto, The
Weathervane Elopes, The Betrayal.

519. *One-Act Plays for Stage and Study*, 4th Series (French, 1928).
Blue Thunder, Reckless, So's Your Old Antique, In-Laws, The Miracle of St.
Martin, The Snake-Eater, The Fourth Mrs. Phillips, The Wily One, The
Witch's Daughter, Cobweb Kings, Fortinbras in Plain Clothes, Three Players,
a Fop and a Duchess, Invitation, A Wedding, Lenna Looks Down, A Tune
of a Tune, Brother Bill, Things Is That-a-Way, The Pipe in the Fields, Christmas Eve, Cured, Love in a French Kitchen.

520. *One-Act Plays for Stage and Study*, 5th Series (French, 1930).
A Diadem of Snow, The Late Captain Crow, It's an Ill Wind, The Stoker,
The Wedding Rehearsal, No More Americans, Art and Mrs. Palmer, Rescue,
Black Oliver, Mrs. Adis, The Widdy's Mite, Angelus, Limping Along, Bab-

ouscka, Hot Lemonade, Jumpin' the Broom, The Man with the Iron Jaw, The Haunted Coal Mine, Maizie, Balm, Words and Music.

521. *One-Act Plays for Stage and Study*, 6th Series (French, 1931).
The Still Alarm, Speaking Terms, Murder! Murder! Murder!, The Moving Finger, Men, Women and Goats, Colman and Guaire, The Willow Plate, The Woman Who Understood Men, Poetry and Plaster, The Bad Penny, The Lost Princess, The Chinese Water Wheel, The Ghosts of Windsor Park, Traffic Signals, Babbitt's Boy, Josephine, St. Cyprian and the Devil, The Wolf at the Door, The Pie and the Tart, A Change of Mind, The Snake Charmer.

522. *One-Act Plays for Stage and Study*, 7th Series (French, 1932).
Boy-Chinnen, Are Men Superior?, Chatterton, Counsel's Opinion, The Way Out, Laid Off, Grandma—Old Style, Smoke-Screens, Some Words in Edge-wise, On the Portsmouth Road, Family, The March Heir, Funny Business, The Tea-Pot on the Rocks, Accidents Will Happen, Here Are Sailors, The Good and Obedient Young Man, Knock Three Times, The Last Refuge, Moses Was an Oyster-Man, As the Tumbrils Pass.

523. *Plays of the Greek Dramatists* (Caxton House, 1946).
Agamemnon, Choephoroe, The Eumenides, The Clouds, The Frogs, Lysistrata, The Cyclops, Iphigenia in Tauris, Antigone, Electra, Oedipus, the King.

524. *Plays of a Half-Decade* (London, Gollancz, 1933).
Autumn Crocus, The Rose without a Thorn, The Lady with a Lamp, The Barretts of Wimpole Street, To See Ourselves, The Improper Duchess, Many Waters, Musical Chairs, Journey's End, After All, Young Woodley.

525. *Plays of To-day*, Vol. I (London, Sidgwick and Jackson, 1925).
Chains, Abraham Lincoln, Jane Clegg, The Voysey Inheritance, Hindle Wakes.

526. *Plays of To-day*, Vol. II (London, Sidgwick and Jackson, 1927).
Prunella, Pompey the Great, The Pleasure Garden, Mary Broome, Rutherford and Son.

527. *Plays of To-day*, Vol. III (London, Sidgwick and Jackson, 1930).
A Hundred Years Old, The Man With a Load of Mischief, At Mrs. Beam's, The White-Headed Boy.

528. *Six Plays* (London, Gollancz, 1930).
Street Scene, The Green Pastures, Alison's House, Down Our Street, Socrates, Badger's Green.

529. *Six Plays* (London, Heinemann, 1934).
Design for Living, Wild Decembers, Dinner at Eight, Sheppey, Dangerous Corner, The Rats of Norway.

530. *Six Plays of Today* (London, Heinemann, 1939).
I Killed the Count, Point Valaine, The Island, Cornelius, Idiot's Delight, The Silent Knight.

531. *Six Plays of 1939* (London, Hamilton, 1939).
No Time for Comedy, The Little Foxes, Rhondda Roundabout, The Man in Half Moon Street, Quiet Wedding, After the Dance.

532. *Seven Plays* (London, Heinemann, 1935).

Conversation Piece, Moonlight Is Silver, Escape Me Never!, Aren't We All?, Laburnum Grove, The Shining Hour, Libel.

533. *The Theatre Guild Anthology* (Random House, 1936).

John Ferguson, Mr. Pim Passes By, Liliom, He Who Gets Slapped, The Adding Machine, Saint Joan, Goat Song, The Silver Cord, Porgy, Strange Interlude, Hotel Universe, Reunion in Vienna, Mary of Scotland, Rain From Heaven.

534. *Theatre Omnibus* (London, Hamilton, 1938).

Amphitryon, Jane Eyre, Pride and Prejudice, The Amazing Dr. Clitterhouse, French without Tears, George and Margaret.

535. *Twelve One-Act Plays* (Longmans, Green, 1926).

The Valiant, Romance of the Willow Pattern, The Grill, The Last Straw, Thank You Doctor, Copy, The Trap, Good Medicine, God Winks, A Woman of Character, Jazz and Minuet, The Most Foolish Virgin.

536. *Twelve Famous Plays of the Restoration and the Eighteenth Century* (Modern Library, 1933).

Love for Love, The Way of the World, All for Love; or, The World Well Lost, The Beaux' Stratagem, The Clandestine Marriage, The Beggar's Opera, She Stoops to Conquer, Venice Preserv'd, The Rivals, The School for Scandal, The Provok'd Wife, The Country Wife.

BOOKS ON PLAY PRODUCTION

GENERAL

BAILEY, Howard, *The A B C's of Play Producing* (McKay, 1955).
A practical producer's handbook, dealing with play selection, blocking, action, settings, castings, rehearsals, etc.

BRICKER, Herschel, *Our Theatre Today: Art, Craft, and Management* (French, 1936).
Chapters written by thirteen different workers in the contemporary theatre on various aspects of the theatre, including production. Arthur Hopkins and Brock Pemberton are among the authors represented.

BROWNE, Elliot Martin and Others, *Putting on a Play* (London, Dickson, 1936).
Various British authorities contribute chapters on different phases of the theatre including a chapter on production by John Fernald and one on presentation by F. Sladen Smith.

CARTER, Conrad, *Play Production* (London, H. Jenkins, 1953).
A small, concrete book dealing with the various jobs of the producer-director; a primer on the preparation of the play, rehearsal technique, etc.

CRAFTON, Allen, and ROYER, Jessica, *The Complete Acted Play from Script to Final Curtain* (Appleton-Century-Crofts, 1943).
A very good, down-to-earth book with exercises for use of the body and voice. There are good sections on makeup, scenery design and construction lighting, and costuming, all with simple diagrams.

CLARK, Barrett H., *How to Produce Amateur Plays*, Rev. ed. (Little, Brown, 1925).
Although the original edition appeared more than thirty years ago, this little volume still has many helpful suggestions for beginners.

COOPER, Charles W. and CAMP, Paul A., *Designing the Play* (Appleton-Century-Crofts, 1942).
An analysis of the problems in producing plays, with assignments and work forms.

DOLMAN, John, *The Art of Play Production* (Harper, 1946).
A very good basic book for actors and directors.

DRUMMOND, A. M., *Play Production for the Country Theatre* (Cornell University Extension Division, 1930).
A valuable little manual specifically adapted for producers in rural communities.

GASSNER, John, *Producing the Play*, with *The New Scene Technician's Hand-Book* by Barber, Philip (Dryden, 1953).
A very comprehensive book on production with Barber's academic program of study used as the outline of the course at Yale.

157

HEFFNER, Hubert C., SELDEN, Samuel, and SELLMAN, Hunton D., *Modern Theatre Practice: A Handbook for Nonprofessionals*, 2nd ed. (Appleton-Century-Crofts, 1959).

A generally good book dealing with organization of a dramatic group, play selection, structure of drama, casting, rehearsing, scenery construction, lighting, sound, costume, and makeup.

HEWITT, Barnard, FOSTER, J. F., and WOLLE, Muriel Sibell, *Play Production: Theory and Practice* (Lippincott, 1952).

A good book on all phases of the theatre, with much concrete material and many illustrations.

KELLY, Mary, *How to Make a Pageant* (Pitman, 1937).

For the teacher who is called upon to produce a pageant, this is a valuable handbook.

KNIGHT, George Wilson, *Principles of Shakespearean Production with Especial Reference to the Tragedies* (Macmillan, 1936).

Producing Shakespeare's plays has its peculiar problems, and this book provides many valuable suggestions for solving them.

MATHER, Charles Chambers, SPAULDING, Alice H., and SKILLEN, Melita, *Behind the Footlights: A Book on the Technique of Dramatics* (Silver, Burdett, 1935).

Especially designed for elementary and secondary school dramatics.

MITCHELL, Roy E., *Shakespeare for Community Players* (Dutton, 1929).

In addition to providing excellent suggestions for producing Shakespeare in community theatres, it contains numerous references and copious bibliographies.

ACTING

ALBRIGHT, Hardie D., *Working up a Part: A Manual for the Beginning Actor* (Houghton Mifflin, 1947).

Especially suitable for the neophyte in acting as he develops his part.

BARNES, Grace, and SUTCLIFFE, Mary Jean, *On Stage, Everyone,* (Macmillan, 1954).

One of the best textbooks on acting, with clear explanations and excellent exercises organized in a good sequence of training. It includes play and character analysis, as well as use of the body and voice. Good suggested courses of study are included.

BARRY, Philip B., *99 Points for Amateur Actors* (French, 1936).

Sensible and practical suggestions of what to do and what not to do.

BOLESLAVSKI, Richard, *Acting: The First Six Lessons* (Theatre Arts Books, 1954).

A primer of the inner development of an actor in charming dialogue form.

BOSWORTH, Halliam, *Technique in Dramatic Art* (Macmillan, 1934).

Written by an experienced actor and teacher, who combines practice with good theory.

BRIDGE, William H., *Actor in the Making: A Handbook on Improvisation and Other Techniques of Development* (Expression, 1936).

Useful in explaining the theories and practices of improvisation as it contributes to an actor's development.

BRIGANCE, William Norwood, and HENDERSON, Florence, *Drill Manual for Improving Speech* (Lippincott, 1955).
Excellent exercises for improving breathing, diction, and tone quality.

CARTMELL, Van H., *A Handbook for the Amateur Actor* (Doubleday, 1936).
A well-known anthologist and lover of the theatre makes interesting suggestions for the beginner.

CHEKHOV, Michael, *To the Actor: On the Technique of Acting* (Harper, 1953).
The distinguished Russian actor and director sums up his philosophy based on long experience on the Russian and other stages.

COLE, Toby and CHINOY, Helen Krich, *Actors on Acting: Theories, Techniques, and Practices of the World's Great Actors* (Crown, 1949).
Various actors and critics discuss aspects of acting. Valuable for getting many points of view.

COSGROVE, Frances, Editor, *Scenes for Student Actors: Dramatic Selections from New Plays*, 5 vols. (French, 1934–1944).
Useful in providing material for actual training, taken from the plays of the 1930's and 1940's.

CRAUFORD, Lane, *Acting: Its Theory and Practice: With Illustrative Examples of Players, Past and Present* (R. R. Smith, 1930).
For those who wish to learn how some of the great actors handled their roles.

DOLMAN, John, *The Art of Acting* (Harper, 1949).
A good, all-round book: the psychology of acting, rehearsal techniques, voice, stage diction, bodily action, etc. are taught with concrete exercises. Bibliography and glossary.

EUSTIS, Morton, *Players at Work* (Theatre Arts, 1937).
Distinguished actors tell how they went about developing some of their favorite roles.

FRANKLIN, Miriam A., *Rehearsal: The Principles and Practice of Acting for the Stage* (Prentice-Hall, 1942).
The art of rehearsing and preparing for performance.

FRENCH, Florence Felton, LEVENSON, William B., and ROCKWELL, Vera Cober, *Radio English* (McGraw-Hill, 1952).
Good speech exercises. Formats for various types of programs: continuity, news, the talk, plays, and television. Good sections on acting, directing, and sound effects.

LATHAM, Jean Lee, *Do's and Don'ts of Drama: Five Hundred and Fifty-five Pointers for Beginning Actors and Directors* (Dramatic Publishing Co., 1935).
Brief, practical suggestions.

SELDEN, Samuel, *First Steps in Acting* (Appleton-Century-Crofts, 1947).
An interesting and practical primer.

SPEAIGHT, Robert, *Acting: Its Idea, Tradition, Technique* (London, Cassell, 1939).
A distinguished British actor expounds his views.

STANISLAVSKI, Constantin, *An Actor Prepares* (Theatre Arts Books, 1955).
The basic book on the psychological preparation of the actor for a part by one of the greatest directors of all times.

DIRECTING

BOYLE, Walden P., *Central and Flexible Staging* (University of California Press, 1956).
A most useful and suggestive book with excellent illustrations of the staging of in-the-round performances.

BROWN, Gilmor, and GARWOOD, Alice, *General Principles of Play Direction* (French, 1936).
A good general treatment of the basic elements of play direction.

COLE, Toby, and CHINOY, Helen Krich, *Directing the Play* (Bobbs-Merrill, 1953).
A compilation of articles and essays on directing and the history of directing.

CRAFTON, Allen, *Play Directing* (Prentice-Hall, 1938).
The basic principles of directing the play, simply expressed.

CRUMP, Leslie, *Directing for the Amateur Stage* (Dodd, Mead, 1935).
A helpful handbook for the amateur director.

DEAN, Alexander, *Fundamentals of Play Directing* (Farrar & Rinehart, 1941).
The most extensive single work devoted entirely to the problems of directing. The theories and exercises were developed by the late Alexander Dean in courses which he taught at Northwestern and Yale universities. A valuable and helpful book, especially for advanced students.

DIETRICH, John E., *Play Direction* (Prentice-Hall, 1953).
One of the best and most thorough books on the subject, including play structure, audience response, stage composition, movement, emotion, tempo, and the entire process of direction from play selection to performance. Interesting chapters on musicals and arena productions. Many helpful, simple diagrams.

DOWNS, Harold, Editor, *Theatre and Stage*, 2 vols. (London, Pitman, 1934).
An illustrated work on the whole range of direction and production. Short articles by many writers make up this useful book.

HUGHES, Glenn, *The Penthouse Theatre: Its History and Technique* (French, 1942).
The story of the development of the "center-staging" idea at the University of Washington and the building of the special theatre to house the productions. It includes a discussion of the technique of production without a stage by the teacher who made a great success with this method.

JONES, Margo, *Theatre-in-the-Round* (Rinehart, 1951).
One of the most definitive books yet produced on this subject, dealing with the history of the arena theatre, methods of organization and management, and its physical requirements, including seating, sound, and lighting. Production notes on plays produced by Theatre '50.

NELMS, Henning, *Play Production* (Barnes & Noble, 1950).
A practical and concise exposition of all the aspects in play production, with many cross references to other volumes devoted to this subject.

OMMANNEY, Katharine Anne, and OMMANNEY, Pierce C., *The Stage and the School* (McGraw-Hill, 1950).

A good basic text for a course in dramatics, dealing with appreciation, pantomime, voice and diction, characterization, with good exercises. The sections on stage settings and makeup are somewhat simplified.

PARKER, Anthony, *Pageants: Their Presentation and Production* (London, The Bodley Head, 1954).

All phases of the production of outdoor pageants.

RAINE, James Watt, *Bible Dramatics* (Appleton, 1927).

Especially suitable for those interested in the ever-increasing field of religious drama and production.

SAMACHSON, Dorothy and Joseph, *Let's Meet the Theatre* (Abelard-Schuman, 1954).

Interviews with outstanding contemporary playwrights, producers, directors, scene and costume designers, actors, and others. Practical suggestions.

SELDEN, Samuel, *First Principles of Play Direction* (University of North Carolina Press, 1937).

An excellent brief treatment of the basic fundamentals of direction by an outstanding teacher and director.

SELDEN, Samuel, *The Stage in Action* (Appleton-Century-Crofts, 1941).

One of the most complete treatments, useful for both the actor and director.

SMITH, Milton Myers, *Play Production* (Appleton-Century-Crofts, 1948).

One of the most comprehensive and useful texts, dealing with choice of script, analysis of script, casting, the rehearsal process, acting, scenery, costuming, make-up, lighting, and organization and management.

WATKINS, Ronald, *On Producing Shakespeare* (Norton, 1951).

Discusses the practical problems in staging Shakespeare's plays.

SCENERY

ALBRIGHT, H. D., HALSTEAD, William P., and MITCHELL, Lee, *Principles of Theatre Art* (Houghton Mifflin, 1955).

Nine valuable chapters deal with the organization of the theatre structure, the nature and function of design, and the practical solution of various problems in staging.

ASHWORTH, Bradford, *Notes on Scene Painting*, Edited by Donald Oenslager (Whitlock's, 1952).

A professional scenic artist of long experience provides some valuable suggestions.

BRADBURY, Arthur Jack and HOWARD, W. R. B., *Stagecraft* (London, H. Jenkins, 1953).

A small, practical book on the construction of sets and furniture, making properties, and creating special effects.

BUERKI, F. A., *Stagecraft for Non-Professionals*, Rev. ed. (University of Wisconsin Press, 1956).

A helpful though brief guide for the new workers in the field.

BURRIS-MEYER, Harold, and COLE, Edward C., *Scenery for the Theatre* (Little, Brown, 1938).
A practical, detailed book on the preparation of scenery and furniture for the professional theatre, liberally illustrated by photographs, diagrams, and charts.

CORNBERG, Sol and GEBAUER, Emanuel L., *A Stage Crew Handbook* (Harper, 1941).
By utilizing the question-and-answer method, the authors have provided a handy and easily understood manual in lighting and scenery. It has many useful drawings and a glossary of technical terms.

EVANS, Ralph M., *An Introduction to Color* (Wiley, 1948).
A practical discussion of theories of color as they apply to both light and pigment colors.

GASSNER, John, *Producing the Play*, Rev. ed. (Dryden, 1953).
Philip Barber's *New Scene Technician's Handbook*, heretofore available only in mimeographed copy, appears in this volume for the first time in book form. The section is a detailed and well illustrated treatment of scenery and property construction, sound effects, and lighting.

GRAVES, Maitland, *The Art of Color and Design* (McGraw-Hill, 1941).
A well-illustrated treatment of line, direction, shape, texture, proportion, value, and color, analyzed according to the aspects of repetition, harmony, contrast, and graduation.

HALSTEAD, William Perdue, *Stage Management for the Amateur Theatre* (Crofts, 1937).
In addition to discussing various aspects of stage management, the author has valuable chapters on scene-shifting, handling of properties and costumes, lighting, and effects.

NELMS, Henning, *A Primer of Stagecraft* (Dramatists Play Service, 1941).
An excellent handbook, especially easy for beginners to use. Well illustrated with accurate and concise discussions of many technical matters pertaining to stagecraft.

STAGE LIGHTING AND SOUND EFFECTS

FUCHS, Theodore, *Stage Lighting* (Little, Brown, 1929).
Although somewhat out of date, it contains a comprehensive treatment of the whole area of lighting, with especial emphasis on equipment.

HARTMAN, Louis, *Theatre Lighting: A Manual of the Stage Switchboard* (Appleton, 1930).
Recollections of the means by which the great Belasco achieved his lighting effects in some of his major successes.

McCANDLESS, Stanley Russell, *A Method of Lighting the Stage* (Theatre Arts Books, 1947).
A good basic book on lighting.

NAPIER, Frank, *Noises Off: A Handbook of Sound Effects* (London, Frederick Muller, 1948).
A very good practical book.

NELMS, Henning, *Lighting the Amateur Stage: A Practical Layout* (Theatre Arts, 1931).

For the beginner a valuable introduction to the subject.

OST, Geoffry, *Stage Lighting* (London, H. Jenkins, 1954).

A small, practical book in the Practical Stage Handbooks series.

RUBIN, Joel E. and WATSON, Leland H., *Theatrical Lighting Practice* (Theatre Arts Books, 1954).

Lighting requirements for all types of theatres, from the conventional to outdoor, area, puppet, and television types. Includes a survey of job opportunities.

SELDEN, Samuel, and SELLMAN, Hunton D., *Stage Scenery and Lighting*, 3rd ed. (Appleton-Century-Crofts, 1958).

An exceptional book, designed for amateurs, but teaching the best professional practices in neither too elementary nor technical fashion; authoritative and sufficiently detailed.

SIMONSON, Lee, *The Art of Scenic Design: A Pictorial Analysis of Stage Setting and Its Relation to Theatrical Production* (Harper, 1950).

A very suggestive and beautiful book for the scenic designer; not for the scenic builder. Profusely illustrated by photographs of some of the most significant settings of recent years.

STEWART, Hal D., *Stagecraft* (London, Pitman, 1949).

A very good practical book on how to design and make scenery, create lighting and special effects, and how to manage the stage, well illustrated by many photographs, drawings, and diagrams.

COSTUMING

BRADLEY, Carolyn G., *Western World Costume: An Outline History* (Appleton-Century-Crofts, 1954).

A kaleidoscopic view of the development of dress from primitive times to the present, profusely illustrated. Arranged in outline form by periods, the book is an exceptionally useful source of information.

ELICKER, Virginia Wilk, *Biblical Costumes for Church and School* (Barnes, 1953)

A sensible book on easy, cheap, and effective methods of costuming.

EVANS, Mary, *Costumes throughout the Ages* (Lippincott, 1950).

Costumes of all times and places, illustrated copiously by black and white photographs of contemporary paintings, sculpture, and drawings.

FISCHEL, Oscar, and VON BOEHN, Max, *Die Mode,* 7 vols. (Munich, F. Bruckmann, 1909–23).

Treats costume from the Middle Ages to 1878. The volumes on the 19th century have been translated into English by Marian Edwards and published by Dutton. One of the most complete books of its kind.

GORSLINE, Douglas, *What People Wore* (Viking, 1953).

Illustrated by 1800 line drawings, 12 color plates and 50 pages of text, this offers a fascinating pageant of the history of costume through the ages.

GRIMBALL, E. B., and WELLS, Rhea, *Costuming a play*, Inter-Theatre Arts Handbook (Appleton-Century-Crofts, 1925).

Very practical instruction in material, color, dyeing and making period costumes; with bibliographies and lists of costume plays. Black and white sketches.

LAMBOURNE, Norah, *Dressing the Play*, How-to-Do-It Series, #48 (Studio, Crowell, 1953).

An excellent book of practical instruction on the making of cheap and effective costumes and jewelry for the stage, illustrated by very good photographs and sketches.

LAVER, James, *Costume of the Western World* (Harper, 1952)

Fashions of the Renaissance in England, France, Spain, and Holland, fully illustrated.

MCCLENNAN, Elisabeth, *History of American Costume, 1607–1870* (Tudor, 1937).

Extremely helpful for those costuming the American historical drama.

NORRIS, Herbert, *Costume and Fashion* (Dutton, 1933–1950).

V. 1, pre-historic and classical European costume to 1066; V. 2, English costume 1066 to 1485; V. 3 (two books) Tudor costume. Volume 6, dealing with the 19th century is out of print. These are the definitive volumes dealing with these periods and places, and cover costume, materials, headdresses, jewelry, and other accessories. They are illustrated generously in black and white and color, and accompanied by clear and detailed description.

WALKUP, F. P., *Dressing the Part* (Appleton-Century-Crofts, 1950).

A general history of costume, with very useful detail drawings in black and white, which make it easy to recreate the costumes.

WILCOX, R. T., *The Mode in Costume* (Scribner, 1942).

Traces the history of fashion in dress since Egyptian times.

MAKE-UP

BAIRD, John F., *Make-up* (French, 1930).
Good for beginners. Has many helpful line drawings.

CORSON, Richard, *Stage Makeup*, 2nd ed. (Appleton-Century-Crofts, 1949).

All aspects of make-up thoroughly described and illustrated with 77 drawings and photographs. The book contains an invaluable Color Chart listing the manufacturers of commercial brands of make-up.

FACTOR, Max, *Hints on the Art of Make-Up* (Max Factor Make-Up Studio, Hollywood, Calif.).

A set of nine booklets on the basic principles of make-up, including the preparation of beards, special effects, special stage types, and characters from fiction and from Shakespeare, plentifully illustrated by photographs and diagrams. One of the most helpful, concrete, and the least expensive of all publications on the subject of make-up.

PARSONS, Charles S. A., *Guide to Theatrical Make-up* (Pitman, 1932).

Although somewhat dated, it is still a useful guide for many phases of the subject.

SEQUEIRA, Horace, *Stage Make-Up* (London, Jenkins, 1953).
A good, simple treatment, but not very subtle.

STRAUSS, Ivan, *Paint, Powder, and Make-Up* (London, Sweet & Maxwell, 1930).
One of the most widely used books on this subject.

WOLTERS, N. E. B., *Modern Make-Up for Stage and Screen* (London, Dickson & Thompson, 1935).
Somewhat out of date but interesting for comparative purposes.

THEATRE MANAGEMENT

BERNHEIM, Alfred L., *The Business of the Theatre* (Actors Equity Association, 1932).
A bit dated, but contains valuable information for the present-day producer.

DEAN, Alexander, *Little Theatre Organization and Management* (Appleton, 1926).
One of the classics of the little theatre movement and still interesting to read.

FLANAGAN, Hallie (Ferguson), *Arena* (Duell, Sloan, and Pearce, 1940).
The director of the Federal Theatre Project tells the story of that gallant adventure in Depression days.

GRUVER, E. A., *The Stage Manager's Handbook* (Harper, 1952).
Covers all the practical details of stage production, including the making of cue sheets, light plots, stage business, rehearsal schedules, managing the performance, and the multifarious problems of touring.

MACGOWAN, Kenneth, *Footlights across America* (Harcourt, Brace, 1929).
A subsidized study of the nonprofessional theatre across America up to 1925.

NADELL, Aaron, *The Master Guide to Theatre Maintenance* (The Author, 130–57 Lefferts Blvd., S. Ozone Park 20, Long Island, N.Y., 1955).
A very practical book for the theatre manager (mostly motion picture), but useful for the manager of a legitimate theatre. Covers theatre maintenance, operation, painting, selling refreshments, heating, law, sound, and lamps for projectors.

SELDEN, Samuel, *Organizing a Community Theatre* (Cleveland, National Theatre Conference, 1945).
A practical man of the theatre and gifted teacher and writer discusses the organization of the community theatre and its problems.

TRAUBE, Shepard, *So You Want to Go into the Theatre* (Little, Brown, 1940).
A Broadway producer writes in popular style of the trials and tribulations that befall the newcomer to the profession.

INDEX OF PLAYS

NOTE: Below are listed the titles of over 700 plays which are summarized and annotated in Parts I–IV of this book. Immediately after each entry, the bold-face number refers to the page on which the summary occurs. Light-face figures correspond to the numbered Anthologies (Part V) which contain the particular play. Some Anthologies are listed that do not contain any of the plays summarized but the titles have been included as useful references for the reader of this volume.

The plays with bold-face numbers from 4 to 60 are Full-length Plays; numbers from 62 to 97 are One-act, Television, or Guidance Plays.

INDEX OF AUTHORS

Folios refer to pages on which plays of the authors listed occur.

BY SAMUEL CHOTZINOFF

Toscanini: An Intimate Portrait (1956)

A Lost Paradise: Early Reminiscences (1955)

THESE ARE BORZOI BOOKS
PUBLISHED BY ALFRED A. KNOPF IN NEW YORK

TOSCANINI: *An Intimate Portrait*

Toscanini

AN INTIMATE PORTRAIT

by Samuel Chotzinoff

ALFRED A. KNOPF, NEW YORK

1956

All of the photographs in this book are by
Adrian Siegel
except for the outdoor snapshot
taken by the author

L. C. CATALOG CARD NUMBER: 56–5784

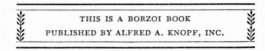

THIS IS A BORZOI BOOK
PUBLISHED BY ALFRED A. KNOPF, INC.

FIRST EDITION

The first four parts of this book originally appeared in HOLIDAY *in slightly*
different form.

For Harry Sions, gratefully

TOSCANINI: *An Intimate Portrait*

CHAPTER ONE

$\mathcal{T}$HE first time I met Arturo Toscanini was in the spring of 1926. I was then music critic for the *New York World*, and I had been sent to Europe to report on musical events. In Paris, one day, I received a cablegram from my editor, Herbert Bayard Swope, telling me to go to Milan to investigate reported trouble between Toscanini and the Fascists. Rumors had reached New York that Toscanini had refused to open his performances at La Scala with the Fascist hymn and had severed his connection with the Milan opera house.

Knowing Toscanini's distaste for newspapermen, I took the precaution of obtaining a letter of introduction from a friend of his in New York. This letter, wrapped in a hundred-lire note, I presented to the concierge at Via Durini 20, the Maestro's seventeenth-century house in the heart of Milan. I was shown into a music room furnished in Victorian style, hung with many Victorian

3

paintings in elaborate gilt frames, and adorned further with bronze figures of Verdi, Puccini, and Catalani; in black boxes, under glass, I saw plaster death masks of Beethoven and Verdi. The Maestro came in after a few minutes, shook my hand warmly, and motioned me to a chair. He was smartly dressed. Though the day was hot, he wore a vest, a starched shirt and wing collar; starched cuffs protruded from the sleeves of his black morning coat. His pants were striped, and his small shoes were newly shined. His sparse, soft white hair was brushed up at the sides, giving him the look of a satyr. His pepper-and-salt mustache was neatly trimmed, with both ends sticking up in points. His face was richly sunburned; although he was almost sixty, there was not a wrinkle on it. Fearing that I might never again have a chance to see him at such close range, I boldly scanned his face and figure. I was struck by the classic mold of his head, the beauty of his face, the dark intensity of his eyes; his look was so piercing that his eyes seemed to shoot out actual rays. I knew I was in the presence of a great man.

I told him frankly the purpose of my visit. He replied with a stream of Italian which I could not understand. A servant brought in coffee and poured two demitasses. I took a teaspoonful of sugar; the Maestro took four. We drank in silence. I began again, speaking slowly and in a kind of pidgin English that I hoped he would be able to grasp. I said I did not wish to pry into his affairs, but that his resistance to Fascism was of great concern to the world. My paper would like to have the privilege of presenting his side of the story, and so on. As I spoke I felt from the perplexed expression on his face that he did not understand a word. When I finished he stared intently at me for a while, and then looked away with the helpless air of a man who had tried his best to comprehend and could do no more. "I see," I said sadly, "you don't understand English." He nodded. Defeated, I rose to go. We shook hands. He saw me out politely, and as I descended the stairs he called out: "See Smeeze." I stopped and turned around, expecting him to say more. But no elucidation followed. "See Smeeze, see Smeeze," he reiterated, and I walked down the Via Durini repeating the cryptic words in an effort to arrive at their meaning.

Near the Scala I ran into Max Smith, the music critic on the *New York American*. Max was the only newspaperman Toscanini could tolerate, and Max in turn was extremely devoted to Toscanini; for him the Maestro was the world's only musical saint, and he, Max, was his self-confessed acolyte. He followed the Maestro wherever he went and kept voluminous notes on his performances, even to the metronomic timings of every piece of music he played, all for the benefit, presumably, of posterity. I was therefore not at all surprised to find Max in Milan.

Max spoke Italian well. I told him about my visit in the Via Durini and asked him if he could make anything out of the Maestro's advice or admonition or whatever the strange words implied. Max laughed and said it was plain enough: " 'See Smeeze' meant 'See Smith.' He was merely referring you to me for information about the La Scala situation."

"But doesn't Toscanini speak any English?" I asked. "After all, he spent seven winters in New York, from 1908 to 1915." Max blushed and turned the subject to the Maestro's present difficulties with the Milan Fascists. It then dawned on me that I had been the victim of the Maestro's extraordinary histrionic powers. Unwilling to discuss his troubles with me, he had pretended he could neither speak nor understand English. He had carried this out with the finesse of a great actor. And to dramatize his ignorance of the language and at the same time to show his willingness to be helpful, he had cannily referred me to his diplomatic acolyte. I could see that Italy had lost a star actor when Toscanini took up the baton.

That winter Toscanini was back in New York conducting the Philharmonic Symphony. I went to see him in the green room of Carnegie Hall after his first concert. I was amused to hear him speak beautiful, if archaic, English. And when I asked why he had misled me in Milan, he replied that he had never in his life given an interview to a newspaperman, and never would. Then, with a mischievous twinkle he added: "But you believed me, absolutely, no?" I told him that he was a wonderful actor and that he had had me fooled, absolutely! He looked very pleased.

I haunted the green room of Carnegie Hall after

every Toscanini concert. Though I was entitled, as a music critic, to a pair of seats, I subscribed to a second-tier box, one practically over the stage, from which I could see the conductor at very close range. For Toscanini had cast his spell over me, as he did over everyone who had access to him. Yet seeing him at close range did nothing to explain the mystery of his power. He did not, in fact, *exercise* power. He *radiated* it, effortlessly, unconsciously, like some absolute monarch of a long, unbroken, unopposed line of absolute monarchs. Nor could familiarity reveal the secret of his personal fascination. There was no one in any way like him, no one to whom I could compare him.

He was (and is) a law unto himself. I have never heard anyone seriously oppose him to his face on any subject whatsoever. One could disagree only silently, for open opposition might risk the most unpleasant of penalties—ostracism. To be shut out from that most exciting, that most exhilarating, personality was a dismaying deprivation. Of course no one would dare question his musical judgments. His knowledge of music was encyclopedic, his opinions solidly founded and therefore irrefutable. His talk on music was not academic. He did not regard music as an end in itself. It was for him a humane art, valid only when it expressed the heart or soul of man. That was why he distrusted purely contrapuntal musical forms. He often quoted Verdi on that very subject. He mistrusted the fugue, except for a few rare instances of what he called "human" fugues like the

7

finale of Beethoven's String Quartet in C Major, Op. 59, and the finish of Verdi's *Falstaff*.

He loved certain Italian music so extravagantly as to make one suspect a tinge of chauvinism. And he was very proud of Scarlatti, Rossini, Verdi, Donizetti, Bellini, and his great friend Catalani. "Only an Italian could have written such music," he said. "Not Beethoven, not Weber, not Wagner, no . . . no . . . and no!" But, though the sincerity of his admiration for his countrymen was beyond question, his protestations were not without overtones of envy. As an Italian, he envied, secretly, the "cold" Teutonic countries their great musical figures of the past. However, his standard for Italian music was very high, except in certain instances when a personal bias made him endow a friend with the highest creative qualities.

Toscanini has always maintained that he has never permitted personal relationship to affect his musical judgments. Yet there is some evidence to the contrary. There is, for example, the music of his countryman, teacher, and friend Giuseppe Martucci. When Toscanini was young, Martucci was one of the first conductors to champion the music of Wagner and Brahms in Italy. Martucci was a very serious man, lofty in character and personally unassuming. Toscanini loved him unreservedly, so much so that he failed to perceive that Martucci's own compositions were unoriginal and showed a variety of influences, particularly that of Brahms. The fact that the public did not take to

Martucci's music saddened Toscanini, but made him more determined to play it. Wherever he went to conduct, Toscanini relentlessly played a symphony or concerto of Martucci. Toscanini's own family did not share his enthusiasm for his old teacher's music. They dreaded, like any audience, having to sit through a long composition that sounded like Brahms yet wasn't. But they dared not say so. However, they would warn me (as NBC's musical director) that the Maestro intended to play a Martucci composition, hoping that I might discover some way to avert what all of us considered rather a disaster. And one year, following such a warning, I tried what I thought was a subtle insinuation of my own distaste for Martucci. "Maestro," I said with an air of innocence, "does Martucci ever remind you of Brahms?" The Maestro regarded me wonderingly. "Never!" he snapped. And Martucci's Second Symphony duly appeared on one of his programs.

The Maestro not only adored Martucci's music; he also revered him as a man. The Maestro remembered even Martucci's wife as a paragon of what a conductor's helpmate ought to be. Mrs. Toscanini generally accompanied her husband to rehearsals, unpacked his valise, set out his things, and acted as valet; but the moment he left the green room for the stage she would go out shopping, returning in time to help him change his undershirt and alpaca rehearsal coat at intermission. Once when she was late in returning the Maestro said witheringly: "Martucci's wife was *always* around. She never left his dressing room for a moment. *Mai—Mai* [never, never]!"

While Toscanini knew everything there was to know about music and could give any musicologist and theoretician cards and spades on the subjects of harmony, counterpoint, musical form, and musical history, his peasant intuition and levelheadedness had, like Verdi's, steered him clear of the lofty tomfoolery that makes some excellent musicians forget the primary objective of music—namely, the expression of emotion through song. The admonition *"canta"* (sing) was always on his lips. *"Canta!"* he forever implored or shouted at orchestras and singers, and he hunted the melody in a composition relentlessly, like a hunter stalking his prey. The architecture of music as exemplified in the symphonic form was, for him, a structure of melodic fabrics. A symphony, from a simple melodic one by Haydn or Mozart to one as complex as Sibelius's Fourth, was a continuous song. Even great composers sometimes unwittingly bury melodic continuity under layers of secondary sound; Toscanini would keep these secondary matters down to a level that permitted the melody to flow unimpeded. At the same time, his patrician abhorrence of sentimentality kept him from adding meretricious luster or passion to melody, whether in symphony or opera. That was why critics and intellectual dilettantes called his interpretation of Teutonic symphonic music "Italianate," and his interpretation of Italian opera "Germanic."

10

In the late twenties, when he was musical director of the New York Philharmonic Symphony, Toscanini lived in a modest suite at the Astor Hotel. A large advertising sign twinkled perpetually outside his living-room window. It did not disturb him in the least. On the contrary, he liked to watch it. He also enjoyed the crowds and the bustle in the lobbies of the hotel and the din of the surrounding Times Square area. In a narrow brownstone house connecting with the hotel lived his friends Fred and Elsa Muschenheim, proprietors of the Astor. The Muschenheims loved music and adored musicians, and gave large suppers for visiting and resident artists. The suppers for Toscanini were very special occasions because of the risk they entailed. Suppers for other musical celebrities held no risk whatsoever. There was rarely any possibility that the guest of honor, no matter how celebrated, would not show up. Nor was there any difficulty about whom to invite with the guest of honor. Not so with Toscanini.

In the first place, it had to be ascertained what Toscanini thought of the guests the Muschenheims proposed to invite. The Maestro had the most definite likes and dislikes. These, however, fluctuated unaccountably. He might look with disfavor today on a person he had cherished only yesterday. It was essential to check with him or his family or his friends. Furthermore, the Maestro held to a rigid code of behavior and morals, the test of which even members of his family and his intimate friends had to meet or suffer ostracism. For ex-

11

ample, he frowned on divorce. While he cheerfully pointed out that marital fidelity was unnatural to man, he insisted that the legal bonds of matrimony were inviolable. A man might have many mistresses, but he could have only one wife. Those of his friends who contemplated divorce had to take into account the loss of his friendship. The Maestro also disapproved of remarriage after the death of a husband or wife, though he might forget his disapproval if the second marriage occurred after a respectable interval of several years. Any shorter period earned his displeasure and inspired swift retaliation. He struck back at one of his closest friends who married again only *one* year after his wife's demise. Notwithstanding their previous intimate association, the Maestro never again saw or spoke to the man. Thus, anyone desiring to entertain Toscanini was obliged to be informed on the up-to-the-minute status of the Maestro's friends.

In the second place, the Maestro's acceptance of an invitation was no guarantee of his attendance, especially on nights when he was conducting. Everything depended on how the concert (or opera) went. He might drive up to the stage entrance of Carnegie Hall at eight p.m. (he was the soul of promptness) in the best of spirits and three hours later leave it in black despair. There could then be no question of supper. The Maestro went straight to his bedroom at the Astor, where, crying imprecations at his orchestra or at himself, or both, he finally went exhausted and supperless

12

to bed. Once, in Milan, after he conducted an opera at La Scala, he returned dejectedly to his home, where the table was set for the usual delayed dinner. As the members of his family made for the dining-room, he placed himself in front of the door and barred their entrance with planted feet and outstretched arms. "What!" he raged, "you can *eat* after such a performance! Shame on you. . . . Shame!" And the family perforce went hungry to bed.

The Muschenheims were Philharmonic Symphony subscribers and attended all of the Maestro's concerts. But not until they heard the very last note of a concert could they be certain he would grace their board a half-hour later. The hazards were many—an orchestral mishap, ill-timed applause, the reluctance of the soloist of the evening to take a bow alone, anything at all. One bitter February evening the Muschenheims left Carnegie Hall secure in the belief that everything was all right, that nothing had occurred to prevent the Maestro from coming to their house for supper as he had promised. They left, alas, a moment too soon. As the Maestro was taking his final bow an overenthusiastic admirer advanced to the stage and placed a floral wreath at the conductor's feet. Quite unaware that his hero associated floral offerings with mortuary rites, the donor was hardly prepared for his idol's strange reaction to his gift. Seeing the wreath, the Maestro blanched, stood irresolute for a moment, then turned tail and fled. Once clear of the stage he did not, as usual, proceed to his dressing-room to

13

change his sweat-drenched undershirt. Instead he ran to the stage-door exit, scampered down the steps two at a time, gained the street, and turned to Seventh Avenue, down which he fled at top speed, followed by Bruno Zirato, the Philharmonic manager, who had tried to intercept his flight and now, winded and distraught, limped helplessly far behind him. Bareheaded, his starched shirt and collar wilted, the frock-coated conductor pushed his way nimbly through the crowds in Times Square, gained his hotel, and shut himself in his room for the night. At the same moment the unsuspecting Muschenheims were greeting their guests. Their butler, holding a tray with a glass and a bottle of wine, stood at the living-room door waiting for Toscanini. (On arrival the Maestro usually declared he was "thirty" (thirsty), and a glass of champagne was always ready for him to put him in a genial humor and thus ease the tension of the other guests.) On this night, however, the tension was eased by a phone call from Mrs. Toscanini saying the Maestro would not be down. Supper was served, conversation was animated and uninhibited. There were several musical "lions" among the guests. But there was a noticeable want of glamour.

On those fortunate evenings when nothing untoward happened at Carnegie Hall and the Maestro did arrive, the Muschenheim abode seemed—to this guest, at any rate—the most exciting place in the world. Aside from the Maestro, one might find oneself seated at table next to Fritz Kreisler, Jascha Heifetz, Vladimir Horowitz,

Lotte Lehmann, or some other world-famous artist. The Maestro was, of course, the focal point, and his presence affected all the other guests, both great and near-great. No one disputed his supremacy and no one ever seriously challenged his views, whether on music or on affairs in general. Mrs. Toscanini might sometimes say quietly but dogmatically: *"No, Papá, non è vero!"* and the atmosphere for a while would grow tense. But by and large the Maestro held forth without interruption.

His opinions of men and events were positive to a degree. Such-and-such an occurrence was a *"scandalo,"* or else, on the contrary, *"una meraviglia."* This or that woman was *"una bella donna—magnifica,"* or else *"una donna bruta—stupida e schifosa!"* Seated at the head of the table and flanked on either side by a pretty woman (the hostess unselfishly saw to that), Toscanini, his eyes flashing, talked quickly and passionately, his hoarse, raucous, guttural voice holding everyone's attention. This voice, by ordinary standards strident and unlovely, seemed to rise from some deep, seething well of the emotions, and it spoke directly to the senses with the force of strange music. Like music, it outlawed reason. However outrageous the Maestro's opinions might actually be, the emotional urgency of the voice which spoke them made them for the moment utterly convincing and incontrovertible. The colleague, the friend, the foe, the political or civil figure, the musician, painter, writer, or composer the Maestro was pillorying found no defender in that room. Any possible defense could but fall flat

15

after the Maestro's hoarsely ejaculated *"Imbecille! Porco! Ignorante!"*

The Maestro especially bore down heavily on musicians in general and on his colleagues in particular. Most conductors, living or dead, were to him anathema. This one was a "pig" because he re-seated his orchestra on unorthodox lines, bunching the first and second violins, thus upsetting the time-honored arrangement of the two string sections on either side of the conductor, which should resemble, the Maestro maintained, "a pair of shoulders with a head between." That one, an *"assassino"* who dispensed with the baton altogether, disdaining honest up- and down beats, made ridiculous, incomprehensible passes in the air with his hands, to the confusion of orchestra and audience. Also consigned to perdition were the extravagantly out-and-out *physical* conductors, the crouchers, the leapers, the forward-and-backward-bending gymnasts—in fine, the whole tribe of show-offs and charlatans "who think only to themselves, to their frock, to how they look from the back" and "think not at all to the music."

Someone would ask him if he had known many great men in his time. The Maestro would look thoughtful. "Great?" he repeated, shrugging his shoulders and jutting out his lips in disdain. "That is a big word." Then his face suddenly brightened. "Great was Verdi. . . . Yes, Verdi. He was also a good man," he went on. "His music is like his cha*rac*ter, strong and honest. He was born a *contadino* [peasant]. He remained a *con-*

tadino all his life. Like me," he added. Verdi had been the Maestro's idol.

"I could have known him better . . . but I was in those days very timid. . . . I did not dare to ask to see him. Now I am sorry. Three times in my life I spoke to Verdi. The first time was at La Scala at the rehearsal of *Otello*. I was a conductor then, but I went to play second cello in the orchestra so I could be near him. In one part I played pianissimo as it was written in my music. Verdi said to me: 'No, no, second cello, I cannot hear you. This is a big theater. You must play louder, *naturale*.' He was right, and I said: 'Si, Maestro.' But he was not happy with the *mise en scène*. No! He was never satisfied. You know, after the first performance of his operas he never came to hear them again. But the *première* of *Otello* was tremendous. I was so excited I could not play my cello. When it was finished I ran quickly home. The house was dark, everybody was asleep. I wake-ed my mother. 'Down on your knees to Verdi!' I commanded her. 'Tonight a miracle happen-ed at La Scala.' My poor mother, she was so frightened. I force-ed her to leave the bed and kneel down on the floor. She thought I must be crazy.

"The second time I saw Verdi? Ah, yes. A long time later I myself was conducting *Otello*. At the rehearsal the *tenore* dragg-ed and dragg-ed, he sing slower and slower. I stopp-ed him. 'Why you sing so slow? That is not the way you sang at the first performance when I play cello in the orchestra.' 'Maestro,' he said, 'I sing

Verdi's own tempo.' 'It cannot be,' I said. 'We will go and ask Verdi.' We came to Verdi. The *tenore* sang. I play the piano. Verdi listen and said to the *tenore:* 'No, no, you are too slow . . . you are too slow. You know, Toscanini, singers forget quickly. . . .'" The word "singers" as he uttered it seemed to bring to mind a spate of musical disasters attributable to vocalists he had worked with; for he now abandoned Verdi and launched into a diatribe against all singers, past and present. Seated around the table were several much-admired concert and opera singers, but the Maestro was not to be deterred by anyone's presence. "They are all *cani* [dogs]," he cried, "*tutti* . . . *tutti* . . . every*bawdy* . . . every*bawdy*."

Mercifully, someone attempted to divert the Maestro's wrath by inquiring about the third time he had spoken to Verdi. The stratagem worked. "Ah, yes!" And his savage expression gave way to one of reminiscent tenderness as he related the circumstance of the last time he saw Verdi alive. He was going to conduct Verdi's last work, the choral *Quattro Pezzi Sacri,* and he called on the composer to discuss matters of tempi and interpretation. "He was very kind," the Maestro said, "so kind. I played the pieces on the piano and he said the tempi were *correct.* I wished to stay longer, but I was too timid. I had not the courage even to ask him for a picture." Here the Maestro's eyes flashed challengingly and he looked at the guests around the table accusingly. "Never —*never* have I asked any*bawdy* for a picture. *Mai* . . .

18

Mai! And I do not like to give my photograph—only imbe*cile* ask for photographs." The guests smiled indulgently at him; for all of them cherished photographs of the Maestro, which he had freely given and charmingly inscribed. Indeed, one Christmas he had sent a gold medal of his head to every member of his orchestra. He had also presented the medal to members of his family and to several favored ladies of his acquaintance. The head, modeled by the sculptor during one of the unsuspecting Maestro's rehearsals, looked savage in the extreme, with the mouth set hard and the eyes, under beetling eyebrows, flashing ecstatic fury or unbridled hatred, or both. It was, in short, a trinket calculated to strike terror in the beholder. But the men of the orchestra, relishing the truth of the artist's representation in metal, received the portrait with gratitude and unselfishly gave it to their wives, who proudly wore it attached to their bracelets. "Yes," the Maestro insisted, "only imbe*cile* ask for photographs." As he spoke, his unheeding eyes rested on a large, elaborately inscribed photograph of himself standing in a silver frame on the sideboard.

There were also supper parties that the Maestro sat through in silence, occasionally sipping his wine, but refusing all food. At those times the conversation around the table was conducted in a low key. One of the bolder spirits there, a very close friend, perhaps, might attempt to draw out the brooding Maestro with some provocative question. The failure of the ruse made the guests even more uncomfortable than before. The self-conscious people around the board hardly touched the food. A second helping in the presence of the abstemious and glowering Maestro was unthinkable. For, notwithstanding a reputation for astigmatism, the Maestro, at certain moments, could see clearly at any distance. He might even launch into a tirade against gourmandizing, beginning with "I cannot understand why people eat so much. I? I do not like to eat. No. For me, sometimes a little soup and bread. This morning at five o'clock I drink a cup of *minestrone* and eat a *grisini* [Italian bread stick]. That is all. I would like to eat *never!*" And he relapsed into silence and looked accusingly at the other guests, some of whom hastily put down their knives and forks, while the anxious hostess made signs to the waiters to clear the table for the *espresso*.

I discovered early that music was the one subject that never failed to dissipate the Maestro's unsocial moods. A disingenuous question on my part like "Do you consider *Falstaff* a masterpiece, Maestro?" would instantly dispel the blackest depression and set him off on a passionate exposition of the glories of that work. "*Falstaff* is a jewel. What a pity you don't know Italian! You must know Italian to understand how wonderfully Verdi fitted together words and music. Do not speak of *Die Meistersinger*. Yes, I know that is also a master*piece*. But not like *Falstaff*. No. *Falstaff* is alone. No Wagner, no German could compose *Falstaff*, only an Italian, only a true Mediterranean like Verdi. *Die Meistersinger* is good, very good, but it is heavy, heavy. *So heavy. Falstaff* is light, it is quick*silver*. You know when I accepted to go to Salzburg I said to Bruno Walter, who was selecting the operas: 'Walter, I wish to conduct *Falstaff*.' He look-ed surprised, because in Salzburg they think to play only Mozart, Beethoven, Wagner, Weber, and Strauss. Why not? I ask-ed him. *Falstaff* is a master*piece*, no? It is a master*piece* like *Fidelio*, like *Magic Flute*, like *Meistersinger*. Oh, yes. If I cannot conduct *Falstaff*, I stay away altogether. No *Falstaff*, no Toscanini."

Another effective gambit was the mention of some-thing that was certain to rouse his ire. "Maestro, last night I went to the Metropolitan . . ." The Maestro did not wait for me to finish. "Don't speak to me of the Metropoli*tan*," he shouted. "It is a pigsty, not an opera house. They should burn it down. It was a bad theater even forty years ago. Many times I was invited to come to the Metropoli*tan*, but I always said no. Caruso, Scotti, would come to Milan and tell me: 'No, Maestro, the Metropoli*tan* is no theater for you. It is good for make the money, but it is not *serious*.'" I broke in to ask why he finally came to the Metropolitan. "Ah! I came be-cause they tell me one day that Gustav Mahler had ac-cepted to come, and I think to myself if a good moosi-cian like Mahler go there the Metropoli*tan* could not be *too* bad." A pleasant expression suffused his face as he began reliving his seven years (1908–15) at the Metro-politan. We listened to the rich and violent memories of those days. He held us with his vivid descriptions of persons and events. We were aware of the privilege of listening to him, all the more as we were certain that what we heard would never be committed to paper by him. Though his talent for writing, as evidenced by the quality of the letters he wrote, is of a high order, he is as averse to writing about himself as he is to others writing about him. "I am a moosician, not a writer." That simple statement also cut short all requests for interviews and the pressure of agents, photographers, and hero-worshippers.

I learned in time to turn his attention to any musical subject about which I sought enlightenment. He was easily diverted. Notwithstanding his undisciplined nature (undisciplined, that is, outside of music), there was a canny streak in him which often put him wise to the hidden motives of people around him. Yet he could be naïve to a degree. I determined to draw him out on the subject nearest my heart, music, without appearing to be importunate. For my own benefit and that of posterity he must never suspect that he was being pumped.

He had known Richard Strauss intimately. I knew he valued highly the tone poems and *Salome* (unaccountably, he disliked *Der Rosenkavalier*), but I wanted his opinion of the composer's character. From experience I knew that a direct question would not produce the subjective opinion I desired to get from him. "Maestro," I asked, affecting innocence, "is Richard Strauss anything like Verdi? . . . I mean in character, not in music." Instantly he reacted in the expected way

—he gave me a look that was a mixture of scorn and incredulity. "No!" he exploded, "not in *music*, and not in char*acter*." I pretended surprise. He went on in a flood of Italian, but, suddenly remembering that I understood very little of the language, he switched to English without pausing and with no lessening of intensity.

"I will tell you about Strauss. . . . In May, the year 1906, May 25th, yes [the fabulous memory was operating easily], I wrote to him. I ask-ed him for permission to give the first performance of *Salome* in Italy at La Scala. He repli-ed yes. I put the date for the *première* in Milan—December 26. . . . He again repli-ed yes. Very good. But wait, wait," the Maestro said dramatically, "*aspetta . . . aspetta*. . . . One day I read in the newspaper that Strauss himself would give *Salome* in Turin one week *before* my performance in Milan! *Santa*. . . . *Madonna*. . . . *Santissima*. . . . I was as*tone*-ied. I was crazy. I could not eat. . . . I could not sleep. That night I took the train for Vienna, and the next morning I stood before him in his house. 'Strauss,' I told him, 'as a *moosician* I take off my hat to you . . . *aspetta* . . . *aspetta*. . . . But as a *man* . . . I put *on* ten hats!' " and the Maestro, his face shining with scorn, feverishly put on ten imaginary hats.

The graphic dumb show delighted the assembly. Other questions about contemporary musicians were asked, and the Maestro disposed of them as vividly and comprehensively as he had of Strauss. So the night wore on to everyone's satisfaction. The party broke up at a very late hour, the Maestro politely remaining till the last guest had departed. This was a strikingly handsome young lady who had sat at his right the entire evening. He had shown her marked attention, often patting her hand and even urging her to eat, in itself a sign of special interest. The young lady now said good-night to the Maestro and told him how sorry she would be to miss his performance of Beethoven's *Missa Solemnis* with the Philharmonic the following Thursday. She had, she said, long ago accepted an invitation to see *Hot-Cha* that evening. The Maestro pressed her hand understandingly. "Yes, yes," he said, "certainly, certainly," and there was a note of envy in his voice. The Maestro read the advertisements in the papers and knew that *Hot-Cha* was Broadway's biggest musical-comedy hit. He was himself very fond of musical shows. He hoped that some night he, too, would be invited to see *Hot-Cha*.

CHAPTER TWO

Some time before I met him I had written a short and highly laudatory profile of Toscanini for *The New Yorker*. As the Maestro disapproved of all persons who wrote about him, I was sure he would sooner or later find a way to punish me. Every time I visited him in the green room of Carnegie Hall, I expected the ax to fall. But months went by and nothing happened. When half a year had uneasily passed, I discreetly asked one of his close friends what the Maestro thought of the piece. To my relief and, secretly, to my annoyance, I learned that the Maestro had not seen the article and, when told about it, had not even expressed a desire to read it. The fancied danger thus averted, I approached the Maestro one day after a concert and boldly invited him to dinner at my house. To understand my astonishment at my temerity, imagine a young baseball enthusiast inviting Joe DiMaggio to dinner, or a student of mathematics offering to entertain

Albert Einstein. Indeed, I was so unprepared for an acceptance that when the Maestro replied: "Why not?" I ran all the way home to tell the great news to my family.

My wife, who shared my awe of, and enthusiasm for, Toscanini, flatly refused to believe me. And when I at last convinced her, her delight was tempered by the hazards of the operation: Whom to ask with the Maestro? What to serve? How to behave? These and other questions had to be faced and settled.

We made a list of possible guests. Many turned out to be questionable: one was once divorced; another was addicted to ultramodern music, which the Maestro heartily detested, and so on, and so on. We finally decided to take no risks. We invited three of the Maestro's closest friends—one lady and two gentlemen—who, as far as we knew, had not at the moment incurred his displeasure. As for the menu, my wife sought the advice of the lady. To show our gratitude for the privilege of entertaining the Maestro, my wife extravagantly proposed caviar for an hors d'œuvre, but the lady raised her hands in horror. Caviar belonged to the fish category, and the Maestro never ate fish. Indeed, his feelings about fish were so positive that he had been known to flee from a house where he had merely *sniffed* its presence. Soup, yes. Perhaps a veal *cotoletto*. When in good mood, the Maestro might eat a mouthful or two of *cotoletto*, but very few vegetables. Perhaps a potato. *Espresso*, of course. For drink, champagne and red wine. Later, brandy. He loved to dunk a piece of sugar in brandy, put a match to it, and call everybody's attention to the blue flames in the glass.

That settled, a situation arose at home; learning of the Maestro's impending visit, my parents-in-law, my wife's sister, and a man who was our best and oldest friend flatly insisted on being present. I said no, categorically. My parents-in-law could come in after dinner (should all have gone well by then), but not the other two. The only way, I said jokingly, my sister-in-law and our best friend could be present would be as maid and butler. The two pounced on the idea. Though my wife and I regarded the proposed deception with misgivings, they begged and pleaded and promised to be letter-perfect in the discharge of their duties; and we finally acquiesced. My sister-in-law spent hours carrying trays from the kitchen to the dining-room, and my friend, after many tries, proved to us that he could open the front door with the elegant obsequiousness of a Park Avenue butler (we lived in an unfashionable street on the upper West Side).

An hour before dinner on the fateful day the "maid," clad in an apron and cap, and the "butler" in starched shirt and tails, presented themselves for our inspection. They seemed presentable enough, though my wife thought her sister looked somewhat too presentable. Indeed, except in musical comedies, I had never seen a maid look so fetching. We sat around nervously smoking cigarettes and wishing we had never embarked on an adventure so fraught with peril. At last the doorbell rang, and our hearts practically stopped beating. The butler ran downstairs, ushered the Maestro and his party upstairs into the living-room, and discreetly retired.

I had never seen the Maestro look so forbidding. He greeted us perfunctorily, sat down in an armchair aggressively, and began twirling his mustache. We hovered about, tongue-tied. The butler came in with champagne and the Maestro silently took a glass. Only when the maid appeared with a tray of hors d'œuvres did the atmosphere lighten. The Maestro took out his pince-nez, held it sideways, and with his right eye regarded her through the upper lens. My sister-in-law blushed, and looked outrageously pretty. The Maestro put away his glasses and chose a slice of Italian salami wrapped around a bread stick. He had brightened up remarkably. He began to talk. Conversation became animated. The butler announced dinner and we filed into the dining-room. The soup was brought in. There ensued a tense moment as the Maestro dipped an exploratory spoon in his plate. He raised the spoon to his lips, tasted the soup, smiled, and, like one conferring a degree, said: "*Buono.*" The dinner was plain sailing after that. The gentlemen followed the maid with their eyes as she moved around the table. The Maestro took a *cotoletto* and gave her an approving look as he helped himself. The guests told anecdotes, mainly about the Maestro, who listened approvingly and supplied accurate names and dates, and sometimes took over and elaborated a story that someone had just begun. The dinner over, we rose and went into the living-room. The brandy was served, the piece of sugar was lighted, and the glass was filled with blue flame, to the Maestro's satisfaction and everybody's delight. The maid came into the room very frequently to empty ash trays and tidy up. This annoyed my wife, who attempted by surreptitious signs to induce her sister not to come in again. But the latter, flushed with success, remorselessly came and went until the party took their leave. When the front door closed on them, the butler ran up the stairs two at a time laughing and fell exhausted on a living-room sofa. The maid lit a cigarette and danced around the room in triumph. The party had been a success; the deception had come off perfectly. We relived every moment of the evening. But in the midst of our rejoicing someone remarked: "What if he finds out?"

That dinner was the beginning of a close friendship. The Maestro thereafter came often to our house, but familiarity failed to dull the wonder and delight we felt in his company. We learned by trial and error how best to amuse him; we discovered, for example, a naïveté we had not suspected. Like most Italians, he was short on humor, but he adored slapstick, practical jokes, and all manner of juvenile games, especially those which involved deceptions. One night when the company rose from the dinner table, we noticed that the fringed silk gown of one of the ladies had been mysteriously chewed away up to her knees. After a moment of bewilderment, we traced the crime to our young mischievous cocker spaniel, who had crept under the table and silently nibbled at the dress. The Maestro, on learning this, grew purple with laughter at the lady's discomfiture, and even pleaded for clemency for the dog.

Somewhere on Sixth Avenue there is, or there used to be, a delightful shop called The House of Fun, where one could purchase trick objects and contraptions designed to fool unsuspecting guests at parties. With these we fooled the Maestro many times, always to his own delight. One object consisted of several pieces of metal loosely tied together. The maid dropped the pieces on the kitchen floor, with a noise like that of many dishes breaking. My wife pretended that she had heard nothing and went on talking to the Maestro, whose sensitive ears had reacted violently to the sound. Five minutes later the metal was again dropped, and again my wife disregarded the clamor. But this time the Maestro could not contain himself. "Pauline," he demanded, "go to the kitchen! Some *stupido* is breaking all your dishes!" He had an uncomfortable experience with a brandy glass that had a tiny hole in it. Each time he raised it to his lips a few drops of the liquor spilled on his shirt front. A most fastidious man, the Maestro could not comprehend what was happening, and furtively wiped the drops with his handkerchief. When we could stand his discomfiture no longer, we revealed the trick, and his relief was immense. But he was impatient to try it himself on some unsuspecting friend.

One day we took him into our confidence and asked him to join us in tricking his wife. The Maestro enthusiastically agreed, and we showed him our latest purchase from The House of Fun, an ordinary table knife that broke in half when applied to the cutting of meat. This knife was placed next to a bona-fide fork beside Mrs. Toscanini's dinner plate. The Maestro could hardly wait for dinner to be announced. He sat opposite his wife at table and watched her narrowly when the meat course came around. To his consternation (and ours), the cook had baked a meat loaf and Mrs. Toscanini used only her fork. There ensued an exchange of words in Italian between husband and wife. The Maestro said sharply: "Carla! Have you no knife?" To which his wife replied that she had a knife, but the meat was soft and did not require one. The Maestro grew angry. "What nonsense! One does not eat meat without a knife! Where are your manners? Where were you brought up?" She looked up in astonishment. "What is the matter with you, Papá? I don't need a knife." "*Per Dio Santo*," the Maestro cried in desperation, "you do, you do! Use your knife, like a civilized person! Like me! Like every*bawdy* here. . . . So!" and he ostentatiously cut into his meat. Completely mystified, she shrugged her shoulders, but to avoid a scene, she took up the knife and used it. The knife did what was expected of it, and the Maestro, who had watched its application apprehensively, laughed with glee; and his wife, who herself was not above enjoying a practical joke, joined in. That winter we drew heavily on The House of Fun. It is true that our plans for gay dinner parties often went awry, for everything depended on the

31

Maestro's disposition during the day, the evening, and up to the dinner hour. But our successes outnumbered our failures. One time we were horrified to learn that one of the guests who had been present at our very first dinner party had in a moment of weakness revealed to the Maestro the trick we had played on him with a false maid and butler. But to our great relief the Maestro, far from resenting it, regarded it as a capital joke, and went around telling it to his friends with vivid gestures and in minute detail. Emboldened by this success, we staged a similar deception. This time my sister-in-law was again disguised as a maid, but an ill-dressed, disheveled, slovenly one, with blackened teeth. When she served the Maestro he could not conceal his aversion, and he refused all food to avoid getting close to her. At the end of dinner, the "waitress" deposited her tray of ice cream on the table and, without warning, seated herself on the Maestro's lap, threw her arms around him, and planted a kiss on his cheek. The Maestro's frozen look of horror defies all description. But the next moment the maid revealed her identity, and his anguished look gave place to one of incredulity and pleasure.

Another evening, he bounded up the stairs to our living-room and was met by a strange sight: our family, all arrayed in eighteenth-century costumes and headgear, stood at the top of the staircase ready to greet him with appropriate period elegance. This was so unexpected that he became utterly confused. "You said not to dress," he murmured, as he began running down the stairs to the street door. Only when he was brought back and got a closer look did he realize that we were outfitted in the formal evening attire of two hundred years back.

These bizarre incidents he never tired of relating. His favorite story concerned one that occurred in our house, but for once without our foreknowledge. We had invited the Maestro and his wife to dinner. At the last moment two of the other guests telephoned their regrets. As we were chatting in the living-room after dinner, there was a violent ringing of the doorbell, and presently our maid hurried into the room. There was a taxicab in front of the house, she said; in it was a horse, and the horse had demanded a dollar and a quarter to pay for the cab. I ran downstairs and into the street, and there indeed stood a cab with the front and rear of a horse protruding out the windows. The front said hoarsely: "For God's sake, pay the driver and let us out of here!" I recognized the voice as that of one of our absent friends. I paid the driver and opened the door; the horse sprang out, bounded up the stairs and into the living-room, which it circled innumerable times, circus fashion, and at last collapsed on the floor in a heap.

All this time the Maestro, who got to his feet in amazement when the horse stampeded into the room, followed its gyrations with eyes starting from his head. (His version of the incident, which he repeated for years at every opportunity, grew in dramatic intensity with each telling, accompanied by flashing eyes and intensive gestures, and was frequently punctuated with the inquiry

33

"*È vero?*" addressed to Mrs. Toscanini, who always listened to the tale excitedly, and always answered solemnly: "*Sì! È vero!*") When the two human components of the horse extricated themselves, they revealed the details of the hoax, which was indeed an elaborate affair requiring secrecy, much persuasion (to get a cabdriver to bring them), and serious practice in equine behavior, especially by the one who was the rear of the horse. But the pair agreed that the reaction of the Maestro as he pointed to the crazily circling horse and shouted: "*Guarda*, Carla! *Cavallo! Cavallo!*" was a sufficient reward for all their pains.

The relish with which Toscanini entered into such innocent pastimes seemed to be in inverse ratio to the ever-present spiritual agonies of his musical life. They offered surcease from the grave soul-searchings that musical scores and their translation into sound imposed on him, and from the great bouts with his orchestra, and his desperate attempts to make it a flawless medium for his own reconstruction of the printed page. The Toscanini who watched the progress of some practical joke with impish expectancy and uninhibited joy was quite different from the one who stayed up half the night wrestling with the scores of the great masters of music, who each morning locked himself in rehearsal combat with his orchestra. For the Toscanini rehearsals were, in the main, deadly battles between conductor and orchestra, and even between Toscanini and himself. And one of the reasons his players did not rebel against the insult and injury he heaped on them was the tongue-lashings the Maestro inflicted on himself when he found he could not communicate his own vision to his men. At those times he castigated himself as an incompetent man, a bad musician, a conductor unworthy to command an orchestra. "It is not your fault," he would say. "No! Not at all. It is mine. I am the *stupido*. I cannot make this pig of an arm" (and he hacked furiously at his right arm with his left) "say what I wish . . . what the composer wants. . . ." And, awed by the agony mirrored in his expressive face, the men pitied him and forgot their own troubles. He could hurt their self-esteem, but they fought against resentment, for they saw plainly that their tormentor suffered, too, as only a man defeated in realizing an ideal of perfection can suffer. After a grueling session with an orchestra he could passionately say to me: "I feel they [the players] are my enemy. I want to *kill* them. It would give me pleasure . . . they are against me . . . they are beasts . . . yes, beasts." His look at that moment was demonic. And just as Benvenuto Cellini (whom the Maestro resembled in artistic rectitude, courage, recklessness, and vindictiveness) harbored—and often translated into action—thoughts of murder against real or fancied enemies, so Toscanini, four hundred years later, often brooded on revenge and bemoaned the effete times that stood in the way of his taking simple, direct action. For him there was something wrong with an age that frowned on dire punishment for miscreants who defiled the sacred art of music.

If he could not actually slay an "opponent," he could at least be brutally pitiless in his abuse. The Marquis de Sade himself would have been hard put to invent anything like the verbal tortures Toscanini visited on some unfortunate player. He staged harrowing inquisitions, which he built up with the deliberation of a crafty playwright. At a rehearsal one day a member of the orchestra had just got through a solo passage, when the Maestro rapped for silence. He assumed a pose, hand on hip and baton touching the end of his nose gingerly, which the men knew from long experience signified displeasure and the framing of a suitable punishment. An ominous silence pervaded the room as the Maestro stood meditatively tapping the end of his nose. Then, suddenly, he brightened up and called the player by name. The man said eagerly: "Yes, Maestro," and rose to his feet. The Maestro contemplated him benevolently for a few moments. Then he said pleasantly: "Tell me, please, when were you born?" The man, wondering, told him. "And in what month?" the Maestro pursued evenly. The man stammered out the month. "And what day?" The man, now completely unnerved, had to think, and the Maestro waited, patiently tapping his nose. At length the man said weakly: "I think it was a Tuesday, Maestro." Then the Maestro pounced. *"That,"* he shouted at the startled musician, "was a black day for music!" He raised his baton in the air and poised it for a downbeat. "And now, *da capo!* [from the beginning]" he commanded. The dreadful moment for the solo passage arrived and passed. This time it was quite another story. The Maestro, still beating away, was heard above the fortissimo sound of the orchestra: "So! So!" and with his left hand threw a kiss to the so recently crucified player. "Like this! Like this! So you are *not* stupid. You *can* play well. . . . Santa Madonna . . . Santissima . . . Now *I* am happy. . . . *You* are happy. . . . *Beethoven* is happy. . . ." At the final chord of the movement the Maestro put down his baton and turned smilingly to the concertmaster. "You know," he began, and the orchestra to a man leaned forward to catch every word, "I remember me a moosician in La Scala, it must be forty years ago . . . yes, in 1906 . . . the month was February . . . yes . . . February the fourteenth, a Saturday . . . I was conducting *Tosca* . . . his name was Bertelli . . . Giovanni Bertelli . . . he was a wonderful player . . . but *stupido* . . . no, not *stupido* . . . *stu-pi-dis-simo!*" The men listened eagerly to the anecdote, laughing loudly and nervously at the humorous moments and exchanging meaningful glances at each evidence of the Maestro's prodigious memory. Forgotten was the vitriolic little dialogue the Maestro had so cleverly staged a moment before. Dispelled was the orchestra's uneasiness. Even the unfortunate player was now forgiving and happy.

There were times when the Maestro shed the four centuries that separated him from the Italian Renaissance in an instant and behaved as uninhibitedly as Benvenuto Cellini. Once, in his younger days at La

Scala, he impulsively threw his baton at the head of an erring violinist, catching him painfully in the eye. The man sued for physical damages and the hurt to his self-esteem. The trial was a stirring spectacle, with all Milan divided on the merits of the case. Toscanini put up a spirited defense, contending that his assault was strictly impersonal, merely the reflex action of a sensitive artist in defense of his art. In the end he was morally exonerated, but he had to pay several thousand lire toward the violinist's medical expenses. It was a considerable sum for those days, but the Maestro paid cheerfully, deeming it not excessive in return for the satisfaction he felt in defending his art.

Many years later he again succumbed to a sixteenth-century impulse. A difference had arisen between two members of the NBC Symphony Orchestra. The Maestro heard about it and generously offered to interview the two and resolve the quarrel. He summoned the men to his dressing-room and asked each to state his grievance. He heard the first one out patiently, then politely turned to the second, who launched into his grievance glibly and confidently. As he proceeded, the Maestro's face darkened. Before the man could finish, the Maestro, trembling with emotion, roared: "Stop! You are not saying the truth . . . you are not a *man* . . . you speak lies!" And with clenched fists he began to beat him about the head. Taken unawares by this sudden transformation, the player stood dazed and rooted to the spot, suffering the blows to rain on his head. Then, recovering, he fled from the room, toward the elevators and safety, the Maestro in hot pursuit. But before the old man (Toscanini was then seventy-five years old) could catch up with him, an NBC official threw himself on the volcanic Maestro, pinned his arms behind him, and led him, wildly protesting, back to his dressing-room. There the Maestro, pale and exhausted, threw himself on a couch, clutched at his head, and for a quarter of an hour breathed stertorously, like one about to give up the ghost.

Yet the injured and aggrieved player harbored no malice. Prudently, for a time he kept at a distance from the orchestra and its Maestro. But some months later he wrote his assailant, politely requesting an interview. This the Maestro granted. He received his visitor at his Riverdale home, chatted amiably, listened sympathetically, and rang for *espresso*. Indeed, the Maestro behaved so charmingly that there could be little doubt that he had quite forgotten the intensity of his reaction to his original meeting with the player in his dressing-room at NBC. As for the visitor, it seemed never to have occurred to him to bring charges against the Maestro at Local 802, the New York branch of the American Federation of Musicians. Local 802 is a tough organization, pledged to uphold the dignity of its members. A harsh word to a member is an insult to the Union, and no complaint of mistreatment is too insignificant to result in immediate inquiry and appropriate action. Once, at a rehearsal with the NBC Symphony, a celebrated guest conductor reprimanded a violinist for inattention. The rebuke was mild enough. But a half-hour later a delegate from 802 appeared and brusquely told the conductor to apologize to the violinist in the presence of the orchestra then and there, or be yanked from the podium. The conductor, somewhat nonplused, acquiesced. But no charges of any kind were ever lodged against Toscanini. The plain truth is that all his life he has been forgiven conduct that would have been tolerated in no other artist. With no outside force to back him up, he was in his own realm an absolute dictator. For one thing, his glamorous hold on the public made victory in any open contest with a disaffected player, singer, agent, or impresario a foregone conclusion. For another, there was the undeniable fact of his unique stature as a musician, his fearlessness as a man, the beguiling charm of his personality, the startling vividness of the figure as a whole. It seemed to be universally agreed that he was not subject to the rules and regulations that applied to other men, even to other celebrated artists.

When the effects of his encounters at morning rehearsals wore off sufficiently during the day for him to be in a mood to come to dinner, we felt more than ever obliged to devise some entertainment that would erase from his memory his earlier session with his orchestra. On one such evening we introduced him to the "murder" game. This consisted in dealing out playing-cards to the participants. The holder of the ace of spades was the would-be "murderer," a fact known to that person alone. The lights went out and players milled around in the dark room, trying to ward off the "murderer." When the "murderer" placed his hands on his "victim," that person would count ten to give the "assassin" time to lose himself in the crowd, then let out a piercing scream and fall to the floor. The lights came on, everyone stood frozen, and the district attorney (previously selected) questioned each player. Only the murderer was permitted to lie; everyone else had to speak the truth.

When the "murder" game was outlined to him, the Maestro showed interest, but declined to be an active participant. Before the lights went out he took up an inconspicuous position between the piano and the wall, as the safest place for a spectator. There followed a few minutes of darkness; a scream duly rent the air; the lights came on. The Maestro had not moved an inch. His face, however, was mysteriously covered with lipstick. The "district attorney" asked him whether anyone had approached him during the blackout. "No!" the Maestro answered simply, "no-bawdy." He came from behind the piano. He listened with grave attention to the "trial" and the "evidence" and marveled at the "district attorney's" success in exposing the murderer. He confessed he like-ed the game, and thereafter always welcomed the suggestion to play it.

The Maestro was enthusiastic about the theater, more especially about musical comedy. During his years at the Metropolitan (1908–15) he saw many Broadway musicals. His favorite was *The Pink Lady*, whose waltz number ("Beautiful Lady") he admired and sometimes played on the piano when in reminiscent mood. Feeling sure that he would welcome an evening at a musical play, I made up a party to dine and to go on to see Ethel Merman in her musical hit *Panama Hattie*. And, indeed, the prospect of an evening at the theater pleased him and he arrived for dinner in the gayest of moods. Sitting opposite him at the table were my nine-year-old daughter Anne and my twelve-year-old son Blair, who had been permitted to come downstairs so that they might carry through life the memory of having dined with Toscanini. Throughout dinner, Anne never took her eyes off the Maestro; Blair, however, was unimpressed. He soon began to exhibit symptoms of ennui; and at one point, in the middle of an anecdote of the Maestro's childhood days at Parma, Blair took from his pocket two little magnets. He laid one of them on the table in front of him and held the other a few inches over it. The two magnets promptly sprang together, whereupon Blair separated them and repeated his game.

The Maestro, still talking, focused his gaze on the magnets. Presently his words trailed off into an incoherent murmur. He was giving his entire attention to Blair. "That's a magnet, Maestro," I said. "Yes," he said, "a *magneto*. I know." "Would you like them?" He nodded eagerly. "Blair, give the magnets to the Maestro." Blair made no move to obey. "Come on, Blair, hand them over," I commanded. But Blair had put the magnets back into his pocket. "Gee, Dad, I can't," he

said, "it don't belong to me. It's my friend Sam's." I
spoke more sternly to Blair, who kept doggedly denying
his ownership and insisting that he could not possibly
do as he was told. The Maestro followed this interchange
keenly, his eyes veering from me to my son and back
again as if his fate depended on the outcome. The situation grew painful. Blair was plainly determined not to
give up the magnets. Concealing as best I could my
chagrin at my son's behavior, I finally broke down Blair's
resistance with hints of enough money to buy a dozen
magnetos. The magnets were grudgingly handed over.
The Maestro pocketed them with satisfaction and resumed his interrupted anecdote.

It was a charming story of his early home life in
Parma, where he was born. The Toscaninis, he said, were
very poor. The little Arturo (he was an only son) went
hungry, the family diet (when it materialized) consisted
mainly of bread and soup. "That is why I like soup and
bread all my life," he beamed. "I am a peasant, like
Verdi. One day my doctor said to me: 'Toscanini, you
are well-born.' He means I was born a peasant, strong
and simple! My mother was strong, very strong, in body
and in char*acter*. My father no! He was very handsome.
In my house in Milano I have a beautiful picture of him
in a Garibaldi shirt and a Vandyke beard. He was a good
man, but weak. He like-ed to drink." (The Maestro
graphically shoved his thumb into his mouth and tilted
his head back, by way of illustration.) "He was a tailor
—in those days, you know, I wish-ed to be a tailor, too,

I would take scissors and cut cloth. The shop was in our living-room. Sometimes the neighbors came and brought their sewing, these people they like-ed to work together in Parma. While they work-ed some*bawdy* read aloud from a book. In this way I learn-ed many, many books. *Ee-van-o-eh, I Miserabili, Il Gobbo di Notre Dame, I Promessi Sposi,* Dante, Shakespeare. I lov-ed these books. And music, too, I learn-ed when I was a little child. Oh yes, in Parma every*bawdy* like-ed music. The people were critical in Parma—more than in Rome, more than in Milano. You know, singers were afraid to come to Parma. The same *tenore* who made a success at La Scala could make a terrible fiasco in Parma." (The Maestro shoved the second and fourth fingers of his right hand into his mouth as if to whistle, to indicate the Parmesan reaction to some vainglorious vocalist.)

According to Toscanini, everybody in his native town knew the standard operas. In the Toscanini workshop–living-room the workers frequently broke into song and little Arturo knew the arias and ensemble numbers of many operas long before he learned to read music or saw the inside of an opera house. Music, so learned at secondhand, was sometimes likely to be inaccurate. Of this Arturo, of course, was blissfully unaware. So much so, that when he was taken to the gallery of the Parma Opera House to hear his first opera, Verdi's *Un Ballo in Maschera,* he was shocked to hear the tenor sing a certain aria in a manner that he, the child Toscanini, considered wrong. "No, no! You are wrong!" the little boy

44

in the gallery, cupping his hands, shouted at the astonished tenor on the stage. "It goes like this . . ." and the child sang out the tune with all the imperfections he had learned at home.

While he was telling us of his early privations and enthusiasms, the Maestro frequently put his hand into the pocket of his jacket to make sure that the *magnetos* were still there. We left our house early and got to the theater while it was fairly empty ("Artists should never be kept waiting"). The Maestro awaited the rise of the curtain with the eagerness of a child. He laughed extravagantly at Miss Merman's down-to-earth deportment and admired her lung power. In the first intermission he stood up and swept the audience with his opera glasses, quite unaware that the people had caught sight of him and were all looking at him. A man came up and said: "Excuse me, are you Maestro Toscanini?" The Maestro, not turning a hair, answered innocently: "No. I am sorry," and the man, incredulous and still gazing at him, retreated.

Near the end of the play I saw that the Maestro was not paying attention to the stage. I whispered: "Is anything wrong?" and he whispered back: "The *magnetos*. I have lost them!" I told him not to worry, that he must have dropped them on the floor, and when the curtain came down we would look for them. Until the end of the play he sat, the picture of dejection, his right hand propping up his head, his eyes closed. When the curtain descended, we waited ten minutes for the theater to empty. We then got down on our hands and knees and searched for the *magnetos*. We called over the ushers and they searched the lobbies, but all to no avail. We left the theater and got into the Maestro's car. Usually, after theater, we drove to our house, where we discussed the play, drank brandy, and the Maestro talked and played the piano until early in the morning. This time the Maestro said he preferred to go home. When the car stopped at our house I suggested that he might have dropped the *magnetos* on our doorstep on the way to the theater. "You think?" the Maestro said, brightening, and he jumped nimbly out of the car and, along with the rest of us, began searching our stoop, illuminated by a street lamp. There the *magnetos* lay in full view. I picked them up and gave them to the Maestro, who hastily put them in his pocket and suddenly decided he was "thirty" (thirsty) and wanted to drink "some*thing*." Mrs. Toscanini demurred, saying it was late and that her husband had a concert the following afternoon. The Maestro packed her off to their hotel. As the car drove away he commented: "Poor Carla! She is always sleeping. She is old." (She was ten years his junior.) We went upstairs, where he drank some*thing*, talked for hours, to our delight, played the piano and sang large chunks of operas in his cracked voice. It was six in the morning before he left reluctantly. The sun had risen and birds were twittering. "I could conduct a concert this moment," he said as he loudly sniffed the morning air. We had no doubt that he could. There was a chill in the air, but he disdained to put on his overcoat. He regarded me pity-ingly as I shivered on the doorstep and magnanimously advised me to go inside before I caught cold. When he reached his hotel suite (he told me subsequently) he removed his shoes like any conscience-stricken husband who had been out late and feared to disturb his wife. An hour later the maid brought him his morning coffee. He spent the morning in study. The afternoon concert went off without incident and to his satisfaction. In the green room later, I asked him if he felt fatigued after staying up all night. "No!" he said. "When I enjoy what I do, I am never tired. Nothing that I like to do can be bad for me."

CHAPTER THREE

$\mathcal{I}$N the summer of 1930 Toscanini was invited by Siegfried Wagner, son of the great Richard, to conduct
Tannhäuser and *Tristan* at the Bayreuth Festival in
Bavaria. This was a revolutionary step. No Italian conductor had ever been remotely considered for the sacred
German festival; but Toscanini's fame and drawing-
power had penetrated even there. He was asked to name
a fee, but refused, saying that he considered the honor
of conducting at Bayreuth sufficient payment. I was
planning to be in Europe that summer and was eager
to go to Bayreuth. The Maestro asked me to call on him
there.

This was the year of the real emergence of Nazism
in Germany, and especially in Bavaria. Adolf Hitler was
an ardent Wagnerite, and he and some of his lieutenants
were to attend the Festival. His presence was expected to
stimulate the box office, but it was Toscanini who proved

48

to be the real star of the season, which had been quickly sold out on the announcement of his coming.

Bayreuth was so crowded that summer that it was with great difficulty that I found a place to sleep. It was my first visit; I had expected to find a lovely town, an ideal setting for a Wagner shrine. In reality Bayreuth was an ugly, smoky little community, its architecture hideous and its inhabitants ungracious and even rude. On the afternoon of the performance of *Tannhäuser* I joined the German and foreign worshippers (at fifteen dollars a head) who walked the mile or so from the town to the Festspielhaus, an unprepossessing wooden theater perched on the top of a hill. From its roof, trumpeters blaringly warned the faithful that the opera was about to begin. The inside of the theater, though an acoustical marvel, was a perfect firetrap; it was enormously wide, with only two aisles along the far sides. Because there was no middle aisle, the people in each row had to stand until the last person had taken his seat. But once the lights went out and the overture sounded from a completely hidden orchestra pit, the magic of Toscanini filled the theater, and I was treated to a performance of *Tannhäuser* so beautiful and alive that it dwarfed any other presentation I had ever seen.

In the intermission I made my way to the green room, but was stopped by a uniformed official, who put me at the end of a long line of people waiting to see the Maestro. Directly in front of me stood an enormous man in a long green robe, and a distinguished-looking middle-aged woman. The official came around with pad and pencil to take our names. To my surprise, the large man said "Ferdinand—of Bulgaria," and the middle-aged lady, "Princess Margherita" (a relative of Victor Emmanuel, King of Italy). The official disappeared and after a few minutes returned. "The Maestro," he announced in German in a loud voice, "will see Mr. Chotzinoff and Mr. Lodi." Mr. Lodi, a drab little Italian, and I stepped out of line and were conducted to the Maestro's dressing-room.

There sat the Maestro, naked from the waist up, his face in an agony of pain. He was subject to attacks of bursitis, and this one looked unusually severe. A heat lamp was focused on his right shoulder. Near him hovered the German conductor Wilhelm Furtwängler. "*Povero* Toscanini!" the Maestro said, trying to smile. "The shoulder is terrible! When I conduct I forget a little. But this moment the pain is terrible. Terrible!" Nevertheless, he greeted me and Signor Lodi warmly, especially Lodi. "*Come sta, caro* [how are you, my dear]?" he inquired. The Italian beamed and bent down to kiss the Maestro's hand. "Lodi was *cameriere* in the Milano hotel, you know, where Verdi died," the Maestro explained. "A fine *cameriere*, and a good man. . . . *Caro* Lodi . . . I thank you for coming to see an old friend." The two conversed in Italian for a few minutes, and the radiant Lodi took his leave. The Maestro then asked me for news of America, and in turn told me about some of the drawbacks he had encountered in Bayreuth. The most irksome was the obligation of the artists to repair after a performance to the great restaurant adjacent to the opera house, there to be inspected at close range by the audience.

"Of course I refuse-ed," he said indignantly. "I told Winifred [Mrs. Siegfried Wagner] I was not an animal for exhibition in a cage. She begged and cri-ed, and said the people are us-ed to see the artists and conductors after the opera. You know, many people come to Bayreuth just to see. Can you believe? I am ashamed for me, for Wagner. But she beg! Ah! *Caro* Chotzie, the life of a serious moosician is *difficile*. . . . Yet I like very much this theater. This theater is serious. Wagner did well when he made an apron to conceal the conductor and orchestra. No*bawdy* can see them. You know, I must laugh. Furtwängler"—Furtwängler had vanished like a ghost—"likes it not, because no*bawdy* can see him conduct. They tell me he would like to raise the platform for the orchestra and take away the apron so that the audience can see him. . . . *Pensa!* [Imagine!]"

The intermission was about over, and I said good-by. I felt sorry for the people who could not get in to see the Maestro. It occurred to me that perhaps the Maestro had not been told about the King and the Princess. "Did they tell you, Maestro," I asked as I was leaving, "that the King of Bulgaria and the Princess . . ." The Maestro cut me short with a disdainful wave of his arms which doubled him up in pain. "Yes, yes," he shouted, "they told me. But what have I to do with kings and princesses? They have no-*thing* to say to me. I have no-*thing* to say to them. No! I am not happy to see them. I am only happy to see my friends."

A few years later, at a supper party after a "good" concert with the Philharmonic, Toscanini, in an expansive mood, invited my wife and me to visit him the following June at the "Isolino," the little Borromean island on the lake of Maggiore he had rented for a term of years. After a fortnight on the Isolino we would all go to Venice to stay with Toscanini's son-in-law and daughter, the Count and Countess Castelbarco. The Maestro, however, would spend only one night in Venice and then fly to Salzburg, where he was to conduct several operas for the Festival. We were to join him there a week later.

In June we sailed for Genoa and from there took a train to Milan. Mrs. Toscanini met us at the station, and we drove on to Pallanza, the town adjacent to the Isolino. It had begun to rain, and by the time we reached Pallanza the rain had become a downpour. We got into a small covered launch and made for the Isolino. As we approached, we discerned a small figure standing at the water's edge; it was the Maestro waiting to receive us. He stood drenched, hatless and coatless, oblivious of the furious rain beating down on him. "At last!" he said solemnly, as he embraced us. "I thought I would never see you again." Servants came running with umbrellas

52

and we climbed the steep hill to the house, the Maestro running nimbly ahead.

It was a beautiful island, full of rare trees and shrubs and exotic flowers. To us it seemed an enchanted isle, the ultimate setting for its magical deity. Toscanini himself showed us through the villa that crowned the island—a redone eleventh-century monastery. Nothing more romantic could be imagined. The terrace and the main rooms and bedrooms opened a hundred feet above Lago Maggiore, its surface now blistered with sharp pebbles of rain. The Maestro enjoyed our delight and promised us greater wonders when the rain would cease and the sun come out. I went to bed that night in a state of unreality, and I could barely close my eyes. Early in the morning, quicksilver fragments of light seeped through the chinks in the shutters. I got out of bed, threw them open, and flooded the room with blinding sunlight. The lake below was a motionless expanse pinpricked by millions of sunbeams. I put on a dressing-gown and went downstairs, stepping softly so as not to be heard. Passing near the kitchen, I heard the Maestro's voice. I went in. The Maestro, in blue silk pajamas, was talking to the cook. I greeted him and asked him why he was up so early. "I came," he said cheerfully, "to order for you an American breakfast—ham and eggs." We then went into the living-room, where he unbolted and threw open all the shutters, arranged chairs, and pottered around busily like a practical servantless householder doing the morn-

53

ing chores. This done, we went outdoors, smelled and admired the flowers, and greeted an aged gardener, with whom the Maestro held an animated conversation. Then we went back and had our breakfast on the terrace, I my ham and eggs, he a cup of soup and bread. He was the soul of solicitude, much concerned that the ham should be to my taste (which it wasn't, though I said it was perfect) and the eggs properly "cook-ed."

After breakfast the Maestro excused himself and went upstairs. He came down again toward noon, dressed smartly in striped trousers, pleated starched shirt, cuffs and collar, and black bow tie. We sat in chairs on the terrace facing the lake. The Maestro's presence on the Isolino drew many sightseers in rowboats and on the ancient paddle boats that made the circuit of the lake. The boats came very close to the Isolino, and people stood up, waved handkerchiefs, and yelled: *"Bravo, Toscanini! Viva Toscanini!"* I was touched by this show of affection, but the Maestro's face suddenly darkened and he shouted back: *"Stupido. . . . Ignoranti. . . . Schifoso!"* However, when a small launch came along and those in it did not speak but waved their handkerchiefs or their arms at us, the Maestro smiled and waved back as if he believed they were waving at two anonymous figures.

The week we spent on the Isolino had a fairytale quality. We were taken to visit the other Borromean islands. We steamed over to the Isola dei Pescatori, a quaint, unspoiled fishing-village, and lunched with the

Maestro's great friend Ugo Ara. Ara was once the violist of the celebrated Flonzaley Quartet. When he left the Quartet he went to live on the Isola dei Pescatori. Born a Jew, he had become a convert to Catholicism and given himself up to good works with a zeal and simplicity that endeared him to the fishing-folk and earned him the name of saint. Toscanini took me to Ara's little house, which consisted of a tiny room with only a cot, a small table, and two chairs. The Maestro called my attention to the austerity of Ara's life, and said: "That is the way we should all live." He said it with emotion; he believed what he was saying. But in America, after a visit to Jascha Heifetz's spacious, comfortable, remodeled farm-house in Connecticut, he told me that such simple sur-roundings did not suit an artist of Jascha's fame. And neither his own house on the Isolino nor his apartment in Milan approximated the modest dimensions of Ugo Ara's monastic cell.

The Maestro was preparing for his Salzburg season. His music room was piled high with many editions of the score of *Die Meistersinger* and books in all languages relating to Wagner. He had long been familiar with the prose works of Wagner. But now he went laboriously through all the composer's articles and letters for what-ever light they might shed on the interpretation, the scenic designs, and the staging of *Die Meistersinger*. At Bayreuth he had discovered a mistake in the orchestral parts of *Tristan*. Since the death of Wagner this error had gone unnoticed. Now he showed me passages in the writings of Wagner which contradicted the traditional staging of the final scene of *Die Meistersinger*. All this was fascinating for me, especially his running comments on Wagner and his music, and his animadversions on the plain disregard of Wagner's wishes by conductors, directors, and singers the world over. The Wagner recitative, which vocalists treated with the freedom permissible only in cadenzas, was meant, he claimed, to be sung in strict time, and he pointed to Wagner's own words to prove it. Though the cast for *Die Meistersinger* in Salzburg would boast seasoned artists, he feared they would be tradition-ridden. They must therefore relearn the opera as if it were a brand-new work. "And what a work it is!" he exclaimed ecstatically. "*Ma . . .*" and he smiled indulgently, "*sempre* C Major [always C Major]. . . . Beautiful, yes . . . but too much C Major."

Suddenly the week was over—like a moment. We left the Isolino and motored to Venice in the Toscanini Cadillac, driven by Emilio, the Maestro's massive Swiss chauffeur and bodyguard. Emilio made the most of his employer's fame. When we stopped for lunch in Verona, he and his car became the center of attention for the passers-by. Surrounded by an eager crowd, Emilio was pleased to answer questions flung at him, no doubt inventing details of the Maestro's habits and idiosyncrasies, though an unvarnished report would in all probability have been even more startling. Actually the drive to Venice was a mixed pleasure for my wife and me. The Maestro had (and still has) a mania for speed, and regarded a seventy-mile-an-hour clip as a leisurely pace. Our expressions of alarm only delighted him. "But we are going *adagio*," he would say disingenuously. "Emilio, a little faster!" And Emilio, who relished his master's pranks, would accelerate the speed of the car to its limit, the unceasing sound of the horn scattering bicycles to the right and left like astonished and resentful chickens.

The Maestro spent only one night in Venice. Early the next morning he flew alone to Salzburg. He carried a valise containing his immediate needs, and his wife tied some money in his handkerchief in the event of an emergency. He departed happily, for he loved traveling, particularly in airplanes. His journey proved safe and uneventful. Some hours later a telegram to that effect arrived from Salzburg.

A week later Mrs. Toscanini, my wife, and I motored to Salzburg. We arrived there toward nightfall and went to the Österreichischer Hof, where the Maestro had stayed the week. Mrs. Toscanini told us to wait in the lobby while she went up to fetch her husband. We would then have dinner in the dining-room. She returned presently, followed by the Maestro. We could read on both their faces that something was amiss. The Maestro looked straight at us with no sign of recognition. We went into the dining-room and sat at a table. A waiter who spoke Italian took Mrs. Toscanini's orders. The Maestro never uttered a word, and hardly touched his food. Nor, for that matter, did my wife and I; we were completely floored by the Maestro's conduct. Dinner over, we bade Mrs. Toscanini good-night and went to our room, where we sat around unhappily trying to figure out what to do in the strange role of unwanted guests. We finally decided to remain in Salzburg on our own, and to avoid meeting the Toscaninis at all costs.

The next morning we went to the Maestro's rehearsal. Afterward, for fear of running into him at the hotel, we lunched in a restaurant on the edge of the town. In the evening there was another rehearsal, which we attended, for we had no intention of letting our personal pique interfere with our enjoyment of the Maestro's art. As we were walking back to the hotel, his car drew up alongside us and Mrs. Toscanini motioned us to get in. The Maestro was sitting up front with Emilio, his usual perch. He now turned on us in a fury. "Where have you been all this time?" he demanded. "Why did not you come to dinner tonight?" This seemed even more incomprehensible than his obliviousness of our presence the night before. "Well, Maestro," I began boldly, when I was able to collect my faculties, "after the way you treated us last night—" "I knew it, I knew it," he broke in triumphantly. "You are people who have no feelings. For a week I was in Salzburg alone . . . it was raining and cold . . . I had no overcoat! I was unhappy . . . and I thought you were in the family . . . you would understand. . . . Well, I was mistaken. . . ." We were by then melted to tears and as contrite as if we had indeed committed some outrageous sin. We said we were sorry—if we had only known. At last he was mollified. "But if you do such a thing again," he warned us as he turned his head to face the road, "I will never speak to you again! *Mai* . . . Never! Never!"

The Toscaninis moved into a villa in Liefering, a village some miles from town, and into it also moved their daughters, Wanda Horowitz and Wally Castelbarco, with their husbands and a small child apiece, also Mrs. Toscanini's sister and brother-in-law, the Polos. My wife and I rented a room in a farmhouse near by, but we took our meals with the Toscaninis. Each morning around ten the Maestro would pick us up in his car on his way to rehearsal in the town. *Die Meistersinger* was being prepared. The artists sat in a semicircle around the Maestro. They sang their roles to the accompaniment of a piano played by Erich Leinsdorf (now conductor of the Rochester Philharmonic), with the Maestro beating out the time by clapping his hands. The cast, which consisted of celebrated and experienced artists, might have been a group of beginners learning their parts, so unrelenting was the Maestro's beat and so intent was he on their being letter-perfect as to the duration of notes, nuances, and phrasing. This classwork went on daily for a fortnight, after which the rehearsals, now with orchestra and stage directions, were transferred to the opera house.

Only a week before the first performance we became aware that all was not going well with the production of *Die Meistersinger*. At home, in the evenings, the Maestro looked melancholy, ate sparingly, and often

59

put his head in his hands and softly murmured to himself: *"Povero* Toscanini . . . *Povero* Toscanini." At last, one night, he spoke out. He was unhappy about one of the leading members of the cast. "He is a good man . . . a good artist . . . but not for this role," he said. "But you yourself chose him," I protested. "Besides, it's too late now. He came here at great expense, rented a villa, and brought his family. You can't send him away now. It would ruin his reputation." The Maestro shot me a look of scorn. "Are you asking me to think to this man or to think to Wagner?" My heart ached for "this man." But the Maestro had scored a point, and any appeal to sentiment would be regarded as an affront to his integrity as an artist. We telephoned to Munich for an acceptable replacement and, finding one, spent half the night composing a letter to "this man." The gist of it was that the Maestro had noticed at rehearsals that the artist was not well. Should the artist decide to leave the cast and go away for a cure, the Maestro would quite understand, and so forth. A reply arrived the following day. The artist thanked the Maestro for his solicitude. It was quite true that he was unwell. He would avail himself of the Maestro's kind suggestion to leave the cast and go somewhere for a cure, and so forth.

The whole Toscanini household was saddened by this episode. But after a satisfactory rehearsal with the replacement from Munich, the Maestro brightened up. A few days later there was a never-to-be-forgotten dress rehearsal of *Die Meistersinger* when the Maestro drove orchestra, chorus, and principals to such emotional heights that when the curtain fell and was then permanently raised for criticism and last-minute touches, as is customary at dress rehearsals, no one on the crowded stage stirred, but all stood frozen like effigies, their eyes tear-dimmed. The Maestro, too, stood for a while stock-still in the pit, his left hand on his hip, his right covering his eyes. He, too, was moved. Altogether forgotten was the poor man who had sacrificially betaken himself to a "cure." Wagner had been superbly "thought to" at the cost of one individual's happiness—and who could say that it was not justified?

The rehearsals for *Falstaff* were not less exciting. There were, fortunately, no replacements. But one incident nearly canceled its presentation. On a certain morning we repaired to the theater to see the sets for *Falstaff* mounted for the first time on the stage. All was well until the curtain went up on the interior of Mr. Ford's house. After one look the Maestro rose from his seat and rushed for the door. The scene-painter, the director, and other dignitaries ran up to him to find the cause of his displeasure. "*Vergogna!* [Shame!]" the Maestro cried, including with a great sweep of his hand the theater and everyone in it in his stricture. "Do you call *that*"—pointing to the offending scene on the stage— "an Elizabethan house! You know no-*thing*, no-*thing*. Go read what Verdi says in the score! No! This is not a theater. It is a place for the *ignoranti!* I will not conduct in such a place. . . . No! No! Never . . . never!" His hoarse voice rose to a scream, drowning out the frightened, protesting "buts" of the designer and *régisseur*. I ran into the street to shoo away the photographers who were always lying in wait to snap the Maestro. One of them had set up his camera on a tripod in front of the motor car at the stage-door entrance. I begged him to leave and told him about the Maestro's belligerent state of mind. He would not be budged. He had been sent by some international news service to get a picture of Toscanini and told not to come back without one. The Maestro was coming through the stage door, his wife behind him. I tore off my jacket and threw it over his head, and pushed him from the rear toward his automobile. Emilio, sensing his big moment, had already started his engine. As soon as we were in the car, he drove straight toward the cameraman as if to run him down. In his haste to avoid what seemed like certain disaster the cameraman tripped and caught his foot in the tripod, and camera, tripod, and man crashed noisily to the street as Emilio deftly steered his car away. I removed my jacket from the Maestro's head. Understanding the necessity for my action, he had not lifted a hand to remove it himself. Emilio, knowing by long experience what to do, headed for the open country. For an hour we drove in complete silence. When we returned to the Toscanini villa we found an elaborately worded message from the Salzburg Intendant that a new set in the authentic Elizabethan style had already been started and would be ready on the morrow for the Maestro's inspection.

When, on the following day, the curtain went up on the new interior of Ford's house the Maestro said triumphantly: *"Ecco!* [There it is]." *Falstaff* gave no further real trouble. A minor flurry developed when the romantic young couple in the opera failed to steal the prescribed furtive kisses in the Ford garden in time with the rapid tempo of the music. The Maestro shouted: "No! No!" climbed up onto the stage, pushed the tenor aside, and nimbly planted rapid kisses on the ingénue soprano's lips. "So!" he shouted. "Like this!" After several tries, the kissing was accomplished to the Maestro's satisfaction. At last the opera seemed prepared to perfection. Yet at every performance, in the intermission before the last act, the Maestro called the principals to his dressing-room and painstakingly rehearsed them in the final fugue. "You know, singers forget quickly," he said each time in explanation.

The Maestro had little privacy in his villa at Liefering. The Toscanini children, their wives and husbands, *their* children with their nurses, the uncle and aunt and *their* daughter and her husband, and numerous friends and friends of friends turned the place into a kind of Italian *pensione*, gay and noisy and uninhibited. Except at those times when some rehearsal or performance "poison-ed," as he claimed, the Maestro's life, the inmates, including *"Papá,"* behaved like any outsize Italian middle-class family. Children screamed and laughed, everybody talked at the same time, the voices trying to outdo each other in pitch and emphasis, often rising to what sounded to non-Italian ears like alarming belligerence. (Actually the subject matter always turned out to be inconsequential. One such verbal free-for-all that I nervously expected to end in blows proved to be an animated discussion about a dress Mrs. Toscanini thought she had sent to the cleaners, but which happily turned up the next day in the Signora's bedroom closet.)

In the afternoons, friends would arrive with movie cameras and someone would whip up a little scenario in which the entire family would act. The Maestro played ball with his grandchildren as the cameras ground away, or acted the hero or villain of a grotesque scenario with the emphasis on facial grimaces, bodily posturings, and buttock-slapping.

The Maestro's hearty willingness to be photographed by his family and friends and his refusal to pose for the press brought frustration and despair to the publicity department of the Salzburg Festival. However, his mere presence at the opera house was sufficient to insure the success of the season. Mainly because of him, the picturesque town was crammed with people of all nationalities running around in leather pants or dirndls. Tickets for the Toscanini performances were at an extravagant premium, and Josef, the factotum of the Österreichischer Hof (the town's best hotel), made a fortune from rich Americans who were willing to pay anything for the coveted tickets. Crowds followed the Maestro's Cadillac. He dared not show his face on the street for fear of being mobbed, and only in the country could he feel free to walk about.

One night after a late rehearsal, he was prevailed upon to visit an inconspicuous restaurant in the town, where there would be little likelihood of his being recognized. But we miscalculated, for his appearance threw the shabby place into an uproar. The crowded, chattering room suddenly grew silent; the proprietor ran toward us, quite beside himself as to how to make us welcome. "What an honor, *Herr Maestro*," he kept repeating as he bowed low to the ground, at the same time waving his arms backward in an effort to spur the gaping waitress into action. When we were finally seated, he ran off, and a moment later returned with a bottle of wine. This bottle, he assured the Maestro, was his special stock, and he wished to have the great honor of the great Maestro's opinion on it. The place was not of a kind to inspire confidence in the quality of its fare. I thought it prudent to taste the wine first, and when I did so my skepticism was fully justified. Never had I tasted a liquid so raw and sharp and rancid. I leaned toward the Maestro and whispered in English: "For God's sake, don't touch it. It's terrible." The proprietor had filled the Maestro's glass to the brim and now stood by anxiously awaiting the verdict. To my horror, the Maestro lifted his glass, said *"Salute"* to his host, and stoically downed the vile concoction to the last drop. A spasm of distaste screwed up his face for a second. The next moment he smiled and put down his empty glass. *"Buono, buono,"* he said. *"Grazie . . . grazie."* The beaming host refilled the glass and the Maestro, after a pause, drank it down. Of course, the rest of us felt obliged to follow suit. To forestall the host's further pressure and the Maestro's gallant acquiescence, I pointed to the lateness of the hour, and our party, greatly relieved, rose to go. On the way home I asked the Maestro why he hadn't heeded my warning about the wine. He gave me a reproachful look. "He was so kind. I could not be rude," he said.

Yet the very next week he proved that he could quite easily be remarkably rude. There was a lunch at his villa, and among his invited guests was old Frau Thode, Richard Wagner's stepdaughter and granddaughter of Franz Liszt. Ever since she had met the Maestro at Bayreuth she had adored him as the greatest interpreter of Wagner's music she had ever heard. I sat next to her at lunch. There was much talk of Wagner and *Die Meistersinger*, which the Maestro had conducted the night before. To please Frau Thode, I steered the conversation to the music of her grandfather, Franz Liszt. At the mention of Liszt the Maestro's face grew dark. "Don't speak to me of Liszt," he said. I was astonished and mortified. I admired Liszt and had thought the Maestro did too. At any rate, I felt he should have spared the sensibilities of Liszt's granddaughter. I tried to change the subject, but the Maestro went on bitterly about Liszt. "He was a charlatan," he proclaimed, looking pointedly at Frau Thode as if she was directly implicated in her grandfather's perfidy. "He was a *poseur*, and

66

his music is insincere." Frau Thode pressed my hand in anguish, and her eyes filled with tears. I rushed to Liszt's defense, but I could not prevail over the Maestro's blazing eyes and scornful invective. When I saw that my efforts only drove him to a more virulent attack, I decided to ease Frau Thode's situation by distracting the Maestro suddenly. I knew he despised Mascagni. He had often inveighed against him and his music. "Maestro," I said, "why is it that I like *Cavalleria Rusticana* so much? I know it is not a great work, but it has a power—" The switch from Liszt to Mascagni was instantaneous, like a montage in a movie. "Why?" the Maestro yelled at me. "Why you like *Cavalleria?* I tell you why. Because you are *stupido . . . ignorante . . .* that is why . . . *Dio . . . Madonna . . . Santissima . . .*" He was off on Mascagni, on Leoncavallo, on the whole Italian *verismo* school—"*degenerato.*" Everybody at the table saw the trick and felt relieved. Frau Thode dried her eyes with her handkerchief and pressed my hand in gratitude. The crisis was over.

I often thought that the Maestro's temperament resembled the Salzburg weather, which was kaleidoscopic in its changes. Without warning it would rain, black clouds would hasten through the sky, thunder would roll ominously close. Then suddenly the rain would cease and a bright sun would sop up every bit of moisture, the green landscape would shine pleasantly, as if it had always shone like that, and the distant mountains would come closer to the town, their milky transparency as immediate as if seen through a telescope. Toscanini, too, presented in a single day transformations without number. He was naïve, crafty, simple, complex, kind, and ferociously spiteful. The moods *inhabited* him without forewarning, and evaporated as mysteriously.

He was most appealing when a prey to a quiet, gentle sadness. When on our last day in Salzburg we came to bid him good-by, he appeared moved, and he embraced us gently. "We shall probably never meet again," he said. He had left the Philharmonic and America for good that spring.

"Oh, yes, we shall," I said optimistically. "If you won't come to America, we'll come to Italy."

He shook his head. "No! I am sixty-nine. . . . I am old . . . too old . . . it is time to die. . . . *Va, vecchio* John!" ("Go, aged John," quoted from *Falstaff*.) He looked old at the moment. His words, I thought, could be prophetic.

CHAPTER FOUR

$\mathcal{I}$N the fall of 1936, at a dinner party in New York, I met General David Sarnoff, then president of the Radio Corporation of America and chairman of the board of the National Broadcasting Company. We talked about music and discovered in each other an admiration for the great voices of the past, a brash addiction to melody, and a reverence for the art of Arturo Toscanini. "What a pity," I said, "that America will never hear and see the Maestro again." He agreed that it was a pity, and thought something should be done about it.

Several weeks later I met Mr. Sarnoff at a concert. He gave me a lift in his car; as we drove along, he suddenly offered me a job at NBC. I told him I knew nothing about radio and asked him what kind of job he had in mind. He said he hadn't the faintest idea, but would I please talk to Mr. John Royal, in charge of programs at NBC. I thought the offer rather strange, but when I got to know Mr. Sarnoff better, I understood that I was one of his hunches. And, while it was perfectly true that at the moment he didn't know just what to do with me at NBC, he was, so to speak, putting me on ice for the time when his hunch would take concrete shape. So I took a part-time job at NBC with duties as nebulous as a court favorite's.

In due time the hunch materialized. Mr. Sarnoff called me to his office one day and told me he had made up his mind to persuade Toscanini to return to America. I could not help smiling in pity for his ignorance of Toscanini's character. "He will never come back," I said. "He told me so himself." I sketched for Mr. Sarnoff a verbal portrait of the Maestro, underscoring his absolute intransigence. I pointed out that once the Maestro made up his mind about something, he could not be budged. When he left the Metropolitan in 1915, for example, Otto Kahn, the opera house's Mæcenas, moved heaven and earth to get him to return. He finally dispatched a cable to Milan begging the Maestro to come back on his own terms as to fees, rehearsals, artists, and anything else he thought important. The Maestro had not even deigned to reply.

My disclosures failed to disturb Mr. Sarnoff. "We'll try," he said amiably, and I told him to remember that I had warned him. I was then commanded to send the Maestro a cable offering him a cross-country tour with the Philadelphia Orchestra, to be sponsored by RCA Victor, the recording company under RCA's banner. To this the Maestro promptly replied: "Thank you dear friend no. Arturo Toscanini." Disappointed but triumphant, I showed the cable to Mr. Sarnoff, who read it without emotion and said: "Let's think up something else." I could think of nothing else. "Suppose," he went on calmly, "we offered to *create* an orchestra for him—a *radio* orchestra. Would he go for that?" I shook my head pityingly. No. I was certain he would not. He had no interest in radio. His Sunday matinees with the Philharmonic Symphony were broadcast, but for him they were just concerts. Radio was mechanical, like recording. For many years he had refused all offers to record. He would refuse to be primarily a radio conductor.

"Very well," said Mr. Sarnoff. "I want you to go to Milan and get him. The American radio listener deserves the very best in music. All we can lose is a few weeks of your time and the expenses of the trip. No more cables. Get on a boat."

However, I did send one last cable in which I told the Maestro I expected to be in Milan early in February and hoped I could see him. He smelled a rat. "Think to my age!" he cabled back.

Believing that I might at some point require feminine co-operation, I took my wife along. The voyage was a stormy one, and I spent most of it in bed alternately dozing and dipping into the books and magazines friends had sent to the boat. In one of the magazines my jaundiced attention was caught by an article on canaries. I am ordinarily indifferent to canaries, but the paragraph that caught my eye recounted the behavior of a flock of canaries in the author's living-room during a Philharmonic Symphony Sunday broadcast of Beethoven's Ninth Symphony, conducted by Toscanini. During the first three movements, said the article, the canaries were silent. But at the entrance of the chorus in the finale, the birds settled themselves on the radio console and sang along. This amused me. Hoping it might also amuse Toscanini, I shoved the magazine into a valise for possible future use.

We arrived in Milan late on a piercingly cold, snowy afternoon and went to the hotel Principe e Savoia, close to the railroad station. So certain was I that my mission would fail that I at once made inquiries about a return passage within a week. Then I telephoned Mrs. Toscanini. She said the Maestro was in one of his somber moods, and that she would be right over. Half an hour later she was in our room. It was obvious that she wished to warn us about the Maestro's current state of unreceptiveness toward whatever scheme we had in mind. Our room being ice cold, Mrs. Toscanini suggested that we all get into bed and continue our conversation in a less frigid temperature. The three of us piled into bed and pulled the feather comforter up to our necks. In that supine position I disclosed the purpose of my visit. My wife, who spoke Italian, was my interpreter. (Although Mrs. Toscanini had spent years in America, she spoke no English, a circumstance that her husband attributed to her stubborn provincialism.) Almost from the start she began shaking her head and muttering: "No, no . . . *impossible* . . . *mai!*"—a reaction I had fully expected. Indeed, what with my deep-rooted pessimism about the project, the piercing cold, the dreary, wet aspect of the city from our bedroom window, and the prospect of facing the ill-disposed Toscanini, I would gladly have seized our still unpacked valises and fled Italy, if that had been possible.

After an hour's conversation in bed, Mrs. Toscanini said it was time for her to go home. She would expect us for dinner that night. She had no objection to my broaching the project to the Maestro, though I must have no illusions about his answer. Perhaps, she said, I had better wait for some more propitious moment. I grasped at the possibility of a respite.

Later, in the Via Durini, we found the Maestro indeed in a somber mood. His greeting lacked even a hint of the old warmth. The conversation at table was strained. Several times I was on the point of making a clean breast of it. Reconciled to the expected refusal, I was prepared for a quick farewell and an immediate return to America. But courage failed me, and we returned dispirited to our icy bedroom in the hotel. The next morning Mrs. Toscanini telephoned that we were to lunch and dine with them during our stay in Milan. Dutifully but hopelessly we drove twice a day to the Via Durini. Some meals went better than others, but none gave me an opening. The Maestro spoke little. When he did speak, it was mostly bitter invective against Mussolini and what he called his *ladri* (thieves), and the misfortunes they had brought on Italy.

One day the Toscaninis took us to lunch in a very large restaurant in the Galeria. This great, high, glass-roofed section of the city was more crowded than usual: the Fascists were celebrating something or other and Mussolini and Ciano had come to Milan for the festivities. Flags and streamers hung from windows, and the city had a holiday aspect. The restaurant was full. As we entered, all eyes turned to the Maestro. He was, as usual, oblivious of the sensation he was creating, but Mrs. Toscanini looked nervous. Although the Maestro was a popular figure, Milan was a Fascist stronghold and there was always the chance that some hothead might start a demonstration against the anti-Fascist conductor.

When we finished our lunch I made an attempt at conversation by describing our recent sea voyage. The Maestro asked me if our ship had called at Naples or had gone direct to Genoa. I told him we had stopped a day at Naples and were surprised at the change in the city since we had last seen it. "Mussolini certainly cleaned up Naples," I said thoughtlessly. I had hardly finished speaking when the Maestro screamed at me: "Mussolini! Do not speak of that *assassino!* That *porco!* I wish to kill him. I would be happy to kill him. . . ." He ranted on in Italian and in English for what seemed an eternity. I looked around me. Not a soul *appeared* to hear the Maestro. No one was looking our way. It was as if the Maestro were speaking in a language none of the diners understood or cared to understand. Mrs. Toscanini kept murmuring: "*Basta! Basta!* [enough, enough] *Papá*," and clutching my hand in despair. He talked himself out at last. His wife hurriedly called for the bill, and we left the restaurant. For the first time I understood why Mussolini suffered his archenemy to go unmolested. I had seen the people in that restaurant *protecting* their beloved Toscanini by pretending to be deaf.

Two weeks went by and I had said nothing. Then the Maestro began to show restiveness at my strange reluctance to say what I had come for. I was sure that Mrs. Toscanini had not betrayed my confidence, for sometimes I would find him giving her sharp looks that said plainly: "Do you know anything? Why don't they speak?" His increasing irritation at meals and in the evenings did not loosen my tongue. It had, in fact, the opposite effect. And as the days passed slowly, the very faint hope of success that I might have secretly cherished vanished. I was waiting for an opening that seemed never to come. But always I took along with me the copy of the provocative magazine article on canaries, and a slip of paper on which I had outlined several different offers for a series of broadcasts with a future NBC Radio Orchestra. Not that I really expected ever to produce these documents. I only wanted to be prepared, in the unlikely event that I should need them.

At the end of this fruitless and depressing fortnight in Milan, the tension in the Toscanini apartment suddenly began to ease. One night we found two other guests at dinner—Mr. and Mrs. Giulio Gatti-Casazza. Gatti (as everybody called him) had just retired as general manager of the Metropolitan Opera Association and had returned (like Toscanini) to spend his declining years in his native land. Impresario and conductor had had a long association, both amicable and warring, in Italy and America. They appeared pleased to see each other, and their reminiscences of their colorful past continued throughout a lengthy dinner. It was a succession of humorous or dramatic experiences prefaced by "You recall, Gatti?" or "Maestro, it remembers me . . ." (They spoke English for my benefit, the Maestro fluently though rather archaically, Gatti with great difficulty and with abrupt excursions into Italian.) They recalled their first years together at La Scala, and how after a performance they would remain at the opera house until dawn, planning new productions and analyzing the merits and defects of the old ones. The faces of the two aging men reflected the bitter-sweet pleasure their recollections (and some excellent wine) induced.

"Do you remember, Gatti . . ." the Maestro said, and his face was suddenly clouded with some disturbing memory, "do you remember the *jettattore?*"

Gatti nodded his large head. "I remember well!" he said solemnly.

I looked perplexed, and the Maestro explained that a *jettattore* was a man who had the evil eye. "This poor man—Giovanni was his name—eh, Gatti?" Gatti nodded. "Si—Giovanni." "This Giovanni ruined my

first performance of Weber's *Euryanthe*. *Vero*, Gatti?"
Gatti nodded. "*Vero!*" he said. I was eager to hear how
the man with the evil eye ruined the *première* of *Euryanthe* in Italy. The Maestro turned to me. "Everybody
was afraid of Giovanni. . . ." ("*Naturalmente*," Gatti
put in.) "I, too. When I see him in the street I go the
other way." ("*Certo!*" Gatti murmured.) "Giovanni
was a good man. *Poveretto!* He could not help it to have
the evil eye. Think! He even married and had children!
Well, well! I was going to conduct *Euryanthe*. It was
the first time the opera would be given in Italy, and I had
many rehearsals. Many. *Vero*, Gatti? At last I was satis-
fi-ed. The theater had been sold out. *Vero*, Gatti? People
were coming from all over Italy to hear it, even from
Germany. Well, came the night of the performance. I
put on my frock and I go to La Scala. As I reach the
stage door I hear a voice from the other side of the street.
The voice say '*Buona sera*, Maestro.' My blood freeze. It
is the voice of the *jettattore*, Giovanni. I stay still. I pretend I do not hear. Shall I go in the theater or go home?
I did not know what to do. Then, of a sooden Giovanni
cross-ed over and came close to me. He put his hand out
to me so"—the Maestro stuck out a hand toward me—
"and he say-ed again: '*Buona sera*, Maestro.' Imagine
how I felt! But I could not deny to take his hand. *Povero*
me! I took it! Then I went sadly into the theater. Ah! I
think to me, what will now become of *Euryanthe!* It will
be a fiasco. Giovanni has put the evil eye on me. I was
disturb-ed. You remember, Gatti, I said to you: 'Gatti,

what shall we do? Shall we postpone the opera?' And you said: 'Too late, the people are all here, the opera must go on. We must take the chance.' *È vero*, Gatti? So I go before my orchestra, but without heart, without spirit. I begin the overture. To my surprise, the orchestra play no bad. They play, they play, they play, and it is no bad. It go well, very well. I am a-stoni-ed. I say to myself: 'Ah, Giovanni, you have lost your power. Your evil eye is no-*thing* no more. You can do no-*thing*.' The orchestra play better and better, eh, Gatti? And I finish the overture, and the people all scream: 'Bravo, bravo!' I am content. I laugh to myself. No more shall I be afraid of Giovanni. But wait! *Aspetta . . . aspetta . . .*" The Maestro had risen from his chair. His face was flushed. He waved his arms at me as if to caution me against optimism.

"The people scream: 'Bravo!' That is good. But they do not stop. I wait for silence to begin the opera. They do not stop. For five, for ten minutes they scream. I do nothing. I stand with my back and wait. They will not let me begin the opera. You must understand I never permit *bis* [encore] at La Scala. *Mai*. Never. The people in Milan know I never permit *bis*. And now at last I understand. The *jettattore!* Giovanni! The evil eye! It had worked. Giovanni had won. The people scream: '*Bis . . . bis!*' I turn around. 'No *bis!*' I scream back, and I break the baton in half and throw the pieces at them. Then I go home to bed. *Vero*, Gatti?" Gatti now took over and related how the *première* was postponed to the following week, when the Maestro and everybody at the

Scala took special precautions to avoid the *jettattore*. And, having steered clear of the baleful Giovanni, the performance went on without interruption and became the season's greatest success.

The Gattis left. I stayed on purposely. I had suddenly decided that the moment had arrived for me to talk to the Maestro. The visit of the Gattis, the old memories, and perhaps the wine had put the Maestro off his guard. He was amiable and talkative. He urged me to have some brandy. He had poured some out for himself and applied a match to a lump of sugar, an invariable indication of good temper. His face glowed with satisfaction as the blue flames spilled over the glass. Now, if ever, was the moment! I must have had a great deal to drink, for, strangely enough, my fears had vanished. I attacked the subject boldly, without preliminaries. I said that all America was hoping for his return. I told him it was useless for him to talk about his being old. He was younger, in spirit, yes, in physical stamina, too, than any other conductor in the world. The NBC would build him a great orchestra. Instead of being played to a few thousand people in Carnegie Hall, his music would reach millions over the radio. I did not let him interrupt. I talked eloquently without pausing for a second. I advanced all the arguments I had been marshaling in my mind for an occasion like this. I anticipated his objections. He stared at me incredulously as I spoke. My wife, too, looked at me in surprise, and so did Mrs. Toscanini.

But I needed a climax, a fortissimo finish. It suddenly came to me. I remembered the magazine article about the canaries. Had I forgotten to take it along? I felt in my pocket. It was there. "Maestro," I said, "did you know that canaries once sang the chorus of the Ninth Symphony? Well, they did!" And before he could speak, I whipped out the magazine and read him the significant paragraph. He listened with mounting excitement. And when I finished he seized the magazine and read it for himself, holding the paper very close to his eyes and underlining the words with his forefinger. "*Senta*, Carla!" he cried to his wife, waving the article in her face. He was beside himself with excitement, and he poured out a stream of Italian, fiery and rapid, in his eagerness to impart to her the news of the miracle of the canaries in Cincinnati. Her wondering "No, Tosca! *Impossibile!*" only heightened his fervor. I heard the words *uccelli* (birds), *Chin-chin-nati, rah-dio,* and *Novanta sinfonia* (Ninth Symphony) with pleasure, and I gathered by the rapid flow of his speech and his vivid gestures that, carried away by his own enthusiasm, he was heightening and elaborating the printed story. At last he stopped, apparently on a triumphant note, for Mrs. Toscanini murmured: "*Incredibile . . . meraviglia.*"

My moment had arrived. "Maestro," I said, taking his hand, "this is one of the marvels of radio. It is touching to know that canaries can be excited into song by the Ninth Symphony played a thousand miles away. But think of the millions of people who will also hear it and be touched and comforted by it . . . millions of people on farms and in little villages who have never heard a live symphony orchestra and never can. And when your music goes over the air," I continued shrewdly, "everyone who hears will know the way the composer *meant* the music to be played, they will hear the difference between your revelation of what Beethoven and Mozart and Haydn and Wagner *intended* and the dreadful misrepresentations of second-class conductors which they call 'interpretations.' Maestro, *will* you come?" There was a pause that seemed an eternity. Toscanini's eyes were probing me like an X-ray, as if to make completely sure of my veracity. Then he looked away and dropped the words "Why not!" like a bombshell in the oppressive silence.

I was taken aback. The situation seemed quite unreal. I needed a moment for recovery. But if what I'd heard was really true, I must leave nothing in doubt, but must clinch the matter then and there. I extracted from my pocketbook a paper that contained the National Broadcasting Company's three separate offers to the Maestro, one for ten broadcasts, one for fifteen, and one for twenty. I handed the paper to him, saying: "Which of these do you like?" He scrutinized the offers carefully and pointed to the first. Mrs. Toscanini, who had behaved with complete impartiality, was suddenly presented with a *fait accompli*. Now she turned her attention to the practical aspects of the engagement. She took the paper from her husband, asked him some questions, and then said to me in studied English, pausing between the words: "*You*—pay—income—tass.*" Too excited at the moment to calculate what that additional burden might amount to, and quite forgetting my obligation to the company I worked for, I said rashly: "Yes, yes, of course. Signora, may I use your telephone? I want to tell the great news to Mr. Sarnoff." A look of apprehension passed over Mrs. Toscanini's face. "Telephone to America?" she asked severely. I hastened to set her mind at rest. "*I* pay for telephone," I assured her. "*NBC* pay." She looked relieved. "N.B.Chile pay," she laughed, making the name sound like the Italian equivalent of "imbecile." She liked her little joke, and we laughed with her.

Mr. Sarnoff was delighted with the success of my mission and congratulated me warmly. "And what do I do now?" I asked him. He replied: "Sign him up." I told him I had never signed anybody up, and would not know how to go about doing such a thing. He said he would leave that to me, and so terminated the costly transatlantic conversation, much to Mrs. Toscanini's relief. Although certain that NBC would foot the bill, she disapproved of extravagance in general. Actually she was the most generous of women, helping the sick and needy, sending underprivileged children to the country in the summer, finding jobs for people, and supporting destitute friends and relatives for years if need be. It was the small sums that bothered her. Thus, in the mistaken belief that she was economizing, she would travel miles, using up a dollar's worth of gasoline, to buy one pound of butter cheaper than she could buy it in a shop nearer home.

I told the Maestro that American business firms insisted on certain routine, impersonal documents such as contracts, and he said he quite understood, that he had once, a long time ago, signed such a document, and would not mind signing another for me. So I borrowed a decrepit typewriter from a friendly neighbor, and on a single sheet of paper I typed three or four paragraphs stating the simple facts of our agreement. This the Maestro cheerfully signed without reading. Although he and his wife and my wife and I were the only persons in Milan who knew the terms of the contract, the *Corriere della Sera,* the city's leading newspaper, carried a story the following morning which told in full detail about my visit, its purpose, its success, and the number of broadcasts and the fee. The Maestro explained with bitterness that the Fascists made it their business to find out everything pertaining to him, and that his telephone was always tapped.

The night before we left for America I gave a dinner at Savini's, the town's best restaurant, to the Toscaninis and a few of their relatives. We drank toasts to one another, to Mr. Sarnoff, and to NBC. Then we went on to the Manzoni Theater, where the Maestro had taken a box. The play was Pirandello's *Six Characters in Search of an Author.* The performance was given in memory of Pirandello, who had recently died, and before the start of the play a man came onto the stage and made a long memorial speech. The Maestro, refusing to sit down, took up a position in the rear of the box. He was at once spotted. People nudged each other and pointed to him, and hundreds of opera glasses were trained on him. The man on the stage, judging by his theatrical gestures and rising voice, was making a significant point, when from behind me the Maestro spoke out loud and sarcastically. I couldn't understand what he was saying. But it was clear that he did not agree with what the man was saying, and was voicing his dissent. In a like vein, the Maestro kept up a loud, running commentary during the course of the play. Such behavior in theaters was not uncommon in Italy. I had heard people at La Scala hiss and boo and advise artists who had incurred their displeasure to leave the stage and abjure their profession forever. But that so public a figure as Toscanini would avail himself of a common privilege that could only achieve what he most dreaded—calling attention to himself—was a mystery indeed. The only possible explanation was the Maestro's naïve unawareness of his eminence and importance. He thought of himself as an anonymous member of the audience, and therefore behaved like one.

Returning to New York, I started at once to put together an orchestra that would be worthy of Toscanini. Symphony orchestras are not built in a day, and we had only ten months in which to assemble one before the Maestro's first broadcast on Christmas night 1937. We had engaged Artur Rodzinski as assistant conductor, and he and I now desperately attempted to make up for the time we didn't have by signing up the very best men available. The best men were not always available, but I did everything possible—rather unscrupulously, I must own—to wean them away from other orchestras. We were asked to pay unheard-of salaries to first-desk men, and we agreed to pay them. And so unequivocal was my belief in the crusading nature of Toscanini's return to America that I assumed that all the other conductors of our symphony orchestras would be as concerned for its success as I was. It was under some such quixotic misapprehension that I called on a famous conductor to release his first bass-player to the Toscanini orchestra. Nor could I then understand the conductor's polite but firm refusal to cripple his own orchestra.

Mr. Rodzinski and I gave innumerable auditions to applicants, and at last I was able to write the Maestro that the orchestra had been tentatively formed. I enclosed a list of the players I would, with his approval, engage. Promptly the Maestro returned the list, but he had put crosses next to many names and had made revealing notations in parentheses underneath: "Be careful, he drinks!" "His intonation is bad." "He is not a good musician." Of course I went into the charges thoroughly. The alleged toper we were fortunately able to keep. For, while the Maestro's memory proved to be historically accurate —the man confessed that he had been too free with the bottle fifteen years earlier, when he had played at La Scala—he had long since taken the pledge. As for the man whose intonation was bad and the one who was not a good musician, there was nothing for us to do but heed the Maestro's warning: they were not engaged.

We were now in the last week of November. Everything was ready. We had assembled a superb body of men. They were being whipped into shape by the severe and meticulous Rodzinski. The country was in a high state of anticipation. The National Broadcasting Company had already spent a young fortune in the creation of the orchestra and in its administration. Pending the final seal of the Maestro's approval upon his arrival, I luxuriated in the realization of an impossible dream and the completion of a difficult job.

From this state of euphoria I was rudely jolted one morning at breakfast by a cable from the Maestro. "I have received news unpleasant," it read, "that because of the high cost of the new orchestra and myself the NBC is causing some of its employees to lose their jobs. This I do not like. Please release me from my contract. I stay in Italy. Arturo Toscanini."

I was dismayed. While I could make no sense out of the message, I realized that, whatever the misunderstanding on the Maestro's part, we might not be able to clear it up in time for the scheduled opening of our season. I hastened to Mr. Sarnoff's office with the cable and we discussed what measures to take. One of the Maestro's daughters, the Countess Castelbarco, was in New York, and we telephoned her to join us. She was as mystified by the cable as we were. Mr. Sarnoff suggested that she talk with her father on the transatlantic telephone. But when the connection with Milan came through, it was her mother who answered. The Countess, on the verge of hysteria, talked to her mother in Italian for a long time. When she hung up, she told us that her father had refused to speak to her. He had been terribly upset by the arrival of an anonymous cable, and he had sworn that he would not be the cause of anyone's losing his job, and would therefore refuse to come to America. His decision, her mother told her, was unalterable. The Countess, wiping away her tears, concluded ominously: "You know Father!"

As a last resort I decided to make a personal appeal to the Maestro, and after many tries I wrote out a long cable calculated to melt a heart of stone. If that failed, we would have to accept defeat and start undoing the labor of many months. I wired that, far from causing one man to lose his job at NBC, his engagement had led the company to take on, besides a full symphony orchestra, a number of people to meet the increased demands of the engineering, publicity, and press departments. I begged him to remember that in our many years of friendship I had never misrepresented anything to him. And I earnestly asked him to consider whether he was justified in believing some anonymous troublemaker and questioning my veracity. I ended by swearing that my only concern was to serve the cause of music, as I believed his to be.

Day after day we waited, and no reply came. During this time the Countess spoke frequently to her mother by telephone. It appeared that my cable had not altered the Maestro's decision, except that his outbursts against me and the NBC had subsided. Several days later Mrs. Toscanini was able to report to her daughter that *Papá* was now *calmo*. This in itself was hopeful, but hardly enough to dispel my fears. For a fortnight the fate of the orchestra and the broadcasts hung on a word from the Via Durini. At last, when I had given up hope, there came a terse wire from the Maestro naming the date of his departure for America on the *Île de France*. The long tension was over, yet I could not rid myself of an uneasy feeling that something more might occur to keep the Maestro from our shores. Each morning I half expected to find an ominous cable on my breakfast tray. Nor was I able to relax until we received word from our Paris office that the *Île de France* had sailed with the Maestro and his wife aboard.

The Maestro's arrival posed the ever-recurring problem of keeping press photographers away from him. Whatever influence the NBC Press Department brought to bear on the editors and reporters of the city's newspapers resulted only in vague promises not to use flashbulbs, provided we could get the Maestro to pose on deck, where the natural light would be sufficient. At six o'clock on the morning of the arrival of the *Île de France*, along with a large contingent of newspapermen and women, I boarded a cutter and steamed out to the bay, where we lay around and waited for the liner. Soon she loomed through the fog and anchored, and we climbed aboard. I knocked at the Maestro's cabin. Mrs. Toscanini's voice asked: *"Chi e là?"* and when I shouted my name she unlocked the door. I went in and she locked it again. The Maestro's greeting was impersonal, not exactly friendly, rather reservedly polite, as if he still harbored a suspicion that I might have deceived him in the matter of the anonymous cable. Presently there was a knock at the door. It was the steward summoning Mr. and Mrs. Toscanini to the ship's lounge to have their passports stamped. I went with them, and we continued our conversation in the lounge. The American immigration officers had received instructions to give the Toscaninis priority, and a few minutes later their passports were stamped and we were headed back to the cabin.

At that moment a man with a camera materialized as if from nowhere and flashed a light bulb directly in the Maestro's face. The Maestro let out a piercing yell, clutched at his eyes, and then, screaming Italian maledictions, ran in pursuit of the fleeing cameraman. Through the door he ran and out onto the long deck, I after him, Mrs. Toscanini a poor fourth behind. The cameraman was very fleet, but the Maestro was steadily gaining on him when suddenly two nuns who were walking briskly toward the salon stood directly in his way. As the Maestro veered to one side to avoid the sisters, one of them put out a restraining hand and clutched at his sleeve. With an imprecation he jerked his arm free and sped on. But the momentary halt had given the cameraman time to disappear. I caught up with the Maestro at the end of the long deck, where he stood irresolute, baffled, fuming and gesticulating wildly. I led him back to his cabin, where he collapsed in a chair, the picture of utter desolation. By now the ship was being maneuvered into its berth. The steward reappeared and led us, by pre-arrangement, to a cabin in the tourist class, from where we disembarked quite unnoticed, while a host of photographers and newspapermen patiently waited for us at the first-class gangplank.

We got into a car that was waiting for us and drove to the Astor Hotel. The Maestro had by this time recovered from the effects of his sprint on deck, and appeared rather to enjoy our having given the press the slip. He looked unusually handsome as he sat in the back of the car, bolt upright, on his head a Breton beret at a jaunty angle, a long flannel scarf carelessly draped around his neck. Although it was a cold December morning, he had refused to put on his overcoat. Now he looked out of the window at the familiar New York scene with obvious pleasure. "I like New York," he said. "I always like-ed it. It is a living city . . . it is like strong wine." His high spirits emboldened me to put a question to him. "You gave us a bad time these last few weeks, Maestro," I began. "Why did you do it?" He turned his head to me in surprise. "Why? Because you make a man lose his job." I gasped. "But, Maestro, we did *not* make anyone lose his job. On the contrary, because of your coming we gave jobs to many." He looked at me sharply.

90

"You are *syou*-er?" he asked. I disdained to reply. He saw that he had hurt me, and hastened to change the subject. "And the or*ches*tra? How is it? You wrote me Silva no longer drink. Are you *syou*-er?"

The following morning I called to take him to his first rehearsal. A large dressing-room on the eighth floor of the NBC Studios had been fitted up for him. Mrs. Toscanini brought along a valise with his shirts, handkerchiefs, rehearsal coats, fans, a half-dozen framed photographs of members of his family, several little photographs of Verdi, one each of Brahms and Wagner, and a miniature of Beethoven. Wherever he conducted these pictures were set up in his dressing-room. I suspected that they were a part of his large collection of superstitions. At any rate, I had seen them in his dressing-room in Salzburg, in Bayreuth, and in Carnegie Hall. Mrs. Toscanini arranged the pictures on the piano, then assisted her husband in putting on his rehearsal jacket, a black alpaca garment with a clerical collar. She brushed his silky white hair toward the back of his head in a kind of cottontail effect. The Maestro sprayed his face and head with an atomizer containing his favorite toilet water. He then selected a baton from a number of sticks of various sizes and weights.

He was plainly nervous when I told him the orchestra was ready. As we were about to leave his room, he hastily took up from the bureau a small crucifix attached to a silver chain, and a set of tiny pictures reposing in a number of little metal frames resembling a segmented bracelet. These objects he first raised to his lips, then slipped into the pockets of his trousers. Silently we made our way through the long winding corridor that led from his room to Studio 8H, the NBC concert hall. As we reached the anteroom of the studio, we heard members of the orchestra tuning up, trying out their fingers or their lungs, and building up the usual atonal counterpoint of snatches from every variety of orchestral and instrumental composition. Suddenly there was silence, the kind of silence that is as blatant as the loudest noise. Not the sound of a breath, a scratch, a movement came to us from Studio 8H. I held open the swing door and said: "Ready, Maestro." He looked quite pale, as if he were a novice about to make his debut. His wife went up to him and kissed him on the forehead. At the door he stopped abruptly and held up his hands for a moment in prayer. I preceded him to the stage and called out in a voice that sounded strange to me: "Gentlemen . . . Maestro Toscanini." The men leaped to their feet, the string-players beat their stands with their bows. The Maestro bowed his head once, cut short the demonstration by motioning the men to their seats, rapped sharply with his baton on the stand nearest him, said in a hoarse voice: "Brahms," and the opening fateful rhythmic measures of the Brahms First Symphony cut the air. He played through the first movement without stopping. At the end he said: "Non c'e male" (not so bad) . Then resolutely, "Da capo" (from the beginning) , he sang out, and brought his right arm down sharply in a downbeat which he fortified with a hoarse "uh," and the rehearsal was on in earnest. For one hour and a half he was on his feet, shouting, swearing, cajoling, his baton describing unorthodox convolutions, straight-up-and-down rapier stabs, delicate sideswipes, long horizontal even undulations like a gently-moving multi-arched snake, or sudden circular movements like a cowboy twirling a lariat. At last he stopped, took his watch from his pocket, held it very close to his eyes, and, realizing that he had overstepped the union regulation of an intermission after an hour of rehearsal, said contritely: "Excuse me," and stepped off the podium. His face and head were sopping wet, and beads of sweat gleamed at the tip of his nose. As we entered his dressing-room Mrs. Toscanini, in fur coat and hat, came in through another door. She had evidently spent the hour and a half shopping, and had arrived just in time to pretend she had not left the room. Never had I seen garments so wet as the rehearsal coat and undershirt we removed with difficulty. "You know," the Maestro said with pride, "I perspire water—pure water!" And, indeed, he spoke the truth. We rubbed him down with a coarse towel, which we then draped over his shoulders. His wife gave him a lozenge to chew, and a straw fan which he wielded vigorously over his scalp all through the quarter-hour of intermission. He seemed at ease, and I hazarded a question. "And the orchestra, Maestro?" I asked. He interrupted his fanning and said: "I am content." A moment later he stopped fanning himself again. "Send me Mischa-

93

koff," he said (Mischakoff was the concertmaster). I ran out and returned with Mischakoff. "*Caro* Mischakoff," the Maestro said, "do not make too much *vibrato* in the solo at the end of the Adagio. I beg of you, not too much *vibrato*. . . . Thank you, my dear. . . ." Mischakoff left and the Maestro leaned back in his chair, closed his eyes, and fanned himself mechanically. Now and again he raised his left hand and beat out a measure, or made undulating motions as if molding a phrase. I gazed at him with emotion. At this moment nothing in the world mattered to him but the contour of a phrase in the slow part of a Brahms symphony. In Studio 8H a perfect orchestra sat waiting and eager to realize his perfectionist's musical dream. In a few days every American possessing a radio would be able to share this dream. For the first time in nearly a year I could afford to relax. Certainly nothing could possibly occur between Wednesday morning and the following Saturday evening to prevent the opening broadcast on Christmas night. Yet I knew perfectly well that many things could happen. An anonymous telegram might arrive, a rehearsal might go awry, or the hapless *jettattore* Giovanni might suddenly appear at the stage door of Studio 8H and offer his baleful hand to the horrified Maestro. Agitated by these reflections, I sought comfort in my own superstitions and touched wood several times.

Eventually my fears proved to be unfounded. No anonymous wire arrived, the rehearsals pursued their exciting but non-catastrophic course, and no *jettattore* materialized at the stage entrance. The Christmas-night broadcast, played before a select and critical audience in the studio and heard over the radio by millions of people in the United States and Canada, took place without incident and to the Maestro's satisfaction.

CHAPTER FIVE

$\mathcal{F}$ROM 1937 to 1954, with the exception of one winter season, Toscanini led the NBC Symphony in history-making broadcasts, benefit concerts, and tours in the United States and South America. Until the outbreak of World War II in 1939, he spent the spring and early summer months in Italy, alternating between his house in the Via Durini in Milan and the villa on the Isolino San Giovanni in Lago Maggiore. In late summer he conducted concerts and opera in Salzburg, London, and Lucerne.

When in Italy, the Toscanini family lived in constant dread of Fascist reprisal, for Toscanini spoke his mind freely about the regime both at home and in public places. He even took part in conspiratorial meetings, which he naïvely imagined were unknown to the authorities. In the spring of 1938, for example, when I was with him in Milan to arrange programs for the fall and winter broadcasts in America, I was surprised to see him leave his house promptly at eleven on certain mornings. I thought he might be going for a walk, and I offered to accompany him. But he said: "No," and looked very mysterious. Later he confessed that he was a member of a group of elderly anti-Fascists who met secretly (as they thought) in the rear room of a small bookshop owned by one of them. As all of Toscanini's movements were closely watched by the police, the Fascists either discounted the seriousness of the little conspiracy or else were under orders from Mussolini not to interfere with him. At any rate, the bookshop was never raided, and the Maestro enjoyed the belief that he was outwitting the secret police.

Many of his old friends and associates avoided him through fear of being branded anti-Fascist by association; but the Italian people did not hesitate to show their love and admiration for him. He had nothing but contempt for his fair-weather friends, but he disapproved also of public demonstrations in his favor, which he took to be political rather than personal. He honestly thought of himself as a non-political person, and he saw no inconsistency in his public and private attacks on Mussolini and the regime.

One rainy night in Milan he accompanied me to the Conservatorio to hear the debut of a French violinist. His car deposited us at the conservatory hall, and Emilio, the chauffeur, was told to come back for us at the close of the concert. As we entered the hall the audience rose in a body and shouted: "Viva Toscanini!" The Maestro turned pale with anger and rushed out of the hall. I followed, of course, and so did half of the audience. In the roofless courtyard of the building the Maestro raged against the "villani" who failed to respect his privacy and used him "politically." He then implored me to return to the hall and let him go home alone. It was raining hard, and he and I and the people who had formed a ring around us were being drenched. The car was nowhere in sight, and I said I would not hear of his going home alone. But he clasped his hands close to my face and, in a voice full of suffering, said: "I pray you, go back. I am very unhappy. You must not fol-*low* me. You must listen to the concert. I pray you . . . let me go. . . ." There was nothing for me to do but obey. He vanished in the darkness, and I and the curious who had followed us into the courtyard returned to the hall.

His hatred of Mussolini was personal as well as political. At the end of World War I, Mussolini, then an obscure Milanese journalist, had persuaded Toscanini to be a candidate for some minor municipal office along with him on a Socialist ticket. Mussolini's powers of persuasion must have been formidable indeed to overcome Toscanini's distaste for politics. In addition, the country had been beggared by defeat, and the situation of the Italian worker and peasant was desperate; and it was unquestionably Toscanini's concern for the lot of the underdog that steered him into politics. In the elections both Mussolini and Toscanini were snowed under.

Toscanini, much relieved, gladly resumed his baton. But Mussolini, not at all disheartened, set about creating the Fascist party and planning his march on Rome.

For years Toscanini had watched with growing hatred the transformation of the former liberal into a Fascist dictator. He now enlisted his reckless courage and his worldwide prestige in a personal war against the spurious Cæsar. From the time of Mussolini's march on Rome to his ignominious death, Toscanini was a thorn in his side. Mussolini could easily have had him put out of the way. In fact, it was rumored that Hitler had expressed surprise that his Italian counterpart tolerated this "senile and irritating musician." Such a man, he implied, would get short shrift in Germany. And the only explanation for Mussolini's sufferance may have been his fear of world opinion and his genuine admiration for a fellow dictator in a different realm, but one with greater personal courage in the pursuit of an ideal as selfless as his was selfish.

However, being unwilling to do away with Toscanini, Mussolini decided to woo him. Through intermediaries he made several advances for a meeting. These Toscanini scornfully rejected. Only once did he give way to pressure and reluctantly accede to a meeting with Il Duce; a committee representing the artists of La Scala had called on him to report on the desperate state of Italy's leading opera house. Il Duce had cut the government's usual subsidy of La Scala to an extent that seriously impaired the livelihood of even top-flight singers.

These were certain that the direct intervention of the Maestro would alter the situation. In fact, they had heard that the Duce was most eager to be reconciled with the Maestro, and they thought that even a formal call by Toscanini would materially improve the fortunes of La Scala. Mussolini happened to be in Milan at the moment. He had already been sounded out about a meeting with Toscanini, and was ready to receive him. The committee pleaded with the Maestro for hours before he yielded. An appointment was arranged, and at last, after many years, the Maestro found himself again in the presence of his former political running-mate.

In relating the incident the Maestro grew as pale as he said he had been when he stood before Mussolini. "I was wet through and through like after a rehearsal. I did not look in his face. He spoke a long time. I did not hear what he said. I did not reply. When I could not longer stand to be there, I turned around and left. It was a fiasco because I forget what I came to say. I wish-ed only to put my hands on his neck and choke him. Ah, *miseria!* It was wrong for me to be persuaded to come. I must always do only what I *feel* to do, not what I *think* to do."

In the late summer of 1938, presumably on Mussolini's orders, the police took away Toscanini's passport. Far from being dispirited, the Maestro was elated by this open reprisal. He was determined to get to America to carry out his commitment to NBC, and he conspired to have a seaplane take him from Lago Maggiore to a

Swiss lake, whence he could proceed unmolested to America. He entered with great zest into secret arrangements for this hazardous and perhaps fatal undertaking. The necessity for escape was, however, soon obviated. Whether because of the pressure brought to bear on Mussolini by Washington or through the intercession of influential Italians, the passport was restored in time for the Maestro to conduct his scheduled broadcast in New York in October. I believe the Maestro rather regretted the turn of events which enabled him to leave Milan by train. He would much have preferred a dangerous escape by plane in the dead of night.

Except for the situations created by his own unpredictable temperament, Toscanini's life in New York from 1939 to 1945 was ideal. In Riverdale, New York, overlooking the Hudson, he had bought a massive, roomy, late-Victorian house that had a central hall two stories high with an old-fashioned grand staircase leading to a balcony in the shape of a quandrangle. The Maestro was proud of the grand staircase, and would find many occasions to show it off by running up to his bedroom or sitting-room to fetch a letter, manuscript, or picture, disdaining all offers of servants or friends to run errands for him. "If I were not asham-ed for an old man, I would run up the stairs two at a time," he would say. Among his many endearing traits was his consideration for servants. I never noticed a hint of superiority in his behavior toward them. He addressed them as he did his family and friends. "Thank you, *caro*," he would say to one who opened the door for him, or "Do not trouble, my dear," and on arriving home after a long absence he might embrace the domestics warmly.

The Riverdale house was the scene of many entertainments and parties, at Christmas and New Year's and in the late spring, when the Maestro entertained the members of his orchestra and their wives. Always a hospitable host, he was never more solicitous for his guests than at his parties for his orchestra. He went about the tables urging everyone to eat and drink; he fascinated his guests with charming anecdotes. It was, in fact, impossible to believe that this benign, silver-haired old man was the same who perhaps only the day before at rehearsal had thundered at his men with the voice of an angry Jove, had broken his baton into bits, upset the heavy iron music stand at his side with a kick of his foot, and blundered off the stage in a blind Olympian rage. At those moments no object on his person or near him was safe from destruction. During a certain historic outburst, after he had deliberately ground a valuable watch to bits under his heel, Mr. Royal presented him with a brace of Ingersoll watches (then a dollar apiece) to break when necessity demanded it, thus saving from destruction a number of expensive timepieces the Maestro owned. Far from being affronted by so pointed a gift, Toscanini appreciated the serious intention of the donor. In due time the Ingersolls disappeared under the Maestro's annihilating heel.

Occasionally the orchestra and the Maestro gave a

live concert in cities not too far from New York. These trips brought with them special hazards and problems. At NBC we had worked out a system that ensured privacy for Toscanini. But away from our offices at 30 Rockefeller Plaza we were faced with such obstacles as the dubious acoustics of concert halls and the persistence of admirers of Toscanini in getting to see him at close range. The flavor of these expeditions out of New York may be sensed in the following typewritten report of a trip to near-by Newark. The writer was Albert Walker, an NBC employee assigned to look after the Maestro. Until he met Toscanini, Walker knew nothing of music; but, speedily falling a victim to the Maestro's charm, he soon began to hum snatches of Beethoven and Brahms as he briskly went about his duties of keeping strangers away from the Maestro and tending to his personal wants.

> *Toscanini Concert*
> *Newark, N.J.*

At 3:16 p.m. Tuesday, December 13th, we left the Astor. (Route taken to Holland Tunnel—West on 45th Street, South on the Westside Highway to Canal Street, through tunnel to New Jersey. Left tunnel at 3:31 p.m., picked up by pre-arranged police escort; after a wild ride—12 miles—arrived at Hotel Essex at 3:42 p.m.—average per hour, 60 miles.)

Maestro asked to drive around Newark; took advantage of this to locate the RR Terminal that Walter Toscanini was to arrive at.

Back to Mosque Theatre for rehearsal 4:30 p.m. Everything went great until 5:45. I was busy with details out front of theatre and Mrs. T. discovered that she forgot the Maestro's suspenders. So she sent the chauffeur to the hotel for same. The chauffeur came back at 6:00, and as he jumped out of the car, shut the car door, the damned thing locked on him. (He did not know this at the moment.) At 6:15 I went downstairs to check on flashlight hounds and told the chauffeur I would bring the Maestro down. I tried the door and imagine my feelings when we discovered the car locked. Not wanting to tell and upset the Maestro, I suggested that we go out front and see the theatre. He fell for it, so simply walked around the foyer and out to the street. Once there, we just walked back to the hotel (6:20). In the meantime we got the door opened!

Up to the Maestro's room and Mrs. T. told me to meet Walter at depot at 7:01. So I took time off for dinner and asked the chauffeur to pick me up at 6:50. Down to the Penn Station, and there was no train due at 7:01. Shot over to the Central of N.J. and no train due at 7:01. So back to Penn RR and found a 7:31. Waited for that one and Walter was aboard. Delivered him okay at 7:45. Went up to my room and hell broke out on my phone. A swarm of press and photographers were in the lobby. They all wanted pictures and were bound to get them. After telling them about the flash and arguing with them, I got a call that the Maestro was going to start for the theatre in about 25 minutes. So I dashed for my room and started to change for concert (time, 8:10 p.m.). Mrs. T. called me and told me they were ready and would send the Maestro's bag to my room. Then I heard a noise outside of my door and opened to behold at least five photo men there. I argued with them and pleaded not to snap the Maestro when he came out. They got peeved and said they would. So I called the Hotel manager to clear the corridor. I made a bargain with the press men, if they saw us in the lobby, okay to shoot. I got dressed at last and called a war conference. The plan was to have Walter T. get off at the lobby and stand there and say out loud that he wished the Maestro would hurry. In the meantime I took the Maestro down in the elevator, putting out the lights and disconnecting the elevator indicator (so the press did not know where we got on or off). We got out through the basement and walked out the alley to the car. Reached the theatre at 8:25 and, holy smokes, the bellhop took the wrong bag to the car! I beat it back to the hotel, up to the room and tried to unlock the door. The g--d--- door would not open as the inside lock was down; did not have time to get master key; looked around for a fire axe and wedged it into the panel, pried it open and unlocked the door and rushed to the theatre, and as I flopped in the Maestro was just going out. The country was saved and I was K.O.'d after running four city blocks with the bag!

Going out of the theatre we had no trouble, as I had the car pulled right into the alley, dispossessing the fire chief's car, and the Maestro simply opened the stage door and into his car. A nice leisurely ride to New York and so to bed about 2:45 a.m.

Albert Walker

The presence of the Maestro offered perpetual excitement for us at NBC. As general musical director of NBC, I was often away from the symphony rehearsals, but in my office I received frequent bulletins by telephone about the condition of the Maestro's uneven disposition. These phone calls sounded like the weather reports of a Channel crossing: "all calm," "blue skies," "sun out," or else "rough sea," "fair to middling," "squalls," or "storm any minute." These messages often sent me hurrying to 8H. Sometimes a squall would have turned into blue skies by the time I got there. At other times I would find the storm raging in full force. My presence had, of course, no effect on the progress of the Maestro's ill-humor. But if, as often happened, he angrily terminated the rehearsal and retired to sulk and rage in his room, I would surreptitiously countermand his order to the men and, by applying a psychological treatment that long experience had perfected, would sometimes mollify him and persuade him to proceed with the rehearsal.

The method I used was simple indeed; it was based on the notorious singlemindedness of geniuses, and consisted of violently diversionary suggestions. I could divert his rage at his orchestra to something quite unrelated, which in turn made him forget the original cause of his unhappiness. For example, I would wait for a pause in his denunciation of his men and remark innocently: "I see the critics are raving about the beautiful tone of the ——— Orchestra." The Maestro would look up sharply and explode: "Don't speak to me about critics! They know no-*thing!* They think because the violins vibrate all the time—" the Maestro would put his left hand on his heart and do an imaginary slow vibrato with his middle finger —"they make a beautiful tone! No! A *fast* vibrato make a beautiful tone, not a slow one. Our NBC violins make quick vibrato. *That* make a beautiful tone." And he would embark on the virtues of his own orchestra, which he had a moment earlier consigned to perdition. While he was talking I would hold up his rehearsal coat, and through force of habit he would slip his arms through it. A few moments later he would follow me docilely into 8H, where the men, already alerted, sat in nervous silence. It was plain that the Maestro had completely forgotten the alleged sins of his own orchestra and was brooding now on the insensitiveness of music critics. The rehearsal was resumed and bade fair to continue without

107

incident. I would go back to my office and await further bulletins.

The excitement, however, was not always induced by his surpassing art. Because NBC is a business operated for profit and accountable to stockholders, Toscanini's demands sometimes—indeed, quite often—interfered with the operations of the commercial programs, the profits from which paid for Toscanini and the NBC Symphony Orchestra.

The orchestra, for example, was assigned to play commercial programs when free from its symphonic duties. And as seventy-five or eighty per cent of its playing-time was given over to the rehearsals and broadcasts of the Symphony, its commercial programs were necessarily few. It happened one winter that Toscanini was rehearsing with the NBC Symphony in Carnegie Hall for a benefit concert that he was unselfishly donating to some worthy charity. The Maestro and the orchestra had been scheduled for the usual two-and-one-half-hour rehearsal from 4:00 to 6:30 p.m. on a certain day. At 8:00 p.m. thirty members of the orchestra were scheduled to play a commercial radio program at the NBC Studios, seven blocks south of Carnegie Hall. The Maestro sometimes ran over his allotted time at rehearsals, and I felt that a one-and-one-half-hour lapse between the end of his rehearsal and the NBC commercial program was more than sufficient leeway.

But at 6:30 the Maestro showed no disposition to finish. Nor at 7:00 or 7:15. The composition was Verdi's

Requiem, and for three and one-half hours the Maestro lavished his interpretative genius on the music and inspired his men to feats of lyric and dramatic expression which Carnegie Hall had seldom witnessed. Yet the eight-o'clock commercial program *had* to be serviced. The Maestro, of course, knew nothing about the *"commer-ziale,"* and would have cared less for anything so mundane, had he known. The orchestra contractor, whose duty it was to see that the thirty men were in their places at NBC in time to play the commercial, had been in a dreadful state for the last hour, frequently coming to me anxiously for instructions. "He must finish any moment," I kept telling him. But now it was 7:30, and we could no longer wait. I looked at the Maestro. He was in a fury of movement, shouting, pleading, singing, and dedicating all of his faculties to the molding of the great threnody. He could no more be stopped than an express train going at a fantastic speed. There seemed only one thing to do. I told the contractor to go down to the rim of the stage and from behind Toscanini beckon the needed players to leave one at a time and at spaced intervals. I had a faint hope that this defection of the men might go unnoticed by the nearsighted, galvanized Maestro. One by one the needed men stopped playing, crouched low, and sneaked off the stage as inconspicuously as they could manage. For a long time the Maestro did not notice the maneuver. Then suddenly, in a pause in the music, he became aware of empty chairs in strategic sections of the orchestra and

109

caught a man doubled up in the very act of leaving his place. With a cry of rage, the Maestro wheeled around and shouted my name. But my nerves were already too shaken for me to face his wrath. I ran from the hall ignominiously, jumped into a cab, was driven home, gained my room, and fell exhausted on the bed. I heard later that the Maestro, finding me gone, tore his collar to shreds, upset every inanimate object that stood in his way, ground his Ingersoll to bits, staggered blindly off the stage and into his dressing-room. However, he was bent on going through with the benefit, and as he never permitted anything, not even his rages, to stop him from doing what he wanted to do, the concert took place. But the next day, taking advantage of one of his calmer moments, I was able to dramatize the need of the *"commerziale"* program for the thirty men who had been spirited away. Any crisis was sure to enlist his sympathy. His mood changed overnight, and all was well again.

During the war years he suffered periods of acute depression, which were reflected in his behavior at rehearsals. He would arrive at the studio silent and scowling, and after a few minutes of rehearsal get into a rage and dismiss the orchestra. It transpired that the Maestro had heard over the radio that morning a report of an Allied setback, in consequence of which he had not touched his breakfast and had talked of conducting as a futile waving of one's arms while civilization was going down the drain.

But he could never long resist the power of music,

which consciously and unconsciously filled his waking hours. I remember the faraway, dreamlike, spiritual ecstasy expressed in his face and body after a rehearsal of Wagner's *Siegfried Idyll*. He had stepped off the podium, dripping as usual from head to foot, and had walked into his room. I attempted to divest him of his jacket and shirt, but he stood immovable as in a trance, his hands clasped, eyes shut and freshets of perspiration raining down from his head and eyebrows. I wiped his head and face with a towel, but he did not move. At last I said: "You must change into dry clothes or you will catch cold." He held out his arms dutifully and I began to remove his jacket. Suddenly he interrupted my efforts by clasping his hands again. "It is more than fifty years since I first conduct this music," he said quietly, as if talking to himself, "yet every time is like the first time for me. I cannot bear it—it is too beautiful. Think! Ima*gine* how Cosima felt on that morning when she was awake-en-ed by the sound of the *Idyll!*" And he again stood motionless for some moments as he gave himself up to the contemplation of that memorable scene at the villa on Lake Lucerne when, on the staircase leading to his wife's bedroom, Wagner conducted a little orchestra of eleven men in the piece he had composed to celebrate the birth of his son Siegfried.

The spell that Toscanini cast on everyone around him during those years was powerful and unflagging. Whether grave or gay, vengeful or beneficent, he magnetized alike players, page boys, servants, executives, friends, and even his family. They trembled at his frown and basked in his smile. At NBC his every wish was attended to in the spirit of a favor conferred by him. To be allowed to remove his sopping garments was like assisting at a rite. To sit next to him in a motor car or at table, to have him address one as "*caro*," to attend a concert or a play with him, to entertain him—all these became memorable events. No one stopped to examine and analyze or question his strange and unprecedented power. He ruled over our hearts and minds. His judgments were accepted like articles of faith. We took to our hearts the people he liked and looked askance at those he dropped. We loved the music he loved, became skeptical about the music he despised, and accepted without question the music that, having summarily cast out, he as summarily restored to favor. When with him we talked about him. We never tired of hearing him talk about himself; when away from him we never ceased recalling his words, looks, gestures, opinions. When he telephoned to one of us, we hastily apprised one another, through a telephone relay, of the happy occurrence. And indeed it was thrilling to lift up the receiver and hear one's name pronounced *sotto voce*, hoarsely, vibrating with the fast tremolo so characteristic of the Maestro's speech.

We spent much of our leisure time in thinking up ways to amuse him. At the end of one season we planned to surprise him with a great party at the Sarnoffs', which was to be in the form of an old-fashioned vaudeville show put on and performed by his friends. The enterprise was of considerable magnitude, and brought with it great anxieties, for the participants were amateurs like myself, and the professionals among us assumed roles quite outside their specialties. Marc Connelly, the playwright, staged the show and acted in one of the sketches; Walter Toscanini, the Maestro's son, danced a Russian Hopak, while Efrem Zimbalist, in Russian peasant costume, played the harmonica. An acrobatic number enlisted the clumsy gymnastics of six amateurs, all dressed in tights and spangles; while I, in white tie and tails that swept the floor, sang Victor Herbert's "Ah, Sweet Mystery of Life" and led the grand finale. Rehearsals went on for weeks, and a professional tumbler was hired to coach the gymnasts in their routine.

All this was kept secret from the Maestro. On the day of the show Mrs. Toscanini told him only that they were to dine that evening at the Sarnoffs'. When they arrived at the house, they found themselves in a press of people all in evening dress. The raucous noise of a jazz band smote the Maestro's ears. He thought they had mistaken the house. But his wife assured him they hadn't, and piloted him into a great solarium on the top floor, which had been fitted up to look like a Broadway night club, with small tables, a dance floor, and a thick velvet rope barring the entrance. At the rope stood Mr. Royal, dressed as a headwaiter and made unrecognizable by a strange wig. He consulted a sheet of paper in his hand, asked the by-now-bewildered Maestro his name, and, on being told, commanded him to spell it. This the Maestro did, and the "headwaiter," glancing up and down his paper, said that no reservation had been made in any such name. The Maestro, utterly at a loss, was about to turn tail when Mr. Royal, fearing the joke had gone too far, removed the rope, passed them through, and showed them to a table in the very first row. The Maestro glared about him, sat down, dropped his head on his chest, covered his eyes with his hand, and remained so for the rest of the evening. The guests, about eighty in number, surrounded him, but the Maestro's ostentatious unhappiness put a damper on everybody, and more particularly on the cast, who were appalled at the prospect of displaying their amateur talents before the grim, unseeing, hostile guest of honor. Some of the actors, having taken a peep at the Maestro through the wings, burst into tears and vowed not to go on. But the feelings of the other guests had to be considered, and at a hurried meeting of the cast backstage it was decided to proceed with the show. So the show went on, unseen by the Maestro, and only nervously observed by the guests, whose attention shifted alternately from the stage to the brooding conductor. The injustice and the unfairness of the Maestro's behavior had their effect on those who had worked so hard to amuse him. A certain bravado now animated the cast as it went through its paces. The acrobats leaped higher than they had at rehearsals. Walter Toscanini executed his Russian dance with a gusto that subsequently laid him up with an injured leg for weeks; Marcia

Davenport, attempting a split during a can-can number, landed on the floor with such force as to be obliged to wear a cast for her injured back for months; and I, with the aid of a concealed microphone in the lapel of my tailcoat, advanced boldly to the Toscanini table and roared "Ah, Sweet Mystery of Life" straight into the Maestro's frozen face.

There was supper and dancing after the show. Still the Maestro sat unmoving, his hand over his eyes. Fair ladies came and sat beside him and attempted to flirt. Mrs. Sarnoff brought him food especially cooked to his taste. It was all to no avail. Mrs. Toscanini, apologetic and embarrassed, attempted to explain that her husband had been upset by the noise and the lights, and that he did not like surprises on principle. At one in the morning, with tears in her eyes, she begged her husband to go home. "I will stay to the bitter end," he muttered gloomily, in the voice of one condemned. So he stayed on, prolonging the pall he had cast over the party, while the jazz orchestra blared away and the people ate and danced halfheartedly and finally melted away. Mr. and Mrs. Toscanini were among the last to go, leaving the indignant cast to express their resentment openly and take what comfort they might in recalling the polite expressions of sympathy from the rest of the audience.

This unfortunate episode had, however, a pleasant sequel. For, having indulged his spleen to the full, the Maestro began to regret the pain he had caused. Some time later he conveyed his repentance obliquely by suggesting that if we ever gave another show, he would like to be a participant. This unexpected offer instantly obliterated whatever resentment we still felt. We hastily made plans for another show with the Maestro as star. We concocted a series of comedy turns and sketches, and recruited a cast of celebrated artists. The presence of Toscanini and a half-dozen popular soloists gave us an excuse for presenting the entertainment as a benefit for the Chatham Square Music School, a non-profit school for talented young musicians on New York's lower East Side. Even so, we failed to grasp fully the drawing-power of a cast that included Toscanini, Heifetz, Horowitz, Tibbett, Milstein, Adolph Busch, Alfred Wallenstein, and the late Emanuel Feuermann.

Although we could have sold out Madison Square Garden, we rented the tiny Chanin Theater, seating two hundred persons. We had printed and mailed out invitations to purchase tickets at fifteen dollars apiece, but the price also included a midnight supper and dance with liquor and food. For a time our ticket sale was negligible. On investigation we learned that most of those to whom we mailed invitations refused to believe that the cast of characters for a revue entitled *Say Ah!* could possibly include some of the greatest musical artists in the world. Believing themselves the victims of a hoax, they had thrown the invitations into their wastepaper baskets. But two or three days before the night of the performance, word got around that Toscanini, Heifetz, Horowitz, Feuermann, *et al*, were actually rehearsing for *Say Ah!* We sold all the tickets in one afternoon, disappointing many persons who telephoned too late.

The Maestro's "number" in *Say Ah!* was called "Toscanini and his Children's Orchestra." It was a take-off on a "Youth Orchestra" then recently organized by Leopold Stokowski. The Maestro's "Children's Orchestra" consisted of some thirty instrumentalists, with Heifetz as concertmaster. They were to appear in short pants and white blouses, and the Maestro was to wear a long, old-fashioned Prince Albert coat, with a bandanna handkerchief sticking out of a rear pocket, an exaggerated starched collar, and a large four-in-hand. The music he selected included short popular pieces such as "*Loin du Bal,*" "Tritsch-tratsch Polka," "Skaters' Waltz," and Mozart's farcical "A Musical Joke."

A dress rehearsal was called for very late in the evening of the night before the performance. Out of deference to the Maestro, we asked him to rehearse his number first, though it came last on the program. This mark of respect almost resulted in the abandonment of the show. For the Maestro rehearsed his little pieces as painstakingly and arduously as if they had been exalted works of Beethoven. If the members of the orchestra had thoughts of enjoying themselves in the preparation of light "hotel" music like "*Loin du Bal,*" they were quickly disabused. For three hours Toscanini and the little band of noted instrumentalists labored to perfect the small pieces until they sounded like miracles of orchestral balance. As we of the non-musical cast listened, we were

117

struck by the inferior quality of our own poor amateur dramatic efforts. Some of us flatly announced that we would withdraw. Mr. Herbert Graf, our stage director, observed sadly that we could not possibly appear on a program with Toscanini and his remarkable players, and he suggested that the Maestro enlarge his portion of the program to a full evening's entertainment. We all agreed, with the exception of one amateur dancer who was to have been the star in a burlesque of a ballet to the music of Debussy's "Afternoon of a Faun." Made unhappy by the decision to abandon everything in the show but the Toscanini "number," this fledgling Nijinsky fled to a dressing-room, where I discovered him lying on the floor dressed in his faun's costume, alternately sobbing and drinking from a bottle of whisky he had thoughtfully provided for himself.

I informed the Maestro of our decision as he took his place in the first row of the theater to watch the rehearsal of the rest of the show. He expressed great surprise, but declared that he would reserve judgment until he had an opportunity to see for himself. By then it was one a.m. I hurriedly rounded up the actors. Nervous and shaken, we went through our numbers while the Maestro watched us intently through his pince-nez, which he held lengthwise in front of him. After the final number I leaned over the stage and with sinking heart asked him what he thought. "Wonderful!" he said gravely. I brought the glad news to my dejected and perspiring colleagues, and we spent several hours celebrating.

118

The next evening I arrived early at the theater. Only the Maestro was backstage, dressed in the Prince Albert (he had spent half a day at Brooks Brothers being fitted) and nervously pacing up and down. Soon the rest of the cast arrived and were crowded into the few little dressing-rooms the tiny theater afforded. Half-dressed actors kept rushing in and out of the corridor, jostling the Maestro, who, having dressed at home, did not rate a dressing-room. He got in everybody's way, but there was no place else for him to go. As his was the last number on the program, he would have been in ample time had he arrived at ten instead of seven. When reminded of this, he said it was his habit to arrive at a performance ahead of the audience.

The show was a stunning success. A sketch in which Heifetz (as a barefoot, tatterdemalion Tennessee hillbilly), Horowitz (as a Dostoyevsky-ish piano student), Tibbett (as a vainglorious singer), and Feuermann (as a Tyrolese cellist) applied for admission to the Chatham Square Music School brought down the house. Heifetz played a Virginia reel on an inexpensive violin, which I, in the character of the school's director, broke irately over his head. Horowitz, looking like a character out of Gorky's *The Lower Depths*, kept mumbling idiotically: "I play the piano" when asked what he would play. Mr. Tibbett, clad in white tie and tails, came out to sing the Prologue from *Pagliacci*, which he did seriously and beautifully. But at a certain point his trousers began almost imperceptibly to slip down. At the final high G,

119

delivered with clarion force and tonal beauty, they fell to the floor as the stage quickly blacked out. The house rocked with laughter. Rachmaninoff, sitting in the balcony, seemed to resent the planned accident at the Prologue's climax, and he left the theater, presumably in displeasure.

Another sketch warmly greeted was "The Maestro Comes to Dinner," which spoofed the terror inspired by the Maestro's acceptance of a dinner engagement. Wanda Horowitz, Toscanini's daughter, assumed the role of her father and looked startlingly like him in get-up and bearing—so much so that many in the audience thought that the Maestro was playing himself. In the skit the hostess discovers, a moment before the arrival of her distinguished guest, that the cook has put too much salt in the *polenta*. Unwilling to face the Maestro's wrath, the family decides to commit suicide in a body. The host draws a revolver and shoots everyone in the room. Each one dies resignedly. But Mrs. Heifetz, the mother of the violinist, injected an impromptu line as she expired: "Good-by, Jascha," she gasped, "I know *you* will understand!"

The climax of the evening came at the end with Toscanini and his Children's Orchestra. Never had light music been played with such brilliance, verve, beauty, tonal balance, and general perfection! In a certain crescendo-decrescendo passage in Mozart's "A Musical Joke," Toscanini made the men of the orchestra rise slowly to their feet and then sink slowly back. The audience stood up and cheered. And the Maestro, loath, as usual, to take curtain calls alone, made his "children" rise innumerable times as he stepped down from the podium and took his place among them. After the show, artists and audience repaired to a large adjoining room for supper and dancing to the music of a jazz band. Our joy at the success of the show was slightly tempered with regret that the Chatham Square School benefited only to the extent of $2,200 instead of the great sum the presence of such stars should have netted.

CHAPTER SIX

$\mathcal{I}$N the spring of 1940 Toscanini and the NBC Symphony sailed on a tour of South America. The Maestro had a pleasant time on the boat. Each morning he appeared on deck dressed in colorful silk pajamas. He talked at great length to the men in the orchestra, and he was generally surrounded by many of them eagerly taking in his every word, while those who had cameras hovered at a distance and snapped the Maestro, catching him in characteristic attitudes. He watched with great interest the activities of his musicians, the shuffleboard contests and swimming in the pool, the noisy rites celebrating the crossing of the equator. One member of our party, a quiet, middle-aged man with a family to support, fell a victim to the lure of a coin machine in the lounge, losing more than he was able to afford. Neither his colleagues nor I could detach him from the machine. In desperation I appealed to the Maestro, who said he would speak to the man. We watched the Maestro enter the salon and go up to the man, who was completely absorbed in feeding quarter after quarter into the insatiable contraption. However, the reprimand that Toscanini had prepared was never delivered. For the Maestro himself became fascinated by the machine, and half an hour later he was still standing at the side of the player, and with him patiently waiting for the elusive jackpot to come tumbling out of the slot. "I said something to him, but he did not listen," he explained rather apologetically later. "You know, I like-ed that machine."

Never before had the men of the orchestra been so close to their adored Maestro, and never before had my wife and I been privileged to see so much of him for so long a time. Except during the five or so hours between four and nine in the morning when he went down to his suite, presumably to rest and sleep, we were with him every moment of the day and night. Mrs. Toscanini would most sensibly retire at a normal hour. Not so the Maestro. He would watch the dancing in the salon until the band and the dancers dispersed in the early dawn. He would then announce that he felt not at all sleepy and meant to walk the deck and look at the sea and sky. We could not, of course—nor did we really ever wish to—leave him to himself. So, protesting that we too were not sleepy (though we might be dying on our feet), we walked on either side of him, back and forth the length of the deck, sometimes until we saw the top of the sun rising out of the sea. Then the Maestro, sensing but

123

not understanding our exhaustion, would say: "Go to bed, you are tired. I? No! But I will go to my room."

One morning the Maestro heard on the short-wave radio that France had capitulated to the Nazis. The news almost robbed him of his senses. He shut himself up in his rooms and for two days refused food and drink; and his voice, cursing and swearing at Hitler and Mussolini, was so loud that it penetrated to the deck above. At last, in the faint hope that I could calm him down or at least divert his rage toward some topic less world-shaking, I went into his room. He was walking up and down, screaming and shouting. I sat in a chair and waited for a chance to speak to him. It never came. With inexhaustible lung power he attacked, in Italian and English, the enemy, the allies and their leaders, and the entire human race. All at once the shadowy figure of his wife stood in the doorway of her bedroom, adjoining the little salon in which I sat. "*Basta! Basta!*" she yelled in a voice that cut through his, and he shut up as suddenly as if someone had placed a hand over his mouth. I sat frozen with apprehension; no one before had dared to raise a voice to him, let alone command him to be silent! Yet nothing happened. The Maestro looked at his wife wonderingly for a while. Then he slowly turned away, sank into a chair, put his hand over his eyes, and began swaying his head from left to right and right to left in the self-pitying manner I knew so well. Not another sound came from him. His wife retreated to her bedroom. I tiptoed out of the room, leaving the Maestro

124

moaning softly to himself. Outside, I told the steward that the Maestro was now in a mood to eat something, and I asked him to bring him a cup of minestrone and some bread sticks.

The vacillating fortunes of the war were reflected in his behavior at home, at the houses of friends, and in his work. But his prophecy that he would one day "dance on the grave of Mussolini" was, in a figurative sense, borne out. One Sunday afternoon, in the intermission of one of Toscanini's broadcasts, the loudspeaker in Studio 8H suddenly announced the capture and execution of Mussolini. The Maestro, on the point of entering the hall to resume his concert, heard the name Mussolini, but could not understand the rest of the announcement. He turned to me in perplexity. His son, Walter, fearing that the shock would be too much for his father, motioned to me not to enlighten him. By coincidence, the program that afternoon was all-Italian, winding up with the Overture to Rossini's *William Tell*. This coincidence appeared to me providential, and I decided to risk telling the Maestro. He stood silent for an instant. Then he said quietly: *"Bene, bene* . . . now we must play well," and he walked briskly into the hall and onto the stage, to the shattering applause of an audience already excited by the news and wondering about its effect on the man who had prayed and hoped and worked for such a moment.

The end of the war brought a measure of serenity

to Toscanini and, by reflection, to the people who worked with him. The republic that succeeded the monarchy in Italy wished to honor him by conferring on him the title of Senator. The Maestro politely declined, as he had previously declined (with one exception) all offers of degrees from leading universities of America and England. "I am a moosician—not a doctor," he said. The presidents and trustees of universities were mystified by his refusals as something altogether beyond their experience with celebrated men. Oxford, in particular, was so pressing that Toscanini was touched. He wrote the trustees that, while he could not possibly accept a degree, he would be happy to give a concert for any benefit they would name. This he did in the little university town, raising an impressive number of pounds.

At NBC we had the recurring problem each year of persuading Toscanini that he was not too old to undertake another season of broadcasts. As early as 1941 he wrote to Mr. Sarnoff that he thought it was high time for him to withdraw from what he called the militant scene of art. He desired, of course, the reassurance of our faith in his artistic vigor and physical vitality, with which we duly besieged him. Almost every year of the seventeen he spent at NBC saw him formally (and in measured, archaic phrases) resigning his post and, following our heartfelt emotional pleas, permitting himself to reconsider. In the meantime he continued to make history in 8H and, later, in Carnegie Hall.

The younger generation of music-lovers had never

heard him conduct opera, and I used this fact as an argument to persuade the Maestro to broadcast concert performances of some noteworthy music dramas. In quick succession he prepared and directed *Fidelio, Orfeo, La Bohème, La Traviata, Aïda, Otello, Falstaff,* and *A Masked Ball.* All of these broadcasts, recorded on wax and, later, on tape, were subsequently released, or will be released, by RCA Victor. The rehearsals, with Toscanini at the piano and the singers grouped around him, offered to those fortunate enough to be present a glimpse of the working methods of a great musician and born stage director. For, while there could be no actual stage direction in a concert performance, Toscanini arrived at the same thing by inspiring the artists to give an illusion of dramatic action even more immediate than in a stage performance. And he could, in illustration, when criticism and suggestion failed, sing a phrase himself with his throaty, guttural voice in a manner that startlingly brought to the surface the dramatic or humorous point he wished to make.

The phrase *"Non so"* (I don't know) in Verdi's *Otello* drew from the Maestro a lecture to the baritone who was singing Iago; then, having failed to produce the result desired, the Maestro sang the two words in a manner that was altogether inimitable. "You see, *caro,"* Toscanini explained, "Iago is a bad man . . . but he is also clever . . . more clever than Otello, who is a child . . . far, far more clever . . . and when Otello ask to him why Cassio and Roderigo are fighting he answer

'*Non so!*' . . . But the way he say it must make Otello to think: 'Ah, he *does* know why, but he wishes not to get Cassio in trouble, he also wishes not to disturb me!' . . . At the same time he must make Otello suspect Cassio. . . . All these things Iago must convey with the words '*Non so.*' It is *difficile, caro . . . molto, molto.* . . . Perhaps it should sound like this . . .'' And the Maestro sang "*Non so,*" and all the shrewdness and evil of Iago were in his voice and diction. At a rehearsal of *Traviata* the Maestro stopped playing, shook his head sadly, went to a bookcase, took down a copy of *Hamlet*, and read the entire "Speak the speech, I pray you" passage with great positiveness and many mispronunciations. "This," he commented, "is true for opera as well as for the stage. *Cari amici*, think to Shakespeare always!"

At the final rehearsals of *La Bohème* I undertook to give the signal for the offstage breaking of dishes in the third act. With the score before me, I watched for the composer's indication "Here a breaking of dishes is heard," and gave the signal to the sound-effects man who stood near me with a barrel of cheap crockery. At the crash I heard Toscanini screaming: "No! No!" and I put my head through the door and asked if anything had gone wrong. "Every*thing!*" the Maestro yelled. "Once more!" I returned to my post, the orchestra and singers began again, and again at the indicated place I nodded to the sound-effects man. The second crash again infuriated the Maestro. "Wrong! Wrong!" he screamed.

"What imbe*cile* is doing that?" Terrified, I had to confess that I was the one. "So it's you!" he stormed. "Don't you know you must wait to break dishes until the soprano and baritone finish their duet? . . . Imbe*cile* . . . Santa Maria . . . Santissima . . ." "But, Maestro," I said stoutly, "in the score Puccini says—" "Ah!" he broke in, "you do not use your brain. . . . *Si* . . . *certo* . . . Puccini say: 'Break dishes,' but he wishes the people first to hear the notes. No? He compose the notes to be *heard*, no? Imbe*cile!* Once more!" For the third try I used my brain and waited for Marcello and Musetta to finish their duet. The breakage this time was acceptable to the Maestro, for he made no comment.

The public performance of *La Bohème* was perfect until the final four bars of the opera. So great was the tension of the orchestra and the Maestro as the opera drew to a close that at the concluding chords the brasses entered a fraction of a second too soon. The error was so insignificant that only the nervous brasses and the Maestro could have noticed it. A moment later the opera was over and the audience broke into thunderous applause. The Maestro, with head bowed, left the stage and went swiftly to his dressing-room, leaving the singers to take their bows alone. Once in his room, the Maestro abandoned himself to an elemental rage more devastating than any I had ever witnessed. Screaming and roaring incomprehensible things, he tore at his clothing and upset every movable object that yielded to his inspired strength. His piano and a large desk resisted all his

efforts at dislodgment, and in exasperation he kicked
them repeatedly with such fury that I feared for his
legs. After minutes of fulmination and wreakage he
suddenly desisted and said: "Send me the *porci* [the
swine]. I wish to speak with them." The erring players
had not dared to leave the hall. There were nine of them,
and I led them into the Maestro's room, where they took
up an uneasy position in a line against a wall, their
faces pale, their heads down. The Maestro walked up
and down in front of them like a sergeant inspecting his
squad, glaring at each one with hatred and contempt.
At length he said with bitter sincerity: "I hide my head
in shame. After what happen-ed tonight my life is fin-
ish-ed. For me it is impossible to look in the face of
any*bawdy*. I can live no more. But *you*—" and he
pointed straight at the man at the head of the dejected
line—"you will sleep with your wife tonight as if no*thing*
happen-ed. I know you!" The Maestro turned away, and
the men sadly filed out.

The telephone rang. It was my wife. She had arranged a supper party for the Maestro and she wondered what had delayed us. In cryptic monosyllables I
managed to convey the state of affairs in the dressing-
room. "Of course he won't come," she said. "I suppose
it is just as well." I assured her that he would certainly
go straight home. I would be home as soon as I had put
him in his car and seen him off. As he slumped dejectedly into the back seat of his car, I said: "Shall I
tell the chauffeur to drive you home?" "No!" he an-

swered bitterly, "to *your* house." I excused myself for a moment, ran back into the building, and telephoned my wife. "You better meet him at the door with a glass of champagne. He needs it. It may save your party."

My wife met us at the door with a glass of champagne in her hand. She kissed the Maestro and handed him the glass. "What is?" he said with an air of innocence which would have deceived anyone who did not know him intimately. "Champagne," said my wife. The Maestro shook his head. "Could you," he asked plaintively, "give me a glass of water? I would like some water." In our twenty years of friendship we had never seen the Maestro drink water. My wife and I exchanged glances. It was now clear to us that the Maestro was still nursing his grievance at the brasses and was determined to prolong his pain and make us share it. We brought him a glass of water. He drank it avidly, like one parched in the desert who suddenly comes upon a water hole. "Ah! Good!" he exclaimed. "Can I have some more?" He emptied two large glasses, and we went in to dinner. He refused all food with excessive politeness, spoke no words except "Thank you, *cara*, no!" and "Is there more water?" The dinner was a nightmare. When it was over, he went into the living-room, sat down by himself, and covered his eyes with his hand. The guests conversed in low tones. The evening was ruined. I was angry with him for his punishment of persons innocent of any musical misdeeds. And, fearing that my anger would impel me to rudeness, I deliberately steered clear of him. My aloofness became so marked as the evening wore on that my wife implored me to pay some attention to the guest of honor. This I refused to do. It was not until one in the morning that the Maestro rose to go. I handed him his hat without a word, and he left. Half an hour later a friend of the Toscaninis rang up. "What have you done to the Maestro?" she asked. "He telephoned me a moment ago and said he had never been so insulted in his life." "Who does he think he is," he had exclaimed scornfully, "to treat a guest in his house with such rudeness? Where was he brought up? Was he never taught manners?" and so forth, and so forth.

There was to be a rehearsal next morning. Assuming that the Maestro would never speak to me again, I asked the lady whether she thought I had better stay away. She said she would speak to the Maestro and call me back. At two in the morning she called. The Maestro was still very angry, but wasn't it my duty to be at rehearsals? he had asked. Next morning, a few minutes before the time of rehearsal, I opened the door of his dressing-room. He was sitting at the piano playing softly the prelude to the last act of Catalani's opera *La Wally*, and pretending not to see me. He looked beautifully serene, and the expression on his face was angelic. I was completely unnerved by his appearance. A feeling of guilt smote me. I went behind him and listened to his playing awhile. Then I succumbed to an expiatory impulse and put my arms around him. He stopped playing, turned around, and embraced me. "What beautiful music!" he said. "How simple and noble. The snow is falling softly, sadly . . ."

In the intermission, after he had rehearsed Beethoven's Eighth Symphony, the Maestro startled me with a question. "What would you think, *caro*," he asked, "if I reinforced the orchestration of the theme in the first movement when it arrives *fff*. You know, I have not slept nights thinking to it. It is very seldom that Beethoven puts three fortes; that means he wants the theme to sound very strong. But what happens? It does not sound strong. Perhaps in Beethoven's mind it sounded strong. But he was deaf, and he never heard it played. Do you think I dare change? I would like to add tympani and brasses. Then it would sound *fff* the way Beethoven really wished it to sound. Tell me frankly, *caro*. Do you think I dare?"

I replied that he was a better judge of such matters than I. We sat silent for some time. "I think to try," he finally said. The next morning he brought with him new parts for the percussion and brasses he had written out. I went into the auditorium to hear the new version of the passage. The Maestro played through the entire first movement. When the controversial passage arrived, it sounded distinctly different from the original. At the finish the Maestro faced the auditorium and called my name in a loud voice. I knew that he was going to ask me what I thought. But my opinion was unfavorable, and I decided not to reveal my presence. I slid under my seat. The Maestro waited awhile and then called my name in a louder voice. Several people around me who knew me began to look at me wonderingly. Realizing that my attempt at deception had failed, I rose and reluctantly made my way to the stage. When I stood below him, the Maestro said: "Have you heard?" I said I had. "What did you think?" I gulped and said weakly: "I didn't like it." I had the impression that everybody—the people out front and the orchestra on the stage—was frozen with horror at my temerity. The Maestro looked down on me remorselessly and said: "Why didn't you like?" I thrashed around in my mind for a reason, and surprised myself and horrified everyone else by saying: "I thought it was vulgar." A fearful silence filled the hall, as if everybody had stopped breathing. There was a long pause. The Maestro then said: "You are *syou-er* you heard?" I nodded. "I will now play the movement in the original, and after that once again with the new orchestration. Stay here and listen." The Maestro turned toward the orchestra. When he had finished both versions, he veered round to me again. I remained silent. "You still don't like?" he asked. "I don't like," I said. "Dolin," the Maestro called to the librarian, "take away what I have written." Nothing more was ever heard about the new version.

He welcomed criticism from any reliable quarter. "You know, I am so close to the orchestra I cannot hear many things." After rehearsals he would ask me whether I heard this or that, whether the "ba*lance*" had been good, and so forth, and he listened to what I (or anyone else who took him at his word) had to say with the detachment of one who is interested only in the end result. When he played contemporary music, he insisted on the continual presence of the composer, whom he consulted frequently. Once, at a rehearsal of a modern work, I was enraged at the many interruptions by the composer, a brash and insensitive young man who stopped the Maestro every few minutes to tell him how he wanted his composition played. He even gesticulated to the players from behind the Maestro's back. When I complained about the behavior of this individual, the Maestro regarded me with wonder. "But he is the *composer*," he said reprovingly. "*He* knows better than I how his music should sound."

When the war ended, the Maestro began spending his summers in Italy. La Scala had been badly damaged by Allied bombs, and he took a direct interest in the restoration of the theater. When it was its old self again —except for the wonderful acoustics, which, the Maestro maintained, unaccountably resisted restoration—he opened it with a great concert for the benefit of the orchestra. The following spring he conducted at La Scala acts from Boïto's *Nerone* and *Mefistofele*. This he did by way of atoning for his fancied (or perhaps real) neglect of Boïto at the time of the composer's last illness and death. Boïto had been his great friend and, in a sense, his mentor and sponsor. "You must hear Toscanini conduct your *Falstaff*," Boïto had once said to

Verdi. "You would be content." Verdi, alas, never heard Toscanini conduct. The preparations for the excerpts from Boïto's two operas turned Toscanini's apartment in the Via Durini into rehearsal rooms. People from La Scala came and went continually; singers were coached, there were sessions with the chorus master, with the scenic designer and the stage director, Toscanini attending to the smallest details of the production. Great outbursts of temper, musical corrections in a raucous voice, and threats of abandonment of the project were followed by expressions of satisfaction and pleasure and a personal show of cordial hospitality, when *"espresso"* and Carpano were brought in and the artists relaxed under the Maestro's paternal smile.

Mrs. Toscanini was generally confined to her room —their room, for the Maestro had no bedroom of his own—with the illness that was soon to prove fatal. She had stayed in Milan under care of her doctor during the winter while her husband was conducting in New York, and when he arrived at the Via Durini she was scarcely able to get up from her bed to greet him. In preparation for his coming she had engaged a special chef, who came by the day, and who could be glimpsed through the open kitchen door in his white jacket and tall chef's hat and, after dinner, in ordinary clothes, passing through the dining-room on his way out, carrying his own culinary tools in a satchel, bowing elaborately and saying: *"Buona notte, Maestro."* To which the Maestro, not recognizing the man in his street clothes, would answer affably:

"*Ciao, caro,*" and look to his wife for enlightenment as to the man's identity.

I had accompanied Toscanini to Italy, and was invited to take my meals at his house. On the day of our arrival Mrs. Toscanini made a valiant effort to sit at table with us. The dining-table was a high one, and the chair his wife had designated for the Maestro was extremely low. Sitting down, he found to his surprise that the table was too high for comfort. But out of solicitude for his ailing wife he said nothing, and all that summer he ate his meals from an inconvenient elevation. His tenderness toward his wife was unfailing. Often at table he would reach out and place his hand over hers and gaze at her with great compassion. And knowing that she would be displeased if he ate sparingly, as he ordinarily did, he made a show of tasting the food elaborately prepared by the expensive chef; and he refrained, when guests were present, from calling attention, as was his wont, to his own abstemiousness. But once, after the departure of a luncheon guest who had eaten well, he forgot himself and said sarcastically: "From the way she ate, you would never believe that she had lost a son in the war!"

The gravity of his wife's condition preyed upon his mind at those scarce moments when he was not immersed in music. He had always taken for granted that he would survive his wife, who was ten years his junior. In the years when she was quite well he would say, apropos of the, to him, pernicious tendency of widowers to remarry: "When Carla dies I will not marry again." But as her illness progressed he began to brood over the separation that would eventually face him, and he often gave way to tears and wondered aloud whether he could live without her.

When the end was approaching, he had just finished his season with the NBC Symphony in New York. A cable arrived from Milan with the dreaded news, and the Maestro flew at once to Italy. I saw him off at the airport. He looked haggard and old. He moved slowly and feebly, and there was an air of hopelessness about him which was the more heartbreaking because I had never before seen him surrender so completely to apathy and almost childish self-pity. I did what I could to console him, pretending that her case was less grave than we both knew it to be. I spoke about his return in the fall and our plans for the season, and I mentioned his pet project—a concert performance of Verdi's *A Masked Ball*. He shook his head sadly, and tears ran down his face. "No, *caro*," he moaned, "it is the end, my life is finish-*ed* . . . finish-*ed*. . . ." He leaned on my arm heavily as I walked him to the plane. Still weeping, he bade me farewell. "*Addio, caro*," he whispered, "I pray you to engage for *Un Ballo* [*A Masked Ball*] Bjoerling [the tenor]. I pray you . . ." He ascended the steps of the gangplank, and a moment later the plane was in the air. Music had triumphed over life and death. I remembered and now understood his astonishing retort to an Italian heart specialist who had pronounced the Maestro's heart in beautiful condition—in fact, quite untouched. "Why shouldn't it be?" the Maestro had said. "It has *never been used.*"

Nevertheless, after his wife's funeral he shut himself up in his gloomy apartment in Milan during one of the hottest summers on record, eating hardly enough to keep alive, listening to no music, and refusing to touch his piano or open a score, weeping bitterly over his loss and protesting that his life was over and that he wished only for death. It was at that time that I went to Italy, hoping to beguile him into music again. And after some days of fruitless exhortation on my part I hit upon a psychological deception that pried him from the somber, shuttered apartment and gave him the justification he required to remove to his lovely villa on Lago Maggiore. I pretended that I was feeling ill because of the intense heat in Milan. And when he suggested that I would feel better in his house on Lago Maggiore, I said that I had come to Milan not for my health, but to be with him. He had, therefore, no choice but to take me to Lago Maggiore. Some days after we had moved to the villa I hit upon another ruse that turned his thoughts to music. Sitting with him in his room, into which a Steinway grand had been hopefully moved, I began to speak about Meyerbeer, and wondered whether he had ever heard the once-celebrated but now completely neglected opera *Robert le diable.* The Maestro replied, with a sudden show of interest, that he had played it once as a cellist in the orchestra of a small theater in Italy more

139

than half a century ago. "I suppose you don't remember any of it after so many years," I remarked with affected casualness. "I remember very well," he snapped, as if I had insulted him. And, sitting down at the piano, he began *Robert le diable* from the beginning and played and sang for a long time, imparting to the text the dramatic flavor of an actual performance. He had broken a two-month musical fast! And, watching his expressive face and eyes reflecting every shade of the words and music of the antiquated, forgotten opera, his three children, Walter, Wanda, and Wally, who were present, were overcome with emotion and had to turn away to hide their happy tears.

From that day he resumed his normal preoccupation with music. In the morning we heard him playing the piano. After lunch we sat on the terrace overlooking the lake. He would gaze silently at the water and then suddenly say something about a score that he had been going over in his mind. "There is something in *Ibéria* I do not understand. . . . You know, at the end of—" and he would run briskly up to his room and return with the Debussy score and point out the place and tell me that he was tempted to double the woodwinds there, but that perhaps it was his own fault, not Debussy's, and the next time he rehearsed *Ibéria* he would ask the orchestra to . . .

In the evening, after supper, we would all go up to his room, where his son had installed a powerful phonograph. I would pretend that we were all going to a concert and arrange a different program of his records for each night. The maid would bring bottles of red syrup and glasses on a tray. Fortified with drinks, we disposed ourselves around the phonograph and listened to his records for an hour and a half, exclaiming "Oh" and "Ah" rapturously (and sincerely) at certain moments, greatly to the old man's delight. He himself sat upright in a chair and conducted the music with the vigor and passion he displayed at rehearsals and performances. "*Accidente!*" (uncanny) he would exclaim admiringly, his right arm still beating time, his left pressing his side to indicate the warmth and insistence of a melody, as the orchestra executed some difficult or subtle passage. And when we said good-night and dispersed to our rooms, we would often be startled by the horrible scratch of a phonograph needle and an ensuing fortissimo blast of exaggerated orchestral sound, and would know that the Maestro, who was congenitally unable to cope with the simplest contraption, was braving the awesome, complicated machine in order to hear again a portion of a record he had either liked or disliked at the recent "concert." Or later, in the dead of night, if one slept lightly, one could hear from the direction of his room the faint, compressed sound of music from his short-wave radio, thus justifying his resentment of those who inquired, in all innocence, if he slept well, and bearing out his claim that in all his life he had slept hardly at all. I had also discounted his boast that he had never, for the reason that he disliked his face, looked at himself in a mirror, even while shaving; until, entering his room one morning, I found him sitting up in bed, wielding a safety razor and gazing unconcernedly the while at Lago Maggiore.

As I had promised the Maestro, I engaged the tenor he wanted for *Un Ballo in Maschera*. Although the opera was scheduled for late in the season, preparations for it were begun even before Toscanini arrived in New York in late September. As the time drew near for the broadcast, the usual troubles attendant upon an undertaking that involved singers descended on us. The artists had previous commitments to fill, and it was difficult to arrange even a tentative schedule of rehearsals. The Maestro could not, of course, comprehend any difficulties where he was concerned. As he gave himself up completely to the preparation of an opera, so he took it for granted that the vocalists, no matter how popular they might be and how much in demand for concert and operatic engagements elsewhere, would do the same and be at all times at his disposal. And on learning that they would not be, he flew into a rage and threatened to abandon the project altogether, leave America, and what not.

Such crises had been usual during his many years at NBC. By dint of pressure, cajoling, and manipulation of schedules, the difficulties had always been surmounted. And now, after a last-minute substitution of Jan Peerce for the indisposed Bjoerling, all matters were

ironed out and the day of the first rehearsal with Toscanini approached. Then, one morning, I was hastily summoned to the Maestro in Riverdale. I found him
slumped in a chair, his face tearstained. He embraced
me and clung to me pathetically. "If you are my friend,
as you say, you must save me," he pleaded. "I cannot
conduct. . . . I am too old. . . . I should have stopped last year with the *Missa Solemnis*. I must go away
and hide myself in a corner and die. This morning I
awo-ked and I cannot remember the words of *Ballo!* No
word can I remember! I cannot remember no*thing!* I
cannot face my artists so." "But you remember the
music?" I said hopefully. He pursed his lips contemptu-
ously. "The music? Yes, I remember the music . . .
but the words, *no!* I cannot look my artists in the face
without knowing the words. I cannot go on. Save me,
caro . . . let me go. . . ." I kissed his forehead and
assured him that his happiness and peace of mind were
my only concern. I would do as he asked. I would cancel
Ballo in Maschera and find another conductor to take
over the three or four broadcasts that remained of the
season. I left Riverdale thinking that it had come at last,
that all things must have an end. I telephoned a conductor who by chance was free to undertake the remaining broadcasts, and I set about canceling *Un Ballo*.

I had completed these sad arrangements when the
Maestro called me on the telephone one morning. He
was very excited. "*Pensa* [think], *caro*," he cried, "I
awake this morning and I remember *all* the words of

143

Ballo! I can now face my artists. Call the rehearsal. *Addio, caro!"* I telephoned the substitute conductor and the singers and countermanded the cancelation of the opera. At the orchestral rehearsal a day later Toscanini, smiling and in the best of humor, sang every word of the entire *Ballo in Maschera* with his familiar expressiveness, the while he guided the instrumentalists deftly and enthusiastically. The broadcast performance went off in great style. Afterward he entertained the members of the cast in a private room in a downtown restaurant. He beamed with satisfaction, professed himself not at all fatigued, and delighted his guests with old stories and anecdotes; and those of the singers who had a flair for mimicry amused him with take-offs of celebrated musicians, including some of himself.

But, notwithstanding this sudden remarkable resurgence of memory, it was clear to the Maestro's family and friends that the time had arrived for him to relinquish his broadcasts. In this the Maestro fully concurred, frowning on any suggestion that he return for another season. His son, Walter, at his father's request, prepared a letter of resignation addressed to Mr. Sarnoff and placed it on the Maestro's desk for his signature. But days and weeks passed and the letter lay unsigned, for the document had become a symbol of abdication to the old man. And it was not until the week of his final broadcast of the season that he summoned the resolution to put his name to it and send it off.

For his farewell broadcast he had arranged an all-

Wagner program, which included the Prelude and *Liebestod* from *Tristan und Isolde*. But at the first rehearsal he summoned me to his room and told me that he could no longer remember the music of *Tristan* and would play instead the Overture and Bacchanale from *Tannhäuser*, which, he said, he remembered quite well. I recalled his recent temporary crisis over *Ballo*, and I suggested that he might perhaps awake the following morning with the *Tristan* music clear in his mind. But he shook his head sadly and said he was certain that it would never come back to him. So the substitution was quickly arranged, and the next day he rehearsed the *Tannhäuser* with his usual power and subtlety. It occurred to me that a desire to prove to the public (and to himself) that he could summon the strength and endurance to prepare and conduct the long excerpt from *Tannhäuser*, with its powerful rhythms and tremendous sonorities, had actually brought about a temporary loss of memory for the less arduous music of *Tristan*. The *Tannhäuser* piece, followed by the brilliant *Meistersinger* Prelude for a finish, would enable him to wind up his career of nearly seventy years with an exhibition of undiminished vitality and with all his artistic faculties beautifully apparent. In effect, he would lay down his baton while still at the height of his powers.

My belief that he had, perhaps, unconsciously adopted this innocent stratagem was strengthened at the actual broadcast of his final concert. For he began the *Tannhäuser* Overture with his customary air of obsessive authority, arrived by inevitable gradation at the climax, and with controlled fury plunged into the maelstrom of the Bacchanale. Whatever anxieties his family and I had had up to his appearance on the stage were now completely routed. From behind the engineers in the control booth I watched at close range the powerful gyrations of his baton, the mystic behavior of his left hand, and the subtle conspiratorial expressions of his eyes and lips. The audience, as if aware of the significance of the occasion, stared at his head and back with frozen concentration, each person seemingly oblivious of his neighbor, like witnesses of some awesome and perilous event.

The frenzy of the Bacchanale gradually died down, the passion exhausted. The piece was nearing its end. At the point where the offstage strings faintly echo the turbulence of the orgiastic night and retreat ghostlike before the thin, uneasy dawn, Toscanini's stick wavered and began to describe unintelligible motions. The orchestra, suddenly frightened, followed for a few bars, through habit, their Maestro's curious, unrelated gestures. Then, instinctively assuming direction, the men tried desperately to coalesce and reach the end in unity, though without the finesse of leadership. The attempt, beset by self-consciousness and fear, was a failure. In the soft cacophony that ensued, the Maestro ceased conducting and put his hand to his eyes. The men stopped playing and the house was engulfed in terrible silence.

Perhaps only thirty seconds passed, but it was like

a year. Then the Maestro, like a Tannhäuser banishing with a gesture the miasma of the Venusberg, straightened up, lifted his baton for a powerful downbeat, and swung the men into the *Meistersinger* Prelude. Slightly unsteady, yet rhythmic and sonorous enough to be unmistakably Toscanini, the Prelude coursed along. Now it seemed that nothing untoward could occur. Then, at the very end, it happened. Toscanini's arm was seen to falter. It came down and rested, motionless, at his side. The baton slipped from his hand. He stepped unsteadily from the podium and walked with drooping head off-stage, while the orchestra behind him screamed out the exultant, throaty C Major jubilance of the Prelude's final bar. It sounded like the world's affirmative judgment on the man who had for so long revealed to it the naked marvel of great music. He was now, before their very eyes, stumbling toward silence, probably forever.

Or so it looked. One last commitment remained for Toscanini—to remake portions of the recordings of *Un Ballo* and *Aïda*. The session had been scheduled for the Wednesday after the Maestro's farewell broadcast. There could now be no question but that the session would be canceled. But on Monday, to our surprise, Toscanini sent word that he would be ready to record. And on Wednesday he arrived at Carnegie Hall, punctual as usual. He greeted everybody pleasantly and changed into his rehearsing coat. Shutting his eyes tightly and screwing up his face in a mock-painful expression, he sprinkled Eau de Cologne generously over head and face, wielding the atomizer with comic vigor. Then he walked rapidly down the long flight of stairs to the stage without touching the banister and quickly gained his podium. With his baton he rapped sharply on the music stand at his side. "*Andiamo*," he cried, and brought his right arm down in a powerful downbeat.

As if mesmerized, singers and orchestra sang and played with an artistry beyond their conscious abilities. And those who only listened marveled at the conductor's flagrant energy, his secure memory and uncanny synchronization of pose and gesture with the design and content of the music. Was it the upsetting ordeal of a public farewell to music which had, only three days before, disturbed for a few moments the fabulous memory, the superb control over his musical faculties, the easy mastery over his orchestra, all now so beautifully evident? The Toscanini who was now recording *Un Ballo* and *Aïda* was in all respects the autocratic, confident, extraordinary perfectionist the world had known for more than half a century.

A NOTE ON THE TYPE

This book was set on the Linotype in ELECTRA, *designed by W. A. Dwiggins. The Electra face is a simple and readable type suitable for printing books by present-day processes. It is not based on any historical model, and hence does not echo any particular time or fashion. It is without eccentricities to catch the eye and interfere with reading— in general, its aim is to perform the function of a good book printing-type: to be read, and not seen.*

The book was composed, printed, and bound by Kingsport Press, Inc., Kingsport, Tennessee. The paper was made by P. H. Glatfelter Co., Spring Grove, Pa. The typography and binding were designed by Charles E. Skaggs.

4/17/57